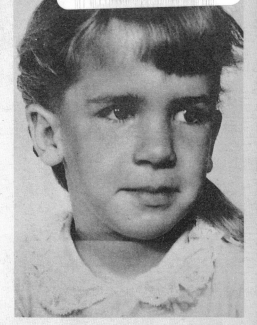

above Jan, aged three
right Rebecca, aged three
below Jan, aged eighteen

top Bill Muller and Rebecca, aged four, in San Cristobal (*Marney Jacobsen*)

bottom, left Harry, aged forty-three, when Jan first met him (*Gertrude Duby-Blom*)

bottom, right Jan, aged thirty-five, in the Lacandon jungle, Mexico

top, left Harry with Rima, Lacandon jungle

top, right Rebecca, aged ten, Lacandon jungle

bottom Cleonisia and Armindo Coimbra, Cucuí, Brazil

top Harry, Jan and Rebecca in 1979, a few months before the disease struck (*George Ball*)
bottom Jan at Rebecca's grave, Homestead Hill, 1985 (*John Man*)

JOHN MAN

Survive!

Penguin Books

Penguin Books Ltd, Harmondsworth, Middlesex, England
Viking Penguin Inc., 40 West 23rd Street, New York, New York 10010, U.S.A.
Penguin Books Australia Ltd, Ringwood, Victoria, Australia
Penguin Books Canada Limited, 2801 John Street, Markham, Ontario, Canada L3R 1B4
Penguin Books (N.Z.) Ltd, 182–190 Wairau Road, Auckland 10, New Zealand

First published as *The Survival of Jan Little* by Viking 1986
Published in Penguin Books 1987

Copyright © John Man, 1986
All rights reserved.
Published in association with I. B. Tauris & Co. Ltd

Filmset in Bembo
Made and printed Great Britain by
Richard Clay Ltd, Bungay, Suffolk

FOR
REBECCA

This world is not conclusion
Emily Dickinson

CONTENTS

❧

ILLUSTRATIONS

MAPS

PREFACE

On the Rio Negro, on either side of the border between
Venezuela and Brazil, everyone has heard of Jan Little. I first
heard about her when I was in southern Venezuela in 1982.
Even in outline, the story was extraordinary.

There had been, I was told, a blind and deaf American lady
who had for years lived deep in the Amazon jungle with her
family – her husband, Harry, and her grown-up daughter,
Rebecca. Their homestead, not far over the border into Brazil,
lay many days of river travel from the nearest settlement.
Husband and daughter had died of disease. Jan had survived
many months on her own before being found.

I found the tale hard to believe. I had once lived briefly with
rain-forest Indians, and had seen how difficult jungle living is,
even for experts. No one – *no one* – chooses to live in isolation,
especially not in a region as forbidding as southern Venezuela
and northern Brazil. All around stretches the Amazon jungle,
thousands of square miles of it, uninhabited but for scattered
settlements along the larger rivers. The border is disputed.
Officials are wary, if not downright antagonistic, to foreigners.
What could possibly impel anyone, let alone a blind and deaf
woman, to choose such a life in such a place? How could
anyone, let alone a blind and deaf woman, survive alone in this
remote and hostile wilderness?

Jan was back home in California. I met her and asked her
those questions. This book is the result.

Her story turned out to be far deeper than I had imagined.
Its roots lay in California, Vermont and Mexico, decades before
the Littles went to Brazil. Jan's return from the jungle involved

9

far more than mere physical survival (although that in itself was astonishing enough). She emerged from twenty years of marriage to a compelling, dominating man, and from a shell of introversion she had built for herself to accommodate his demands, her disabilities, and her deep-rooted habit of compliance. She had survived a relationship that, in a strange and exaggerated form, reflected the relationship of men and women across the Western world.

Her emergence, her decision to give herself to this book, her astonishing memory and her uncompromising and moving commitment to the truth (though there are still things that remain hidden from us both) reveal a richness of experience and strength of character few people who knew her ever guessed at.

The book is dedicated by her to Rebecca; and by me to Jan.

John Man
Oxford,
February 1986

BOOK
I

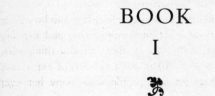

1

HARRY

High up in the mountains of southern Mexico lies San Cristobal de Las Casas, a jewel of a town sparkling in a pine-fresh clasp of wooded mountains. Whichever way you look, down any of the narrow lines of red-tiled houses and out over the surrounding grassland, you see the mountains, emerald green in sunlight, or looming grey through chilly mist. The town itself is remote and exotic, even to most Mexicans, a highland fastness, a backwater, where Indian and Spanish cultures meet without mixing. On opposing hills perch two colonial churches, brooding benignly over the roofs and courtyards below. In the market, tiny Indian women with faces gnarled as walnuts sit among heaps of vegetables; while in back streets cubby-hole shops sell machetes, meat wrapped in banana leaves, and cloth smuggled in from Guatemala. The town has more people and traffic now, for the Pan-American Highway runs right past it, but the heart of the place has changed little since 1958, when Jan arrived there from California with her three-year-old daughter, Rebecca.

The two of them had been there a few months when someone asked Jan if she would pick up a package from Harry Little. She would find him at a hotel on the central square. His name was unfamiliar to her, but not to others. Harry Little – 'Oh, yes, the jungle adventurer! And that hair! Peculiar to say the least!' The raised eyebrows and the knowing hint of disapproval made her curious, and a little apprehensive.

It was a perfect November morning, crisp, clear, bright. She put on a smart grey skirt, dressed Rebecca in neat blue overalls, tied her plaits, took her hand and strolled off with her

MEXICO

See pages 130–31

VENEZUELA

GUYANA

BRAZIL

Manaus

YUCATAN

MEXICO

BELIZE

CHIAPAS

GUATEMALA

Tuxtla
Gutierrez

San Cristobal
de las Casas

Rio Jatate

Rio Perlas

MEXICO

San Quintin

L. Miramar

Las Margaritas

Caverna

Comitan

0   30 miles
0   50 km

GUATEMALA

14

through the sun-drenched little streets to the Hotel Jardin in the Zocalo, the central square. She was expected. The clerk handed her the package, and then pointed out across the square, as if to say '*Si, si*, Don Enrique is there, *señora*. Look! Right there!'

Jan peered through her black-rimmed glasses from the hotel's shadowy doorway across the sunlit square. Even in those days, when she could still see quite well, the contrast between shadow and bright sunlight baffled her. Slowly, glancing to left and right, she scanned the familiar scene: the octagonal bandstand; the paths radiating outwards between little diamond-shaped gardens; minute Chamula Indian women shuffling to market beneath bundles of charcoal and vegetables; boot-boys calling '*Señor! Señor!*' from beneath the trees at ponchoed and sombreroed passers-by.

She moved forward, and then paused uncertainly, staring between the passing cars until her gaze was caught by a scene across the road. On the wide paved area that surrounded the square's little gardens, a man stood, his right foot raised on a boot-boy's block. Harry Little, no doubt about it: green shirt, dark trousers tucked into calf-length jungle boots, and an African safari hat. He had a light, well-trimmed beard, and, yes, they were right – that hair! – shoulder-length blond hair shining golden in the sunlight.

At that moment, he looked up, spotted the two standing on the edge of the road, and waved. Jan smiled, raised her package in acknowledgement, and stepped forward, her foot fumbling briefly at the edge of the sidewalk.

The man paid the shoe-shine boy, and turned, smiling, to greet them. 'You're Jan,' he said, firmly – a statement, not a question – and introduced himself.

She stared. He had the most startling blue eyes.

'I see you have it all right,' he said, glancing at the package. He spoke with a patrician East Coast accent, almost English, and with deliberate clarity. With her poor hearing, she was grateful for that. 'You're happy to deliver it?'

A passer-by stepped between them. Harry stood back.

'Oh, yes, it's no trouble.' Jan kept her gaze on his face. Peculiar? He didn't seem peculiar. With those eyes, he was compelling, intriguing; and familiar, somehow, like someone she'd seen in a Bible illustration long ago.

He gestured, and said something she didn't catch.

For a moment, she hesitated. Even with her hearing-aids, which were built into the stems of her glasses, she found it hard to separate talk from background noise. Then she stepped forward to close the gap between them, pretending she had heard, as she always did when trying to avoid embarrassment, and carrying the conversation forward by introducing Rebecca.

He looked down, and smiled, a frank and open smile. 'Hullo, Rebecca.'

Rebecca smiled back shyly, in silence.

Harry glanced round, as if about to leave.

'Will you be in San Cristobal long?' she asked, to keep him talking.

A passing car drowned his reply.

'Pardon?' she said, craning forward.

'A few days. I have to get back home to the jungle.'

'The jungle? You *live* in the jungle?' She moved forward again, and almost bumped into him. He stepped back.

'Yes. I have a big job ahead of me . . .' Again, traffic blurred his words. She took another pace towards him, concentrating on him, picking up scattered phrases about a thatched roof, and Indians, and cutting trees. As he talked, he stepped back again, and she followed, pressing attentively forward, his face filling her vision, while Harry, in defensive retreat, talked on about wet thatch and the problem of dealing with Indians. Suddenly, he broke off, and looked to his right. 'I go this way,' he said.

Jan glanced around, and was surprised to see they were at the corner of the sidewalk. She turned back to Harry. He was already moving away. 'Would you like to come to lunch?' she said, quickly.

🦁

What impelled her? Was it, as she believed, no more than a determination not to let her disabilities cut her off from a fellow American? Or was there more? No attraction, no, certainly not, it was too soon for that. But perhaps desire of a different kind, a desire to wrest information from him, the long-term resident, the jungle dweller; a vague sense, even in that first visionary glimpse, that she might, through him, be led to, or towards, that which she most needed: a home for herself and Rebecca, a home of a particular kind, a homestead.

The dream of a homestead had been with her from childhood, a part of growing up in the small rural Californian community of Carmichael. Carmichael is a suburb of Sacramento now; but back then, in the 1930s, it was mostly chicken ranches and orchards of almonds, oranges, olives and peaches, interspersed with sweet-smelling hayfields, rolling land that seemed to a child's eyes to roll right up to the snow-capped Sierras shining along the eastern horizon. Summer was the best time. With a friend, she spent summer days roaming the orchards, climbing trees, filching fruit, and lazing away long, hot afternoons looking out over the American River. Condemned to seclusion by her poor vision and hearing, she found peace in the orchards of Carmichael.

But the countryside was more to her than a sanctuary. It could be the basis of life itself. The Deloziers taught her that.

She came to the Deloziers quite by chance. Late one winter's night, when she was seven, Jan was woken by strange sensations and noises: urgent voices, something coarse enfolding her, arms around her, hasty movements. She was in a blanket, being carried by her father. She had an impression of lights flickering in the sky; and remembered her parents had said something about a party. Perhaps, she thought sleepily, perhaps the lights were to do with the party. Her father was talking, a rush of words she didn't catch. There were other voices, bumps and jolts, a jumble of sensations, then silence. She looked round. She was in a neighbour's house. Everyone was at the window, looking at the lights in the sky. Jan joined them. 'We're having a party,' she said, proudly, pointing to the lights. 'Party?' someone said in a surprised voice. 'That's not a party. That's your house burning down.'

It was after that, while her parents were arranging somewhere else to live, that she went to stay with the Deloziers. They were homesteaders from the Ozarks, the forested hillbilly country of southern Missouri, and had brought their way of life with them. A family of four – an elderly couple and their two granddaughters – they lived in a one-room shack, a living area divided from two big beds by a sky-blue bedspread hung over a pole. They had a vegetable garden, and animals – chickens, pigs, bees and a cow. There always seemed to be plenty of good, fresh, home-grown food. The house smelled of turnips, butter and corn-bread, baked fresh each day in a huge black oven. Most evenings, the old lady would produce warm sweet potatoes from the bottom of the oven, and then, after supper, she would sit in her rocking chair and tell stories and sing hymns. Each day was placid, predictable and reassuring. If the Deloziers had worries, Jan knew nothing of them. Their poverty, ignorance and piety – qualities her parents implicitly urged her to despise – were the very qualities that gave the little house its glow of warmth and security. Her brief stay printed on Jan's young mind a powerful, if unformulated, message: if you live on a homestead, you don't need money, you are at one with your surroundings, you have enough food, and you are happy.

All this made a stark contrast to life in her own middle-class home. Her father, Bill Muller, always seemed to be on the edge of financial disaster. He was a determined individualist – he had run away from home in Amsterdam at thirteen to go to sea – but once removed from the imposed orderliness of shipboard existence, he was lost. He ran a tile business, but he was no businessman. He was generous, but generous to a fault. Money meant little to him. Jan would see him pushing bills into drawers, and hear her mother scolding him for it. It was her mother, Jessie, who earned regular money, as an accountant for the State of California; and Jessie who paid the bills Bill didn't pay. When he called her too damned practical, she'd say it was damn lucky for him she was, him and his Robinson Crusoe mentality. To Jan, it made no sense for her parents to be out of the house most of the day, leaving home to hold the home together, finding only unhappiness in the pursuit of happiness. If only they could all live together in simple security, working in harmony, and rely on the bounty of the countryside, like the Deloziers!

That notion stayed with her for the next twenty years, sometimes no more than a vague and dormant longing, sometimes insinuating itself into her mind like new growth.

For much of that time, it vanished from her mind entirely, overlaid by the business of growing up and by the problems imposed on her by her poor vision and hearing. At fourteen, she was told what was wrong with her – tunnel vision, with related deafness. There was no cure. She did her best to ignore the condition, hiding her confusion and her fears, eager to cover her vulnerability, eager to win approval in a male world. After graduating, she tried college for a semester, took secretarial jobs, dabbled in politics, and had several brief and painful affairs. At twenty-one, in 1952, she sought independence in San Francisco.

There she found liberation, of a sort, in new friends and the excitements of the city. She had her first hearing-aid, and could at least make a pretence at being normal. It was a good time to be young. San Francisco was the home of the Beatniks. There was theatre everywhere. In North Beach, the Bohemian area of poets and artists, you could have a five-course meal, wine included, for a dollar. It was good to feel a part of the heady, hothouse rebellion against middle-class values. Finding she could fund a college course from a state rehabilitation programme, she registered for aid under a social security scheme for the blind and gave up her job.

She still felt she had no direction in life. It was Donald –

Donald Fall – who unwittingly gave her that. He was a troubled and introverted man, and their affair was more friendship than physical passion. She became pregnant and, despite Donald's indifference, insisted on having the baby, as if determined that by giving life to another she would assert her own normality and independence. She wanted to marry. But Donald would not accept the roles of husband and father. On his insistence, the marriage was intended to do no more than legitimize the child. It was over before Rebecca's birth in April 1955. Rebecca was her consolation. In Rebecca, Jan found the direction she sought.

With Rebecca to raise, she found the city barren. With only her meagre social security payments and Donald's $30 a month, she foresaw raising Becca as a ghetto child. She could not return home – Jessie could not have borne the embarrassment. Fair Oaks, where her parents had moved to escape the growing city, was no place for a fatherless grandchild. It was now that her childhood dream resurfaced, with overwhelming force. She needed a homestead, in some cheap and healthy place, where she could function on her own, build life anew away from Donald, and give Rebecca the sense of life she remembered from her own childhood. Friends suggested San Cristobal. In 1958, at the age of twenty-eight, she took Rebecca and headed south.

San Cristobal was everything she could have hoped. In that glorious setting, beneath the sparkling sun and sudden, clean showers, her sombre past faded. She had enough to live on. She rented a house, and let rooms to American academics drawn to San Cristobal's Indian cultures and its still unadvertised charms. Rebecca, at a local kindergarten, began to learn Spanish, and Jan allowed herself to dream that one day she would find her homestead.

It was then that she met Harry.

☙

Harry came to lunch; and then, uninvited, to supper. Her academic house-guests were there, and he was wary, revealing almost nothing about himself. He was a naturalist, he said, always on the move; he was married, though his wife was not around; he financed himself by returning to the States each year to work; he was going to write a book about his jungle explorations – 'I think I've bled enough to do the book justice,' he declared grandly; he praised Gandhi, and pacifism; he came from Vermont. She'd never met anyone from Vermont. No, he said, with pride, not many of us ever leave. Those few snippets of information, and his startling biblical good looks, fed her curiosity.

For the next three months, however, Jan saw nothing of Harry Little. He might have slipped from her mind entirely had not one of her visitors, a young American who had stayed for a few days with Harry, revived her interest by telling her that Harry lived on a jungle homestead. '*Homestead*?' she cried in amazement. Why, he hadn't said one word about home-steading!

Intrigued, she wrote him a letter asking him if she could visit him sometime and inviting him to call next time he was in San Cristobal.

🦌

And then forgot him again, the memory of him buried for a while by devastating news from home. Her father had developed cancer of the throat and had had an operation for the removal of his larynx.

Jan, reading her mother's letter, was horrified and saddened, more by the knowledge of what the operation would do to him emotionally than by its physical effects.

Physically, Jessie wrote, he had come through well. Jan would have expected no less. In this, although she hardly guessed it at the time, she and her father were a match for each other. He was astonishingly resilient, and proud of it. Her childhood had been full of his heroic stories of seafaring adventure; and she remembered vividly how, when she was thirteen, he had survived an accident that would have killed most men. It was war-time, 1943, and he had gone back to sea. He fell into the ship's hold, landed on a pile of lumber, and broke a dozen bones: ribs, collarbone, skull. For three hours he lay unconscious. When he came round, he managed to climb sixty feet to the deck, where he collapsed again. In hospital, he was given up for dead. He said later it was hearing a priest pronounce the last rites – over him, an atheist! – that made him determined to live. After a week, to the doctors' astonishment, he walked; after three months he was back on board. Jan had no doubts that, physically, he would be fine. 'I'm very proud of daddy,' she wrote home, 'I hope I have inherited some of his stamina.'

Emotionally, though – that was another matter. The operation had left him with a hole in the lower portion of his neck through which he breathed. He could talk, Jessie wrote, but only in a series of modified burps that were hard to produce and hard to understand. Without his voice, he would have lost the very essence of his charm. Feckless he may have been, but he had great charm, too much for his own good, Jessie said. Emotion came easily to him. He used laughter, and tears, and charm, and generosity, to win approval. Even as a child, Jan had mixed feelings about this side of his character. He adored Jan, taking her around on his working trips, talking to her volubly as though she were a grown-up, demanding her uninhibited approval, imposing on her a responsibility to protect him from disapproval. This duty was both reinforced and undermined by her mother. He might have his faults, but his feelings were not to be hurt. He's the father I wish I'd had, Jessie said, and stuck by him for Jan's sake. The truth was he used emotion to sow confusion, and to protect himself. He was very good at it. Without his voice, he would be lost.

Jan determined to do what she could to help. She suggested that Jessie bring Bill to say in San Cristobal. It would do them both good to get away from Fair Oaks for a while. And they would love her house, the Granja del Carmen, with its tree-lined driveway and surrounding orchard of pear trees. She had space enough to put them up. The Granja had five rooms, white painted, all in a line along a veranda, with a kitchen and a lean-to bedroom joined by a covered patio to the house. Soon, moreover, she would have the place to herself. All her guests had returned home for the summer, and her teenage maid, Soila, would be leaving shortly as well.

The only problem with having her parents to stay was her own health. After she had issued her invitation, she began to suffer from aches, night fevers and recurrent vomiting that kept her in bed for weeks, lonely and depressed. Her father's visit would have to wait.

※

The very first day of her convalescence, she was in the dining-room writing home, repeating her invitation to her father, when she heard Soila's call: 'Doña Juana! Don Enrique is here!'

She was surprised and pleased, glad for company, glad in particular for his company. She stepped towards the veranda, and saw his shining blond hair haloed in the doorway. 'Harry!' she exclaimed in delight, and raised her arms to give him the formal Mexican embrace.

He held back. 'Careful, Jan,' he said, 'I have a sick child here.'

She looked down. Only then did she notice that he had in his arms a little Indian girl of seven or eight, wrapped in a blanket. She was a striking child with olive skin and a mane of black hair. But her face was sunken and drawn, framing great, dark almond eyes, wide with apprehension.

'What's wrong with her, Harry?' Jan asked.

'Not sure. She'll be all right with nursing. Do you have a bed for her?'

'Of course,' she said. 'She can have my room. Becca and I can share.'

Inside, Harry laid the child gently on Jan's bed, smiled down at her, and introduced them. '*Se llama Juana*,' he said. 'Juana, this is Es, Es-s-s.' He lengthened the sound out. 'Like the Spanish for "is". She's had a very bad time. There, little Es, sleep now.' Es said nothing, but relaxed as Harry settled her and stroked her hair. 'She'll sleep,' he whispered tenderly. 'She's weak and we've been travelling.'

Jan was touched by Harry's affection for the girl, and fascinated. Over a lunch of beans and tortillas, Harry explained. 'She's a Lacandon Indian,' he said. 'You know about the Lacandones?'

Jan nodded. 'A little.' Everyone in San Cristobal knew a little about the Lacandones, the Indians who lived in the great swath of jungle on the lowlands to the east of San Cristobal. They were the last of the forest-dwelling Mayas. A thousand years before, when the Maya civilization collapsed, most of the Mayas migrated. Cities, temples, pyramids were left behind, to be swallowed up by the jungle. Only one group stayed – the Lacandones. They had kept their way of life, fighting off outsiders, until quite recently. Now, there were only a few hundred of them left, and they had in recent years become of considerable concern to a number of people in San Cristobal, among them Jan's academic house-guests.

'There's a group of about a dozen near where I live,' Harry went on, fixing Jan with his startling blue eyes. 'They're in a bad way, and Es has suffered terribly. Her mother died. Her father, Jorge, took another wife and both of them maltreated her. I first saw her months ago on the trail to San Cristobal. Her scalp was riddled with bot-fly sores and her hair was matted with pus. She also had malaria. I told Jorge to leave her with me. I treated the malaria, squeezed the pus from her head sores, shampooed her hair, made her healthy again.'

Jan stared at him, riveted by the novelty of being the focus of such attention and of being involved in such intriguing events. She responded not simply with interest, but with emotion that matched Harry's.

'She's so beautiful.' Harry's voice began to tremble. 'When

24

I was dealing with her head, I gave her candy to suck. She would cry, and suck all the harder, and look up at me . . .' He put his head in his hands. 'This is an incredible child, Jan. I taught her some Spanish. We had wonderful times together. She used to love swimming, and she was always picking flowers for us. It was idyllic, Jan, idyllic. If she had been a little older, I would have married her.' Harry paused, his head still in his hands. Jan, amazed at his words, waited for him to explain himself. 'She knew what it was all about,' he continued, seemingly unaware that he had said anything to occasion surprise. 'She thought that's what she was there for. It was hard – that quality of primitive innocence and playful seductiveness is almost irresistible to a man. But she's only a child, only a child.' He gave a sob, and tears ran down his cheeks. 'When I came out last time, she went back home. I gave her a ribbon to tie in her hair. She was so pretty – too pretty! The next I heard of her, she . . .' He shook his head, and wiped away tears with his fingers. For a moment, she wondered if there was something she could do to ease his pain, but there was no need. He was in a world of his own. 'Her father had abused her, and she'd fled into the forest,' he went on. 'I told him if he didn't go back and find her and bring her to me, neither he nor anyone else in his house would get another thing from me, no machete, no cloth, not even a fish-hook. Jorge knew I meant it. He took some other Lacandones, found her and brought her to me. She was terrified. Her eyes and lips were swollen. She looked as if she'd gone through a prize fight and then been crucified. She was broken, utterly broken. And changed. He'd raped her.'

He paused to regain his composure, drawing a deep breath. 'I took care of her again, but it didn't do much good. She'd begun to eat dirt. I couldn't believe it. Every time I looked away, she would start scraping up handfuls of refuse and dirt, and just stuffing it into her mouth. I was beside myself with worry. All my work for her, lost. I have to go back to the States to earn some money, but I couldn't leave her like that. I brought her out for treatment, and there was your letter. It was providential, Jan. It gave me an answer. I could leave her here.'

He spoke as if he took her agreement for granted. She never thought of refusing. She was too flattered by his attention to consider refusal, too sympathetic to Es's need, too awed by his assumption that there could be no other place for Es to be left. 'I'm sure I can arrange something,' she said.

🐝

Later, after supper, Harry commented, 'You don't look all that well. Will you have trouble looking after Es?'

'I've been ill, but I'm better now. I'll manage,' she said.

He didn't seem reassured. 'I'd heard about your eyes and hearing,' he said. 'What's the trouble exactly?'

She paused. To admit her disabilities was like a confession of guilt. She had long ago learned it was better to avoid conversations like this. They made her feel too exposed.

'Best you tell me,' he said, decisively.

How much should she tell, she wondered. Where should she start? At the beginning, when she was five, when she had nearly died of pneumonia? Soon after that, she began to notice that the world was different. Strange lights would explode inside her head, and she would shout 'The lights! The lights!' and no one would know what she meant. There were times when she felt as if she were walking on a glass sphere, with everything falling away on either side of her. It gave her a weird feeling. It was as if she were being swallowed by the world. Once, a teacher said something that gave her a clue to the problem. She and her friends were fooling round in class while he was writing on the blackboard. 'Stop that,' he said. 'I can see you from the corner of my eye.' After class, they all said, 'What does he mean, corner of his eye?' They flicked fingers about beside their heads, right round by their ears, and all the others said yes, yes, they saw what he meant. But Jan didn't see at all what he meant. She didn't seem to have any corners to her eyes.

And the hearing – what should she say about that odd

26

sensation of living in a confined space, about feeling constantly puzzled, constantly cut off, constantly guilty? She remembered once not catching what her teacher said, and leaning over to see what page her neighbour had turned to. 'Jan! You have to stop looking over other people's shoulders! That's cheating!' The words, descending on her like the wrath of God, snatched away her only means of keeping up. The next day, rather than face school, she fled screaming down the road. It had taken all of Bill's authority to compel her to return. Some time after that, another teacher realized she had impaired hearing. But there was nothing to be done. In those days, hearing-aids were huge, ungainly things, seldom worn by children. She was just always the clumsy one, always the one who was behind. 'Jan, you never know where you are' – the comments were like a daily litany – 'Jan, why don't you look where you're going?' 'Jan, why don't you *listen*?'

No, she couldn't talk about all that, couldn't confess to her feelings of rejection and failure, not yet, at least. Best keep it simple. 'Tunnel vision,' she said, brightly. 'Retinitis pigmentosa. With related deafness. I was fourteen before I was diagnosed. Even then, I didn't realize what it meant. No one discussed it. My parents pretended I was fine. I pretended I was fine.' She smiled. 'I even drove for seven years, until my ophthalmologist found out.' It was her ophthalmologist who had told her the truth about her condition. It had never occurred to him that she might drive. He said he had to report her as blind. 'Am I going blind?' she had asked, horrified. 'You *are* blind,' he said, 'Legally blind. You've been blind for as long as we've had records of you.'

When Harry protested that she could hardly be blind if she could see, she smiled, as she always did when asked to explain. She saw things on a narrow beam, as if she was looking through a gun barrel. Less than twenty degrees of vision. Narrow enough to make her legally blind.

🐾

Es's condition did not improve, and Harry stayed, sharing Es's room. Each day, he carried her round the garden, teaching her Spanish words – *sol*, *zacate*, *cielo*, *fruta*. The girl gazed round with lacklustre eyes, too ill to do more than echo his words in a whisper.

At lunch on the fourth day of Harry's stay, Jan asked what he'd meant about the Lacandones being in a bad way. They'd been terribly brutalized, Harry said. First it was the *chicleros* – the gatherers of the *chicle* latex used as a base for chewing-gum. The *chicleros* had opened up the forest during the war. 'But they were criminals, plunderers, the off-scourings of civilization. What did they care for Indians? The Lacandones were never conquered by the Spaniards, but they've been conquered by the *chicle* gatherers and the anthropologists and the missionaries and all the others who came after them hawking the benefits of civilization. That's where I come in. They need someone who can provide them with a few essentials from outside without exploiting them. If I can save this group from extinction, if I can –'

Suddenly Es cried out. It was an odd, despairing cry, odder because she had been so silent over the previous days.

Harry pushed back his plate, and strode into her room, leaving Jan to follow. She found Harry massaging Es's feet. Es was breathing heavily, in a rasping, uneven rhythm. Her eyes were closed.

'Her feet are terribly cold,' he said. 'You hold her head. She needs to know we are with her.'

Jan knelt down at Es's head and placed her hands along the little sunken cheeks. Es's eyes flickered open, without focusing, and closed again. She began to breathe in short, sharp gasps which gave way to a single, long, bubbling breath. She relaxed.

'That's right,' Harry said gently, reaching up to touch her eyelids. 'Sleep.' Then, in the same flat tone, he added: 'She's dead.'

So unexpected was the announcement, so matter-of-fact, so

unconsidered, that Jan made no move. It had never occurred to her that Es might die. Unable to believe Harry's words, she stared down at the hollow face still cupped in her hands. She saw that he was right. There was no movement, no flicker of an eyelid, no breath.

Slowly, Jan released her hold, and sank back on her heels, incapable with shock.

Now Harry, still kneeling at Es's feet, began to weep. 'She suffered so,' he whispered. 'She kept asking me: "*Porque duele*? – Why pain?" I told her it was the dirt. I didn't know she was dying. I will have to live with this for the rest of my life. If only I had stopped her eating dirt . . .' His words became too distorted by sobs for Jan to hear what he was saying. For several minutes he knelt sobbing, while Jan, still in shock, waited for him to regain his composure.

When he was calm again, he asked for her assistance. He wanted her to arrange the burial. She nodded. It was a simple enough task. For an Indian child, there would be no need for anything official. She knew who to approach, and was grateful for a chance to do something positive.

When she returned, an hour later, Harry was wandering slowly through the pear orchard that surrounded the house. She watched him for a few moments from the shadowed driveway, and decided it was better to leave him to his sorrow. To stop herself brooding too deeply on what had happened, she began to sweep the veranda.

A few minutes later, she saw three men approaching up the cypress-lined drive. They carried a small white pinewood coffin, and some other objects. The men nodded at her, and she directed them into her bedroom.

She was about to move away when she saw that the men were setting up a high, draped stand. They lifted the coffin on to the stand, and then began to place tall tapers on either side. Suddenly she understood what was happening.

'Harry,' she called, running towards him. 'They're making a Catholic wake for Es – I didn't think you'd want . . .'

Harry strode quickly past her to the house. 'Stop this!' he exclaimed, as he reached the bedroom. The men paused, grinning, embarrassed. 'She is Indian!' Harry went on. 'She is not from San Cristobal! She is already with God in Heaven! I don't want this!'

The smiles vanished. The men hastily set the coffin on the floor, gathered up the funeral trappings, and fled.

Jan remained where she was, looking down at the body on the bed, waiting for Harry to break the silence.

'You can help me, Jan,' Harry said, at last. 'In the jungle, the Lacandones cover their dead with branches. Do you have something suitable you can spare to wrap the body in?'

She thought for a moment. 'I have a reed skirt,' she said. She went to a shelf and reached down the skirt. 'I think it's long enough to cover her.'

'Don't say *her*!' he said, abruptly. 'This isn't *her*! This is her body! *She's* not here!' Jan looked up at him, abashed, nervously handing him the skirt. 'Yes, good,' he said, mollified. 'This is appropriate for her. Help me with the body – poor wizened little body . . .' And he began to sob again as he reached down to lift Es's corpse into the coffin. Jan felt for the shoulders. It was the first time she had touched a dead body. Her mind closed for those few seconds to everything except the task in hand: the careful lifting, the setting down, the folding of the cloth. Harry closed the lid, and they slid the coffin against the wall. Only afterwards did she realize she was shaking.

She left him to mourn alone then, busying herself round the house until she saw him come out on to the veranda, and lean, head lowered, against one of the pillars, the image of sorrow. Her heart went out to him. 'Harry,' she said, 'placing a hand on his shoulder, 'I'm so sorry –'

She felt the tension in him immediately. His shoulder muscles quivered like those of a horse dislodging a fly. He stepped away from her, as if rejecting her sympathy.

'I didn't know it would be so *hard*,' he sobbed. Then, with

30

his next words, it was as if a chasm suddenly opened before her – no: as if the chasm had always been there, and the words had suddenly revealed its presence. With a strange formality, as if he were making a momentous announcement or stating a grand truth, he added: 'You haven't lived until you have lost a beloved child.'

She recoiled. How could anyone *benefit* by the loss of a child? Didn't he know it was every mother's nightmare? She was afraid at the darkness he had unfolded, and angry at Harry for arousing her fears. I live for Rebecca's *life*, she thought fiercely, not for her death.

⚘

Jan was curious about Harry's past, and would eventually have asked him about himself. She did not have to. With the removal of the coffin the next morning, as if freed from a great weight, he began to talk.

Jan had seen enough of life and death in San Cristobal to know what would happen to Es's corpse – an open field, a hasty hole, an unmarked mound – and couldn't understand how Harry, feeling as he did, could allow Es, a child of the forest, to be treated in that way.

'You have to accept it can't be like an American funeral,' he said. 'It's more direct here. American funerals are so artificial. My mother's funeral was so stage-managed I didn't even know it had anything to do with my mother.'

'Oh?' she said, feeling suddenly out of her depth, as if she just missed some vital link in his train of thought. She sat down slowly at the table.

'My mother died young,' Harry went on, sitting down opposite her. 'It was fighting that subarctic climate for six months at a time that made her ill, I'm sure of that.' For his mother, Lunetta Lee, was the only one of his family who was not a Vermonter. She was a soft southerner, from Florida, with large brown eyes and long auburn hair. But it was Vermont that moulded Harry Little. Before any of the land

31

was his, he was the land's, a part of the ancient, wooded hills, the fiery fall horizons, the icy winters and the Puritan heritage of hard work and rugged independence.

The family was ruled by Fremont Little, Harry's grandfather, old 'Mont', as he was called, lover of foxhunting, crony of state politicians and master of the Vermont Grange, the local branch of the national farmers' cooperative. Mont would have been governor of the state, Harry said, if he hadn't been so crazy about foxhunting. He was a spellbinder. When he talked, everyone listened (like Harry himself, Jan thought: loud voice, eloquent gestures). He had only one eye – took the other one out with a bull-whip driving oxen. When he was twenty-one, he got TB and was given a year to live. But he cured himself. Died at sixty-nine when he drowned in a spring freshet. Advocated a milk diet, whole-grain foods, no meat. Had no use for doctors.

Harry had been scarred by the death of his mother. She was thirty-six, and he eleven. She developed cancer, and had a breast removed. 'The doctors butchered her,' he said, bitterly, his face twisting in pain and anger. 'She showed me. That *hacked flesh* – the horror of it. At the end, the doctors had drugged her so that she didn't even recognize me.'

The week his mother died, the Little's farm burned down. The next few years were harsh ones for Harry. When the Depression struck, his father, Leland Stanford Little (he was named after the founder of Stanford University), worked in the stone quarries of Barre until the quarry-workers went on strike. At thirteen, Harry saw working men impoverished, hounded by National Guardsmen on the streets of Barre, rejected by the culture, the country and the government of which they were a part. The experience turned the embittered Leland into a socialist, and aroused in Harry a passionate belief in the value of labour. 'I was born a peasant, Jan. I live as a peasant. I will die a peasant, so help me God!'

Later, Harry went to the University of Vermont. There, he decided that he was not like other young men of his generation.

He had considerable intellectual gifts. It was only a question of knowing what to do with them. He found his inspiration at a lecture given by one of the great men of the 1930s, a Japanese Christian pacifist named Toyohiko Kagawa. The experience changed Harry. He abandoned univeristy – he'd never taken to the maths course anyway – and decided to pursue his grand-father's interest in cooperatives. With the help of a grant, he set off to study the movement first-hand, at the Cooperative College in Manchester, England.

On the way, he met Elizabeth Barnett, a Canadian. She was twenty-six, six years older than Harry, had a Masters in English literature from McGill University, Montreal, and was on the verge of what she was sure would be a brilliant career in writing. 'I was just a callow youth,' Harry went on, modestly. 'But she saw something in me, and she opened my eyes to many things. Literature, history, Christianity. We made a bi-cycle tour of Europe. What an experience, Jan! We visited Danish rural co-operatives, then on to France. We roomed with Nazis once, arrogant louts ignorant of the peasant culture around them. We saw it was doomed. War was coming, an-other war, and there were all those ruined villages and endless graves from the first one! We saw how evil the modern world was, how nations tore people away from their roots, turning peasants into soldiers. My mother had told me: "Never be a soldier. A soldier is a murderer," and now I saw why.'

At this moment, Soila came in, carrying two plates of fish and rice. Jan realized with a start that it was lunch time, and that she was very hungry. Harry had been talking for two hours. Without so much as glancing away from Jan, he went right on talking. He and Elizabeth married in Washington soon after they got back from Europe. He went to work for the cooperative movement in Greenbelt, Maryland. But he was too much of a firebrand for them, and had to quit. Eliz-abeth was pregnant. It wasn't what they'd planned, but it made them think more seriously about life. It was obvious war was coming. They couldn't raise a child as part of a society that spawned such evils. After the baby was born – a boy, Bronson Alcott – they used their savings to buy a broken-down farmhouse in Tunbridge, Vermont.

He paused. She pushed a plate towards him. He waved a hand. 'I can't think about food,' he said. 'Suffering takes away the appetite.' She looked longingly at her own food, but decided, out of politeness, to wait until he was ready to eat. It was a beautiful place, he was saying, magnificent, unique, up on a hill where you could see for fifty miles across the Green Mountains. But there was no escape for a pacifist, even there. They did what they had to do, and took him off to prison. The capable Elizabeth was left to look after Bronson and the homestead on her own.

After the war, Vermont changed. City people moved in, setting up vacation homes, driving up the taxes. Harry decided that Vermont was too harsh for homesteading, the wood supply too limited, the growing season too short. He wanted a new homestead in the tropics. First, he worked his way to Cuba, then Paraguay, where he lived briefly with a Christian community. But they had all the old faults, tedious specialized tasks, people telling other people what to do, a real theocratic élite. He came back across Peru. There he learned something he'd had to live with ever since. 'Imagine, Jan –' and a sudden intensity of word and gesture imprinted the scene on her mind with photographic clarity '– I'm in the Andes, high up. I'm sleeping in a hostel, a wooden shack of a place. All around, towering, icy peaks. I'm woken by a pain, right through the heart.' He tugged at an imaginary dagger in his chest. 'Nailed to the bed. But I have to keep moving, live or die. I crawl to the shower, reach for the shower knob. Kill or cure! The water's *ice-cold*, right off the peaks. *Bam!* The shock! But I stepped out free of pain.' He leaned back, and flung his arms wide. 'After that, I knew I had to live with a weak heart. Could die any day.'

Weak heart? With his glowing good looks and boundless energy and dramatic gestures? Why, he didn't even appear to

34

need food. She glanced again at the fish on the table. She wondered: would he really think her insensitive if she –

But the search went on. The Pacific, that's where he went next. Across the south Pacific as the crew-member in a twenty-six-foot sailboat. After searching in vain for paradise on a number of Pacific islands, he returned by way of Central America, visiting a community of Quakers in Costa Rica. *That*, he decided, was the place. Back to Vermont he went to fetch Elizabeth and Bronson, now aged thirteen. Sold the farm, and made it to Louisiana, to an island at the mouth of the Mississippi. It was there . . . He broke off, and his expression darkened. 'I was building a raft to take us across the Gulf. I knew what I was doing. I had enough faith for all of us. But it was there that *her* faith broke. She couldn't match me. She left, with Bronson. She should have waited. If she'd waited just one more day, there wouldn't have been any raft. It was burned the day after she left. That shows the importance of faith. You can never let go, never. But I have no recriminations.' He paused again, then added emphatically: '*None whatsoever*. She gave me *carte blanche* to go homesteading in the tropics.'

He fell silent, lost in thought. Her attention wandered again, back to the fish, until she suddenly registered his last words: *homesteading in the tropics*, and saw a chance to mention her almost forgotten scheme to visit him.

'Harry, I –'

But she wasn't quick enough. Harry cut her off, launching into later chapters of his life-story, hardly pausing even when Soila appeared to clear away the untouched meal. For another hour, then another, then another, he bombarded her with quick-fire anecdotes, sparkling with odd characters and dramatic descriptions, of how he had heard of the Lacandones, worked his way to Mexico, gone on several expeditions into the jungle, and finally found the spot where he now lived.

Suddenly he stopped, and looked around. 'It's getting dark,' he said. 'That's enough about myself. Let's talk about you.'

She drew a breath. 'Harry, there's –'

'You're very thin,' he said, with sudden concern. 'That fever set you back. Sunbathing would help. I have a friend here, a painter, who ruined herself in the States, corrupted by the city, by drink and cigarettes. I watched her recover her vitality sunbathing. Just half an hour a day. And a good diet. You could do a lot for yourself if you would look after your diet.' He stood up. 'I think I'll sleep now. Can't afford to miss the bus.' He yawned enormously and stretched. 'It was a good talk, Jan. 'Night.'

After he left, she went to the kitchen to check on Becca and Soila, and at last find something to eat. Exhausted by the seven relentless hours of monologue, her mind was a turmoil of emotions. As she settled Becca for the night, she tried to analyse her feelings. It was exhausting to be so battered with words, and might have been humiliating to be given so little say. But he had after all been grief-stricken, which excused his behaviour. Besides, he was undeniably fascinating. It was as if he couldn't help it, as if he had no way of holding back the power of his personality. It had kept surging across at her, catching her moth-like in a beam of passionate words, blinding her, and binding her. Her final impression, as she fell asleep, was positive. He seemed so gloriously self-confident, so blissfully free of the doubts and anxieties that beset her. Es's death seemed a world away.

In the morning, he was gone.

🦌

Even in his absence, Harry continued to weave himself into her life. He sent her a New Testament from Mexico City inscribed 'with undying gratitude, Enrique and Es.' When he got to the States, he began to write to her. There were letters from New York, and then from San Francisco. He told her he'd shaved his beard and had his hair cut in order to get a job, and was working in a gardening service. The letters were terse and splashed with exclamations. 'I've noticed a growth on my neck!' he told her in one letter. 'If it's cancer, I'll return to the forest to *die*!!!'

She replied promptly, as she did to all her friends. Only once did she delay, explaining that she'd been short of money for stamps. In his next letter, Harry surprised her, yet again, by sending her a five-dollar bill, together with some rose petals 'to take away the smell!!'

But there were more pressing things to think about than Harry Little. She was approaching thirty, and felt the need to take stock of her life. Of one thing she was certain: she wanted family life, with more children. She did not want Rebecca to grow up without brothers and sisters.

She saw her prospects without illusions. She was handicapped, and had a child. She had no money, and no career. She knew she was no beauty. High cheekbones, a full face and a broad nose gave her her father's Dutch burgher looks rather than her mother's refined dignity. On the other hand, there were assets: a shapely mouth, a classically good figure, long legs, naturally curly hair, and a manner that she liked to think was direct and outgoing.

Those who knew her then would have gone further. She had a definite appeal, no doubt about that. It derived from her determination to wrest as much information as possible from any situation or conversation. Men often found that flattering. But there were other, less obvious consequences. Fearing to make inappropriate responses, she was wary about imposing herself on others. In male company, the combination of intense concentration and an equally intense eagerness to please seemed to suggest a beguiling compliance, or even – with a certain type of man, as she had several times discovered to both her interest and her baffled shock – a seductive vulnerability.

San Cristobal itself, however, offered few possibilities. Most of the more interesting men were either married or in transit. In her early days there, she had had only one brief involvement, with a local Spanish shopkeeper – a single hasty encounter that became an instant embarrassment to her.

37

Now, as if on cue, a friend of a friend arrived, with a letter of introduction. David was a gentle, well-built man of thirty-two, a physicist, who retained an endearing, boyish charm. She fell in love with him; and when he left, it took all her determination to reassert her decision to remain in Mexico.

Not long after he left, she thought she might be pregnant. The idea did not disturb her. Indeed, she felt challenged. Once before, when she had become pregnant with Rebecca, she had decided to determine her own destiny in the face of far greater difficulties – anger and then indifference from Donald; opposition from her doctor, who accused her of recklessly risking the transmission of her disabilities to her child; and disdain from a society in which single-parent families, at least white middle-class ones, were a despised rarity. But she had been right to refuse abortion. Rebecca had been a perfect baby, and she, Jan, had been strengthened by the experience of raising her. Here, it would be easier. Her pregnancy would (she told herself) be perfectly acceptable to the intelligent, liberal, artistic community of foreign residents in San Cristobal. It was with real regret that after a couple of months, she discovered that she was not pregnant, just missing periods as a result of her illness.

Through the summer, as the impact of the affair faded, Jan's health improved. She recovered her appetite, and took care to eat well. She sunbathed, as Harry had advised. She went on answering Harry's letters.

Harry. Somehow, he always seemed to be there in the wings, waiting to re-enter her life.

In the end, she herself gave him his cue.

He wrote that he would be returning in September. That gave her an idea. She needed some things from home – another hearing-aid to replace her hearing-aid glasses, which had developed a fault; a watch; a fountain-pen. Harry was still working in San Francisco, just a hundred miles from Sacramento. Surely, she thought, he would be willing to bring her things back for her, if Jessie sent them to him. She wrote to both Harry and her mother to make the suggestion.

At this point, events acquired a momentum of their own. Jessie decided she wanted to meet this person who could tell them so much about San Cristobal and their daughter's new life. Harry made a favourable impression. He still had his hair short, and was, as always, careful to appear tactful, courteous and sociable. With Bill, whose burping speech often embarrassed new acquaintances, he was patient and understanding. Meeting Harry gave Jessie another idea. What if Harry escorted Bill south for the promised trip to San Cristobal? By the time the news reached Jan, it was all agreed. Bill would drive his pick-up truck south, and Harry would act as guide and helper.

On the day of their departure from Fair Oaks, 14 September, Jan received another note from Harry. She opened it sitting at the dining-room table, expecting to read nothing but the final details of their travel plans. It was written in red, and, like all his letters, was in a hurried, cursive scrawl.

'Dear Jan,' she read, and then, with astonishment that almost instantly gave way to shock: 'I have come to love you for your simplicity, sincerity and poverty. Let's get married. I will accept your choice of a ceremony, religious, civil or informal. When you greet me on arrival, kiss me on the mouth if your answer is yes, lower your head if no. Sincerely, Harry.'

She sat, not moving, unable, for a moment, to believe the evidence of her eyes. She checked the address, just to make sure it was actually meant for her. Convinced by what she saw, she thought of escape. No: too late. No time to reply. She was trapped, trapped in an intolerable dilemma.

She wanted to marry, of course, eventually, but she would never have considered *him*. She was all wrong for him. He had no idea what she was like. Simple and sincere! Oh, God, he made her sound like a placid half-wit. And what did he mean by 'poverty'? Since when was poverty a virtue? Anyway, she wasn't poor, not compared to the local Indians. To praise her for poverty sounded patronizing. She would just have to refuse.

But the idea of rejecting him, in the way he proposed, in

cold blood, was equally impossible. She had never been able to say no, straight out, to any man, not her father, not a lover, not Harry. Besides, she saw, behind Harry's terse words, a desperate need. To reject him would be to hurt him, and he'd been hurt enough.

Why had he put her in that position? Why couldn't he have waited until they had a chance to discuss the matter? Why – she thought, as the conflict of emotions and the fearful knowledge that she could not escape a confrontation built inside her – why has he *done* this to me?

Her hands trembling, she reread the letter, and tried to argue herself out of the chaotic welter of fear, her old fear of finding herself in conflict with a man. What was important here, really important? Should she really be angry with him? He obviously hadn't meant to anger her. Obviously, he thought he was offering a gift, something that she should value. A formal, if odd, proposal. She should consider it in that light. What exactly was he offering? He was a good man, a Christian, she knew that. He would certainly not oppose her decision to have more children. Even with her disabilities, he would accept another child as God-given. He loved children – she'd seen that in his behaviour with Es. He'd be a good father for Becca. And he was a home-steader, the first one she'd met since the Deloziers. Surely, the two of them would understand and want the same things. Perhaps she could, after all, accept.

No! My God, she wasn't at all sure she even liked him. He was so . . . so *absolute*. There hadn't been even a hint of tenderness between them. She couldn't possibly say she loved him.

But that could change, if they were working together, and . . .

And round and round the ands and buts revolved, without conclusion. Fear clouded her reason and her will. There was no easy 'yes' or 'no'. He was both the trap and the escape, the chasm and the safety-net. Hypnotized by her looming fate, imprisoned in the shell of her passivity, she could make no decision.

The next few days brought card after card, marking their progress: Palm Springs, Nogales, Los Mochis, Guadalajara, Mexico City. They were on schedule, and would arrive early on 19 September, a Saturday.

That morning, to disguise her inner turmoil, she dressed in a bright red jumper and put on lipstick. She would at least *look* cheerful and confident.

She was still putting away laundry in her bedroom, wondering nervously how to greet the two men, when her father walked in.

2

MARRIAGE

'Daddy,' she whispered.

The operation hadn't aged him. He was still the same sturdy figure, with hardly a trace of grey in his beard and close-cropped brown hair.

He came across the room and embraced her. There were tears in his eyes, as always in moments of emotion. As he put his arms round her, she heard how changed he was. The breath wheezed through the hole in his neck, which was covered by a cloth. He tried to speak, but no sound came. He stood back, and huffed to clear his throat, sounding like a horse.

'Daddy – it's wonderful to see you. Are you all right?'

Again, he tried to speak. His jaw moved, but she heard only grunting noises. She couldn't understand him, not a word. She was appalled. His vibrant, sustaining voice had been so much a part of her childhood, penetrating her deafness, giving life to her world, that its absence was like the loss of childhood itself. He saw her desperation, and blinked away tears, his anguish inducing in her such a feeling of emptiness that she felt her own tears rising. She closed her mouth tight, and glanced away, at a loss.

Harry was leaning against the doorpost on the opposite side of the room. He had the beginnings of a new beard. She looked at him, her eyes pleading: *help me*.

'He'll be all right in a minute,' he said. He was watchful, but aloof. 'He's been doing fine on the trip.'

Bill grunted.

'What, Daddy? I don't have my hearing-aid.'

Harry answered for him, loudly and clearly. 'He was just

saying it's good to be here, and he wished he could talk properly.'

'Yes, Daddy, yes.' She needed to do something. 'Let me . . . let me show you your room.' She led the way for Bill through the door. Harry followed them.

'Very – nice,' Bill said. This time she understood, and saw how he talked – by swallowing air and then burping it up, modifying the sound into a hoarse, staccato approximation of words. The consonants were blurred and there was no way he could raise his voice to make it easier for her to hear, but at least they could communicate.

'Thank you, Daddy,' she said, squeezing his hand. 'Where are your things?'

Bill waved an arm. Again, Harry interpreted: 'In the truck, outside the gate. It'll have to be brought in.'

'I'll do that!' said Jan quickly. 'No problems with traffic here.' She was bright and assertive, needing to escape both of them. She hated her father's inadequacy, and her own. She hadn't kissed Harry on the mouth, nor had she lowered her head.

'No,' said Harry sternly. 'I'll do it.'

As he left, she turned to Bill, and asked about the trip. This time she had no trouble understanding him. 'It – would – have – been – much – better – with – Donald.' She was surprised by the comparison with Rebecca's father, and by the suggestion that something had gone wrong. She felt obscurely guilty – for what? For Harry's defects? 'He's so – EMOTIONAL!' Bill waved his arms in exasperation.

She didn't want to hear the details. Harry had finished parking. Still shaking with apprehension, she went out on to the veranda to meet him, wondering what she should do about his proposal. She hadn't mentioned the letter. But surely he wouldn't expect a reaction from her yet, under the circumstances?

'I'll go find a hotel room,' he said as he came towards her. He sounded detached, defensive, as if he had seen her restraint as a rejection. She certainly hadn't meant to reject him, couldn't let him just walk out.

'There's no reason for you to go, Harry,' she said. 'There's a place here, Soila's old room by the kitchen.'

'All right. If you say so.' He sounded grudging. Then, 'Jan,' he said, abruptly, 'Let's go to the park. We have to talk.'

'Now, Harry? I can't leave Rebecca, and besides my father has only just arrived.'

'Let your father take care of Rebecca. He'll be glad to. Let him be a grandfather again.'

'All right,' she said, feeling her stomach knot with renewed tension. 'I'll tell him.'

She found her father sitting with Rebecca on his knee. Harry was quite right; they were perfectly happy to be left alone.

As she and Harry made their way along the drive and down the road, Jan tried to control her nervousness by asking him about his trip. Harry answered tersely. There had been misunderstandings. Bill was a novice in Mexico. He had needed guidance in how to behave. It was fortunate –

He broke off, for at that moment they reached a small square in the lee of a hill, up which a long flight of steps, flanked by trees, led up to the Templo de Guadalupe, one of San Cristobal's two hilltop churches. Here Harry stopped. Ignoring the stares of passing Indians, he put his foot up on a stone bench and, as she turned to him, began to address her.

'You got my letter?' he asked.

'Yes.'

'I asked for a direct answer, and I meant it. We don't have to play the games other people play, all those little vanities and indecisions. You and I have been through too much in life to inflict that on one another.'

'Yes?' she said, waiting.

'When I leave for the forest, things must be completely settled between us. Ours will be a higher form of friendship than anyone in San Cristobal can understand. You will be

44

living out a reality swept clear of commonplace trivialities, responding to real challenges. The Lacandones will be very excited to see you. You don't have to worry about them. They will treat you well. Not for the world would I risk anything happening to you or Rebecca.'

His words were a torrent of assumptions, rushing her along. She wanted to say: wait. We've left something out. I haven't agreed to anything. 'Harry . . .' she began.

'One thing I have to tell you, Jan. When we're there, in the forest, it will be a vegetarian table. I've made up my mind I'm not going to compromise on that. In the jungle, I insist that no one does any hunting near my house. Here in San Cristobal, you can live as you want, keep the kind of table you want. But I've seen too many situations where the man was subverted into abandoning his principles.' Now what was he talking about? She frowned. 'I mean,' he said, 'I can't have you bribing the Lacandones to bring you meat on the side.'

For a moment she thought he had made a joke, but then saw that he was serious.

'Oh, no!' She shook her head fiercely. 'I wouldn't –'

He broke in: 'I won't give you any cause to regret your decision, and I shall honour my part without fail. Our life will be together, in the jungle. I'm not at home with streets, never will be. I don't want to begin love-making here. The jungle is the place for that.'

Love-making? She'd never even thought of such a thing. There'd been no mention of love, or emotion of any kind. Now, suddenly, he seemed to take intimacy for granted, without even changing the impersonal tone of his voice. Everything was happening much too fast. One consequence of her deafness was that words seemed to take an age to work their way to her brain along the degraded auditory nerves, like strangers picking their way over rough and unfamiliar paths. She needed time to make sense of what he was saying.

'Harry, I know you're religious,' she began. 'I'm not. If that's what you want . . .'

'I'm not religious in the way you think. I haven't been in a church for years. I was not raised in one. I couldn't lead my life by a creed or dogma, and I wouldn't ask you to either. Christian virtues have nothing do with established religion. People forget the essence of Christianity: GOD – IS – LOVE.' He emphasized the words. 'I try to live by that. Sometimes, it's very lonely, but I wouldn't trade it for . . . for all the tea in China.' Suddenly he smiled. 'But we'll have all the time in the world to talk about that.'

The change utterly disarmed her, and she found herself smiling back at him.

'And talking of tea,' he went on, 'Let's see if Pepe's wife has any hot chocolate.' Pepe, a wizened Spaniard in his late fifties, often acted as Harry's local helpmate.

'I should get gack to Becca,' she said, weakly.

'All right,' he agreed amiably. 'I'll be back later.'

She walked away, her mind in turmoil. If she had been in a fit state to analyse her reactions, she would have blamed herself for letting him talk on like that. As it was, she was hardly even aware that she had allowed him to assume they would be married, that she had implied 'yes' by not saying 'no'. All she knew was that he had re-stated his proposal, and that fact left her uplifted, flattered, and challenged. As for the rest, her responses were a mystery to her. She was aware only of her uncertainty, and on that she began to build a tenuous rationale. Her whole life seemed mired in uncertainty compared to his. He was all clarity and certainty. Perhaps, after all, it was just as well she had not given him an answer then and there, for she might have said 'no'. She recalled her reactions after reading his proposal. She was sure that he meant well, that he was genuinely offering important things – a father for Rebecca; a home; more children. Perhaps, she thought, she should trust the clarity of his reactions, a counterweight to her own confusion. After all, he was a man of high standards. God is love – yes, she could accept that. Clarity of thought, high ideals – those were things that had been missing from her life. It would certainly be challenging to be guided by him. Perhaps, she concluded, as she walked back beneath the cypresses to the house, perhaps that was the way to go.

She was clearing Rebecca's lunch when Harry returned. Bill was in the garden. Jan, calm once more – for she assumed there would be more discussion about the proposal later – looked up from the table. His face, she noticed, was alight with happiness. She smiled a welcome and offered him some food.

'Nothing for me, thanks. I had something with Pepe,' he said, beaming. 'I told Pepe I'm going to marry you. I asked him if he knew anything against you I should beware of, and – this is wonderful Jan, I wanted to tell you right away – you know what he said? *"Ella es muy noble"*!'

In an instant, her joy at his mood turned to anger. This was her first inkling of how he had interpreted their talk. What presumption! She turned away to hide her reaction. Damn it, she thought, if you want –

'Isn't it wonderful? "Very noble"!'

– if you want to know something about me, ask *me*, not someone else! How could he show such little trust in his own judgement, and in her judgement of herself? He'd talked to Pepe as if their marriage was a fact. What had she said to give him that idea?

But looking at him again, seeing him smiling, luminous with delight, she couldn't bring herself to speak, couldn't undermine his obvious happiness, couldn't expose herself and her anger in front of Rebecca and her father. I'll talk to him later, she decided. It'll be easier later.

She smiled at him to disguise the sudden rush of conflicting emotions, picked up the dishes and walked past him to the kitchen. He was quick to follow her, offering help with the dishes, with the fire, with Rebecca. As they worked together, he began to talk, and her anger drained away, unexpressed. He talked about cooking in the jungle, about Vermont kitchens, about his father. Sometimes he broke off to comment on something Rebecca was doing. Sometimes, Rebecca would

47

interrupt him by tugging at his trousers or his hand. But the steady all-embracing, overpowering accompaniment to that afternoon was Harry talking, talking, talking on through the evening, and the next day, while Bill wandered the town and wrote letters and entertained Rebecca, talking through meals, and shopping, and household chores, talking about visiting the Paris Exhibition with Elizabeth, about returning from seeing his dying mother and finding the farm burned down, about harvesting apples at the Tunbridge house, about the jungle. For Harry, it seemed, the past was always present, and everything he talked about was charged with meaning and emotion and significance.

After two days of this, Jan began to feel as if she were drowning in a sea of words. She decided it was time she contributed something about her own past. She couldn't talk so easily about herself, of course, and her past was no match for his, but he would surely want to know about Rebecca's father. In all honesty, she should tell him. She waited for her moment, then began to speak. 'I was married, too,' she said, 'But only for a few months. Donald was one of my group of friends. We became close . . . I loved him, but – but we were more friends than lovers. He had – problems, that is, with women he knew personally.' She wasn't doing this very well. Donald had been impotent with her, except on two occasions. 'Just when I decided to break it off, I got pregnant. The doctor, my friends, everyone assumed I would have an abortion –' She stopped. He was watching her with a fixed expression. 'But I couldn't,' she went on, tensely, suddenly unwilling or unable to explain further. 'Donald said if I had the baby it would be my decision. We married to give Rebecca a name . . .'

'But you're free to marry now?'

'Oh, yes.'

That was enough for him. He was off again.

All this talk excluded her father, and she felt guilty on his account. Several times, she'd made a point of trying to talk to him on his own. She'd found it hard going. Much of his speech was incomprehensible to her, and he was still angry about Harry's behaviour on the journey – in particular, his disapproval of drinking. But over the next three days, Bill began to mellow, won over by Harry's solicitousness for Jan and Rebecca, and Jan felt she could tell him, formally, what was going on.

Her chance came on the third evening, after supper. Jan left Harry to finish in the kitchen and came back into the dining-room. Her father was at the table, reading.

'Daddy.' She sat down beside him and took his hand. 'Harry and I are talking about getting married.'

'I thought something like that was going on,' he grunted.

'Well,' she asked, 'What do you think?'

He patted her hand. 'If that's what you want . . . Whatever you want to do, you do that.'

Suddenly, Harry was there by the door, as if he had over-heard their moment of intimacy, and had deliberately intruded to assert control. 'Come to the kitchen, Bill, and you, Jan. It's warmer there and I'll fix you some hot chocolate for the night.'

They followed him across the patio and pulled chairs up to the glowing hearth, with Jan still mildly resentful at Harry's intrusion.

'Bill,' Harry said at once. 'Jan and I are planning to get married. You know me, you know what I am. I'll take care of Jan, and Rebecca will be my daughter. You know I'll do everything in my power to make them happy. Will you and Jessie give us your blessing?'

It was an impressive speech, Jan admitted to herself, a clear, formal statement, even if he had taken the initiative away from her. She looked expectantly at her father. Bill was silent for a few seconds. He might at that point have asked Jan what she felt about the suggestion. Instead, he offered what he clearly intended to be reassurance. 'This – man – will – never – leave you,' he said.

Never. The word rang in her mind like a knell. Vistas of

time opened before her, stretching away into a dark and cavernous future. She suddenly felt out of control, as if both men were combined against her, forcing her towards an inevitable fate. Never! Again, fear washed through her, and again the emotion itself, disguised by a nod, inhibited her response.

Bill added something about signed papers, waving his hand, writing in the air. Very important to Jessie.

'That settles it!' Harry declared. 'I wouldn't have your mother unhappy for the world. We'll have a formal ceremony.' He began to stroke Jan's hair. It was a gesture of possession, a sign, Jan felt, that she had been passed from father to husband; but it was also the first expression of tenderness. Curious, she responded, leaning her head back against his hand. 'We'll be married by a judge!' Harry went on. 'We'll find one tomorrow!'

Tomorrow. That was too soon. She wanted an engagement, she wanted time to think. 'But, Harry, my father hasn't been here a week. We can't just leave him –'

'He'll be all right! He'll be happy to see you married! No reason to delay. It doesn't take long to be married. First time I was married, it took fifteen minutes. We have to settle a date quickly. The Lacandones are waiting.'

'But, Harry, the Granja, all I have here –'

'You'll be surprised how fast things go when you get started. It's a mistake to be attached to property!'

'But –'

But I don't even love you! The words were on the tip of her tongue, when another thought intruded: Who said anything about love? No one. The fire flickered in the hearth; the beams above were black; out there in the streets Indians slept under cotton blankets; Es had died; she herself had been ill for weeks. She was in a harsh world. Wouldn't it be better to accept what was on offer? It was, after all, more than she had. Companionship would do for the time being. Love could come later.

'But not tomorrow,' she said, with studied calm. 'How about in a week?'

'A week then,' said Harry, 'The twenty-ninth.'

'Good,' said Bill, and stood up to say goodnight.

When he had gone, she walked beside Harry out on to the patio. He turned towards her. 'Now I'm going to kiss you goodnight,' he said. 'A kiss to seal the engagement.'

He put his arms around her and kissed her on the mouth. She, feeling that an expression of affection was in order, would have kissed him warmly, and waited for his guidance. None came: no warmth, no desire, no search for a response in her. The gesture was exactly what he had said it would be: a seal, cold and impersonal.

※

His action puzzled her. She had no idea what he saw in her, no idea how strong his feelings were. But he would not insist on marriage without feeling some desire for her, she reasoned. There had to be more.

There was, as she discovered the following day.

Throwing himself into the arrangements with infectious and boyish enthusiasm, he hurried her into town to see the judge. They'd be married on the veranda at the Granja! They'd invite friends! Make it an occasion!

An occasion indeed, with matching accompaniment, for later, when delivering invitations, they overheard gentle music. The sound came from a nearby open doorway. Inside, four men were practising on a huge, double keyboard marimba, a local variant of a xylophone, their rubber hammers softly coaxing a Mexican folksong from the wooden bars. 'Wouldn't you like to dance to that at the wedding, Jan?' He strode inside, and within a minute he had it all arranged.

On their way home, they were overtaken by dusk, and the mood changed. A chill breeze from the mountains caused Jan to shiver and make some inconsequential remark about San Cristobal's climate. Her words set Harry off on a monologue about Chiapas architecture. The houses were built all wrong.

Impossible to heat. New Englanders were much more practical. Good builders. They kept each other warm as well. Had Jan heard of the old courting custom of bundling? Perfectly proper, of course, best way to keep warm, boy and girl each wrapped up in a blanket next to each other. Wouldn't have been any young men left to marry if they all had to stumble home in the snow after midnight. Best way for two people to get to know each other.

At first Jan thought he was just reminiscing about his boyhood. Only as they turned up the Granja's grass-covered driveway did she realize his thoughts had taken a more serious turn. 'I think we need time together, Jan,' he went on. 'We ought to relax, become better acquainted. I'll ask Bill. He'll understand.' No mistaking what he was suggesting now. She smiled to herself. Perhaps he was not going to leave love-making to the jungle, after all. 'Instead of going to your bed tonight,' he finished, 'You come to mine.'

That evening, after she had settled Rebecca, and Bill had tactfully retired to his room, she showered and put on a long cotton dress she had made for summer evenings. What did he expect, she wondered, checking herself critically in the mirror. Bundling might be perfectly proper, but sleeping all night together . . . What if something happened? I want to get pregnant, she thought, applying a final touch of lipstick, but maybe he wouldn't want it to happen so soon. Better if I took precautions.

As she crossed the patio, the cold night air, carrying the scent of evergreens from the mountains, made her shiver. She remembered the reassuring warmth of lying with Donald. It would be good to lie like that with Harry, letting the talk flow easily, without tension.

She tapped at his door, and pushed it open. 'Come in,' he said. His light was still on, and he was sitting up in bed, reading, covered by a single blanket. Uncertain what to do, she sat, still shivering, on the edge of the bed. It was a narrow bed, pushed up against the wall. 'I don't want to go on this side,' she said. 'I'll fall out. Let me climb over.'

'Here,' he said, and raised himself, shifting to the foot of the bed. She noticed he was wearing shorts and a T-shirt. 'I'm happy on the outside.'

When she had settled herself against the wall, Harry spread the blanket over her, tucking the edge of it chastely around her. Then he lay down beside her.

'It really is cold,' she said, teeth chattering. 'I should have brought another blanket.'

'This is fine for me,' he replied.

Their heads came together on the single pillow. 'I should have brought another pillow, too,' she added.

'This is fine. Life isn't going to be all pillows and blankets in the jungle. It's steamy down there.'

An image came to her mind: a Chinese laundry she had visited as a child. She imagined the jungle with steam issuing as if from vents and drifting up in random plumes.

'I promise you,' Harry went on, 'if you can't make it, I won't sacrifice you. I've seen women broken by climate before. I saw what happened to my mother struggling in a climate she couldn't adjust to. That's what broke Elizabeth: she was afraid of the heat. If it's too much for you, we'll come back here. Find a house. I could write.'

She felt cold air on her back, where the blanket had come loose, and resettled it, pulling it over both of them. But no sooner had she done so than he set about tucking the blanket back between them. She realized he must be shy. She understood that. But he would be cold. And she would be quite happy to lie close, as she used to with Donald, allowing conversation to come at its own pace, unforced and honest. She needed his warmth, nothing more. She pulled up her twisted gown, untucked the blanket and moved closer to him.

'No!'

He grabbed her gown, tugging it down vainly; then he pushed her away, and wrapped the blanket back around her. 'Harry,' she said, with mock seriousness. 'I'm freezing.'

She pulled the blanket away again, and for a few seconds they tussled foolishly.

Suddenly without warning, he was on her, and then thrusting at her and into her, and in another few seconds he had finished. He moved off her, and lay beside her, utterly quiet.

She lay with her head on his arm, too shocked to speak. With part of her mind, she was still wrestling with that wretched blanket. She'd thought it was a game, and couldn't all at once adapt to what had happened. Another part of her complained bleakly: He didn't even ask.

'The thing about San Cristobal,' he said after a minute. 'Is that the altitude hasn't affected my heart.'

She said nothing, waiting for him to make some acknowledgement of what had just happened.

'It's good here,' he went on. 'I could even live here if it wasn't for the noise. Every fiesta is a pandemonium of fireworks and church bells.'

This time, she felt she should respond. Perhaps talk, even on a theme as bland and evasive as this, would lead on to more significant matters. 'The noise doesn't get to me,' she murmured. 'I have a good feeling about the place, too. The lonely stretches never last long.'

There was another silence. She felt him tense.

'Don't they?' he said. 'Don't they, indeed? Why do you say that? Were you with someone this summer?'

She said nothing. It was really none of his business. But her silence was an answer of a sort, and he was not to be put off. 'Were you *with* someone this summer?' he repeated, louder.

'With someone? Harry, you have no right to . . .' Her own emotion, and fear of his reaction, made her inarticulate. 'It wasn't easy . . . I had to try to work things out in my own way . . .'

'Don't get psychological with me!' He knelt up and gripped her shoulders. 'Were – you – with – someone – this – summer?'

He was talking not simply as if he owned her, but as if he had already judged and condemned her. The realization made her suddenly angry. 'Yes, I was!' she said, defiantly.

'All right!' He pushed the blanket back violently and stood up. 'You can say you had me too, if you like, but I'm leaving, right now!' He grabbed his shirt, and began to rummage round for his trousers. 'I'm not going to play the fool for you! I trusted you! I didn't know you were *that kind of woman!*'

'Harry . . .' She pulled the cover up around her, as a protection against the cold, and the coldness in his voice. 'Harry, I'm not promiscuous.'

'How can you say that?' He hunted around on the floor for his shoes, talking angrily and much too loudly. 'You know what your behaviour is. I didn't intend for anything to happen. You were the one who started it! I went along because I thought you had to know I wasn't like *your Donald.*'

'Oh, Harry.' Her voice broke. 'That's not why I told you about him. You told me about your marriage, and I thought you should understand –'

'I understand better than you think! I'm leaving as soon as I've got my things together!'

'Harry, be reasonable!' Her resolve began to crumble. Her father would almost certainly be awake by now, and able to hear everything Harry was saying. 'I'll go back to my bed,' she said, in a hoarse whisper. 'There's no need to leave. All the hotels are closed.'

'I'll find a place. Don't you worry about me.'

She couldn't let him go like that, wandering around the cold streets in a fury, an easy victim for the town's drunks. What would she tell her father? What would she tell Rebecca?

He was still trying to find a shoe. 'You've changed,' he said bitterly. 'I should have realized. You're just like all the rest of them, out to use a man. And to think Pepe told me you were *muy noble*! I believed him! But your behaviour . . . with another man . . . What we did, what happened between us . . . . *that* was marriage. The ceremony is nothing.' His words gave her

55

time to gather herself. 'My mother told me never to take a woman unless I was willing to marry her,' he went on, jerking a shoelace tight, 'and on that basis I took you, I *married* you . . .'

'And on that basis you divorce me!' She cut in scathingly, not bothering to keep her voice down. At that moment, she would have been happy to see him walk out and never come back.

But in that same instant, he changed. His anger evaporated. He knelt by the bed and put his arms round her. 'God put those words into your mouth, honey,' he said, gently. 'They couldn't be your words. You couldn't have said them.' She was speechless with astonishment, baffled by the change. 'That was God telling me I should not leave you. God took Es from me and gave me you and Rebecca to take care of. It was wrong of me to speak as I did. I don't know how, but we'll work it out, somehow. Help me.' She stared at him. He was genuinely begging forgiveness, she was certain of it. Seeing him like that, kneeling beside her, she had to soften, and drew a breath to speak. But before she could utter a word, his hand came up. 'Be quiet for a moment,' he said. 'Let me pray.'

He lowered his head. She lay back, too afraid to say or do anything, afraid that any word from her would provoke another outburst, that any gesture might inspire another baffling change of mood.

After a moment he raised his head. 'It's no good,' he said, giving her shoulder several heavy, insistent pats. 'You can't always pray when you want to.' He sighed, took a handkerchief from his pocket, and began to wipe her lips. 'No more lipstick for you. I didn't want to say anything before, but when we arrived and I saw you standing there . . .' He paused, as if appalled at the image she had presented to him. 'You were changed. You looked . . .' He seemed to search about for the right word. '. . . *beefy*, dressed in red, with red lipstick, you looked like . . .' He stopped. A *scarlet woman*, she thought ruefully. 'There: that's the last of it,' he murmured. 'You will be as the white doe.'

'I'm so pale without it, Harry.' Her surprise, anger and bitterness had all receded. She felt nothing but sudden and overwhelming exhaustion.

'You don't need it,' he insisted. 'Once you're in the jungle, you will brighten up. The jungle cures everything.'

Jan remained silent, grateful that he was calmer, that she didn't have to pit herself against him any more. There was no thought now of rejecting him. She was too relieved that the crisis was over, too relieved that she herself had not been rejected.

'And I don't want you cutting your hair,' he went on, putting the handkerchief back in his pocket. 'You will have to take your new life seriously. You've lived here as you want, without thinking of the consequences. You have a little girl to consider, and now she is my little girl as well. You will have to work, but there will be a *purpose* to everything. You will learn what it means to be responsible. Are you ready for that, Jan? Are you ready for a true family life? Are you ready to accept maturity when it is offered to you?'

'Harry, I . . .' She searched around for a phrase that would be true, and would also satisfy him. 'I do want to grow, as a person.'

'Then I will help you. Come.' He took her hand in his. 'It's late now. You need to get some sleep.'

She got up, and put on her robe. 'We'll save our love-making for the jungle,' he said, as he walked her to the door. 'I feel so tense in the city. Was that —?' He stopped and looked inquiringly at her. 'I thought — a diaphragm?'

She nodded.

'You won't need it,' he said, matter-of-factly. 'I had an operation in Washington after Bronson was conceived. In all the years since, nothing has ever happened.'

He didn't wait for her reaction. He kissed her on the fore-head, murmured 'Goodnight, Jan,' and closed the door.

She pulled her robe tight around her. Nothing has ever happened! And now nothing ever would. She gave a short, sharp gasp, something that might if unrestrained have become either a bitter laugh or an equally bitter sob. Her bitterness, though, was directed not at Harry for dashing her most precious hope with an offhand phrase and quick escape, but at herself. Grateful to have found acceptance, well trained at concealing disapproval of vulnerable males, it did not occur to her to reject Harry. How foolish of me, she thought, to build up my expectations without knowing where I stood. Biting her lower lip in self-recrimination, she returned shivering through the empty darkness.

Early next morning, she was woken by Harry. 'You have to make coffee for your father,' he said gently.

'Yes.' She was relieved at his tone of voice, but was still nervous about how he would treat her after the previous evening's débâcle. 'How did you sleep?' she asked, anxiously.

'I slept well. I had your scent next to me.'

No mention of his anger. No apology. But his soft tone and romantic turn of phrase reassured her, and she locked what had happened away in her mind, where it could not threaten her commitment to him.

There was nothing much to do before the wedding itself, except prepare the food. Harry said he would take a few days off to buy some cacao pods for the jungle, and left by bus that same afternoon.

And if, in his absence, she felt any reservations about the impending marriage, when he returned three days later he bound her to him again. Towards evening, during one of San Cristobal's sudden, torrential showers, while Jan, Bill and Rebecca were having supper, Harry burst in upon them, dripping wet. Grinning hugely, as if he were the bearer of a wonderful secret, he pushed the door shut, one hand behind his back. Rain ran in rivulets off his windbreaker.

As Jan rose to greet him, he swung up his arm, and flourished a huge glistening bunch of red-and-cream gladioli. 'I bring you the sun!' he announced.

'Harry, Harry!' Rebecca cried, running to him.

He laughed. 'Here, Jan!' He handed her the flowers, took Rebecca's hands, and danced with her round the room. Then: 'Hungre-e-ee!' he said, throwing off his windbreaker. 'What have we here?' He peered over Jan's shoulder. 'Rice. Vegetables. Wonderful.' He sat down, and Jan, still smiling, handed him a plate.

'No ripe pods,' he reported. 'But I've got eighteen seedlings, delicate little things. Oh, no! I left them outside. They'll die of cold.' He got up, strode outside, and returned seconds later with a large canvas sack. Straightaway, he began to unpack little pots, setting them in a line along the counter that ran the length of the wall. 'Couldn't carry these and the flowers *and* open the door,' he laughed. 'The bus didn't even slow down. I just waved a peso bill out of the window at the woman, and she ran alongside shoving the flowers at me. I felt terrible when I saw what she had given me. All these flowers! Now – heat, humidity. That's what cacao seedlings need. Jungle warmth. The fire. Jan, a kettle. Keep it boiling, all night. Don't know if it'll work. Be a miracle if it does!' Jan watched, smiling. When he was like this, he was magical, *luminous* – for the second time, that was the word that came to her mind. 'Now,' he said, boyishly eager, 'where's that rice?'

※

Next day, after selecting wedding clothes in San Cristobal, they began to sort through Jan's four cases of books to choose those they would take to the jungle. Conan Doyle met with Harry's approval. The Merck medical manual. Good. Mark Twain. Good. He paused leafing through Toynbee's *A Study of History*. 'We had walls lined with books in Tunbridge,' he said, in a meditative tone. 'In the evening, Elizabeth and I

59

would take turns reading to each other. I would read while she sewed; then she would read while I did repairs.'

Jan, making her own selection, smiled and nodded. She liked to hear about Vermont. It sounded so blissfully happy. She seized upon his picture of unalloyed domestic harmony as proof that he had built a fulfilled and harmonious married life before, and would do so again. Surely, she reasoned, when they were in the jungle, and she had her well-defined role as mother and wife in a close-knit family, all the stresses imposed on Harry by city living and the impending marriage would fall away, leaving those fine qualities that had defined his life with Elizabeth.

And clearly he would make a wonderful father for Rebecca. He was forever calling Jan over to watch her play with her dolls. Sometimes she was so quiet he would tiptoe to a doorway and peer round to see if she had fallen asleep. It pleased him to be responsible for her. 'I'm your daddy now, Rebecca,' he told her several times. 'You mind what I say.'

In the face of Harry's warmth and enthusiasm, Jan's reservations faded. As that week passed, and the wedding approached, she kept Harry's virtues firmly before her. She blamed only herself for her suffering, resolutely reasoned away all apprehension, and stared down the restricted tunnel of the present towards a future that, given Harry's qualities, would surely be a bright one. 'I really hadn't had enough experience to realize what an exceptional man he is,' she wrote home to Jessie, insistently, the day before the wedding, 'and how completely devoted a man can be to the idea of family life. It is hard to put such overflowing emotions into words. I love him very, very much and he loves us, Rebecca and me. He is completely loving, understanding, responsible and with the strongest sense of human values I have yet known.'

Jan and Harry were married on the afternoon of 29 September 1959, on the veranda of the Granja. The guests began to arrive soon after two o'clock. All of them had been shocked to learn of Jan's engagement to the eccentric jungle adventurer, and all, seeing nothing but unhappiness in Jan's future, poured good wishes on her, as if she could be saved by wishes. Slowly they gathered: Marcey and Janet, Jan's greatest friends; Vicente, the Spaniard with whom she had had a brief encounter, and who was there because he was a friend of Harry's; the Barocos; Wilfred and Marcia who were going to take over the Granja; Bobbie Montague; a dozen others and, of course, Trudi Blom, San Cristobal's doyenne. Trudi, a diminutive and combative Swiss with a redoubtable reputation as defender of the Lacandones and their forest homeland, had recently been in dispute with Harry over the treatment of some members of the tribe, and Harry had been avoiding her. Indeed, the package Jan had collected from the Hotel Jardin that morning had been for Trudi. But now there she was, wishing them well in her deep Greta Garbo voice, bringing a basket of vegetables from her own garden to set alongside the *tomales*, turkey, salads, bread and cheeses. On the veranda, chairs were set out, and at the far end, the marimba band stood ready to play.

The judge was late. When he did finally arrive, he said he had to get permission from the state capital, Tuxtla Gutierrez, to marry two foreigners, and promptly left again.

'First time I heard of *both* partners being left at the altar,' Jan said, to a ripple of laughter. 'Don't worry, Daddy,' she added in an aside to her father, 'He'll be back.'

'No problem,' Bill rasped. 'I'll serve some drinks.'

'Well,' said Harry. 'There's always the chance he won't come back. I've been waiting for six years for this day. Let's do it ourselves. We don't need the judge.' At this point, John Baroco stepped in. John was an American anthropologist with a winning smile and a direct, sometimes cynical, manner. 'I always wanted to perform a wedding,' he announced. 'Let me do it.'

'You just got yourself a job, John. Do what, exactly?'

There was a flurry of voices and laughter.

'I know,' Harry shouted above the noise. 'You read a text for us. It'll be a Quaker ceremony. I know what I want: the wedding verses from St Matthew.' He hurried inside to find a New Testament. 'Do you have something, Jan?' he asked on his return.

She thought for a moment. Yes: some lines of Walt Whitman. She hastily scribbled them out for John.

By the time everything was ready, the judge was walking back along the drive. 'Never mind,' whispered Harry, taking Jan by the hand, 'We'll have both ceremonies.'

John Baroco took charge. Harry and Jan were to go out along the drive, and make a formal entrance when the guests were all ready.

Harry held out his hand to Rebecca, while Jan took her other hand, and the three walked to the gate, where they turned. John Baroco waved. The marimba band struck up a Mexican folk tune. Harry smiled down at Jan. 'Let's show them how happy two people in love can be,' he said. She smiled back, and the three of them walked back towards the house.

As they stopped in front of John, he began to read:

'"And he answered and said unto them, Have ye not read, that he which made them at the beginning made them male and female,

"And said, For this cause shall a man leave father and mother, and shall cleave to his wife: and they twain shall be one flesh?

"Wherefore they are no more twain, but one flesh. What therefore God hath joined together, let no man put asunder."'

Then came Jan's quotation:

'"Camerado, I give you my hand!

I give you my love more precious than money,

I give you myself before preaching or law;

Will you give me yourself? will you

come travel with me?

Shall we stick by each other as long as we live?"'

When John had finished, the judge stepped forward, and opened a book. He explained that the ceremony would begin with a simple, formal goodbye between father and daughter. This would be followed by a reading of the duties of husband and wife.

Harry summarized the judge's remarks to Bill, and then turned to Jan. 'You might not hear too well,' he said. 'I'll hold your hand. Whenever you have to say yes, I'll give it a squeeze.'

The judge launched into a rapid stream of Spanish, then paused, and looked at Bill.

'Bill,' Harry prompted. 'Your turn. This is when you say your goodbye.'

Bill stepped forward on Jan's left, and placed his arms protectively round her shoulders. He tried to speak, and failed, choked with emotion.

'Daddy,' whispered Jan, 'It doesn't matter.'

Harry spoke again, louder. 'Say goodbye, Bill. This is when you lose your little girl.'

Again Bill tried to speak. She saw the tears glistening in his eyes. He shook his head apologetically.

'It's all right, Daddy,' Jan said, freeing her hands.

Suddenly, Harry leaned across her, and called cheerily, 'Goodbye, Papa!' She drew back, appalled at his insensitivity, wondering if the guests would notice. 'Goodbye, Papa!' Harry called again, grinning and waving. Bill, still shaking his head at Jan, retreated, while Harry laughed and waved theatrically, 'Goodbye, Papa, goodbye-e-e-e!'

Jan, painfully embarrassed for them both, smiled her understanding at her father and watched him retreat to his place. She turned back to face the judge.

His eyebrows were raised in surprise. He blinked, glanced down, and began to read again. Jan couldn't begin to follow him. She responded with an automatic '*Si*' whenever she felt Harry squeeze her hand, but her mind was elsewhere. Soothed by the stream of Spanish, she began to wonder how in years to come she would look back on this day. The judge's voice droned on. I do get into the damnedest situations, she thought. The damnedest situations.

※

Harry's plan was to fly as soon as possible to the jungle, to prepare the house. Jan would close up the Granja and follow with Rebecca in a month.

The three days before his departure were easy enough. Harry moved into Jan's room, where they slept together on a double mattress on the floor. There was love-making of a sort, but Jan, remembering Harry's words, decided not to regard his hasty, silent attentions as a true indication of his capacities once they were established in their jungle home. She was grateful enough that he seemed relaxed and happy, now the strain of the wedding was behind him.

On the day of his departure, however, he woke Jan early.

'Couldn't sleep,' he said, taking her hand. She was astonished to feel that he was trembling. 'Jan, I was . . . Jan, don't say you're coming and not come!' His voice caught, and he began to sob. 'Jan, don't desert me!'

'Harry . . .' She was moved by the intensity of his feeling, but also puzzled. 'Of course I'm coming. I wouldn't . . .'

'Don't lie to me, Jan.' He was not accusing, but pleading. 'Don't ever lie to me. If you're not coming, say so now!'

For a moment she was too bewildered to reply. She'd known from the beginning that he was vulnerable, but it amazed her that he should doubt her sincerity, even now, after the wedding vows.

'Harry,' she said, after a few moments, 'It never *occurred* to me not to come. I want to come. I'm longing to be there. That life is the life I want.' She held a hand against his cheek.

'That's a wonderful thing to say, Jan. If only I could believe it.'

'It's true, Harry, of course it's true.'

'Then you are coming? You won't do what Elizabeth did?

You won't fail me?'

'No, Harry. You must believe me. I made a promise, and I'll never go back on it.'

'Yes. Yes. Thank you.' Her words seemed to calm him. After a few minutes, he got up to finish packing, leaving Jan astonished at this sudden glimpse of his anxieties. She had no idea they went so deep. Such pain – a mirror, in a way, of her own. He needed her, she realized with surprise and more than a little relief, he genuinely needed her. She had hoped, for the last two weeks, that he would be her salvation; now she also began to hope that she would be his.

❧

When the time came for Harry to leave, Bill drove them all down to Comitan in the pick-up. From Comitan, fifty miles south and 2,000 feet lower, flights were cheaper than from San Cristobal. As the truck wound down through the mountains, Harry, with Rebecca on his lap, pointed to the east. 'There!' he shouted above the noise of the engine. 'See the first range of mountains? Over that, there's another, and then – jungle, the Selva Lacandona! Pure fresh air and sweet water! It's as close as you can get to Eden!'

In Comitan, they had time to spare. The plane was scheduled for the following morning. The temperature had risen as they descended, and, after checking in to their hotel, Bill suggested a beer. They strolled to the town's main plaza, which had a pavilion where the locals drank and listened to music. Inside the pavilion, there was a jukebox. As they sat down, someone put on a record of marimba music.

'It's like the wedding,' Harry said. 'Let's dance.' He held out his hand to Jan, drawing her on to the dance floor. As they danced, she fixed her eyes on his face, on his shining hair and brilliant blue eyes. He was smiling, radiantly. She knew the tune – a Mexican folksong – and danced as she had danced at the party after their wedding. Then the tune changed, and she began to improvise. 'You're good!' said Harry 'You're *very* good! You dance like a true peasant!' And he began to match her step for step. He laughed, and threw back his head, and sweat streamed down his temples. The music played on, tune succeeding tune, and all the while her eyes never left his face. He filled all there was of her vision.

3

ON THE SANTA MARIA

Below the little Cessna, the jungle rolled out over ridges and
hills, as endless as desert, until it vanished into haze. Scattered
clouds, and their shadows, dappled the canopy beneath. No
road, not a single house, only the rough carpet of green, torn
here and there by the glistening ribbons of rivers. It was an
awe-inspiring sight, and frightening. A forced landing in that
trackless wilderness would mean certain death. Jan gazed
down, astonished by her suspension between two worlds:
behind her, the safe and the known; ahead, the dangerous and
obscure. Rebecca turned apprehensive eyes to her mother.

'I want to get down!' she wailed.

The pilot smiled reassurance, and pointed. Ahead, two large
rivers, the Jatate and the Perlas, wound their way southwards.
On the tongue of land formed where the rivers joined, a
rectangle had been cut in the long grass to make an airstrip.

'San Quintin!'

The pilot banked the plane into a turn, passing low. Below,
people stood, all watching, all motionless, all but one in long
white Lacandon tunics: Harry, both arms raised in welcome as
if to snatch them out of the sky.

The plane touched, bounced, touched again and bumped to
a stop. As the engine died, the door opened to humid heat, the
rich smell of cut grass, and Harry, his beard longer after a
month in the jungle, smiling hugely.

'Jan! Becca! Wonderful! No, no, leave the baggage – the
Lacandones will bring it.'

She gripped his hand – he was trembling, she noticed – and
stepped down gingerly. He took Rebecca in his arms, and led

the way towards a shelter past the silent Indians. They stared at her in frank curiosity, their serene self-possession contrasting with Harry's electric exuberance.

As the Lacandones unloaded the bedding, kitchenware, clothes and boxes of food, Harry pointed out the Indians, whose names were familiar to her from conversations in San Cristobal. There was Bor, Harry's neighbour, his hair, uncut for years, almost obscuring his wizened face. Like all the men, he was wearing a dirty-white cotton tunic, a *couton* that might, if clean, have passed for a nightgown back in the States. He spoke to Harry in a heavily accented, guttural Spanish Jan couldn't understand. With him was his wife, Margarita, who was no more than thirteen. And the others – Na Kim; little Eska; Pedro; Jorge –

'Jorge?' Jan glanced quickly at a grinning, gnome-like character with a load of food on his shoulders. 'Es's father?'

'Yes. He's really repentant. He couldn't face me. Just put his hand through the thatch. I took it. For a Christian, there was no other way. And that's Chan Bor and Na Bora.' He nodded at a shy couple carrying boxes into the shelter. Husband and wife, Jan knew, but also brother and sister, for in a group of this size there was little choice of mate.

It was too late to go anywhere that evening. While the Lacandones set up camp, Harry led Jan and Rebecca to a hut near by.

The next morning, after breakfast, the Indians were already waiting. When Harry gave the word, the men piled goods into net bags, stretching them extravagantly. Then, with the help of the women, they hoisted their burdens on to their backs, settled tump-lines across their foreheads with grimaces and grunts, and pattered off down to the swirling brown water, where two canoes lay moored.

With Harry's help, Jan, nervous at the unfamiliarity of it all, found a seat on the cargo, while Harry climbed in with Rebecca. The Lacandon men took their places, standing statuesquely at the ends of the dugouts with long oars.

As the canoes began to drift downriver, rocking in the current, Jan preserved an anxious silence. Not Rebecca, who came alive at the sight of the jungle, shouting and pointing at things that caught her eye: a lone giant tree towering above the rest, huge blue butterflies fluttering erratically past, a solitary vulture wheeling above the canopy.

After fifteen minutes, at a spot where the river curved round an island of trees and bushes, the canoes drifted into the western shore. Harry swung Rebecca to safety and held out a hand to Jan. 'Come on!' he called, as the Lacandones vanished ahead into the jungle, 'Let's see some parrots!'

Jan, smiling at his excitement, followed warily up the muddy bank, and stepped for the first time into jungle. Large, soft leaves brushed her face and arms. She took a deep breath, expecting some reminder of the woodlands of her youth, a recollection of pine in the Sierra Nevada or the hills of San Cristobal. There was none, just the humidity impregnated with the smell of leafmould. She was in a universe of greenery, of dense-packed saplings, shrubs and ferns, of older trees with odd roots like stilts and buttresses. From trunks and branches, lianas trailed down, forming a tracery of strings, ropes and gnarled old cables. Around the slippery, root-entangled trail, vivid patches of sunlight turned the shadowy foliage into a baffling mosaic of bright and sombre greens. It was strangely silent. Trees dripped, insects buzzed and zoomed, but there were none of the raucous whoops and screams she had expected. She had no time, however, to admire the dark and intimate beauty of the forest. Harry was off, with Rebecca on his shoulders. Behind them, Jan, unused to exercise, began to pant and sweat.

After half an hour, they emerged from jungle into more open country on the edge of a savannah, a sun-drenched prairie of waist-high grass that groped with whiskery fingers at the fringes of the forest. Harry, talking effusively about the glories of the jungle and his fears for its future, paused to point out the Beehive Hills, beyond the savannah, where his stream originated, and then, as the trail plunged back into deep jungle, on he went again about how ranchers were moving in on the savannah, and how roads in twelfth-century Italy were churned up by pigs, and how pigs would ruin this trail if the ranchers had their way, until, after another half hour, Jan, to her relief, made out in front of her a bank of red clay leading gently down to a little river: the Santa Maria.

She leaned against a tree to recover her breath, her shirt clammy against her body, and gazed down. Below, a rocky step had created a pool twenty feet across. The water spilled over the step past three little islands of bush and fern to form a shallow waterfall. Beyond, on the opposite bank, the trail picked up again.

'It's beautiful,' she said. 'Is the house much further, Harry?'

'It's right here, don't you see?' He pointed up the opposite bank, and urged her on. Jan, picking her way across the shallow ford, could see nothing but vegetation, until, at the top of the steep, muddy bank on the other side, she found herself almost up against an untidy expanse of palm leaves.

'Your new home!' Harry announced proudly.

She saw then that the palm leaves formed a huge roof that came almost to the ground. The hut was so tightly enclosed by jungle it had been invisible to her until she was right beside it.

Harry took Jan and Rebecca by the hand and led them round to the open gable-end, waving a hand towards an acre of citrus trees and banana plants. In the shadowy interior, Jan, peering round, could make out only a few things – a ten-foot table with pole benches, shelves, a hearth made of clay-lined logs, a confusion of support posts, the glint of pots, a pole angling up into the roof.

'I'll make coffee,' said Harry, and began to light a fire.

Only then, when she was about to walk right into them, did Jan notice that the Lacandones were already ensconced on the floor, staring up at her. Smiling to cover her embarrassment, Jan sat at the table with Rebecca, who was so awed by her new surroundings she had said not a word since their arrival.

Together, they watched the Lacandones, while the Lacandones watched them, in fascinated silence, until Harry asked her to help unpack gifts: pocketknives, fish-hooks, files, ribbons, pins. Jan found their composure impressive. There were murmurs and guttural exclamations, but no one shouted or intruded on anyone else.

By now, the light was beginning to fade. 'Looks like they're going to stay,' said Harry. 'They don't usually, but this is a special occasion for them. I'll show you where we wash, and fix our beds in the loft,' which, Jan now saw, was a shelf running the length of the house. The slanting pole she had seen on her arrival was notched to form a rough staircase.

Later, as Jan lay back beside Harry, with Becca asleep behind a curtain further along the shelf, the exertions and worries of the day faded into a delicious feeling of peace. Harry had been everything she could have asked. Her new home, though utterly strange, was orderly and welcoming. She breathed deeply, almost asleep. The Lacandones were smoking cigars, and the aroma wafted up soothingly along with the murmur of their voices.

'Where the hell did all these Indians come from, Mrs Custer?' muttered Harry in her ear.

She laughed. Yes, she thought drowsily, she could be content here.

🦊

But there was little laughter on subsequent evenings.

She had hoped that their arrival in the jungle would mark a new beginning to their relationship. She was soon disillusioned. Each time she welcomed him to her, she was surprised, as she had been in San Cristobal, by the briefness of his love-making. It was a meaningless and painful business. He seemed unaware of the problem. He talked all day long, but at night, during and after sex, he was utterly mute, as if locked away from her. She realized, with increasing nervousness, that she would have to broach the subject herself.

One night, two weeks after their arrival, she summoned up her courage and said, 'Harry, I have to talk to you about . . . about when we are together . . . in bed.'

'What's the matter?' he snapped.

'It's not that something's the matter.' She didn't want him to think that she was complaining. 'It's just that . . . that there's no room –'

'Room! You don't need room for that! A place in the haymow is big enough when the biological urge hits you.'

'I didn't mean that.' She was painfully aware that she wasn't being direct enough. She'd been going to say 'room for me in our relationship,' but her courage had failed her. The problem was that he never gave her any hint that he desired her. All he did was reach for her, and then it was over before she was ready to begin.

'What *do* you mean, then?'

'Harry.' She was pleading now, almost wheedling. 'If we could start more slowly, like . . . like courtship –'

'That's what I wanted for us in San Cristobal, but you were in too big a hurry. We can't go back now. You want me to whisper sweet nothings in your ear? I can't do it. You should have had all that when you were younger.'

'Well, I didn't,' she said, flatly. 'Anyway, it's us I'm talking about, not the past.'

'If you don't want sexual intercourse, say so! I was celibate for six years, and I can be that way again. If you're not interested, don't encourage me! Anyway, you shouldn't move. I'm a very sensitive man. Too much stimulus isn't good for my heart. What would you do if I died? I have to consider you and Becca in the long term. We can't let ourselves be preoccupied with – *that*.' He stretched out on his back and tried to breathe deeply. 'You have to remember that prison damaged me. I've just begun to realize how much.'

She thought of the pain she had seen in him that morning before his departure from San Cristobal, and the sympathy his fears had aroused in her. 'I'm trying to understand.'

72

'You can't.'

'I can, Harry. Enough has happened to me, enough bad things, for me to –'

'What bad things?' He was suddenly alert, up on his elbow, looking down on her. 'What?'

'Oh . . . something . . . a long time ago.'

'Tell me!' he demanded. 'We are one flesh! I have to know!'

'Well, I . . . I was seventeen, the summer after high school. I was living in town, renting a room from a friend's family.' She felt almost suffocated by tension. But there was no escape; the only way out was to tell him.

She was helping her father in the campaign for Henry Wallace in the run-up to the 1948 election, the one in which Truman so unexpectedly beat Dewey. It was a good time, a time of excitement, and shared commitment. Her boss, Harold, a short, fat man with glasses, was like a big brother to her, protective, understanding, and unfailingly polite to her father. ('I bet he was!' Harry interrupted, scathingly.) One afternoon, after a meeting, Harold told her she could have his apartment for an afternoon nap while he went on some errand. She went to sleep. The next thing she knew, he was in bed with her and –

'You got into bed?'

Yes. It was stupid of her, but she was utterly inexperienced. She'd never even been kissed, never even had a date. Anyway, she had looked on Harold and his wife as friends. He began to kiss her, telling her what a pretty thing she was. Even then, it took her a few seconds to realize what was happening. She started to fight him off. At that moment, Harold's wife came in. By the time she was at the bedroom door, Harold was up, pretending nothing had happened. Jan, too stunned to think clearly, left as soon as she could, saying she'd get a bus back to her friend's house. She had hardly gone more than a hundred yards down the street when he came after her in his car, and offered her a lift, insisting there were no buses running. Then, then . . . she broke off, as the memory wrung a sob from her.

73

Harry urged her on: 'You have to tell me, Jan! You can't carry it alone any more!'

She took a breath. She'd read Freud, like all her friends, and thought she ought to act broad-minded. Perhaps, she reasoned, he wanted to apologize. So she got in. He went right past her turning, and on across the river. There, he stopped the car. She tried to get out, but her door was jammed. He didn't say anything. He just reached for her face with both hands, and pulled her down, until her mouth –

'I don't know why I didn't fight him!' she sobbed. 'I just remember thinking "people in concentration camps have been through worse than this," and let it happen. I don't know why . . .'

'I do,' Harry said, quietly, the tension released. 'He recognized you as a victim. I saw men like that in prison. White slavers, pimps. They had it down to a science.' He paused, then added, 'I should have realized when I first met you that you couldn't be unstained by the world.' She felt a wave of relief. He had accepted, and understood. It really did seem that a burden had lifted, that the confession had brought them closer. 'You told no one?'

Afterwards, Harold thrust his handkerchief to her mouth as she retched and spat. 'Your hair is a mess,' he said, absently. Then he drove her still weeping to her lodging. Her friends, seeing her expression, drew from her a hint of what had happened. 'One of the boys said he'd go round and beat Harold up,' she finished, with an attempt at a smile. 'But his girl-friend stopped him. "You can't do that," she said. "He wears glasses." So no one did anything.'

🐞

She lived not for the nights, therefore, but the days. No deny-ing the stimulus and novelty of her waking hours, under Harry's rigorous and enthusiastic guidance.

Since visitors were so infrequent – the Lacandones came by only once or twice a month, and ranchers or would-be settlers making the tortuous five-day journey from Las Margaritas were rarer still – Jan's world was defined by Harry. Under his tutelage, she learned to use a machete. Together, they extended the clearing and planted beans, parsley, spinach and turnips, to add to the bananas, sweet potatoes and cacao Harry already had. He explained in elaborate detail why certain things had to be done in certain ways. He was a meticulous housekeeper, with everything in its place – writing things, hammocks, alcohol for rubbing on insect bites, wood supply, mats, blankets, pots, food. He expected her to match his competence, and she, planting and clearing and managing the fire, took pleasure in doing so.

Practical skill, though, was only a part of what he taught. He talked incessantly. Jan had never heard anyone talk so much, so persuasively, or, to give him his due, so entertainingly. He exploded with ideas, and dazzled her with them. He'd read so much, absorbed so much. While working and resting, he explained at length why he refused to hunt or to clear by burning, as the Indians did. Never be a predator, Jan, he told her. He could accept eating fish, for her sake, but never any mammal or bird. Eating flesh meant killing, destruction, war. He wanted not to destroy the forest and its creatures, but to live in harmony with it.

Every activity involved a lecture. A session of tortilla-making became an excuse to elaborate on the significance of corn. As they sawed wood together, he talked about Hardy and peasant life in England. As Jan stood over the fire, he alternated advice about the use of hard and soft woods with comments about Darwin. While they washed clothes, he told her the story of Alexander's campaigns. Interwoven with instructions to Rebecca about not running where she couldn't see for fear of snakes, and orders to them both about not being out of sight of him, were monologues about Vermont, and peasant economies, and medieval Europe, and local birds, and the Lacandones, and the time a jaguar stole his smoked fish. He was, in speech, a superb performer – sage and savant, her

75

declared superior in intellect, in morality, in religious thinking.

Only slowly, almost incidentally, was she given chances to reveal more of herself to him.

One afternoon, for instance, three months after their arrival, when they were lying in their hammocks during siesta, Harry began to complain about their need for money, for Donald's monthly contribution had ceased when they married. They'd just about have the place established when they would have to take off for California. That was the part he didn't like, working for money to buy food and seeds. 'I'm not made for handling civilization, Jan. Bus travel! Noise! I hate it!'

'Maybe . . .' A memory came to her, a suggestion made by a friend in San Cristobal. Maybe Jessie would be willing to take them as dependents on her income tax, she explained, and give them the deductions. It wouldn't cost her anything, and might provide them with almost all they needed.

'You could ask,' he said, pleased at the notion. 'She's the person to make it work, if anybody can. The thing is, if it worked, would you be content? No more trips to the city. Your life would be that of a homesteader, pure and simple.'

'But that's what I've always wanted!'

'Oh? Why haven't I heard about this before?'

She shrugged. The truth was that he'd talked about himself so much that she was still not in the habit of plunging into her own past, unless he forced her to do so. Now, for the first time, she told him about her Carmichael childhood and the Deloziers and other sharp, sweet memories – about the time when she was four when her grandfather showed her how to plant a peach stone, and her astonishment when the next day, the very next day, as it seemed to her, it had sprung from the earth, a fairy-tale fruit tree, a treasure; and about visits to an aunt's ranch on the American River, where there were pears, and a meadow, and an old barn, all of which had vanished when the ranch was drowned fathoms deep beneath a lake created by the Folsom Dam across the American River.

'Astonishing,' he said. 'The way you work, I knew you were a born peasant. *Now* I see – you just wanted me for my homestead!' He shook his head in mock dismay. 'Anyway, you wouldn't mind staying away from that awful place?'

'San Cristobal, Harry? I thought you liked it.'

'I never said I like any town, or city. They are places of evil.'

'What do you mean, Harry? Cities just *are*, aren't they? Some are pretty, some ugly, but they serve essential purposes.'

'No, Jan, that's where you're wrong. If you stop and take a serious look, you'll see cities are a mistake! God put Man in a Garden, not a city. The trouble is, Man materializes his existence, exploits his environment far beyond his need, and creates a world that enslaves him. Think about it. What do you need to make a city? Power! Power to enslave! Men make cities, make kings and priests, invent time, make themselves slaves, slaves to Tomorrow, slaves to the business of More and More! Americans call it the American Way of Life, and they're so certain it makes them *go-o-o-d* people they build a religion and a politics and morality to tell them how good it is. But it's not good. Cities murder families. It's as the Bible says, the first city was built by a murderer.'

She listened, spellbound. When he talked like that, he seemed to tower above her. He could talk more penetratingly about more subjects than anyone she'd ever met. He was more alive to his surroundings than anyone she'd ever met. He surprised her, frightened her, shamed her; but always he interested her, and always he challenged her.

'You talk so much about God, Harry. Don't you have any doubts?'

'Not in the least.'

'Was it Elizabeth who converted you?'

'Partly. But mainly it was prison.'

He often mentioned prison, with sudden graphic descriptions of places, people and events that seemed like beacons lighting the way towards the core of his character. There was no doubting their significance, for he had made it all explicit in a manuscript, which he kept stored with his books and jungle journals. *Love Your Enemies*, it was called, *The Prison Memoirs of 13727.*

When he and Elizabeth bought the ramshackle farmhouse outside Tunbridge, Vermont, in the fall of 1941, they were already committed vegetarians and pacifists, with a mystical approach to Christianity. For Harry – Henry, as he was known then – and Elizabeth, life's meaning lay in God and God-in-Nature. Their guide was one of the great American prophets of peasant intellectualism and self-sufficiency, Bronson Alcott, father of Louisa May Alcott, who wrote *Little Women*. (Not heard of Bronson Alcott, the man he'd named his son after? He was surprised at her. Alcott, farmer's son, vegetarian, advocate of poverty, nature mystic who lived in imitation of Christ. She would have to study him.)

When war broke out, Harry refused to sign his registration papers. He was arrested and eventually taken to Danbury, Connecticut, where he was held for four months.

'I told them to put me in solitary,' he said. 'I said I'd be fine, as long as I had books and paper. That's when I learned the meaning of Christianity. One has to be in some way removed beyond the pale of normal, respectable life before Jesus becomes real, Jan. I saw that the world pursued riches and war, and that Christ was both the Prince of Poverty and the Prince of Peace.' His delivery was becoming more intense with every sentence, words capitalized by emphasis and gesture. 'I saw that in his life lay the Way. And once I saw that, Jan, I saw the Creation as it truly is.'

Harry went into prison in the depths of winter. He was released on 25 May, and stepped out into a fine spring day. The impact of the change utterly overwhelmed him.

'It was a rebirth, Jan, a miracle. Listen. This is what I wrote.'

He turned pages of the typescript, and began to read. ' "The trees were *alive*." ' He declaimed the passage as if to a hushed congregation. ' "They were standing with branches flung like arms to the sky and they sang a hymn of perpetual praise in chorus to their Maker! Strange I had never noticed this obvious fact before. And the little green hills were dancing in the spring sun; they reached out and took hold of me by some invisible spiritual embrace and lifted my heart in love and joy.

' "And the people in the street, the old silver-haired clerk at the railway station, were all God's glorious, divine creatures, as for the first time I comprehended Life bathed in the alchemistry of the Eternal. I was for the first time living in Vision, Imagination, Spirit, Love, the natural holy plane of existence – the one from which Man fell into corruption. That it was the daily experience of Jesus, I have no doubt." ' He looked up at her. 'I don't think I'll ever express it better. What do you think?'

Jan, mesmerized by the power of his voice, was beyond criticism. She heard in his words no suggestion of self-indulgence or sentimentality. After all, there was something in them that corresponded to her own experiences when wandering the rolling orchards of Carmichael, and there was no denying the intensity of his experience. 'It's . . . it's the way the world was when I was a child,' she said.

'You follow my thoughts so well,' Harry said, pleased. 'My Illumination became my bedrock. I didn't know how much I was going to need it.'

※

On that foundation, Harry had been transformed from a Christian into Christian himself, a pilgrim progressing through a world of evil, armed with Truth. Now, he set about transforming Jan. As they both acknowledged, it would be no mean task, for interest in religious matters had been crushed in childhood by her atheistic father. With surprising gentleness, for in this as in many other ways he played the teacher well,

Harry encouraged Bible readings. After their morning's work, while Rebecca slept, they would take it in turns to read out loud to each other. Jan had never studied the Bible, but she found, to her surprise, that it interested and challenged her. For someone raised to reject God, however, the very concept was hard for her to grasp.

'Don't try to understand God, Jan!' Harry explained, after she had put forward some rational objection to faith. 'God's presence is everywhere, impossible to understand in rational terms. The best you can do is imagine. Life without God is life without imagination. But you can *live* God. Look at Jesus for the answers.' In him, he said, she would see our purpose: to re-establish the harmony between Man and God which was lost at the Fall. Not that she should look upon Christ as a saviour. That was too easy. Redemption was something to be achieved only by the individual. It was hard, no question. It meant struggle, and toil, and suffering. Being a Christian was the hardest thing in the world, and civilization only made it harder. 'Christian civilization' was a contradiction in terms. Established religion, civilization, industry, cities, war – it was all one. Best reject it all, and return to the ideals of St Francis: Simplicity, Humility, Poverty and Prayer.

Oh, she said, the words in his letter of proposal. Yes. He had left out Prayer, because he had known she was not a Christian. 'But you've made a start, Jan. It's up to me to help you, because I'm so much further along than you.'

He talked to her of his favourite religious writers – he was studying Jakob Boehme at the time – and encouraged her to read from his collection of devotional books. She began with the teachings of Meister Eckhart, the fourteenth-century German mystic, and *A Serious Call to a Devout and Holy Life* by an eighteenth-century English theologian, William Law. Both men wrote of the need for self-discipline and for the willing acceptance of suffering to strip away all ego, to expose oneself totally to God's will, to achieve unity with God.

Those were teachings she felt she could respond to. She had

suffered. With her disabilities separating her from others, she had found it hard, sometimes impossible, to defend herself against suffering. It was good to find a justification for that inability, to see that her passivity could be understood not as a failing, but as a virtue.

As she read, and as they talked, her interest matured into commitment. She would, under Harry's tutelage, attempt to re-order her emotions and attitudes, guided by Christian discipline. She could do this, she told herself, only on the basis of uncompromising honesty, with God, with herself, with Harry.

She knew, of course, that she was living a deception, several deceptions. For one thing, she was painfully aware that her love for Harry had not blossomed as she had hoped. For another, she had kept quiet about that grubby, hasty little encounter with Vicente, the shopkeeper in San Cristobal. Perhaps, by ridding herself of her new-found sense of shame, she would be able to build a truly loving relationship with Harry.

Now that the time was approaching for them to make their first trip out to re-stock their supplies, the problem weighed more heavily. If anyone in San Cristobal should let slip some odd suggestive remark, if Harry should find out about Vicente by chance, the consequences hardly bore thinking about. It was a risk. In the month after the wedding, when she had been packing up the Granja, John Baroco had commented sarcastically on that very possibility. 'So he doesn't know about Vicente? And what, my dear, Jan, do you think he will do when he finds out? I'll tell you. The end! *Fin-i-to!*' She felt, increasingly, the need to pre-empt that possibility and make a new beginning.

'Harry,' she said one night, when they were bedded down in the loft. 'I have to tell you something.'

'What is it?' She felt his sudden alertness, almost as if he knew what form her confession would take, and was hungry for it.

'It's been weighing on me terribly.' Best be straight, and

quick. 'It's about Vicente . . .' She had gone to him because, as a Spaniard, he said he could tell her how to find out something about an uncle who had disappeared in the Spanish Civil War. Her father's beloved brother, Gerrit, had joined the Republican Abraham Lincoln Brigade in 1938, and vanished, never to be heard of again. 'He said we couldn't talk politics in public and told me to come to his place. I wanted advice and information. He interpreted the visit differently.' She stopped. Harry had gone utterly still beside her in the dark. 'What I'm trying to tell you is that I let him . . . have me.' She hurried on, trying to make light of the whole thing. 'It was a terrible mistake, and . . .'

Instantly, the tension broke. Harry burst into loud, convulsive sobs.

Oh, no, Harry, she thought, you'll wake Becca. She put out a hand to seek, and give, reassurance. He pulled away, still sobbing.

She had hoped to convince him that the incident had been utterly without significance. But her effort to make him understand – 'Harry, it was all over in fifteen minutes!' – only seemed to make it worse for him. He choked back his sobs, and banged his head down on the bed, shouting 'You and your lust!' again and again, as if in a temper tantrum. 'You and your ungovernable lust!'

She lay very still, shocked into helpless silence by what she had unleashed, afraid that anything she said would re-fuel his passion, and with Rebecca just near by . . .

She didn't hear the whimper, but Harry was already up, still crying. He pushed aside the sarong divide, and went to Rebecca. Jan heard him reassuring her in unctuous, martyred tones that might have been intended as much for her discomfort as for Rebecca's comfort.

When he came back, he lit the lantern, and held it up. She saw his face, like an eerie mask, wet with tears. In a sepulchral voice, he said: 'You were alone for a month after we were married. Was there someone else?'

Fear froze her stomach. She seemed to shrink before his inquisition. 'Harry – I couldn't – there couldn't be –'

'Then there's no hurt to me as a husband.' He lay down again. 'I don't know how, but we'll have to find some way to continue our lives.'

After a few minutes, as his breathing became more regular, she realized he had fallen asleep, and the tension slowly seeped from her.

Next morning, he still seemed to be in shock. Listless and depressed, he went about the household chores with hardly a word. Jan watched him with a heavy heart, wishing she'd never mentioned the subject. Rebecca, too, was affected. On their way down to the stream to bathe, when Harry turned back to fetch a towel, she said 'Harry cry,' watching him with wide eyes. 'Yes, Becca,' Jan replied sadly. 'Let's hope he'll be all right.'

But Harry was not all right. When they returned from the river, and Rebecca went off to play with her dolls, Harry motioned Jan to the table.

'I'm not as strong a Christian as I thought I was,' he said morosely. 'All the faith I have, and still I'm tempted by the idea of suicide. But I can't do that, leaving you and Becca alone. Becca's far too young to understand this blackness that has been loosed upon the family. That's why adultery is so bad. It's worse than murder! It kills whole families!' He paused, ominously. She prayed he wouldn't cry again, or throw more recrimination at her. He didn't; but as so often before, his words and actions took her totally by surprise. 'Jan,' he went on, 'You have to help me. I want you to sit with your mouth on mine.'

Surprise gave way to relief. She was willing enough to comply with what might be a gesture of reconciliation. She turned her head. He placed his mouth on hers. That was all. He made no movement, applied no pressure, gave no indication that the kiss was affectionate. She opened her eyes, and saw that his were closed. She looked around, from his long hair to the palm-leaf thatch. A minute went by. She felt a growing urge to break off, scream, stand up, anything.

He suddenly pulled away. 'This is helping,' he said, and leaned forward again.

❧

But Harry could not forget about Vicente. Her lapse coloured his moods, his questions, his judgements. When she managed the fire, the wood was always too small, or too big, or not mixed right, or burning too low, or burning too high. Her carelessness was an outward sign of her *degraded character*. Were there others? he asked. She had to tell him. She couldn't be free until she had told him everything!

Of course, there had been others, several others, all disastrous. There had, for instance, been Tom. Tom had also been part of the Wallace movement. After the fearful experience with Harold, she had turned to him for comfort. For a year, she was desperately in love with him. He told her it was just for the summer, but she couldn't accept that. In the end, her intensity undermined the relationship, and her. She dropped out of college and went to work.

Harry seemed hypnotized by her revelations. She had to go over every part of every incident a dozen times. He worked at her for every detail – how did you meet, where did you go, what did he look like, when was this exactly – forcing her to relive each experience, until she could not hold back the tears.

Then there was Bruce, Bruce who was such fun, and who found the truth so *dull*, and therefore never told her (it was her mother who found out) that he had bought marriage licences with a dozen other women. And Bob, her boss when she was working as a secretary in the Sacramento Signals Depot. Tall; nineteen years older than her; and with the kindest face you could imagine. It was after Bob that she'd found out she was legally blind, and moved to San Francisco.

It was all a great burden, Harry said, a great burden for them both. 'I can bear my share. Since Jesus forgave Mary

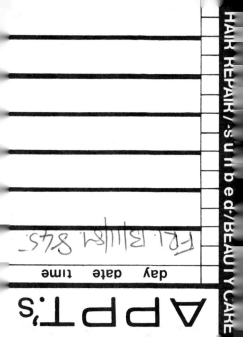

Xception

hair design

11 Comiston Road, Morningside, Edin.

tel:031/447·3177

Magdalene, I must work to forgive you. "The believing husband sanctifieth the unbelieving wife." But you, too, must work to rid yourself of the stigma.'

There was no question of arguing with him. It saddened her that she had lived such a terrible life, that her actions (or inactions) before they met caused such pain. But she saw that the only way to raise herself from the emotional morass of her past to the shining high ground on which Harry stood was to confess, and confess again, reliving each painful incident, in excruciating, tearful detail.

※

Despite the pain (or perhaps as a defence against it), despite Harry's unremitting pressure (or perhaps because of it), Jan's commitment to the homestead never wavered.

On their return from San Cristobal, laden with supplies and books – more of their own and others borrowed from Trudi Blom's library – Jan began work on the banana grove, cutting the grass and turning it into a glade of sweet-smelling hay. Weeks passed, weeks of work, and talk, and reading. During siesta and on rest-days, Jan immersed herself in a new course of study: Bailey's *Hortus*, a huge compendium of plants in North American collections, which Harry had brought with him from Vermont. She began to write to research centres in Florida, Puerto Rico and Hawaii for seeds. As months passed, her determination seemed to reassure Harry. Perhaps they would, by working together, grow together in harmony.

It would take time, of course, for it was never possible to relax for long with Harry. He lived with constant anxiety, manifested by heart pain, and skin rash, and a knot in the muscles of his solar plexus, a dense bunching of muscle fibres that prevented him from taking a deep breath. The knot was like a stopper on his emotions. Too much pressure, too much pain from his heart or an inflamed patch of skin, and he would explode. Jan used to wonder whether he was exaggerating, but she could actually feel the knot with her hand. Some nights, she would sit beside him after Rebecca had gone to sleep, massaging the muscles in a vain attempt to ease them.

'It was prison, Jan,' he said, when she asked him why it happened. 'It's something I carry with me all the time. Prison became part of me. I knew it would. There was no avoiding it. It was a stone-crusher. I had to lie down and let it roll over me. The four months in Danbury was only a prelude.'

As usual, he did not tell her all at once, and completely. He returned to the subject again and again, now talking, now reading from *Love Your Enemies*, focusing on different facets of his experience each time. That first description gave her the gist. But it took many conversations, and many weeks, for her to understand fully.

After Danbury, they left him alone for two years. Then he was re-arrested. This time, he went on hunger strike. They took him to Lewisburg, Pennsylvania. Lewisburg! The home of Giant Despair! Twenty-five-foot walls! He knew it would test him to the limit, from the moment he arrived. He refused all cooperation, refused even to walk, and had to be taken inside in a wheelchair. Still refusing to eat, he was carried to the psychiatric ward, which prisoners called the Blue Room. There, he found himself in the hands of a sadistic, scar-faced doctor named Train, known to the inmates as Choo-choo. A thick-set, round-shouldered man, with a brisk professional manner, Choo-choo tested the skin of Harry's arm between finger and thumb. How long had Harry been without water, he asked. Eleven days? He pronounced Harry suicidal, and ordered him to be force-fed.

Harry had some warning of what was in store for him. A male nurse, himself a prisoner, had described the effect of Choo-choo's methods. 'I saw 'em get to work on a guy, big husky guy. He wouldn't eat. They strapped him down and force-fed him for weeks. He got to where he would cry like a baby when they brought in the tube. In the end, they took him to the bug-house. He wasn't crazy when he came in, but he sure was by then.'

But that was no preparation for the shock of the treatment itself. When Choo-choo returned, he had with him an assistant who carried a rubber tube, a funnel and an enamel pitcher. They strapped him down. 'You can take this by yourself,' Choo-choo said, 'Or else I'm going to tube-feed you.' Harry liked to think his melodramatic reply – 'Get thee behind me, Satan' – plunged a dagger into Choo-choo's heart. But all he said was, 'Down your throat or up your nose?' at which Harry opened his mouth. Choo-choo began to push the tube down Harry's throat, making him retch and gag so overwhelmingly that Choo-choo whipped the tube out again and began to force it up Harry's nostril, until Harry felt it curl round inside his head and slide down his throat. Oh, Jan, he said, grimacing with the memory, it was like being buried alive. Worst thing he ever felt. Then Choo-choo put the funnel on the other end, and poured liquid from the jug. Harry felt a rush of cold in his stomach. The tube was snatched away and his straps released. The men were gone. At once, racked by convulsions, Harry threw himself across to the toilet bowl.

That was enough for him. 'I thought, he's trying to break me. He's not concerned with keeping me from dying. He's trying to torture me into insanity, and if I don't yield he will succeed. I had come prepared to offer my life for peace. But I didn't have to give my sanity. God wouldn't have wanted that. So I told them I'd eat.'

'Harry, I had no idea such things went on.'

'Terrible things, Jan, and all for war. No wonder I'm all knotted up.' He tried to take a deep breath.

'That's right, Harry. Relax,' urged Jan, as she massaged his stomach. She pressed with both hands as he exhaled. His body shook and the loft floor quivered, but the knot remained. 'Never mind. We'll keep working at it.'

'No use,' he said. 'I'll take it with me to the grave.'

Jan was still hoping for a second child – a child for herself, a companion for Rebecca.

The question had received hardly a mention since his agonizing, offhand words: 'Nothing has ever happened.' From Harry's silence, Jan developed the notion that they held one another emotionally hostage, Harry wishing Jan could acknowledge the rightness of his decision not to bring children into a war-ravaged world, she feeling that such an admission would be to deny her decision to have Rebecca. Perhaps. But the issue also opened doors to Harry's fears, fears of sexuality, his own and hers. It was as if sexuality was a threat to his carefully rationalized world. Women could not be relied upon to control their own anarchic urges, and sought to foist those urges and their consequences upon men. To fulfil their higher calling, men therefore had a duty to quell female sexuality. Since affection only aroused a woman's passion, he withheld it. 'There's no time for that!' he would say, abruptly, if, as they awoke, she so much as rolled against him for warmth.

One way out of this emotional impasse would have been adoption. Their second trip out provided an opportunity. In San Cristobal, awaiting them in the post office, was a letter from Jessie. She had accepted Jan's suggestion, and would be sending $30 a month. 'Thirty dollars! We're set!' Harry exclaimed happily. 'We can make it fine on that!'

So delighted was he that he agreed to adopt a child, if they could find one. Inquiries produced a possible candidate – *una gringita*, a little girl whose mother was a prostitute and whose father was an American, one of Harry's acquaintances. There followed a brief visit to the brothel, where a hard-faced and suspicious madam directed them to a back room. There, in bed with a client, was the mother. While the embarrassed man held the covers over his head, Harry explained that they wanted to give Rusty's child a good home. The mother said nothing, but shook her head adamantly until Harry led Jan out. Meanwhile the word had spread. In the front room the other girls paraded their children for sale to the *gringos*. Terrible,

88

muttered Harry as they left, medieval. Brothel-born children being sold off like animals. With that sordid little episode, any intention Harry may have had to adopt a second child began to fade away.

Jan was not the only one to be affected by the failure. Back on the Santa Maria, Rebecca became listless. She'd picked up a cold in San Cristobal, but there was more to it than that. When they were all walking together down towards the stream, Rebecca lingered, dragging her feet, until Harry scolded her for it.

'I'm lonely, Harry,' Rebecca said, her voice shaking. It was about the closest she ever got to the tantrums of most five-years-olds, for she was a quiet, self-contained child, the very image of the demureness Harry expected in females.

'Of course you're lonely, Becca!' he said forcefully. 'You had a good time in San Cristobal and now you're back on your own. I'm lonely too. But we can't have everything. Your friends don't have *this*, do they – the clean water and the beautiful forest?'

As she went glumly ahead, he added to Jan that Rebecca had to learn. It was going to be hard for her, and it would get harder as she grew older. They would just have to trust that God would send a companion for her.

🐾

Lonely or not, Jan pondered as the weeks went by, Rebecca showed a remarkable capacity to adapt, as if accepting that the forest would always be her only true companion. She knew the names of the flowers, especially the orchids, and for those she didn't know she would invent names. 'What do you call these, Harry?' she asked once, showing him some small fragrant blue and white flowers. 'You're the first one to see them, Becca,' he replied. 'You name them.' 'All right, Harry. Let's call them "morning-sweets".' She learned the names of birds from Harry. She made friends with a young tayra – a weasel-like creature – that took to raiding the banana garbage. She would put out four or five bananas for it every morning, and then watch for the teddy-bear head to bob up from behind a log in search of breakfast.

Now that she was five, though, she needed to begin her formal eduction. Jan had no worries on that score. She already had books, and looked forward to teaching Rebecca herself. Sure, Harry said when she raised the subject, personal teaching was the best. The tutorial system. That's what the English élite had. Bronson did much better once Elizabeth started teaching him. In Rebecca's case, though, what should be taught? Well, for a start he wanted her to have phonetics, to help her spelling.

'I never had phonetics, Harry,' Jan replied. 'I was taught word patterns.'

'That's part of your trouble, Jan. You're too confused. I don't want Rebecca growing up like you. I'll teach you first, then you can teach her.' So he explained to her in formal terms some of the relationships between sounds and letters. 'There,' he said, when he finished. 'You can start teaching her while I get on with my writing.'

Harry's writing. That was no new passion; but now he was working on a novel, *Strange Child Marietta*, inspired by their brief foray into the brothel in San Cristobal. He had scribbled away for an hour, and then announced: 'I think I've got it! Listen!'

'That's fine, Harry,' she'd said, when he'd finished. 'But why are you beginning a story about a Mexican brothel in the middle of the Korean War?'

'Oh, that's just to get the reader's attention, battles, that sort of stuff. It'll be fine, you'll see.'

So, while Harry wrote, Jan taught Rebecca up at the far end of the loft. They had to whisper so as not to disturb him. At first, Rebecca was happy matching letters and sounds. Then, after only a week, she began to make sense of individual words. Jan was astonished by the speed of Rebecca's progress. For a child of her age, she had extraordinary perseverance.

But Jan's exhilaration was short-lived. Two weeks after the lessons had started, Harry decided to make a banana pie for a weekend dessert. Rebecca watched him.

'You made my cake,' she reminded him. 'For my birthday.'

'Yes,' he replied. 'But cakes are different. For pies, you have to make a pastry. We'll make the pie together. Can you spell "pie", Rebecca?'

'Um – P – um – I,' she said.

'Jan, did you hear that?' He raised his voice accusingly. 'Pie – P-I! Really, all that time up there and the child hasn't learned *anything*. What have you been teaching her? Long i *always* takes an e.'

'Becca knows what I've taught her, Harry,' she said, defensively. 'She's really very –'

'I can see I'm going to have to take over!' Her mild opposition as usual inspired in him an anger that frightened her. 'I told you I don't want her growing up with your sloppy ways.'

'I did not –'

'You neglected her, Jan. How can you say you didn't? Don't you remember that time in San Cristobal I found her running around outside in her cotton slip and you were nowhere around?'

'Harry, I –'

'Jan don't *counter* me! You're always countering me! That's why marriages break down! You should know by now that the man is the head of the house! He's the one who uses his head! Why can't you accept my direction? You are subject to me, just as I am subject to God. I've told you before, a woman who isn't dominated by a man is dominated by her own femininity!'

To which, for the next twenty years, she had no ready answer.

Their third trip out, in October 1960, was to be their last for five years. Harry wanted to avoid the business of renewing their visas – they'd been in Mexico so long now that they should, by law, have opted for residency. That would take time and money. They would be safe from the attentions of Mexican bureaucracy in the jungle. Besides, it was cheaper to have supplies flown in to San Quintin twice a year and transported up the trail than to visit San Cristobal themselves. Harry was delighted with the scheme. No more pestilential air, he exulted. No more city, no more noise.

Now, at last they could make a long-term commitment to jungle living, and to Harry's lofty ideas.

For Jan, life acquired a regularity, a rhythm it had not possessed before. She found an intense and increasing satisfaction in the labour demanded by the homestead – washing, wood-gathering, collecting water, tree-felling, weeding, planting, cooking. In a letter to her parents, she confessed: 'I always knew I would like homesteading, but I hadn't realized there were *so many* interesting things to do!'

Not that there was anything easy about the life. There were bouts of malaria, which would confine one or both of them to their hammocks for days, until doses of Aralen suppressed the symptoms. There were clouds of the microscopic 'no-see-um' flies that, at some seasons and some hours, enveloped them like a mist, forcing them to retreat to the smoky protection of the hut. Harry's labours gave him heart pain, and he could not bear to work too hard or too long, especially in the heat of the day. There were attacks on their growing trees by their greatest enemies, the leafcutter ants. Citadels of leafcutters would form in hidden places, and then suddenly, overnight, advance by the million on new plants and saplings, stripping them bare, snipping leaves into sections and carrying them off in columns of trembling green mosaic. Harry and Jan waged unceasing rearguard actions against leafcutters, digging, burning, poisoning and boiling in a vain struggle to defend their vulnerable plants. The attacks sometimes reduced Harry to tears. 'Those saplings, Jan! I shouldn't have admired them! You shouldn't cling to *anything* in this life!'

Jan, however, was learning to take such difficulties in her stride. Leafcutters, and malarial fevers, and no-see-ums were minor distractions in the context of her new life. She had begun to read *The Naturalist on the River Amazons*, Henry Bates's classic nineteenth-century description of eleven years in the jungle. She revelled in the thought that they were a part of the huge rain-forest system that spread from southern Mexico to the equator; and part, too, of a vast, unconnected community of peasants farming the tropics. Even more exhilarating was the knowledge that so few tropical farmers tried to live in the forest without burning it and without destroying the wildlife. They were true pioneers. They were in the forefront (perhaps) of a revolution in tropical horticulture. Eager to increase her knowledge, she extended her contacts with seed houses and research stations, seeking advice and asking for seeds as yet untried in their area. She began to experiment with dozens of new plants – cashews, lychees, cherries, limes, papayas, guavas – hoping that one day a few of them would survive to maturity.

She was encouraged in this by her realization that in peasant communities, it was often women who did the planting. Harry shared her enthusiasm. It's always been that way, he said. Think of neolithic woman! Give it a try! But, if she wanted more seeds, they had to find some way to earn more money to pay for them. He who imports must export! 'Well,' he concluded. 'The only thing I can export is my writing. When I get a book published, you can have all the seeds you want, and adopt all the children you want. Better plan on putting in some time on the typewriter.'

🐾

So Jan started typing for Harry. Every morning, instead of working outside, she sat at the table and typed, with Harry hanging over her shoulder to check for errors. He allowed her only two corrections per page, and then only if she could make them cleanly; otherwise she had to retype. Before starting on the next page, he would read it aloud, letting Jan suggest improvements.

'This is a very good way to do it,' he said one day. 'You're giving me help Elizabeth never did.'

Well, that was something. Elizabeth was such a paragon. She had judgement; she had moral force; she had developed as a Christian; she could cook with any stove; she was practical and organized; even her final act of 'disloyalty' Harry now dismissed as 'the will of God'. To exceed her in anything was quite an achievement.

As the weeks passed, Jan typed two books for Harry, *Green Frontiers* – Harry's account of his jungle expeditions – as well as *Strange Child Marietta*. Harry sent both manuscripts to an agent. After many months, and the exchange of several letters, the agent returned them. Harry waved an arm, undismayed. 'He's miffed by my independent attitude,' he said.

'Never mind,' Jan commiserated. 'I'm sure you'll have better luck with *Opal Mountains*.' *Opal Mountains* was Harry's current labour. It would, he threatened, be a saga of redemption involving three generations of a Nevada ranching family. He had sketched out the plot for her approval. A survivor of the San Francisco earthquake is befriended by a mystic in the mountains. The hero goes prospecting for gemstones. He finds one in a skull. But the skull also contains a rattlesnake. The hero is bitten, has an Illumination, says 'I understand it all,' and dies. Harry intended to subtitle the book 'An Evangelical Novel', and give himself a portentous pseudonym: Adan DeMiramar, Miramar being the sacred lake of the Lacandones which lay not far beyond the Jatate.

'But Harry, why don't you write about Vermont?' she suggested. 'You know that so well. America's only peasantry and no one to write about it, isn't that what you said?'

'I don't want to write my family into a novel,' he said,

94

dismissively. 'One good thing about Elizabeth. She never said anything about the way I wrote.'

Had more sense, I expect, thought Jan, hunching back over the typewriter.

❦

As time passed, she found that Harry's probing and her own soul-searching had a curious effect on her mind. It was like peeling off old wallpaper. The past became part of the present. Remembered scenes and words would arise into consciousness of their own accord. They were often little memories without significance, but they commanded her attention, forcing her, in the midst of present activity, to relive the past.

For several days, she was haunted by long-forgotten soap operas, the radio shows she'd listened to when she was ten and eleven, when she was alone in the Carmichael house, cleaning for her mother, carrying the radio with her from room to room. She was assaulted not by the plots but by the inane questions asked by the announcer to hook listeners on the next episode. 'Will Our Gal Sunday from a poor mining town in Colorado find happiness as the wife of a wealthy and titled Englishman?' For a while, life was reduced to a series of cheery rhetorical questions.

On one occasion, Harry was talking to their friend Tomas, a Tojalabal Indian in his fifties who had come to live on the savannah with his grown-up daughter and small son in the wake of an increasing influx of ranchers and settlers. Tomas had a drink problem and had got himself into debt with his drink vendor. The vendor had sold him to a rancher, to whom he was now bonded as a cow-herd. He'd been given a hut and a clearing, but relied on Harry for extra goods in exchange for the occasional odd job.

On this particular day, Tomas arrived just after breakfast, and Jan was in the loft, sorting clothes. She could hear the vague mutter of conversation below as she worked. It was then that the voice began to come at her, that silly announcer's voice and his idiotic comments. She caught glimpses of Tomas as he moved about down below. He was a broad-faced man, with a strange secretive smile. As always, he wore a sombrero and a shirt buttoned right up to his neck.

'Jan!' Harry called. 'Tomas says Louisa is having trouble with malaria. Do we have any more Aralen?'

Will Louisa get the medicine she needs? Will Tomas reach home in time to save his daughter?

'I'll check!' she shouted, to drown the words rising from her memory.

'He wants some fishing line. I think he traded the last lot for drink. When did I give him some?'

Is Tomas deceiving him? Will Harry's worst fears be realized? Tune in tomorrow as we . . .

'It was Chan Bor you gave it to last time! I think we can give him some.'

'All right! I'll give him some! You cut it! But not much!'

Will Tomas suspect there is more line? How will this affect the life of Our Pal Tomas?

'I need the scissors!' yelled Jan.

'Here.' Harry poked the scissors up through the flooring. 'No need to get excited.'

Is Jan excited? Has she reached the breaking point?

She cut the line and passed it down.

Is there anything in that head but trivia? Tune in tomorrow to see if help will –

'He's gone.' Harry shouted. 'Jan! Becca! Let's have our baths!'

✻

'I find this helps me,' said Jan, late one afternoon. ' "The soul which is stripped of all things will receive no less than God himself." '

Rebecca, now seven, was laying the table for the evening meal. Harry and Jan were reading in their hammocks.

'Is that Eckhart?' Harry asked. 'Stripped of all things. Very

96

good. You're on your way, Jan. There isn't anything you haven't told me, is there? There isn't another shadow lurking, is there?'

Another shadow? Somewhere in her mind a door began to open on to a dark hallway. She got up, and went to the hearth. 'I'll fix the chocolate drink for supper,' she said. A figure stood outside the door. *No.* She shut her mind to the memory. It was time to eat. She picked up a bowl, filled it with bananas, and called Harry and Rebecca to the table. They sat, held hands, bent heads. In the silence, the door inched open again. Harry began to talk. She turned to him, listening eagerly.

After supper, Jan cleared the dishes and began to wash, and as she worked she remembered other dishes at another sink. A second-floor apartment in San Francisco. A small kitchen. Above her, the clatter of little feet. Somewhere, a would-be opera singer practising scales. Her hands trembled.

She finished the dishes and returned to the table for their reading from the New Testament. This was Jan's task. She read, but drew no consolation from the words.

The reading over, they went up to the loft. Harry lit the lantern and began to read to Rebecca from Kipling's *Jungle Book*. Jan lay in bed, listening.

The door. Why had she opened the door? She knew there would be no help.

Harry kissed Rebecca goodnight, and settled down beside Jan. 'Our jungle seems tame after Kipling's,' Harry said, looking out at the forest through the open end of the gable, 'But it couldn't be more beautiful. You probably can't see, Jan, but the moonlight is almost as bright as day.' He was beginning to drift off to sleep. 'I thought I heard spider monkeys in the distance,' he went on, yawning. 'A bark like a terrier. They'll be talking to the moon.'

No one would have heard her, no one would have come. She was frozen by fear the moment she saw him and he knew it, the instant she opened the door to him.

Harry was asleep. She lay silently beside him. Slowly the

memory crept further out of the dark. She remembered why she'd buried the experience. It had been so senseless and horrible. She had no name for what had happened. He'd pushed the door open against her contemptuously, grabbed her wrists, pushed her back . . . His skin sickened her. It reeked of hostility.

The memory, sharp and violent, wrenched sobs from her. She pressed her face into the pillow, and lay quivering.

'Jan! Jan, wake up! You're dreaming!'

She shook her head, pushing her hand to her mouth. He pulled it away. 'Tell me – what is it?'

She went on crying, her face against his shoulder.

'What is it? You have to tell me. Is it another man?'

'Ye-e-es,' she sobbed. 'I'd never thought about it, until tonight.'

'Have you never told anyone?'

'No.'

'What was his name?'

'I never knew.' She got her breath, and blew her nose. 'He worked in the grocery store, doing home deliveries. He said he would deliver my groceries. I said no. He said, "Do you have the day off?" I said, "No, I'll take them." But he came anyway. I was the only one in the building. He wasn't violent. He didn't have to be. He was cold and angry and . . .'

'You had been broken before. I told you – to some men, that's a visible thing.'

'I hated him! I hated him! I hated him!' She heaved the words out, as if to expel the loathing from her.

He stroked her hair, and then got up. He came back with a dampened washcloth, and wiped her cheeks, gently touching her eyes. 'Sin is so damnable,' he said, explaining and soothing. 'It's destroyed you and cut you off from happiness. We'll pray. You'll be at ease now you don't have to carry the burden alone. It'll be hard, but God wouldn't have given you and Becca to me if he hadn't known I could bear it.'

Then: 'You realize this means an end to our sexual relations.

I see the problem. You've been too damaged. You equate me with the men who abused you.'

He kissed her lightly on the temple, bid her goodnight, and turned away, leaving her to her silent grief.

🦇

Harry had always forbidden Jan to use the axe. It was far too dangerous, he said. A big three-pounder like that – she could do herself terrible damage. It would be irresponsible if he let her even touch it. But that changed, when many other things changed, in the New Year of 1963.

A few days before Christmas, Harry had gone down with malaria. When he was back on his feet, he found he couldn't work for more than an hour at a time without heart pain. The hot season had begun, and he never liked the heat.

Then, one morning in March, shortly before Rebecca's eighth birthday, Harry announced he would split some logs. It was his Vermont boyhood, he said. Never let yourself get behind on wood. He stood up, went to fetch his boots, and was half-way back to his hammock when he stopped, and clutched at a crossbeam, his face creased with pain.

'It's no use, Jan,' he said, grimacing, 'I can't do it. Here: take these boots.' He handed them to her, and grabbed on to the beam with both hands, panting. 'And there's the axe. If we go on homesteading, it's up to you.'

'It's all right, Harry,' she said reassuringly. 'You lie down for a while. I'll take care of the wood.' She settled Harry in his hammock and brought him some lemon-grass tea. She was concerned for him, as she had been for the last three months. But she couldn't help feeling pleased at his trust in her, and at this chance to prove her competence. She'd always wanted to try out the three-pound axe, and had never doubted her ability to handle it, if only she had the chance. And she had always wanted a decent pair of boots instead of the tennis shoes she always wore.

Of course, the boots were far too big. She laced them as

tight as she could and took a few lurching steps, feeling as ungainly as a toddler. Reaching the chopping block, she lifted out a log. 'Start with a small one!' he called. She turned her back to him, to prevent him seeing, and laid the log on the block with one end towards her. She aimed at the top of the curve and, as she raised the axe, she heard Harry yell: 'I DON'T WANT ANY ACCIDENTS!' She struck. The blade clipped the log, ricocheted sideways, and embedded itself in the left boot. Pain shot through her foot. She made no sound (a reflex built into her during childhood, when a cry of pain only emphasized the helplessness she was so determined to conceal). Keep moving, she told herself. He's watching. If you falter, it'll be the end of this.

'ALL RIGHT?'

'YES!'

She jerked the axe free, and glanced down to check for blood. None. She aimed again, and struck true. After that, with each successful attempt, her confidence grew. She went on chopping, for several minutes.

When she felt she could trust herself to conceal the pain, she walked back to the house, disguising her limp by clumping along as nonchalantly as she could in her oversized boots, wondering what she would do if she discovered her left foot squelching in blood.

'All right?'

'No problem.' She eased the toe of the boot out of sight under the edge of his mat. 'Becca can bring the wood in now.'

'Good. Guess you can do it. Peasant women have always carried on when their men were sick. You better get used to the idea that you and Becca may have to go it alone.'

Later, when Harry was asleep, she checked her foot. The blade of the axe had nicked her toe nail, but failed to reach the flesh. She would lose her nail, nothing worse than that.

🐀

For another three months, the heat held the rain away. Harry sought relief by sleeping out at night and by showering several times a day with water Jan carried up from the creek. 'If I go down to the creek myself, I might not make it back up,' he said. When would-be settlers came down the trail – which they did with increasing frequency – he would sit and talk with them and then, when they'd gone, he would remain sitting, his arms round a post, complaining that his chest felt full of broken glass.

Once, when the pain was particularly bad, he called Jan and Rebecca over. 'Jan, you have to be prepared. I don't think I shall live much longer.' His tone was perfectly straightforward. His pain – caused as often as not by some piece of minor opposition from Jan or Rebecca, and relieved by their compliance – was now such a constant accompaniment to life on the homestead that there was nothing macabre about the subject. 'I just want to tell you what to do. I want to die in the jungle. If anyone comes to take me out, even if I'm unconscious, you must promise not to let them. I don't want to be taken over by doctors.'

'All right, Harry.' There was no cause to object. Objection, if she had considered it, could easily have brought on his pain, foreshadowing – even hastening, he would say, with an emphasis implying that she was doing it deliberately – the very circumstances for which he was preparing them.

'When I die, all you have to do is make sure that I'm dead. It's quite easy. Just check the pulse. Then roll the body up in a mat and drag it out in the yard. The Lacandones will help you deal with it. Don't cry, Rebecca. Death is part of life. You have to learn that.'

One night in mid-June, Jan woke with Harry's hand on her shoulder. 'This is it,' he said. 'I stood up to urinate and I felt my heart stop. Get my New Testament. I'll light the lantern.'

Her heart pounding, she reached for the book. He opened it, took her hand, and read: ' "Let not your heart be troubled: ye believe in God, believe also in me. In my Father's house are many mansions: if it were not so, I would have told you. I go to prepare a place for you," ' He paused, panting. ' "Where I am, there ye may be also." '

She moved her hand, feeling for his pulse.

'I'm here,' he said in a husky whisper. She raised her head and leaned towards him. 'You must never think . . . I harbour ill feelings towards you . . . we had to go through it for your sake . . . and Rebecca's . . . I have always loved you . . . you know that.'

She had a sudden vision of their house as if from above, a spark of life in the dark immensity of jungle. Their nearest neighbour, Tomas, was a good hour away, impossibly far for her and Rebecca to go for help, even in daylight.

'When I'm gone,' he whispered. 'Remember: Don't worry about respect. Just drag the body out.'

He drew a long shuddering breath.

'Are you . . . all right?' she asked.

'I'm fine. Couldn't ask for more. You on one side, Jesus on the other.'

She lay motionless, listening to his laboured breathing, her hand clasping his, holding her own breath in concentration, willing him to live, until she could endure no longer. She released her breath with a sudden explosion.

'What?' said Harry, waking suddenly. 'What? Oh – toad – close by – woke me up – like a message – needed to wake up. Jan . . . coffee. Make me coffee, hot, strong coffee.'

Startled, she got up, pushed the fire together and brewed up coffee. He had never drunk much coffee, and had anyway always liked it weak. But he took the cup, drank it, and then lay back, exhausted.

When he woke again, it was dawn.

'I'm still here,' he said, in surprise. 'It may take a while. But I don't ever want to sink into such a blackness again. Make me more coffee.'

She got up wearily, and did as he asked.

'Now help me stand up,' he said. 'I think I can get out to

urinate if I can stand.' As he raised himself, teetering, he dropped both arms over her shoulders, like a battered boxer. 'Gre-e-e-eat fight, man!' he drawled, then added in a stage whisper: 'Who won?'

That evening, at bedtime, he said: 'I won't sleep. If I sleep, I'll die, and I want to die conscious. The early hours are a low point for everyone. That's when most people die. I can't sleep, Jan, can't afford the risk.'

'Harry, you *have* to sleep.'

'I don't want the oblivion. If I fall asleep, I won't wake up. If I could be sure of waking up every hour or two . . .'

'I'll wake you up. I don't mind. But you have to sleep.'

'If you can promise to wake me up every two hours and give me a cup of hot, strong coffee, I'll sleep.'

They had no watch or clock, certainly no alarm. Jan, setting her mind to the task, prayed she would not fail him. It seemed to work. That night, she woke three times, and made coffee, heavily sweetened. Around dawn, Harry woke, lit the lantern, and sat up to read, leaving her to sleep for another hour.

That became their routine. While Jan fought off her tiredness, Harry kept death at bay. It was, he felt, only a temporary respite. His voice sounded weaker. He was still determined to prepare her as best he could for his passing. Often, when she awoke, she would find farewell notes: 'Not much time left . . . Feet very cold . . . Take good care of Rebecca . . . Entering eternity now. Goodbye.' For hours at a time, he would discuss his symptoms, trying to explain what had happened to him. At first, he wanted to believe that the force-feeding in prison had weakened his heart. Later, Jan, looking through their medical manual, described the symptoms of rheumatic fever, which could affect the valves of the heart. Harry remembered he'd had an illness like that as a child. Yes, bad valves: that would explain why strain was bad for him, why he'd had his first attack high in Peru, why heat was bad for him, why contrary females, and sex, and work, and powerful emotions were all bad for him.

As the weeks passed, however, he began to admit he might have some time left. 'I discovered something,' he said one night. 'You can *will* your own death, Jan. Like an old car, I might last a while if I don't have to take steep hills.' But he couldn't survive another dry season, he said, not down there in the valley. He'd always wanted to get to the source of the Santa Maria, up in the hills. It would be even better there, he promised. Every move he made was better than the previous one. The Lacandones would take them. He'd ride in a chair, like a Chinese mandarin! Yes: that was where he would find life, if anywhere.

4

THE CAVERNA

The tree leant, cracked, and crashed to the ground with a rending of branches and vines. Light spilled around her. Jan, sweaty with the effort of chopping, looked with some pride at the hole her work had torn in the canopy above her. She had expected to see sky, nothing but sky. Instead, her view was partially blocked by a dark shape looming above the horizon of foliage. She stared for several seconds, puzzled, moving her head from side to side to bring the image into focus, and suddenly understood.

'Harry! Becca! I've found a mountain!'

The forested peak was only a thousand feet above them, and so close that their campsite was on its lower slopes, but they had never guessed at its presence. It was a sweet sight, a breath of freedom, a token that the second homestead – Jan's homestead, Harry insisted, since he was incapable of work – would be all they hoped. They'd call it Jan's Mountain! When Jan shook her head doubtfully, he insisted: he was finished, done for, but her grandchildren would look up at the mountain and remember who pioneered this place.

A token of good times. They certainly needed good times. Their first weeks at the Caverna had been a misery. It was a fine site – a large limestone cave up on a slope, and below, bubbling up from an underground stream and winding away to the south, the source of the Santa Maria. But they had had no house, and it had rained almost unceasingly. Immersed in the dripping forest, hidden away from whatever sun there was, their tent had never dried out, nor had anything in it. Harry wanted help building a house; but there were people living at

San Quintin now, surveyors working on a dam site, and the Lacandones had all gone there to work. It was Jan who had taken on the bulk of the heavy chores, she who had chopped the firewood, she who had insisted, in the face of Harry's reluctance, that she could 'make sky.'

And better times came. The rain stopped, the forest dried out, the Lacandones returned at last to fell trees, build a house, and bring in shoots from the old homestead for Jan to plant in the cleared spaces. The plants grew. Every month or two, deliveries arrived – mail, books, seeds and back numbers of the *Christian Science Monitor*, the only paper for which Harry had any admiration. Jan had her gardening; Becca her lessons and her books; and Harry, cosseting his damaged heart, his writing. (He had begun to draft another novel, a monumental work about the Essene sect, *They That Watch For the Morning*, and immersed himself in Jewish history, bemoaning his ignorance of Greek.)

Jan worked outside for six days a week, in the mornings, and again, after a siesta, in the late afternoons, breaking only during rain or when there was correspondence to do. She did no more typing for Harry. She had work enough without that.

So it was from the start Jan's homestead, in more ways than one. It was she who provided what little financial security they had. There was the income from Jessie, of course. In addition, Donald, the father Rebecca never knew, had died, leaving a pension that would be saved by Jessie to pay for Becca's college education. Then, just before Christmas 1965, after they had been at the Caverna a year, Jan happened to be reading a feature in the *Christian Science Monitor*, a thousand-word essay on the 'Home Forum' page, when it struck her that she could write something like that. Their life in the jungle was a kaleidoscope of little incidents, any of which would be ideal for the 'Home Forum' page. With Harry's offhand agreement, she typed out a description of Jan's Mountain, looming up 'as intimate as a relative,' adding an account of a visit from a pair of white hawks that lived on its flanks. To her surprise and delight, the next batch of mail contained a letter from the editor of the *Monitor* thanking her for her essay, asking for more contributions, and enclosing $50.

Her plantings flourished. She had made contact, through the Fairchild Tropical Garden in Miami, with a tropical fruit enthusiast, Toni Martin, who became so intrigued by Jan's way of life that she sent packets of seeds by every mail, together with pages of advice, the beginning of a regular exchange and a lasting friendship. Over the next eight years, Jan was to experiment with over eighty different sorts of fruit and vegetable, planting and transplanting in sun and shade, in newly exposed ground, in ground fertilized by leafmould, in deep soils, in root-filled soils.

Never in her life had she worked so hard, nor found such satisfaction. She felt that her work – building a way of life that might show colonists from outside the jungle how to live there without destroying it – was of real practical significance. But beyond that, she felt, increasingly, that she was doing God's work, forging her own links with the natural world, with the forest, which was becoming for her as much a spiritual as a physical entity, a beneficent intelligence, a Presence from which she drew inspiration and guidance.

※

It was not to last. Unknown to them, their cherished isolation, and the forest itself, was already doomed.

Jan and Becca came upon the first evidence of change. To check on a delay in supplies, they had made the twelve mile trek to San Quintin and were on their way back across the savannah, when, to recover from the exertion and the heat, they stopped on a hillock in the shade of a broad and sturdy tree. While Jan lay down to drowse in the long grass beneath, Rebecca climbed the tree. She began to make occasional, inconsequential remarks that scarcely penetrated Jan's mind until she heard Rebecca say: 'I see little men, Janny.' She had called her mother Janny for some years now, at Harry's suggestion: he and Elizabeth had raised Bronson to call them both by their first names.

She's playing some game, Jan thought sleepily. There aren't more than a score of people in the area, and Becca knows them all, even the surveyors. She imagined that Becca was joking about something close to her.

'You mean . . . bugs?' she asked.

'No, Janny. A line of little men, and they're coming this way.'

Jan sat bolt upright. Now she could see them: fifteen men, Indians in trousers and T-shirts, with string-bags slung by tump-lines from their foreheads. In six years of jungle living, neither of them had seen so many people all at once. The Indians wound their way across the rolling grassland and up to Jan. One of them addressed her politely in Spanish. '*Buenos días, señora*. Please, can you tell us, where is the village?'

There was no village near by. Puzzled, she decided to take them to Tomas's house, twenty minutes away, where Tomas's sister, Leonarda, explained matters. The surveyors at San Quintin needed labour, and the men were going there to work. They had got lost. That was all.

But where had they come from, Jan asked, as the men filed away over the savannah. Leonarda pointed back towards the hills. Over there beyond the Caverna, she said, were people, many people, Tzeltal Indians, living in a village.

The news astonished Jan. That there should be an Indian village so close to them, without them knowing! Agua Zarca it was called – ' "Clear Water",' said Harry bitterly, when he learned the name from the first visitors to the Caverna a few days later. 'Clear Water'! If only he could believe that! As a pig village, as all Indian villages were, it was bound to be degraded beyond belief. Pigs! They consumed the crops, they ate the village crap, they spread disease, they impoverished their owners. Harry hated them.

Over the following weeks, more people appeared. Settlers

on the Las Margaritas trail heard of Agua Zarca, and were drawn to it. In small groups, once or twice a week at first, and then daily, people came up the trail, right through the clearing, on their way across the savannah to the new village. Sometimes, they even asked to sleep on the house floor overnight.

Not that the Littles would wish to turn anyone away. Indeed, Harry saw Agua Zarca as a challenge. It suited his image of himself as a patriarch to see it as God's will that he should help these people to a better life. He began holding reading classes in Spanish. Not many Agua Zarcans showed a lasting interest in education, but scores were drawn by the chance to earn a little money doing odd jobs for Harry, and many were impressed enough by Harry's Old Testament looks – his shoulder-length hair and long beard were turning white with age – to seek his company. Soon, there were so many people around – especially on Sundays – that, to ensure a day of relative peace, Harry ordained that they would observe the Jewish sabbath, on Saturday. ('And if they keep coming, we'll turn Muslim and keep Fridays holy!').

Harry's ideas made no great impact. Far from abandoning their traditional ways, the villagers followed them relentlessly. They shot the wild life, allowed the pigs to scavenge the Caverna's plantings and darkened the skies with smoke in the dry season.

Bugs, Jan had said to Becca. It was just the right word. The jungle had been fatally infected, with people.

🜚

While Harry, still the invalid, entertained, and taught, and talked, Jan worked, and watched Rebecca grow, and still, on occasion, resurrected the hope of creating with Harry not simply a worthwhile life, but a loving relationship. If his actions were anything to go by – never a word of endearment, no sexual contact at all – there was no relationship. But she nurtured the stubborn belief that there could be, for occasional tiny gestures from him kept hope alive.

At dusk one Friday afternoon early in 1967, a few months after the first contact with Agua Zarca, Jan was carrying tools back to the hut. It was the end of the working week. Firewood had been stacked, newly gathered bunches of bananas tied up in the hut, the sugar-cakes broken and ground to paste. She was stiff with fatigue, looking forward to the loaf of sweetened corn and white flour that Harry had baked for supper. Suddenly, she heard a crash, and a cry from Becca: 'The beehive stand, Janny!'

'Oh, no!' The bees, acquired on a recent trip to San Cristobal, were Jan's responsibility. She hurried into the house, put the tools down, picked up her long gloves and veiled bee-keeping hat, and – to the accompaniment of a stream of advice from Harry – hurried along the path through the shadowy forest to the clearing where the hive was.

Even in the quickly gathering gloom, she saw at once what had happened. One of the legs supporting the hive-stand had come adrift. The three-tiered hive was lying open on the ground, with the bees buzzing angrily above it. She would have to set the hive upright on a couple of branches for the night, and repair the stand the next day.

She reached for the base of the hive. The bees, already disturbed by the fall, clustered on her. Suddenly, she felt a touch on her arm, glanced down and saw a hole in the elbow of her shirt. She let go the hive, stood up quickly, and turned to go back to the house. Too late. She felt stabbing pains in her forearm – already, several bees had worked their way down her sleeve and inside her glove. In a silent frenzy, she began to run towards the house, then stopped. No. She mustn't lead the swarm there. Water. She had to get to the creek. But first, she should get the bees from under her clothing. Goaded by stings, she tugged frantically at her glove. The action untucked her shirt, leaving her waist exposed. Within seconds, bees were swarming over her bare skin, dozens, hundreds, stinging angrily. 'Don't come to the hive!' she yelled. Throwing her glove aside, she stumbled the hundred yards to the pool. She couldn't see a thing in the darkness of the riverside forest, but she knew the way. She felt for the guard-rail, all but fell down the steps, and sank gratefully into the cool water.

The relief was instantaneous. The bees, several hundred of them, floated away from her. The fire of their stings died to a steady, but bearable, glow. She undid her shirt and let it float up under her arms. I must look a strange sight, she thought, up to my chin in water, with a veil over my head, like a creature from outer space. It was completely dark now, and utterly silent. She was used to the water, and, as the pain of the stings subsided further, she decided it was quite pleasant, sitting cocooned by the river and the dark jungle.

After half an hour or so, it occurred to her she ought to get back. She waded out, and stood dripping on the bank. She felt weak. Shock, that was all, she told herself. She would be all right in the house. She walked back slowly, trailing water.

In the darkened hut, a single candle burned. Harry was in his hammock, Becca on a camping stool.

'Janny!' Becca called out in relief at the sight of her.

'Thank God you're *alive*,' added Harry in heartfelt relief. 'We heard you shout, then nothing. We thought you'd run off and knocked yourself out against a tree. Becca wanted to go looking for you, but I couldn't let her do that, not in the darkness.'

'I'm sorry, Harry. It didn't occur to me you'd be worried.' She sat down heavily. Her flesh was beginning to burn again, and she felt light-headed. There seemed to be something wrong with her breathing.

'Here,' said Harry, solicitously. 'Hot, sweet coffee, Becca, get some dry clothes.' Jan sipped at the cup, grateful for the warmth of the hearth. While Becca hunted up clothing, Harry came to her. 'I should never have sent you out like that. Are you sure you're all right? Bee stings . . . my father just about died of bee stings. My mother had to pack him in ice. But don't worry. You'll be all right in a day or two.'

Then, to her surprise, he kissed her, warmly, on the mouth.

He had never displayed such tenderness. She relaxed against him, shivering, and grateful.

※

The truth was, though, that her hopes were kept alive not simply by such rare and miniature gestures, but by her increasing dependence on him. She had to admit it: her sight had been 'getting blurrier' for some time.

The degeneration was, she assumed, the result of decay in her retinas, a development that commonly marks the progress of tunnel vision. The decline had been so slow and so variable that she could never say for sure that today was worse than yesterday. Sometimes, she could read well; at other times, she had to use a magnifying glass. Sometimes, she would walk out into the clearing and find that her surroundings were nothing but blurs. She would stumble about for several minutes, feeling for trees and staring round to pick up some familiar detail – a trunk, a faded label, a plant – to orient herself. She seldom called for help, not wishing to impose on Harry and Becca. Besides, she knew her way around well enough not to be frightened, and took comfort in the fact that sometimes she saw quite clearly. What she most deplored was the waste of time.

One day, however, in August 1967, she knew, with dreadful finality, what was happening. Harry was checking through an article she had written for the *Monitor*, a series of images and events to do with the savannah. 'You have a mistake here,' he said, handing it to her. '"Spongy" has no e.'

She took the sheet of paper, and began to read, peering through her magnifying glass. '"Through the ages few men have walked there,"' she read. '"Grass spent in each season has folded down to make room for the new, making a spongey carpet . . ." No e, Harry? It's "sponge" not "spong". Looks odd.'

She wound the page back into the typewriter and searched for the word. She scanned with the magnifying glass, leant back, moved the glass from side to side, tilted it, and turned the typewriter, yet still the typescript remained a blur. Panic rose in her. She tried again.

'You're taking your time, Jan.'

Jan stood up. 'I can't see!' The words suddenly made it real, and her throat constricted. 'I . . . can't . . . see!'

Harry, hearing the tension in her voice, went to her and guided her back to her chair. 'Now sit down. Don't worry. I should have been doing that. No reason for you to do it. I can type. Used to earn money doing it for a professor in college. No reason to break down.'

'I'm sorry.' She stifled a sob, and blew her nose. Harry hated it if she or Becca broke down. 'I almost did it – if I keep trying –'

'No need to get upset! Just makes it harder for Becca and me. Remember what Mrs Eddy says.'

Jan gave him a tight smile. Several months previously, Harry had bought a copy of Mary Baker Eddy's *Science and Health*, the fundamental text of Christian Science. It had intrigued him. Mary Baker Eddy was one of New England's great philosophers, in the same tradition as Bronson Alcott. There was much in *Science and Health* that appealed to him – the mysticism, the rejection of medicine, the doctrine that disease was an illusion to be cured by clarity of insight. Christian Science discipline, he said, helped him cope with both his heart pain and the growth on his neck, which he was convinced would otherwise have become malignant. At his behest, *Science and Health* joined the Bible as a source of daily readings. Not that he accepted all Mrs Eddy said – for one thing, it was impossible to see how being infected by a malarial mosquito could have anything to do with Sin – and her teachings hardly seemed applicable in this case. 'My blindness has nothing to do with my spiritual state,' she said grimly. 'I just can't see, that's all.'

It was not so much blindness itself that disturbed her, but the sudden, unexpected shocks that showed her how close she was to danger, how easily disaster could spring at her from the gathering gloom.

One sunny day in May 1968, she went out to help Becca with a hair wash, taking with her a small saucepan and a kettle of warm water. She was looking forward to being alone with Becca, who had gone on ahead, to the stump of a fallen buttress-root tree. As her mother came up beside her and filled the pan with warm water, Becca leaned over and let her hair fall forward.

Jan poured the water, slowly and luxuriously, so that it soaked the whole mass of Becca's hair. She was thirteen now, and her hair was thick and long, with a glorious copper tint. Donald's hair. It's not just companionship she would need soon, Jan thought, but *male* companionship. Becca had filled out over the last year, and had taken to wearing a slip when bathing in the creek, like the Indian girls. Once, when Becca was small, Harry had said, 'When nature is ready, she can have her boyfriends in the jungle.' But he wouldn't say that now that the time had come. And what chance was there of finding a suitable mate here? I wish we could talk about it more, Jan pondered sadly, watching the water stream over the glinting tresses. But so far Becca had showed no interest in the subject.

Becca began to soap her hair. 'I wonder what the Orchid Society will say about me wanting to join?' she said from beneath her soapy locks. Over the years, her interest in flowers had acquired a sharp focus, and she had recently written to the Orchid Society of America. 'More water now, Janny, please.'

Becca rinsed the soap out of her hair, wrung out the water and threw her head back, eyes closed.

Jan had told her about periods, told her how to use a cloth attached with a belt when she started. Becca had accepted it all without comment. That was Harry's influence. He was direct about bodily functions. 'Here – this piece of old sheet will be fine for your menstrual rags. That's what Elizabeth used to use.'

But as for the *meaning* of periods, that was something else again. Becca's interests seemed to be contained by the homestead, Harry's talk, and their books.

'There are some bauhinias up on the hillside,' Becca mused, splashing water over her eyes. 'You know the ones I mean? That line of purple.' She opened her eyes, blinking. 'Sometimes you see yellow –' She broke off, and yelled: 'Janny! Big snake! Quick!'

Jan, seized by fear, leaped back, turned and ran, still gripping the saucepan and the kettle.

'Janny!' Becca called, running after her. 'Janny! It's all right. It's not coming after us, but I was surprised – it's so BIG!'

Harry, who was in his hammock mending a pair of slacks, saw Jan's expression. 'Who's chasing you? Oh – snake. Let's see.' He put down his mending and led Jan gingerly back across the yard.

There, lying snugly curled in the crook of the root, was an eight-foot boa. 'That is one *big* snake,' said Harry, awed. 'Here, Jan, you're not looking at it.' He put his fingers to her temples and redirected her head. 'See?'

'No. I see the root, but I can't tell there's anything there.'

'Good grief. If you can't see that snake, Jan, we're in trouble. You're going to have to slow down, or have me and Becca check the area for you whenever you work. Well: how do we get rid of him?'

'Fire?' Jan suggested.

'Great idea,' Harry said sarcastically. 'Who's going to bell the cat? You want to build a fire under him? Wait. Pieces of wood with kerosene-soaked rags round them. We'll set them on fire. They'll scare him off.'

But Harry's pungent little firesticks had no effect. Then Rebecca noticed another head. Not one eight-foot snake, but two four-foot ones, mating, oblivious to their surroundings. 'Let's leave them be,' said Harry. 'I know when I'm bested. We better pick up this mess later, or those snakes will make our name mud throughout the forest.'

Back in the hut, Harry continued with his sewing, helped by Jan. 'My ears are burning,' he said, after a few minutes silence, and, seeing her puzzled look, put on a falsetto cartoon voice. '"What do you suppose is the matter with *him*? All worked up over a bit of sunbathing!"' His voice changed to a basso profundo. '"Oh, forget him, my dear. Old spoilsport! Can't stand for others to enjoy themselves." "Goodness, but was he bothered! Such a rude man."' They both laughed. 'Becca, do you think they'll forgive and forget?'

'They've already forgiven, Harry. They'll forget soon enough.'

Such shocks, though, were rare. For the most part, on the surface, she found her life rich and rewarding. There was no more chopping, of course, but she had her plants; Harry busied himself with the Agua Zarcans; Becca did her schoolwork and helped in the gardens; there were letters and articles, and books, and daily prayers, and readings from the Bible and *Science and Health*. All that was good. Yet there remained inside her another world, a landscape of emotions, scarcely touched, waiting for kindness, and receiving only a promise of kindness, or none. As her eyesight clouded towards total blindness, as her growing dependence kept her trembling on the brink of devotion, Harry displayed with apparent randomness flashes of genuine sympathy that contrasted with hurtful, incomprehensible impatience and cold rejection. Despite herself, she could not escape from her hopeless, hopeful dependence. He could, unwittingly, whiplash her from intense desire to agonizing and inexpressible bitterness.

One morning, while Jan was milling maize in the pre-dawn gloom, Harry came and put his arms round her. '*Pobrecita*,' he said, kissing her tenderly, 'Poor little one.' Moved by this demonstration of affection, she leant against him. He sighed and went back to his hammock. She was touched, but also puzzled. It was as if, after all this time, he needed her again.

Three days later, while Becca was out working and Jan was sitting beside him talking, he said, 'I'm much better now, Jan,' in the authoritative way that signalled the introduction of an important issue.

'Yes, Harry?'

'And you have made good progress – spiritually, I mean. You are no longer the woman you were in your old life.'

'Yes, Harry?'

'We could be together, I think, with moderation. I could manage a position comfortably enough on your bed. It hasn't been fair to you. You're still a young woman. I don't want you to feel that life has passed you by.'

She felt a surge of gratitude. Perhaps for the first time he was preparing to acknowledge both her needs and his need for her. For all the past ten years, he had set a guard upon any expression of love. They had not slept together for seven years. His heart had seen to that. She had given up expressing affection. They hardly ever touched. Yet she had never accepted. She believed he could give more, and would, if only she could build the relationship right. It was still, she believed, up to her to create the circumstances in which Harry would express the affection that, for whatever reasons, he kept hidden. If only she could escape her own needs, her own selfish needs, and love Harry as a Christian should! Loving him would be ultimate proof of her maturity and religious development. Now, to her secret joy, he himself had indicated a way forward. She wanted to tell him how willingly she would come to him, how readily she would make a new beginning, if only . . .

She stopped herself. She had been hurt before too many times. Tenderness was what she needed now, and that could only grow slowly. She couldn't take any more unpredictable outbursts. She wanted to tell him of her reservations, delicately, without provoking the very reactions she feared.

'Harry,' she said, nervously, 'I think it's good we're talking like this . . . But I have something to ask you.'

'Yes?'

'Will you – I want – well, let me put it like this – I want to be with you, truly and completely. But it seems – it seemed, even when I was first in love with you – something always happened to destroy it. When that happens, I close up. I retreat. I don't want to do that. Will you help me not to do that, by being . . . careful with me . . . kind to me . . . If you could just, I don't know . . . not criticize me for two or three weeks?'

'All right. I should think you should have learned to trust me by now, but I can see you've had problems.' He sounded not unsympathetic, and took her hand. 'It's almost lunch time. I think I'll bathe in the stream before lunch. We've got a hard afternoon ahead of us' – they were in the middle of digging out a nest of leafcutters – 'so we'll talk more tomorrow.'

Next morning, while Becca went out to the clearing, Jan set about mending part of the thatch, feeling a tingle of anticipation at what might happen later that evening. She pulled out the old leaves, and was piling them into a basket when Harry spoke from his hammock. 'I've been thinking about what you said yesterday,' he said.

'Yes, Harry?'

'I'm not going to have anything more to do with you sexually. I didn't realize just how damaged you were. We have to forget it, Jan.'

The shock of his words, the sudden annihilation of her hopes, was like a physical blow. Her eyes slammed shut, and she sat in stunned silence. *I will not show him he has hurt me, I will not.* She took a slow breath, opened her eyes, gave the basket of leaves a sudden shake, and walked past him without a word or a glance. I will never let that man near me again, she told herself, her mouth clamped shut to lock up the tears. Never. I will not be vulnerable any more.

From then on, she determined to detach herself from Harry, to accept that in an emotional and physical sense their marriage was a waste-land. She would love him only for what he was, to work with him, to struggle with him if need be, to seek strength through prayer and the creation of the homestead, and no longer be weakened by doomed expectations.

🐝

Another year passed. Rebecca, approaching fifteen, was now a force in her own right, silent, uncomplaining, accepting her mother's physical dependence and Harry's prickly, patriarchal guidance. She decided not to go away to school, but to do a correspondence course arranged by the American School in Chicago. Later, after taking her high-school diploma, she would consider college. Her course books arrived, and she worked hard at them. Her reports were full of praise, her marks almost always As and Bs.

Self-contained, strong, intelligent, patient: that at least was how she seemed to Jan. Others, those who met Jan and Rebecca on their rare visits to San Cristobal, saw her qualities and traits differently. Unused to human contact, she seemed painfully reticent, keeping her eyes down and herself apart, as if she couldn't bear to be touched. She spoke in a strange way – from Jan she had inherited a deliberateness of speech as if she herself were deaf, which combined with a tendency to pronounce her Rs as Ws. From Harry, she had acquired an old-world formality of style, choosing a vocabulary and simple sentence structure that owed nothing to the modern world. It was as if she had been transported, not from the jungle, but from nineteenth-century rural America. There was clearly nothing wrong either with Rebecca's intelligence or her education. It was simply that she had been taken over by Harry (the jungle tyrant, as they called him in San Cristobal, the man who thought he was Jesus) and brought to a life of isolation so young that she never had a chance to know anything else. That terrible man, they said, and those poor, poor women.

Becca certainly deserved more companionship and appreciation than she was ever likely to receive. Jan knew well enough that her daughter was not conventionally pretty. With her strong jaw, she would never be that. Yet she had qualities of beauty. Her sturdy figure was full-breasted. Her long hair, browner now, still had highlights of auburn. When pulled back – as it always was in company, for Harry would never allow her to wear it loose – it gave her an austere look, but that was softened by the warmth of her smile and her gentle brown eyes. She had a direct glance that could be disconcerting. With men, she was – as Harry wanted – withdrawn. Her reticence sometimes gave an impression of naïveté, and some-times of a secret wisdom beyond her years. She delighted in children, and in her Indian friends, and they in her.

The Agua Zarcan girls were the only people of her own age and sex she had met since coming into the jungle ten years previously. Although she spoke no Tzeltal and they spoke little Spanish, she felt at ease in their company. It was to them, as much as to Harry, that she owed her habit of demureness, for they, too, had grown up in a male-dominated society.

During this year, Becca found an additional interest. Harry heard of a Guatemalan pedlar who had a marimba for sale, and bought it. With the help of a couple of young *marimberos* from Agua Zarca, Harry and Becca began to learn to play. Becca worked as hard at the marimba as she did at her books, prac-tising tunes on her recorder and then transferring them to the new instrument. Harry lacked musical training, but had a reason-able ear and would point out her wrong notes. Their practice time together became part of their daily routine. Within a few months, Becca was playing a repertoire of the Chiapas *ranchero* folksongs, mellifluous tunes that became for Jan the natural accompaniment to homestead living.

One day, early in 1970, when Becca was just fifteen, a group of villagers trooped over from Agua Zarca to listen to the marimba. There was to be a fiesta in the village later, and they were all in a cheerful mood. While the boys came into the house, the girls, all dressed in their traditional indigo skirts and best white blouses with ribbons in their hair, stayed discreetly out in the woods, away from the boys. Becca, who had been working in the garden all day in her baggy, hand-made slacks and sweat-stained shirt, washed and changed into a skirt and her favourite blouse – a white one, with a design of big red roses – and went out to join her friends. Jan, as usual, went on working until she saw Rebecca coming back. The notes of the marimba died, and the boys drifted outside, ready to leave. As Jan entered the house, she heard Harry berating Becca. 'I didn't say anything when you put on your prettiest blouse, Rebecca,' he was saying, 'But look at you now – flowers in your hair!'

'But, Harry, the flowers were so pretty. We –'

'I told you to be careful not to attract the attention of those boys.'

'But I wasn't! I was only –'

'There's only one reason a girl puts flowers in her hair: to tell the males she wants to be looked at, wants to be admired. What am I to do if some father comes over with an offer of marriage? He'd say you asked for it. And if you marry one of them you know what your life will be – on your knees in ashes making tortillas and a baby every year.'

Listening to him, Jan felt sick at heart. Becca's friends were outside, waiting to go back to the village. It would have been wrong to start a row. Besides, Becca wouldn't have wanted it. Like Jan, Becca knew only one defence against Harry's anger: withdrawal. She turned and climbed the stairs, leaving the others to return to Agua Zarca without even a goodbye.

Jan followed her discreetly to offer what comfort she could, and found Becca was changing back into work clothes. The print blouse lay to one side, torn down the front, ripped almost in half in sudden anger now contained behind a grim expression and too-urgent gestures.

'I can mend this for you, Becca,' Jan said, as matter-of-factly as she could.

'No.'

'It's a lovely print. It's my favourite. There's more material, and I can make it nice again.'

'No. I'm not wearing it any more.'

Jan sighed inwardly. From Becca's tone, it was clear that there was nothing more to be said. Like Jan, she had learned not to burden others with her emotions, to accept Harry's strictures with as much grace as she could muster. Grimly, she climbed back down, and returned to her work in the garden.

⁂

'What's going on up there?'

'Where, Harry?' It was an early afternoon in January 1971, approaching Becca's sixteenth birthday. Jan was knitting in her chair by Harry's hammock. Becca was sleeping in the loft.

'Up on the other side of the banana grove. There are men cutting through the jungle. I'm going up to see.'

He was away for half an hour.

'Do you know who they are?' he said, as he strode back in. 'A survey crew! For Jaime Bulnes!'

Jaime Bulnes – Bulnes-Flanagan, to give him his full name – had become Harry's *bête noire*. He was the scion of an old and rich Mexican family. He was a cultured man who spoke English perfectly, for his mother had been of American–Irish stock and he had been educated in America. His grandfather was Quintin Bulnes, after whom San Quintin had been named, who had been granted the rights to cut mahogany in the Selva Lacandona by Porfirio Diaz, the last President before the 1911 revolution. On that basis, Jaime Bulnes now claimed the whole valley of the Jatate, a claim that made Harry tremble with anger whenever he thought about it. Harry had even helped their poor, drunken Indian neighbour, Tomas, make a land claim, a claim that included the Caverna, in an attempt to give them all security of tenure.

'All that work for Tomas – for nothing! Bulnes has no right to this place! He only sends his men in because Tomas is an Indian! It's iniquitous! Anyone would think the revolution hadn't happened.' He stood at the washbasin, sponging sweat off his bare torso. 'I never wanted a fight over land. I loathe the

122

idea, I loathe it! You know what it'll come to, Jan? Violence. Someone is going to get killed. If I had my health, I'd walk away, let them have it!'

'But, Harry, we can't just give up.'

'It's either that or be involved in a land war.'

By this time, Becca, disturbed by Harry's voice, had woken. 'But where could we go?' she asked plaintively.

'That's just it. Where?' He grabbed an atlas from among his books, threw himself back in his hammock and began to turn the pages angrily. Jan heard him muttering about Costa Rica and New Guinea and the Caribbean, all the places he'd once considered as possible homestead sites.

Suddenly, he shouted: 'Look at that! That's where we ought to be!' He swung out of his hammock, brought the atlas across to her, and stabbed at it with a finger. 'That blot of green! A 10,000-foot mountain on the Equator! I never saw that before. Just imagine it! Why, there might even be snow on the top. You could have any temperature you wanted there, going up and down that mountain. How do we find out about it? I know. Write . . .'

'Harry, wait.' She peered in dismay at the page. All she could see was a blur. 'I can't see any mountain.'

'Brazil, northern Brazil, on the border with Venezuela, right where my finger is. A 10,000-foot mountain! Pico da Neblina! The Mountain of Mist! And there's nobody there! "Less than one person per square mile," it says. Paradise! Seems to be right on the border, but a place like that should belong to the world! We could start all over again, live undisturbed. Think of the wildlife! You could grow tropical fruits. Good, rich soil, untouched jungle, like the Lacandon forest when I first came. No one's going to trample us to death with pigs there. Becca could have her orchids –'

'Harry – how do we *get* there?'

He hesitated, then slammed the atlas shut.

'You're right,' he said, sombrely. 'We're not going any-where. We have to live with what we've got.' He sighed. 'We had our paradise, and now it's gone, destroyed by those who are lost in ignorance.' He put his hands over his face, and dissolved into tears. 'All the wildlife, gone!' he sobbed, 'Jan, Jan, I'll never hear the howler monkeys again!'

※

It was hardly surprising then, with the jungle going up in smoke around them and Jan keeping her emotional needs so carefully hidden, that a pet monkey should have become so important to them.

She was a baby spider monkey, but by some genetic accident she lacked the long prehensile tail that spider monkeys are supposed to have. She had a sweet, wizened face, with buff rings round her dark eyes and round her mouth. Her chest was light-coloured, too, though the rest of her was black. Only a few days old when she came to them, she needed gentle care if she was to survive. Harry fed her, using a cotton pad soaked with milk, while Jan nestled the monkey, no bigger than the palm of her hand, into the crook of her arm. The baby sucked the pad dry, again and again, staring up into Harry's eyes. It was like looking into her soul, Harry said, into the soul of the forest itself. The analogy reminded him of Rima, the nature-girl, spirit of the jungle in W. H. Hudson's *Green Mansions*. Rima: that would be her name.

Within a few weeks, Rima had become the focal point of the household. At night, she slept lying on Jan's neck, her tiny heart fluttering against Jan's own pulse. Soon, she gained strength enough to swing on hammocks and jump on knees to be tossed and tickled. Jan, like a mother with a child, loved to blow on Rima's stomach, to hear the husky, high-pitched gurgle, a rudimentary laugh which developed, as time passed, into an elfin chortle.

In some ways, Rima seemed much more than a monkey. When visitors came, she would delight them by teetering up and down the hut like an ungainly mannequin, arms waving to keep her balance. She was intrigued by speech, and would stand on Harry's chest, hanging on his beard when he delivered his monologues, staring at his moving lips, glancing backwards and forwards during conversation as if trying to make sense of the flow of sound. She learned that by pestering Harry, she could get him to shout for Becca to squeeze out some sugar cane juice for her. Sometimes, as if copying Harry, she would put her face right up to Jan's and babble in imitation language.

It was Jan who weaned her, though the idea seemed to come from Rima herself. One day, Rima handed Jan a leaf and passed a hand across Jan's mouth. 'What, Rima?' Jan asked in surprise. 'You want me to chew this for you? Is that it?' Again Rima brushed Jan's mouth. Jan, still wondering what it was all about, chewed the leaf; then, quelling her squeamishness, she offered it to Rima with her teeth. Rima leant forward, took the chewed-up morsel with her own mouth and swallowed. Until she acquired teeth of her own a few months later, that was how she ate her solid food.

Harry, who took her around with him in a sling, was besotted with her. He began keeping detailed notes about her progress in his journal, and promised he would write a book about her when he had the chance.

In late 1972, nine months after Rima's arrival, the land dispute came to a head. They had been expecting a confrontation. In reply to their letters written on Tomas's behalf, they had been told, no, no, of course the land belonged to the Indians and the peasants; Tomas could not be evicted, even for a million pesos. In San Cristobal, Trudi Blom had even whipped up support to turn the Caverna into a nature reserve, to preserve at least a corner of her beloved Lacandon forest, and give the Littles the protection they needed. There would be an inquiry.

On 26 October, Harry heard the noise of a plane swinging in over the savannah and guessed the inquiry team was on its way. An hour and a half later, people began to file out of the jungle, Indian peasants mainly, with a few ranchers on horseback. Harry went out to welcome them, leaving Jan to hold Rima, who was trembling with anxiety at the sight of the crowds.

The ranchers tethered their horses on the other side of the stream, and everyone walked over the log bridge to crowd into the house. Eventually, there were seventy people standing in the gloom of the hut and around the outside – the elders of the rural councils, neighbouring ranchers, dozens of villagers, all of them facing Harry in silence. Outside, Jaime Bulnes himself, a tall, aristocratic, broad-shouldered man well dressed in a plaid shirt and dark trousers, waited with the three members of the commission. When everyone was still, Bulnes and the commission members came forward. The crowd parted and formed a pathway. Harry welcomed them with a handshake.

At this point, Rima struggled out of Jan's grasp and leaped into Harry's arms. The officials, ignoring the disturbance, sat down on a bench and chairs. One of them opened a briefcase, and began to speak. 'We are here today in order to –'

'Wait a minute,' Harry interrupted. 'Where is Tomas?'

'Tomas?'

'Tomas Perez who claims this land. Where is he? He must be here before we go on.'

There was a murmur of conversation. Tomas was at the back. Twisting his sombrero in his hands, he pushed his way through. He was dressed in his soiled work clothes. Jan had known him only as a friend, who would offer and accept help when the need arose. Now, beside the gentlemen from Tuxtla Gutierrez, in their laundered shirts and well-creased trousers, he looked like a bedraggled, poverty-stricken, drunken old Indian. He said '*Buenos dias*' respectfully to Harry and Jan, and then squatted down on his heels, facing the three officials.

Harry, meanwhile, was struggling to control Rima.

'Do you want me to take her?' asked Jan.

'She won't go. She's much too frightened,' Harry answered quickly.

The official began again. 'We are here today to decide on the claim made by Tomas Perez. This land is part of the Bulnes Concession, and –'

'It is *not* part of the Bulnes Concession,' Harry snapped, picking Rima off his head. 'I have a map here. I will show you.'

The official looked at him coolly. 'That will not be necessary,' he said. 'We have our own maps.'

'This is national land,' Harry insisted. 'Tomas's documents are all with the land-claim office in Tuxtla.'

'The governor says you can stay, Don Enrique,' said the spokesman, evenly. 'He has much respect for you.'

'ME!' Harry exploded. 'Who am I? I am nobody. I am a foreigner. I cannot even hold land legally, and he has respect for *me*? It is Tomas who needs respect! He is a Mexican! It is his land!'

'Don Enrique –'

'This is a problem of land rights. This is fundamental in the Third World. The eyes of the whole world are on Mexico to see if Agrarian Reform will be honoured for the poor, the Indians, the landless. If the land stays with the barons, as before, all will be lost!' He was shouting loudly now, and Rima, disturbed by the noise, wrestled to free herself from his grasp. 'Indians, whites and mestizos all gave their blood for the revolution, and still nothing changes! What I say is *right*! If after three years of fighting, you can't see that, we shouldn't be here at all. We'll simply . . . leave!' Rima had begun to bite his hands and tug at his hair. There was no dealing with her in that mood. 'I have said what I have to say,' Harry said, with as much dignity as he could muster. 'You will excuse me.' He clasped Rima firmly to him, shook hands with Bulnes and the officials, and walked outside.

Jan looked on in dismay. Harry had spoken for Tomas, for the Agua Zarcans, for all the poor. He had said what they believed, what they had fought for over the last few years. But there was more, there had to be. He couldn't just walk out like that. He should at least know what the commission had to offer.

Silence.

Perhaps *she* should say something. But what? Should she ask what the man meant when he said 'You can stay'? Stay on what terms? What guarantees would there be that their own land would not be taken over? Could they guarantee protection for Tomas and the others? Would they listen to her, the only woman in a crowd of seventy men? Was her Spanish good enough? Perhaps she should –

Jaime Bulnes exchanged glances with the officials and shrugged. He stood up. The crowd fell back, opening a pathway. Bulnes and the officials filed out. Slowly, everyone began to drift away, across the stream. Those with horses mounted them. Within minutes, they had all disappeared down the trail.

Harry brought Rima back into the house. 'Well, that's it,' he declared, as Becca stifled sobs. 'Rima decided it. I just had to get her out. We did what we could. That's the end of the homestead. We're bought out, bribed out, pigged out. Any ideas where we go from here?'

🐝

Day to day, week to week, life went on, but not as before. To prepare herself for her increasing blindness, Jan sent off to San Francisco, to the Lighthouse for the Blind organization, for the Grade 1 Braille textbook. Jan and Becca still gardened, but without zest. They began to give away their plants. Packing took weeks. There were over 800 books, most of which they planned to give to Trudi Blom in San Cristobal for her library; pounds of manuscripts; box after box of tools, utensils, clothes, and pots. The plane was ordered, a departure date set.

While they packed, they discussed, obsessively, where they should go. Neblina, the jungle mountain Harry had pinpointed in northern Brazil, seemed too remote for consideration. Arkansas was one possibility; it had good homesteading country, and Becca could have the education Jan wanted for her. But Becca wasn't enthusiastic. 'I want a tropical homestead,' she said. 'I want a creek and a mountain.' Guyana, then: in Guyana, there would be no language problem, and there was wilderness enough. Becca could go to school, and Harry could write, and Jan could garden.

At dawn on the morning of their departure – 24 January 1973 – the crowd was larger than ever. Agua Zarcans and the Lacandones arrived to carry what was needed and scavenge what wasn't. Becca's Indian girl-friends clustered round to help her with her things. Harry, girding himself for his first long walk for ten years, gathered up Rima. Preceded by their caravan of helpers, they made their way slowly up past the cave. Behind them, the waiting crowd descended on the house to remove whatever scraps of clothing, plastic, rope and sacking they could find.

'Don't look back!' Harry ordered. 'Remember what happened to Lot's wife.'

'It's all ruined,' came Becca's voice from in front. 'Time we were gone.'

'Yes,' Jan replied. 'Don't let them see you crying, Becca.'

'I'm not crying, Janny. I've done all my crying.'

So had Jan. The paradise had long since vanished. What had once been virgin forest was now a patchwork of burned clearings. What remained of the homestead – the mangoes, guavas, avocados, cacaos, jackfruit, breadfruit, oil palms, date palms, lucumas, pineapples, mameas, sugar apples, guanabanas, oranges, lemons, limes, tangerines, cashews – would soon be gone. Harry was right: they mustn't look back. Becca's future must be on some other homestead, Jan told herself. Her own relationship with Harry could bloom only in some other, more peaceful setting. Perhaps transplanting would bring new life.

A creek and a mountain. Pray God we find them, thought Jan, for Becca's sake.

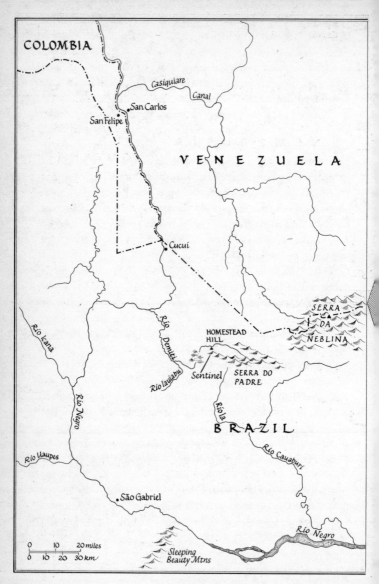

5

JOURNEY

Later, much later, their journey into the Brazilian interior seemed to be predestined, inexorable, a destiny dictated by their shared determination to find pristine wilderness, where no hunters, or loggers, or pig villagers, or road-builders, could ever, *ever* disturb them. At the time, there was no such logic, for there was no single journey, no certainty about where they would live, simply a kaleidoscope of travel and tension and exhaustion.

Now that Jan was almost completely blind, and had to be led through a world of shadows, hearing only the loudest of speech, baffled by the speed and babble of the outside world, travel, any travel, was gruelling enough; but her ordeal was doubly cruel after the pain of leaving the homestead, the bumpy flight over the fire-scarred jungle, a whirlwind visit to San Cristobal to arrange new passports, and the six terrible weeks in a rented house in Las Margaritas.

Terrible, because there Rima died. Once, Las Margaritas – The Daisies – had been a charming and quiet village, isolated high up at the head of the jungle trail. Now it was made filthy and noisy by lumber trucks hauling away the Lacandon forest. Filthy and noisy, and chilly and damp. Jan had fallen ill, and the infection had passed to Rima. The disease settled on her appendix. Despite all their care, Rima slipped into a lethargy disturbed only by little whimpers of pain. On the third day of her illness, she died. Back to the jungle, Harry had said, handing the tiny corpse to Jan, Rima's gone on ahead of us. And Jan had sat through the night cradling the body, mourning not simply Rima herself, but also what she represented: the child

Jan might have had, the homestead, the soul of the once-pristine forest.

On then, by fits and starts, to Guyana. First, by bus, train and plane to the quayside at Progreso. There, crisis upon crisis: not a berth to be had this side of Jamaica; the decision to fly; a flurry of repacking; their possessions shipped off to Georgetown; at the airport, a wrangle over emigration; the plane held back just for them; a mad dash over the tarmac; and, at last, take-off.

Thinking back, Jan wondered whether she shouldn't sometimes feel a perverse gratitude for being half deaf and mostly blind – it kept her from knowing exactly what impression they made on people. Harry, now fifty-six, had been in the jungle for ten years without a break. Those years had sharpened his loathing for cities, crowds, airports and traffic. His Old Testament mane of white hair, his jungle clothing and his safari hat made him an eccentric figure, an eccentricity compounded by the presence of Becca and herself – a sturdy, solemn, withdrawn eighteen-year-old and her haggard, prematurely aged, nearly blind mother, both of them dressed in long peasant skirts.

Only in Georgetown did Jan begin to relax. Harry was always better with other people around him. Local Christian Scientists, the Moores – Derek, Johanna and their sixteen-year-old daughter Josie – befriended them. Becca, under Josie's cheerful influence, seemed about to blossom. (Jan was once astonished and delighted to hear Josie say she wished Becca could stay for ever and ever, because Becca was always laughing.) When the Moores offered their house, while they were away on holiday, Harry seized the opportunity to begin work on Rima's life-story. In this graceful city, with its fragrant, tree-lined streets, its bright wooden houses, and its easy-going mixture of races, Jan allowed herself to dream of a life freed of the crippling tensions generated by Harry, a life in which their marriage could bloom.

It was a dream, nothing more.

In Josie's absence, Becca became unhappy. Harry was partly to blame. He had become eager to find a helper for their future homestead, and knew that the only way he could get one was to see Becca married off. Like a clan patriarch, he took to commenting on the supposed advantages of young males, men he happened to meet socially, or even by chance in the street. His behaviour embarrassed Rebecca acutely, which only annoyed Harry more. 'He was obviously a gentleman,' he'd say, parting from another likely candidate, 'Probably one of the old families, and what does she do? Scowl and look the other way! I don't know what's wrong with the girl.'

Jan had her own reasons for unhappiness. She was still weak from her last malaria attack in Mexico. In addition, to her dismay, she had, at the early age of forty-two, entered the menopause. She was totally unprepared for the strange and extreme effects the changes had on her. Often she felt sexual desire with almost painful intensity, yet knew Harry would simply not acknowledge the existence of such a problem. At other times, she felt ready to collapse into old age. 'The juices have gone from my bones,' she told Becca mournfully. The thought of homesteading again in that state filled her with dread.

As time passed, Harry's initial optimism died. He became disillusioned with both the country and the city. In the wake of the 1973 elections, racial tensions of which they had not been aware surfaced. He complained about the chlorinated water, which he said aggravated his skin rash, and about the noise. Buses rumbled, scooters whined, dogs barked. He couldn't sleep. It was only his work on Rima's story, he said, that kept him sane.

Finally, it became clear that the opportunities for home-steading were simply not there. The remote borderlands Harry coveted were also coveted by Venezuela or Surinam. The government didn't want colonists there. All it would offer was land along the highway leading south-west to Brazil.

The highway? Harry exploded at the suggestion. He

wouldn't live on a highway if it were paved with gold bricks! They had to get out. What was the alternative? Sit there on the street and listen to the cars roaring by? They'd talk to the Venezuelans! They'd go to Neblina!

In the Venezuelan consulate, Harry's request to settle received an astonishing response. Almost before Harry had finished talking, the official spread his arms and said yes, Venezuela had a colonization policy – official, government backed – and yes, they would be welcome to settle. *No hay problema, señor!* No need for special papers! All they had to do was get to southern Venezuela, to a little place called San Carlos on the Rio Negro, and register their claim.

That seemed to leave only one problem: how to get there. Air travel was expensive, and bad for Harry's heart. Harry suggested they go by river. There was a way – complicated and slow, but at least cheap, and one that would provide them with an introduction to Amazonia. They would take a 300-mile plane ride over the border to the Brazilian town of Boa Vista, head south on the Rio Branco for 400 miles to Manaus in the centre of the Amazon, and backtrack for 600 miles up the Amazon's greatest tributary, the Rio Negro, to the border. San Carlos lay only a few miles further north.

'Harry,' pondered Jan. 'Won't it take rather a long time?'

'All the more reason to get on with it,' he replied, testily.

🜨

Thus, by plane and truck, and then as passengers on a cargo-boat, chugging out of the creamy-grey Rio Branco into the sluggish and inky Negro, they came to the heart of the world's greatest natural wonder, Amazonia. On either side, a universe of water and jungle hinted at the unseen immensity of the wilderness. What at first seemed the far bank of the Negro, a grey-green slash of vegetation two or three miles away, turned out, as the boat travelled on downstream, to be merely an island. Beyond that was another channel, a mile, two miles wide; and beyond that again, lay more islands, and more channels, and more islands, all lying polarized by the sluggish current, like the finger-scratchings of a Titan, forming an archipelago which in times of flood spread back forty miles or more, bounded not by banks but by an undifferentiated muddle of trees and water and spits of land.

The Negro, the Black River, is an extraordinary entity, and not simply because of its size. In some lights, and in bulk, its waters are indeed black. But the darkness is often more brown, or grey, or red, or purple than black. Sometimes, on cloudy days, the river seems as sombre as tea; at other times, when the sun strikes through shallows on to sand, the water glows a gorgeous deep ruby. It looks tainted; but it is pure, as pure as any water anywhere, for it flows from ancient highlands scrubbed so clean by aeons of erosion that it is practically devoid of sediment. Its colour derives from the tenuous remains of vegetation. It, the whole 1,400 miles of it, is an infusion of leaves, a river of tea, pure tea, in essence as well as in colour, with two contrasting consequences. By comparison with the white-water rivers that flow from younger mountains, the Negro sustains few insects, in particular mosquitoes. It also sustains relatively few fish; though it contains more species than any European river, the individuals are scattered, and fishing is a job for experts. With good reason, Brazilians call the Negro the River of Hunger.

If Harry had appreciated all this, if he had been the sort of man to admit ignorance and plunge into research, he might have discovered, or guessed, that the Negro offered some clues to the nature of the Neblina highlands and of the problems they would have to face as homesteaders. He might have done; but it is not surprising he didn't. The immensities of forest stretching away in every direction prompted only positive thoughts – here was an untouched wilderness, a wealth of trees, a treasure-house of plants, an infinite resource for anyone willing (as the Littles were) to live in harmony with it.

🐁

So they came to Manaus, a city astonishing not for its looks, but for the fact of its existence. It lies 750 miles inland in the heart of the Amazon, yet it is also, in effect, an ocean port. The city's core is of elegant stone and wrought iron, turn-of-the-century monuments to a society grown rich on rubber. Caruso sang in the ornate opera-house; its wealthy merchants dressed wives and mistresses in Parisian fashions. When the Littles arrived, Manaus, after years of neglect, was again a boom town, revitalized as a free-trade zone. Downriver, factories ranged along the high banks. The opera-house had regained its Viennese splendour. On the exuberant waterfronts, dignified high-prowed double-decker launches loomed over sweaty Indians bearing grain, bananas and fish up stone steps slippery with squashed fruit.

Upriver, 500 miles away, a week's slow travel by a river-launch bearing fruit, soft drinks and hardware to the river's pinpoint settlements, lay an altogether different world: São Gabriel. For all that week, there was little to watch but the distant line of jungle dividing the sky from its mirror image, the glassy river. But shortly before São Gabriel, the landscape changes. On the left, steep and angular mountains jut from the jungle, a ridge of peaks that locals see as the profiled outline of a reclining woman, and name them accordingly: the Sleeping Beauty Mountains. To the west rear other mountains, equally angular. At São Gabriel itself, the river, forced in upon itself by two headlands, breaks up into white-water rapids. Shooting by in great flat sheets, then surging up in standing waves four or five feet high, the waters sweep past the little town, making a natural division between the upper and lower Negro. Only the most powerful vessels can force their way up, and navigation is always dangerous. Every year, a few people – over-confident outsiders, the occasional drunk, a trader whose engine fails – are swept to their deaths.

São Gabriel's dramatic setting gives the isolated little town a grandeur out of all proportion to its size and architecture. Most of the houses are shacks of tin or plastered mud-brick;

but they roam picturesquely over several little hills down to a huge white-sand beach, and they are benignly overseen from one of the hills by the white church and monastic courtyards of a Salesian mission. There are no roads in or out, and few cars.

For outsiders, life in such a place – indeed in any of the little settlements along the hundreds of miles upriver from Manaus – is an odd combination of relaxed charm and indefinable tensions. There are no telephones. It is almost impossible to obtain accurate information about local affairs. There is very little money. As everywhere in backwoods Brazil, mineral wealth – particularly gold – is an obsession, for only in some lucky find could a local hope to become wealthy. Those residents – like missionaries – who have money and radio-phones and spare parts for their cars are objects of wild rumours, for on what else could their wealth and power be based but some secret cache of gold?

Harry, strolling into town from their camp on São Gabriel's huge sandy beach, discovered that a family of six brothers, the Coimbras, dominated the river trade from São Gabriel to the Venezuelan border. The Coimbras – Alfredo, Antonio, Arnaldo, Walter, Armindo, and a teenager, Germano – had stores in both São Gabriel and the border town of Cucuí, 130 miles north. From one of the brothers, Harry hired a canoe and a pilot, a *motorista*, who lived upriver.

Two days later, the *motorista* – dressed in shorts and T-shirt, for there is seldom any need to wear more – drove them all to the other end of town, to a backwater above the rapids. From there, with the canoe crammed full with baggage, they purred away west and north. This was back-country indeed. The jungle on either side was now broken only by the occasional clearing: a maize field, a thatched hut, barefoot children. Otherwise, there was nothing but river and jungle. A clearing was nothing against it. Here, the wilderness was all, a force that would, given the chance, embrace, permeate and ingest anything that intruded upon it – clearings, people, life itself.

After a night at the *motorista*'s clearing, and after another full day's travel beneath searing sun and tepid showers, there loomed above the jungle ahead a 1,000-foot pinnacle of rock, steep and bare of all cover: the Rock of Cucuí. Minutes later, the canoe, cutting in along the right bank, passed a neat, white-painted store; a sawmill, set back behind a macheted grass area; thatched houses scattered along an unpaved street of red earth; and, finally, Cucuí's *raison d'être*, the military headquarters, a three-storey block decoratively guarded by half a dozen antique muzzle-loading cannon.

To the east, somewhere off beyond unmapped jungle, hidden in haze and cloud, was Neblina. Ahead lay Venezuela.

And sudden, disheartening reversal. Venezuela was a dead-end, a waste, best forgotten.

By the time they had reached San Carlos, bought supplies, arranged permissions, and were ready to leave for the Neblina highlands, they were too late. Elections had paralysed the country, every official branch and nerve of it. No sooner had they set out in their hired canoe than the local commander hauled them back, and searched them. Had they found diamonds, they were asked. Or gold? Angered and scared by these incomprehensible suspicions, they fled back downriver, leaving their newly purchased supplies to follow, with nothing to show for six wasted weeks but a replacement for Rima – an adolescent woolly monkey whom Harry had rescued from captivity. Harry named him Hanuman, after the Hindu monkey-god. Any other family would have instantly regretted the acquisition, for even before they had passed the Rock of Cucuí, heading back into Brazil, the monkey had proved as pesky and recalcitrant as any Venezuelan official.

Harry was not downcast for long. Back in Cucuí, where they set up camp in a zinc-roofed hut beside the sawmill, he insisted their failure was a blessing in disguise. It was God's way of telling them that they were meant to settle in Brazil. Proof lay in the presence of Armindo Coimbra's store, which would provide them with all their homesteading needs. Everything about the Coimbras encouraged confidence (at least that was the impression Jan received, from Harry's lyrical descriptions). The store – the neat, white-painted stucco-and-brick bungalow they had seen on their first arrival in Cucuí – was about the only decent civilian house in the whole place. Armindo was a solidly built man, well-to-do, established, seemingly much older than his twenty-eight years. His wife, Cleonisia, was a fine-looking woman, three years older than Armindo, with deep-set eyes and an aristocratic nose. They had several children, and seemed happy, settled and prosperous. Once the Littles had a place of their own, Armindo would supply them.

To stay in Brazil, however, they would need permission to become residents. That was available only in Manaus. The *commandante* kindly offered them free seats on a military plane, but Harry, to avoid flying, said he'd stay and look after Hanuman. Jan and Becca could go. Besides, he added, he could stand by to receive the supplies bought in Venezuela and ask about a good place to homestead.

🔆

That decision, many tedious weeks later, led Becca to a brief but momentous meeting.

Jan and Becca arrived back in Manaus on the last day of 1973, and settled again into the hotel Harry had found for them on their first arrival in the city. The hotel, the Lar, was a seedy place. A hole-in-the-wall gate gave on to a passageway and a line of wooden rooms. It was administered by a desk-clerk named Osmar, who had a crippled foot. But it was cheap, and conveniently close to the waterfront.

Having spent most of their money on supplies in Venezuela, Jan cabled her parents to send more. Then, cheerfully ignorant of the town's Kafkaesque web of overlapping and conflicting bureaucracies, military and civil, national and local, they set out to obtain permission to live in Brazil.

All bureaucracy maddens; in Manaus, it inspired in Jan and Becca new and undreamed of categories of frustration. They had intended to stay two weeks. It took them two months of exhaustion, confusion, rage, and fear before they found out how easy it might have been if they had known what they were doing in the first place. Jan, walking everywhere with her hand on Becca's shoulder, would have despaired had not Becca proved so resilient, and so adept at learning Portuguese. Success — a letter allowing them to stay and promising that their papers would follow — was crowned with success: the next day, $1,000 arrived from Fair Oaks.

Jan handed over the money to Osmar for safekeeping. Osmar, delighted to be of service, at once asked to borrow $250.

Jan hesitated. What would Harry say? Osmar pressed her, smiling, assuring her he would repay her in a couple of weeks. She capitulated, telling herself that Harry would want him to have the money. That was the Christian thing to do. He had a wife and three children to support. He had been generous with his advice to them. Besides, they would need an agent in Manaus. Osmar would do very well.

Their mission completed, and finding all the military flights to Cucuí full, they had three days to spare before their boat left. They decided to use the time to find seeds and seedlings. Some they simply bought in the waterfront market: cacao, jackfruit, taro, pineapple, Brazil nuts and a bunch of gorgeous, red, firm-fleshed, peach-palm fruits. But there were numerous other plants that might be obtainable, if only they knew the sources. Advice might, they decided, be available from the government's Agricultural Extension Service, which promoted commercial farming in the region.

Here occurred the meeting that so strangely affected Rebecca. For the first and only time, she fell in love.

At the institute, which lay within a few minutes' walk of the Lar, they were shown into a back office. There they were greeted by a young man who introduced himself as Dr

Carlos Roberto Bueno. Jan guessed from the softness of his voice and his warmth of manner that he was young – mid- to late-twenties, she imagined – and very attractive.

After the introductions, Becca retreated into a demure silence, as usual in the presence of a man, leaving Jan to explain why they had come, and to ask in stilted Portuguese about seeds for their future homestead. Bueno seemed intrigued. Speaking carefully and slowly, he explained about Brazil's National Research Institute for Amazonia, INPA, and its work studying wild jungle plants to find species for domestic cultivation. 'Perhaps,' he finished, 'you would like me to show you around INPA?'

Jan turned to Becca and asked in English: 'What about it? That's what I'm interested in, and –'

'We don't have time,' said Becca, quickly. After a brief moment of surprise, Jan accepted Becca's judgement. From the tone of Becca's abrupt reply, she didn't want to be pressed on the matter. Jan had no awareness, at that moment, that Becca's abruptness was dictated by entirely different emotions.

Oh, replied Bueno in Portuguese, when Jan passed on their decision, well, as for seed sources, had they tried the local seed shop?

Becca, who had as yet given no indication that she understood the conversation, suddenly glanced up and said in near-faultless Portuguese: 'We've been there and they don't have what we want.'

As she spoke, she met Bueno's surprised gaze. She dropped her eyes immediately, abashed, and said nothing further. He was, perhaps, taken aback, even intrigued, for thereafter, although addressing himself scrupulously to Jan, she gained the impression that he was trying to draw Rebecca out or catch her eye again.

After perhaps twenty minutes, Jan brought the fractured conversation to an end, and the two women stood to leave. Bueno came round to the front of the desk to say goodbye. He took Jan's hand, then, in the Brazilian fashion, placed his other hand gently on hers. He shook hands with Rebecca in the same way. Again, their eyes met. For the first time in her life Becca found herself touching and looking at an attractive, intelligent man with whom she had an interest in common. No doubt he was used to making an impression on women. Perhaps he enjoyed doing so. In any event, his obvious charm, combined with Jan's limited perception and Becca's naïveté, ensured that the two women had no reason to doubt his sincerity.

Much later, Becca described to Jan her feelings at that moment. The details had seared themselves on her memory, marking her as intensely as Jan had been marked by her first meeting with Harry. And, lacking her mother's emotional complexities, Becca's response was one of childlike innocence; pure, simple, and quite devastating. 'When our eyes met,' she told Jan years later, 'I knew I didn't have to be afraid any more.'

Outside, Becca stood for a moment to let Jan take her shoulder. 'He had grey eyes,' she said, wistfully. 'You don't see that very often.' Then, as they set off, she added: '*That's* the kind of man I'd like to know.'

🦌

They arrived back in Cucuí on the last day of February.

In the intervening two and a half months, things had not gone well for Harry. He had all but run out of money. Of the stores bought in Venezuela, only half had arrived. The other half had simply vanished, as if consumed by the wilderness.

On these reduced supplies, they would, he had learned, have to travel much further, because as foreigners they would not be able to settle closer to the frontier than 100 kilometres. To comply, and yet still be near the highlands, would mean an immense journey of 400 miles down the Negro and then north, up smaller rivers, another 150 miles.

There was another good reason to be off as soon as possible. The Brazilian military were planning a road through the jungle joining São Gabriel to Cucuí. A road. The very word summoned up all the horrors they sought to escape – civilization; death and destruction; the end of wilderness. Even a simple dirt track through uncharted jungle would be a formidable undertaking, and would take years to complete, but work had already started. South of the town, rough young men in T-shirts and shorts were carving into the jungle with bulldozers. Once they knew of Rebecca's presence in Cucuí there would be no peace, of that Harry was certain. They'd have to get out, fast.

He'd done his best to ensure they could leave just as soon as possible by buying a solid thirty-four-foot dugout, which he'd named *Rima*. The canoe, which had been abandoned before completion because of a slight imperfection in the grain, needed a stern, and a coat of paint. The repairs, and the replacement supplies, would cost money. For a number of reasons, therefore, he was eagerly anticipating Jan's return.

When Jan handed him what was left of her cash, he exploded into an apoplexy of rage and frustration, releasing upon her a torrent of anger and invective that was without precedent even for Harry. He'd never lent money to a city person, he said. How could she imagine they would ever see the money again? It would never have occurred to him to do such a thing. What were they going to do? They had to get more money. Jan had to write home for another $1,000, and while she was at it, she would have to say exactly why she needed it and why she was writing. And she had better not say that he was angry about it, because that would make him sound sinful – no, *she* had to take all the responsibility. What had she been doing down there all this time? Permissions? What was this piece of paper she had? A letter, nothing more! Worthless! Worthless! Not permission to reside at all!

For hour after hour, repeating himself endlessly, he vented his anger and frustration at her, with occasional verbal side-swipes at Becca, whenever she wasn't collecting wood, washing or cooking. Jan, anchored to her hammock by her disabilities, endured Harry's high-pitched diatribes in total silence, waiting in vain for him to burn himself out.

'We have nowhere to go, nowhere!' he ranted. 'We'll have to sit here for another six months! I thought after all this time I'd put some sense of responsibility into you. You should never have done *anything* without consulting me, your husband. Becca should have told you that. Then we'd have had the money. What are we going to do? I was waiting here, suffering, while you've been down in Manaus having a *good time*. What are you going to do about it? What would happen if I die? What are you trying to do? Kill me? You don't have to endure what I endure, the heat, the noise . . .'

And on he went, right through the next day, each speech a replay of the last, while Jan sat in helpless, humiliated silence, the tears rolling down her cheeks. How could she, she thought bitterly, how could she ever have believed that there was any hope of revitalizing this wasteland of a marriage? With his words blasting away the withered remnants of her affections, she accepted finally that she would have to revert to the decision she had taken so long ago in Mexico. To remain in possession of herself, she must look only at Harry's virtues – his religious values, his ideas about living with nature, his refusal to compromise on his ideals. All this she had accepted long ago. She must affirm them, and reaffirm them, and stop, finally, having any other expectations of him.

Her greatest comfort was Becca – her self-possession was an added inspiration to endure. But comfort also came from a more suprising source: Hanuman. He sat on her stomach, put his arms round her neck, and with exquisite gentleness licked away each tear as it rolled down her cheek. After that, for all his faults, he became to Jan as much of a child as Rima had been. From then on, no matter how badly he behaved, Jan would always regard him more as a wayward child than a monkey.

Eventually, towards the end of the fourth day, Harry lapsed

into fitful moans of 'What are we going to do? What are we going to do?'

The answer had long since become obvious. There was nothing to do but eke out their remaining supplies, and wait until they received confirmation from their bank in Manaus that the money had arrived.

Days stretched into weeks. Jan wrote letters and studied Braille. 'I do have trouble understanding Mrs Eddy's "Divine love always has and always will meet every human need",' she told the Moores. 'It seems to me it ought to be true, but I don't see it.'

Rebecca read – she had grown particularly fond of Emily Dickinson's poetry – and wrote letters of her own, expressing to Josie Moore feelings she revealed only in part to Jan: simple faith, love of the wilderness, conflicting emotions about marriage. 'I know God *is*, but do not yet *know God*. God simply is, like space and light. Sometimes, in moments of calmer thought, I am aware of glimpsing something beyond mere material perception, something beautiful and precisely ordered and perfect in loveliness . . . It is hard to wait . . . but we have so many blessings to be grateful for, the marimba, the canoe, the peace, the river, the shelter . . . I will be nineteen in a few days, and it is past time I came to grips with life on adult terms. Maybe my father is right, but I'm still skittish about marrying. But I'm wasting my breath. When the time comes, and the person – until then I mustn't worry or regret, just try to live each moment the best I know how.'

Several times a week, when the weather was clear, Harry would take out his binoculars and stare out over the jungle towards Neblina and the range it guarded, talking about the possibility of establishing a nature reserve there. He read right through Bates's *Naturalist on the River Amazons* again, and then through Alfred Russel Wallace. Wallace had seen the very wilderness they were about to enter, and was a particular inspiration. ' "Give me five stalwart Englishmen," ' Harry quoted to Jan and Becca, ' "and I could show the people of the

Rio Negro a flourishing garden," That's what Wallace said. Shame about the stalwart Englishmen. We'll just have to show what three not-so-stalwart Americans can do.'

Still, after six weeks, there was no mail from Manaus. Why not? It was enough to induce paranoia. One of the officers said as a joke: 'I think they hate you in Manaus.' But it was no laughing matter. It seemed all too likely that he was right.

Only after two months did they receive the news they needed. For unfathomable reasons to do with the relationship between the civilian and the military postal systems, the letter had taken seventy-eight days to travel from Manaus to Cucuí.

There was, of course, no word from Osmar.

🦋

By early July, they were ready. *Rima* was painted and canopied with plastic, supplies bought, seeds packed, young food plants set out in boxes. They themselves each had a large paddle, Canadian-woodsman-style. The paddles were supposedly to provide the sole motive power for their 500-mile journey to the highlands.

They set off, finally, on 5 July 1974, eight months after their arrival in Cucuí. As the morning haze gave way to bright sun, they paddled gently south with the sluggish current. Even Jan could paddle well enough, as long as Harry and Rebecca steered. After a few hours, Harry spotted an abandoned *sítio* – a tumbledown wattle-and-daub hut surrounded by a scattering of achiote trees and some overgrown manioc – and ordered a halt. Weather looked good. No point getting the tent out. Just sleep on the bank.

After Harry had made a fire and cooked supper, they settled for the night. Harry was in his hammock, with Hanuman snuggled at his feet.

Far into the night, Jan was woken by a deep, chesty snort, like a sneeze, or a cough. Why did Harry have to make such a noise, she wondered. He'll wake Becca. At that instant, she heard more noises – Harry rattling pot lids and fanning the fire.

'Harry,' she whispered hoarsely, as the flames leapt up. 'Why so much noise?'

'Oh, it was you,' he said.

'What was?'

'That sneeze. Woke yourself up.'

'I didn't sneeze. You did.'

'No. I was dreaming you and Becca were in danger from a jaguar. I'm letting him know we're here.'

Jan felt every limb freeze. There was no doubt in her mind that he was right: the noise had been a jaguar, close by. The creature, perhaps the size of a small tiger, must have emerged from the darkened jungle, drawn by the unfamiliar presence in this abandoned spot. It would have been curious, nothing more. But if frightened it would have been quite capable of killing. Was it still there, somewhere, waiting, watching? Or already padding away, warned off by Harry's racket?

Nothing happened. Harry stopped his noises. The darkness around them remained silent.

She felt again a tingle of awe at Harry's qualities. He had dreamed of a jaguar, and therefore there was a jaguar, and he had sprung awake in time to warn him off. It had happened before. Once in Mexico he had dreamed of a jaguar, woken with a start, and discovered huge pug-marks near the house. She shivered, not so much out of fear now, as relief at his presence. He not only saw and heard so much more than her, he knew so much more, intuitively. He seemed to have an affinity with the natural world, even jaguars. No need to fear the jaguar, he used to say. He has his place, we have ours. We're vegetarian – no rivals of his for food! Only meat-eaters need fear the jaguar! She trusted his assurances. With Harry, the dangers of the forest receded. It was one more reason to go forward with him into the unknown, despite everything.

🐾

They paddled on, making a few miles each day, and camping at night in clearings until, on the afternoon of the fourth day, they spotted a little flat-bottomed dinghy travelling towards them in midstream. Harry knew the dinghy's owner slightly. He was around sixty, and worked as a carpenter.

'Fidel!' called Harry, as the dinghy came abreast of them. 'Is there a good campsite near by downriver?'

Fidel nodded, described the spot, and asked where they were going.

'You won't get to the mountains that way,' he said when he heard Harry's ambitious scheme. 'The river begins in a swamp and ends in a swamp.'

Anyway, he added, they would need a pilot to take *Rima* down the São Gabriel rapids. And there weren't any pilots because there was an epidemic down there. Many people had died. He had orders for seven coffins. Harry was silent, digesting this dire news, while Fidel's eyes roamed over their extensive cargo. 'Do you have any crackers?' he asked cheerily, referring to the little dry biscuits that Brazilians like to offer with coffee to guests.

'Yes, we do.'

'I have bananas. Would you like bananas?'

'Yes.'

'Good,' said Fidel, as he pulled away. 'I will bring them to you later.' He paddled off in his little skiff, a leaf against the unbroken expanse of the Negro.

The Littles journeyed on in gloomy silence for a few minutes before finding the spot Fidel had described. It was a better site than most – a steep bank, a shed for Jan and Becca, two trees for Harry's hammock – but that was no compensation for Fidel's news. They had nowhere to go. Depressed, sapped of purpose and energy, they made camp and fell asleep.

In the morning, it was raining. Clouds shrouded the river. Their universe had shrunk to a mournful grey blur. No one stirred. There seemed no point in doing anything or making plans.

Fidel visited them briefly to trade his bananas, and said he'd be back with some fish the next day, but there was no other relief from gloom. For all that day, and most of the next, they sat glumly talking over the possibilities. Progress downriver had been abysmally slow. They'd been out a week and covered just twenty-five miles. If they went on downriver to São Gabriel, even if they wanted to risk the epidemic and the rapids, it could take them another three weeks to get there. And if they headed back upriver, they'd be fighting the current. There seemed to be no solution.

That afternoon, however, the rain stopped and the clouds began to lift. For the first time since their arrival at this dreary spot, they could see across the river. As the skies cleared, the jungle emerged, fresh and green, stretching away and away in the sparkling air.

'Wait a minute!' Harry said all of a sudden, raising his binoculars to his eyes and fiddling impatiently with the focusing-ring. 'Becca! Look at this!'

Becca took the glasses and peered through them.

'That,' she said, after a moment's silence, 'is where we have to go.'

'What *is* it?' asked Jan, impatient at her exclusion.

'A mountain!' Harry declared. 'Crystal clear and not too far. Could be Neblina itself!' Neblina. The name, so often spoken, now seemed like a magnet, a beacon, a grail, beckoning them on. 'And foothills!' Harry cried. 'Gently rounded foot-hills!' Yes, Becca was right – that's where they had to go.

But how?

'You go up the Rio Demiti,' Fidel said, on his return.

'Aha, yes.' Harry peered at his map. 'I thought we had passed it. But I didn't see any river. Where is it?'

Fidel raised his arm and pointed straight across the Negro. 'You cannot see from here. There is an island, a long island across the mouth. Behind the island is the river.'

From Harry's voice, Jan could sense his growing excitement. 'Fidel – will you take us?' he asked.

There was a long pause: Then: 'Yes, Don Enrique.'

※

Two days later, Fidel joined them in amidst the half-drowned forest where the Demiti debouched into the Negro. He tied his little dinghy on behind *Rima*, climbed in, and swung the bows to point upriver. Feeling the strength of his stroke, they all began to paddle with renewed confidence. As if to welcome and encourage them, a pair of freshwater dolphins appeared, puffing and snorting as they played around the boat, making Hanuman squeak in alarm.

But even with Fidel's powerful assistance, progress was slow. The Demiti, no more than a hundred yards across, was faster flowing than the Negro. In the first two days of travel, they made no more than ten miles.

On the third day, a boat came by, a motorized canoe that held a party of hunters. The *motorista*, an outgoing bright young man called Nilo, slowed down long enough to tell Fidel that he better get back home – the epidemic that had struck São Gabriel had moved upriver, and members of his family were affected.

Fidel, masking his anxiety, left them at the next campsite, a hummock called Black Rock. For three days, they languished there, and had just decided they'd better declare Black Rock their new home when Nilo reappeared from upriver. They couldn't stay there, he said. The place flooded every year. In that case, Harry suggested, perhaps Nilo would tow them to high ground with his motorized canoe?

Yes, he would.

He returned, as he promised, a few days later, and again they pressed on, ever deeper into as yet uncharted regions.

At every bend, Harry peered ahead to glimpse mountains. But, as they wound their way along, between unvarying walls of flooded forest, there was never a hint of hills. After three hours, Nilo moored at another occasional camp-site, a 50-foot hillock surrounded by swamp. Apparently, Nilo thought this was what Harry had meant by 'high ground.'

'No, Nilo, we can't stay here!' Harry exclaimed, doing his best not to let his frustration show. 'The mountains. Where are the mountains?'

'You have to go further. Beyond the place where two rivers join.'

Two rivers? He must mean there's a fork, Harry said. Yes, that was it. A fork, four hours further upriver. 'But, Nilo, we stay on the Demiti?'

'Yes. But the river is narrow there, and blocked by many fallen trees.'

'And after that?'

'I do not know. There is a place where the old people say the river turns back upon itself. Beyond that.'

'Can you take us?'

'I do not know the way,' he said, shaking his head.

'We don't seem to be getting anywhere,' Harry said, turning back to Becca and Jan in exasperation. 'Every good general has to be prepared to retreat. I'm all for retreating and regrouping.'

'No!' Becca spoke with surprising vehemence. 'No. There's nothing for us back there. I don't want anything more to do with the big river.'

That did it. Harry turned back to Nilo. 'Is there someone else who can take us?' he asked.

'My brother-in-law, Pelon, has been there.'

'Will you ask him to come?'

'I will, Don Enrique.'

So, for the third time, they were left on their own. But at least the place – Jahauri, Nilo called it – could be turned into a comfortable campsite. Indeed, it had apparently once been lived on, for there were signs that it had been cleared many years before.

There was virtually nothing to do. To pass the time, Harry began to read *The Pilgrim's Progress* out loud. It was a good choice in the circumstances, for Christian's adventures seemed to mirror their own. The three of them were Christians, after all, and they, like Christian, had listened to Evangelist, left behind the City of Destruction and were seeking, if not a Celestial City, at least a consummation of their own ideals. Ahead of them lay the Delectable Mountains, which they could surely reach if only they could clamber out of this particular Slough of Despond.

After a week of waiting, the jungle's silence was broken by the throb of an engine. Pelon had arrived.

Pelon, his broad features a mixture of Indian and Mediterranean traits, was only twenty-two but he had an authority and competence beyond his years. He squatted down and drew a map in the mud to explain where they were going. Here was the Demiti, here the join with the Iauiabu, here the North Fork of the Demiti, and over here another river, the Igarape Preito, the Dark Stream, which was connected to the North Fork of the Demiti by a narrow canal, a *paraná*.

'It must all lead somehow to Neblina,' Harry mused, squatting down to look at the squiggles in the earth. 'There are mountains, Pelon? Proper, high mountains?'

'Oh, yes, there are mountains! Very high!'

'Will you take us?'

Pelon nodded slowly, and then frowned. 'But you cannot take this canoe through,' he said. 'The *paraná* is too small. I must get someone to help. Sometimes, that is difficult. The older ones are afraid of Indians.'

'Indians? Are there Indians?'

'Who knows? Once, there were. They killed a missionary family here – yes, right here, Don Enrique – and took the little girl away with them. Don't worry. I will bring someone, and another canoe, gasoline, food . . . I will return, Don Enrique, in one week.'

Pelon was as good as his word. In a week, he was back, with his younger brother and Nilo, towing Nilo's canoe and two dinghies behind his launch. He stopped long enough to help repack *Rima*, tie her to the stern, and take the Littles on board.

Then, at last, they pulled away, pressing on towards the Delectable Mountains.

𝕽

The four-hour journey to the place where the two rivers joined was straightforward. At that point, however, it was clear at a glance that further progress would be painfully slow. One fork, the Iauiabu, headed south. It looked clear, and was apparently in occasional use. But in the other direction, along the North Fork, the river narrowed to a mere thirty feet, snaking along in bends that were too tight, and too dense with overhanging growth, for large craft. Every few hundred yards, fallen trees made tangled barriers of branches, or treacherous underwater snags.

Pelon moored, and transferred the expedition to *Rima* and his own canoe, leaving his brother to look after the launch. Slowly, with the two canoes lashed together, and with Nilo's outboard just ticking over, they edged past fallen trees and round bends so tight that the canoes almost touched both banks.

Pelon and Becca took the prow positions. While Becca swung her machete, cutting back branches and trailing vines, Pelon stared down into the water to check for sunken logs that might damage the boat or the propeller. Every hour or so, they would find their way completely blocked by trunks and branches. Then Pelon and Nilo would have to haul out axes, climb barefoot on to the tree, and hack a passage through it.

It seemed to Jan, sitting amidships, feeling the canoe wobble and shake with every movement, that Becca rose wonderfully to the challenge of the journey. She stood, wielding a machete, slashing away with almost the strength of the cargo-men themselves. Not however, with their skill. At one point, the bows suddenly rose up on a hidden log just as Becca was swinging at a vine. She was caught off balance, and without a sound – no cry of alarm, no shriek for help – she fell over the side and vanished with a splash beneath the black water.

'Becca!' yelled Harry. 'Becca's in the water! That mach-ete . . .'

Even as the spray settled, Nilo cut the engine.

Jan, imagining a hidden log, a cracked head, a machete wound, swung her head in a vain attempt to see what had happened. The canoes drifted silently for a couple of seconds. Then there was a second splash from behind, and a laugh. The next moment, Becca had a hold of the side. She was still laughing. 'Look!' she said, proudly, and swung up her arm to show that she had kept hold of the machete. 'I'm all right, Janny! Haul me in!'

As Becca levered herself up on the side, Jan, weak with relief, joined in Becca's laughter. That set Becca off again. Within seconds, as Becca lay flopped over like a gaffed fish, they were both gripped by such uncontrollable giggles they could hardly move. It took a good minute for them to recover and for Becca to find strength enough to haul herself into the boat.

For four days, they worked their way along the North Fork, until they reached a point, some twenty miles on, where the river seemed to give out completely. Here, in a little pool entirely surrounded by trees and bushes, with little waterways winding off in all directions through the shadowy jungle, the northern fork of the Demiti seemed to have its origins. Harry named the place the Source Pool.

But after setting up camp on a slight mound no more than a foot or so above the surrounding water, Pelon showed that it was not, in fact, a source pool. He and Nilo pushed off in their canoe towards a wall of trees and bushes, levered aside some light branches, and revealed a dismal little ditch, perhaps six feet wide: the *paraná*. It seemed extraordinary that this could be the way to their goal, but Pelon was not in doubt, assuring them that this was the last barrier.

As Pelon had said, *Rima* was indeed too large to take through. She would jam at the first bend. Harry decided that Pelon and Nilo should ferry supplies through in several loads, find a suitable hill, build a house of saplings and palm leaves, and then return to pick them up.

Once again, they resigned themselves to waiting. This site, Hummock Camp as they called it, was a miasmic and sunless spot, a miserable place to spend even a few hours. After four days of mud, damp and gloom, Pelon and Nilo declared themselves ready for the final run. The remaining load – a food box, bedding, typewriter, a few personal items, together with Hanuman and themselves – weighted down Nilo's canoe until there was just an inch of precarious freeboard. Harry gave *Rima* a last affectionate touch, and they set off gingerly along the *paraná*.

After five hours of ducking overshadowing branches and sliding the canoe over submerged logs and tangling roots – a progression so gloomy that Harry nicknamed the canal the River Styx – the *paraná* acquired a current, running against them. They all paddled furiously, until suddenly, brushing through bushes, they skimmed out into open water, under open sky.

As Harry described it to Jan, the change was astonishing. They were in the Igarape Preito, the Dark Stream, the upper Demiti. On their right, the river vanished into a maze of boggy channels and half-drowned trees. To their left, lay a broad highway, a good forty feet across, reflecting sky and jungle walls in its smooth, dark surface. It was like escaping from a dungeon into fresh air and freedom. 'Must be the only river in the world that gets bigger as it goes up,' Becca remarked.

Pelon replaced the outboard. As he swung it into action, he pointed. 'Buto!' he called. The grey shape of a freshwater dolphin rose briefly alongside.

'One traveller saluting another!' Harry said, as Pelon pointed the canoe upstream. 'The mountains, Pelon. Where are the mountains?'

'Not far. If there were no clouds, you could see them.'

It was late August 1974, eighteen months since they had left

Mexico, almost a year to the day since their departure from Guyana. Jan had ended her last letter at Hummock Camp: 'By the grace of God, it looks as if we'll get there. Soon we shall be planting our precious seeds and baby plants. My cup runneth over!'

And there, round a bend no more than two miles from the end of the *paraná*, was the first of the hills.

'Your *sitio*!' shouted Nilo, as he eased the canoe in to moor amongst the bankside vegetation. 'Here we are!'

6

DIFFICULTY HILL

From the shallows, a rocky ledge, overhung with bushes, rose abruptly to a steep slope that vanished into the forest above.

'Stay where you are while we check it out,' Harry called to Jan, 'I'll see if I can find a better place for you to come ashore.'

Jan listened as he and Becca clambered up through the bushes with Pelon and Nilo. The sound of voices faded above her. She turned her head, and glimpsed sunlight striking through plum-coloured water, open sky, shadow upon shadow of river and jungle. The forest was silent, except for the electric hum of some nearby insect.

Suddenly, she heard Harry's voice, loud and aggrieved. 'There's this quartz ledge and thin soil! This *isn't it!* There are no mountains to be seen, no mountains anywhere! I don't know what to believe any more! The soil's so thin you can scratch down to rock in seconds! There isn't even a house site!' He emerged from the bushes, flapping his hand at insects. 'But there's nowhere else. They're going to leave as soon as they get paid. You better come ashore.'

'But, Harry, we can't let them go until they've done what they agreed. Didn't they say they'd build a hut?'

'A Chinese matchbox! It's their idea of a store hut. We can't possibly live in it. Give me your hand. Put your foot on the gunwale and jump. It's muddy, but . . .'

'But Harry, they can't just *go*.'

'What can I do? They're out of food and want to get home to their families. The water's dropping. They only have three hours before dusk. It's a wonder they didn't dump us before this.'

'But what . . .?'

'Jan! Don't make things worse!' He took her hand, helped her ashore, and guided her up between bushes towards the little hut Pelon and Nilo had built. 'I thought we were going to get our place at last,' he grumbled as they climbed. 'I thought by now we'd have white water, steep slopes. And here we are on a rock island in the middle of a swamp. You should have seen Becca's face. She's really broken up.'

They arrived, panting at the hut. Becca was standing to one side in sullen silence.

'We are very unhappy about this place,' Harry said forcefully to the two guides.

'We will come back in a month,' Pelon answered quickly. 'We will take you on to the mountains. It has been *much work*.'

'But you didn't tell us what we would find.'

Pelon shrugged.

'The mountains are there,' put in Nilo, quietly. 'You can't see them because there's a hill in the way.'

'Another hill?'

'Yes. You could walk there from here.'

'You will take us when you return?'

'Yes.'

'Good.' Harry relented a little 'You've both worked hard. How much do we owe you?'

Nilo glanced at Pelon. Pelon hesitated, then said: 'Three hundred cruzeiros a day each – fifteen days – 9,000 cruzeiros.'

Harry turned to Jan. 'I knew it,' he muttered. 'He saw us as rich Americans. He's trying to take us for all we've got, and more.' He turned back to Pelon. 'Three hundred . . . *each*?'

'Two hundred and fifty, Don Enrique – 7,500.'

'Very well,' Harry agreed. But, he went on, they'd agreed to find the mountains. He would pay them 1,000 cruzeiros now, in cash, give them a cheque for 5,000 cruzeiros, and pay the rest when they'd fulfilled the bargain. 'Damnable business, carrying a cheque-book,' said Harry as he made out the sum.

'Makes them think we're rich. Sign right here, Jan, by my finger.'

'We return in one month, Don Enrique.'

'No, Pelon, we can't afford that now. Come back in two months, in November. And make sure you bring the supplies. We don't have enough food for longer.' Harry handed them letters to be posted and an order for supplies, and they turned to leave.

'Goodbye!' Harry shouted, as they climbed down the bank. 'We know you did your best!'

'Goodbye,' Jan echoed forlornly. The engine started. There was a final shout of '*Adeus!*' from below, and the noise of the engine faded. Jan was suddenly aware of the gloom and the silence. They were on their own, isolated as they never had been in Mexico. No trail, no canoe, no contact with the outside world at all.

Becca's voice broke the silence: 'I'll get some water.' She picked up a bucket, and climbed down to the river.

'Is there a way for me to get down on my own, Harry?' Jan asked.

'No. You'll have to wait until we make an access. Maybe tomorrow I can help you to have a bath. Right now, a fire, food, and your tent. I'll have to put a shelter over my hammock. There's no room for anything but stores in the little hut.'

After their meal, with a fire going, Jan began to clear a smooth base for the tent, feeling for roots and then chopping them out with her hatchet. Harry hung his hammock, with a tarpaulin over it. Then there was the tent to pitch and the remaining boxes to be carried into the hut. It was good to work. It kept despair at bay.

When the camp was established, Harry reviewed plans. 'We'll have to make a nursery clearing,' he said. 'And then get beds started to plant seeds. Maybe we ought to do that first.'

'No,' said Becca, 'The seeds will keep. The bananas are more important.'

'Well, you'll have to take care of the onions. Everything depends on them. They'll be our first fresh food.'

Next morning, Harry and Becca walked up the hill to see if they could open a trail to the hill Nilo had mentioned. They returned after an hour or so.

'It's too up-and-downy,' Harry panted. 'We'd never make it carrying all our gear. Besides, we might get lost exploring, and even if we didn't, the men might miss us when they return. Better get established here and be ready for them.'

He was right, of course. They had no choice but to make the best of things. Jan started making little 5 × 3 ft nursery beds for vegetables, feeling for the tangled roots, cutting them, pulling them out and re-spreading the quartz-sand soil. Becca began clearing the underbrush with her machete, while Harry started chopping. He hadn't chopped for years, but he said it was a job he, and he alone, had to do, if only to teach Becca. To Jan's surprise, considering how often he had said he'd never chop again, he managed well. By the end of that day, they had cleared enough to set out the banana plants, the coconuts and a pineapple.

But those few hours of industry couldn't disguise their situation. It was a bad site. The soil was poor. The insects were oppressive. Though there were few mosquitoes, as on all black-water rivers, they were pestered by sweat-bees, lazy, fly-like creatures that wander harmlessly but infuriatingly over exposed skin, and by horseflies, which deliver sharp stabs and leave small bloody spots.

'I can't understand why such a curse should be allowed in Creation,' Harry muttered angrily, smacking at his neck. 'There seem to be so many different sorts. Whose blood were they sucking before we came along?'

After two days of work, Harry decided to set out the onions. Jan was down at the river, washing clothes. Becca had helped her down, carrying a plastic tub, and then climbed back up to work with Harry. Suddenly she heard Harry shout, 'The onions are gone!'

'Gone?' Had the cargo men lost them, or what?

'Dead. Didn't survive the trip. Becca just jammed then in clay and they were there too long. This is a terrible loss . . .' Jan returned to her washing as Harry fulminated on, becoming more emotional with every sentence. ' . . . should have taken personal care of them myself. She was careless, just jammed them in, and they couldn't take it. What are we going to *eat?*' She could hear he was in tears. She sighed to herself. He was always telling them to detach themselves from worldly concerns, and he was the first to break down. If he cried over onions, what was he going to do if things really got serious?

As, indeed, they did. The third day, it rained, heavily. Water streamed down the hill in a torrent, dowsing the fire and running right into the tent. Two of Becca's schoolbooks were soaked. She returned from chopping to discover the mess, and dissolved into tears of frustration. But by the time Jan reached her to offer comfort, she had herself under control again. 'It's all right, Janny,' she said, opening a sodden geography book to assess the damage. 'I'll dry them out somehow. I'll just make sure it doesn't happen again.' She went out, fetched a spade and set about digging a drainage ditch.

Harry, meanwhile, with Hanuman squeaking on his shoulder, was trying to save the fire. 'We can't stay on this site,' he said, fanning the embers with a piece of cardboard, 'When the rainy season comes, we'll just be flooded out all the time. I'll scout out a better site further up the hill in a few days.'

They tried to make the best of it. As well as saying the Lord's Prayer together every evening, Harry reinstated the habit, established in Mexico, of observing the Jewish sabbath. It would remind them, he said, of their affinity with other exiles. So on Friday evenings, Harry lit a pair of candles, and they treated themselves to a cup of cocoa each and a biscuit with guava jam. They tried to remind themselves how lucky they were to have got so far when they might have been trapped by low water somewhere along the North Fork.

Imagined blessings soon withered in the face of real affliction. There was no fresh food. The lettuce seeds germinated, but died as soon as they were transplanted. The taro would not be ready for a year, the bananas not for eighteen months. Their staple diet was mainly starch – rice with bean sauce twice a day and noodles on the Sabbath. The few cans they had were eked out in miserly fashion. On 29 September, their fifteenth wedding anniversary, they allowed themselves their only real extravagance – some tinned peaches, a purchase made by Harry weeks before in Cucuí and kept secretly for just this occasion. Peaches! It touched Jan that Harry was still capable of such gestures. Harry rationed out half the tin, keeping the remainder for the following evening.

After three weeks, it was clear that they were in for a time of great hardship. Jan noticed she was losing weight with remarkable speed. The slacks she wore as a protection against the horseflies became loose at the waist. There was no doubt, yet, that they could endure – 'since we are here under Guidance,' Jan wrote, 'I'm sure we shall be given the help and strength we need'. But there was no denying that in their own pilgrimage this was to be their Hill of Difficulties; and so they called it.

As if the lack of food and shelter were not enough, Hanuman made himself practically unbearable. He yanked up Becca's precious shoots. He dragged newly washed clothes into the mud. He snatched tools, books, anything he could lay his hands on, scattering them randomly around the site, or – worse – dropping them among the bushes.

Becca, forever on the alert to protect her young plants, was driven almost beyond the limits of her patience. But Jan had the hardest time of all, for she could never see him coming. Her hands, forearms and neck were already raw with nips. Now he began a campaign of seemingly deliberate torment. Inspired by any action that left her vulnerable – changing, or bathing, or squatting to urinate – he would leap on her shoulders and bite her right through the skin before being scared off by her agonized shouts and her flailing arms.

Yet there seemed to be no alternative but to endure him. To kill him would have been unthinkable. On the contrary, since they knew themselves to be under Guidance, there had to be a purpose in their suffering, some benefit to be derived from Hanuman's torments. 'Remember St Paul,' Harry said. 'All things work together for good to them that love God.'

It took him a while, but eventually he devised reasons that would enable them to look upon Hanuman as a blessing. Firstly, enduring him would strengthen their self-discipline. If they could tolerate him, that would be a guarantee that they could never be dispossessed of their self-control. But there had to be a more positive purpose than that. 'I think I've got it,' Harry said, after rummaging through his convictions for further rationales to justify his attitude. He'd always walked in the footsteps of St Francis, treating all living things with equal sympathy. Man could never achieve true justice towards man, never achieve true and lasting peace, until he ceased to mistreat animals. Hanuman's kind had suffered more from humankind than the Littles would suffer from Hanuman. To atone for the sins of humanity, the least they could do was love Hanuman, their brother primate, whatever he did.

🐾

To make the new camp, Harry wanted to move uphill, where there were two areas of level ground divided by a step of quartz. On the top area stood a flat rock that could serve as a hearth. It should be possible, he said, to suspend a roof over both areas to form a split-level shelter. Behind the site was a small stone plateau with a couple of pits that could be used to store water.

He was keen to get started. Once the trees had been cut, he said, it should be possible to gain a view over the surrounding forest to the mountains. The air was cooler up there, and that suggested the presence of foothills. He was sure the mountains were near. On the few clear days, at dawn, they seemed to be touched briefly by a huge shadow cast, perhaps, by Neblina itself, or at least one of its nearer neighbours. If only they could get a good view, they would be able to see where they should be going.

The area was dominated by three huge trees that would have to be felled, and felled in the right direction, eastwards, to ensure clear ground where they wanted to build. The first two came down as planned, though they took two days each to fell. The third was trickier. Jan had been warned to keep clear of the site to avoid possible danger. She heard the chopping stop. Then there was silence, such a long silence she wondered what had happened.

She waited, tense with anxiety. Then after another half minute, there came a tremendous crash.

A minute or two later, Harry and Becca arrived, panting. Even as Harry strode into the campsite, he began a dramatic description of what had happened. 'I shot my bolt before we were half-way through, so I put Becca to finishing it and just stood off to watch the tree. She chopped to the last few inches and the tree just stood there, perfectly balanced – incredible! No telling which way it would fall. Could have snapped, jumped its stump, anything. Becca was really frightened. Hanuman knew we were in trouble – just sat there without saying a word, didn't you, boy? It took ages to go, and when it did, it fell right across the house site. Only place we could have built, all smashed up.'

'You can't clear it?' Jan asked.

'Take us months, the hardest wood you can imagine. No, it's God's way of telling us the place is not for us.'

Jan really didn't mind. It was enough that they were both out of danger, and that Harry had accepted the disaster so readily.

Right then and there, Harry decided on a makeshift solution. They would move a mere thirty yards along the hillside, to a spot where they would not be washed out in the next storm.

The move had to be done at once, he said. Couldn't risk

even one more night in that spot. Good opportunity to make other changes as well. Since the tent was never dry, he explained, it would be better if Jan and Becca lived in their hammocks from now on, protected by a tarpaulin.

Eager to complete the move before dusk, he worked much faster than usual, laying the tent out to dry, carrying hammocks and equipment, helping Jan and Becca reset their hammocks and string up their tarpaulin. He got so hot he twice went down to the river to bathe.

Next morning, Harry seemed tired. He hardly spoke over breakfast. Then, while sharpening machetes, he said in a subdued voice: 'I don't seem to be strong enough for this any more, Jan. These emergencies drain me. You don't know what it cost me in nervous energy just to get this far. After all, I'd never reckoned on homesteading again on our own, without extra help.'

'Take a rest, Harry,' Jan advised, anxiously.

'No, no. Work will see me through.'

Soon, however, she realized that he was feeling worse. 'Jan,' he said, lying back in his hammock. 'If anything should happen to me, take Becca back to Fair Oaks.' Jan's heart sank. His tone was casual, but he had hardly mentioned the possibility of his death since leaving Mexico.

He finished his sharpening, and took Becca off to lop branches from the fallen tree up the hill.

On his return for lunch, he asked Becca for a cup of lemongrass tea, saying he had a fever. 'Feels like malaria. Thought work would do the trick. Must have been the effect of overheating yesterday combined with those cold dips. Should have learned by now.'

Jan, fearing the worst, helped settle him in his hammock. He hadn't had malaria for years. He must have been weakened by the months of travel and the recent lack of good food.

For three days, he hardly moved, regularly sinking into fever with a cloth spread over his face, consuming nothing but

lemon-grass tea. He couldn't force down any of their mono-
tonous, starchy food.

'Harry,' she pleaded, 'You have to eat.'

'Can't. No appetite,' he muttered, eyes closed. 'No future.
Starve to death.'

With the onset of Harry's illness, after they had been on Difficulty Hill for a month, Jan's spirit all but failed her. Bit by bit,
she sank into an emotional and psychological morass, her own
inner Slough of Despond.

There were reasons enough for her collapse, reaching back
almost two years – the debilitating bouts of malaria in Mexico;
the loss of the Caverna; her worsening vision; the death of
Rima; the bitter disappointment over her relationship with
Harry; the onset of the menopause; the long, frustrating search
for a site; the steady retreat from civilization and immersion in
the unknown; Hanuman's plaguy habits; Difficulty Hill itself,
a place so steep and broken she could hardly move without
help, where an unwary step could tumble her into the river.
This was not like the Caverna. Here, she was practically useless.
The cooking – on an open fire, where pots would easily be
spilled and she could burn herself – had to be left totally to
Becca. The significance of her blindness came home to her
with renewed force – her isolation from the world around her,
her utter dependence on the others for her food and safety, her
inability to contribute just when they needed help most.

And now Harry was on the point of death. If he died, how
would she manage? If she was incapable now, what would she
be like if Harry's death made her responsible for both herself
and Becca?

A phrase of Harry's surfaced from her memory, a phrase he
had read out when first looking at the area on the map: 'Less
than one person per square mile.' Then, it had seemed an ideal;
now, it had become a nightmare. They were specks in a void,
outside human existence, cut off as few others ever are. Like

prisoners of conscience, they had placed themselves in solitary, isolating themselves in place, and – more terrible still – in time as well.

The wilderness around them was not simply empty right now – it always had been. This ancient land, inconceivably older than the youthful wildernesses of North America, had never been touched by anyone. They were lost in vistas of geological time that ranged back into a hidden past and forwards into an obscure future.

What could ever end their isolation? Pelon had said he and Nilo would return in two months. How could she believe that? Why should they remember, what reason to return if they did remember? The questions prompted only further questions. Her thoughts ran wild. How could she be certain Pelon and Nilo were still alive? If they were dead, why should anyone come, ever? What proof was there that Cucuí had not been wiped out by malaria?

Step by step, the outside world fell away from her, as if she had become the victim of some Cartesian demon destroying the possibility of knowledge. Nothing was certain. If Cucuí was gone, what of more distant regions? What of those worlds they had once inhabited, in Mexico, California, Vermont? There was no proof that they still existed. She saw the world empty of all people but themselves whirling through a dark and meaningless void. The void was round her, and inside her, and there seemed no way to fill it.

A memory came to her. San Francisco. Her apartment bedroom. Night. She was pregnant, her brief marriage over. She was alone, uncertain of her decision to bear her child, tormented by feelings of inadequacy and guilt. Then, too, the world had seemed an empty place, without meaning. Overwhelmed by the need for immediate release, she had thought of the pills in the bathroom cupboard; opened her eyes; seen a ray of light. The light came from under the bathroom door. She fixed upon it, and was about to move towards it when she felt the baby move inside her. She thought:

168

you don't create life and then consider suicide. With that, her panic had left her, never to return, until now.

And now, was there not still Becca to live for? I live for Rebecca's *life* – she remembered that fierce assertion made after Es's death. If she could live for Becca before she was born, move to Mexico for her, marry to give her a home and a father, she could surely stay sane for her.

For Becca was real enough, right there beside her, bringing her food and cups of water. And if Becca was real, if the food and water were real, other things were real: the ground, the trees, the leaves.

She made her way to a fallen tree, and threw herself along it. Arms outstretched, she felt beneath her fingers, beneath her clawing fingernails, the roughness and the solidity. No denying that this, too, was real; it had once been alive; its past was, or had been, a reality. If the forest was real, then so were the rivers, the distant towns, and Nilo and Pelon, and their promises.

Strengthened by its solidity, she returned to that tree day after day and, by the ritual repetition of the certainties she derived from it, she conjugated her way back to sanity.

🦎

Harry's recovery was effected with vinegar. Becca, listing what food they had, suggested he try some pickles. He did, and discovered he liked the vinegar. With this as a relish, he found he could get down enough of the starchy foods – *farinha*, rice and noodles – to regain his vitality.

But he remained terribly weak – 'I haven't been this thin since prison!' – and could do no further work on Difficulty Hill. Indeed, as far as this site was concerned, he seemed to give up on it. His mind was set on getting to, or nearer, the mountains. 'If only we were higher,' he would say, 'We would be cooler, and free from these horseflies.'

Jan agreed with him. Though she never told him of the extent of her inner struggle, she did mention that she found things hard. 'It'll be better in the mountains,' he said. 'You'll have creative work to do. We'll all be happier.'

But what if the men didn't come? she asked once, remembering her fear, and then tried to quell it with a wild suggestion: perhaps they ought to plan to build a raft and float downriver through the *paraná* to *Rima*?

'Why shouldn't they come?' asked Harry, puzzled. 'Even if they didn't want to, Armindo would tell them to come. Besides, we're under military authority here. The Commandante would organize something. He'd have to.'

He was right, of course. Over and over again, she told herself he was right. He didn't have to understand the depths of her agony to be right. She struggled to absorb his words, to attach his logic to her own. She paced back and forth beside her tree trunk, arguing with herself. When Becca grew impatient with this neurotic pacing – 'For goodness sake, Janny, at least sit down when you eat!' – Harry said: 'Let her be. She has to work it out this way.' Jan was grateful to him for that.

A week passed, then another. Harry recovered enough to joke again. When he heard a plane go over – one of the regular commercial flights to Manaus – he said, 'Manaus, anyone?' and Jan smiled, thinking longingly of fast travel, safety, the immediate response to tiny whims, food, other people, a destination, a sanctuary.

Sanctuary. That was what she needed.

As his health improved, Harry began to read to them again. Christian and Faithful escaped from Vanity Fair and reached their Celestial City. Christian was now far beyond Jan. She could not see how, given their present strength, given her own inner darkness, she could continue directly on to another homestead, unless . . . Unless she did something that Christian never considered: retreat in order to regain strength.

Her mind plucked from the recent past Harry's remark about where she and Becca ought to go if he died. Well, why not do it anyway? Why not draw breath at Fair Oaks?

She was wary about suggesting the idea. After all he had only mentioned it when he thought he might die. Again, it was Harry who provided the opportunity, during a conversation about plants.

Becca, who showed no sign of strain or discouragement, had been working hard enough to have an impressive range of vegetables planted, if not grown. The lettuces had failed, but the taro was coming along, and the squash and the bananas looked promising.

'There are a lot more plants I'd like to get from the Rio Negro,' Becca said, one afternoon after work. 'Maybe we can get Pelon's mother or sister-in-law to collect for us?'

'Sure,' Harry replied, 'But don't be in a hurry. You've enough to take care of right here. Even if we left for two years, you'd be surprised how much you'd find when we returned. Maybe that's the way to do it. We could go away and come back to a harvest. Start upriver with new plants, come back later to harvest Difficulty Hill.' Jan listened in amazement. He was extraordinary, no doubt about it. Despite the malaria and the starvation, his enthusiasm was undimmed. 'And this time there won't be any ranchers coming in to rob and ruin,' he went on. 'That's one of the blessings about this place we should never forget.'

We could go away and come back to a harvest. The words sanctioned her own thoughts. The work on Difficulty Hill need not be wasted. Retreat need not mean failure. For her parents, it might even be a blessing. The five-acre lot in Fair Oaks could surely do with their labour. And there would be advantages for Rebecca – friends, education, wider experience.

'Harry.' She spoke diffidently, barely raising her voice above a whisper. 'I've been thinking . . .' Harry turned. 'While our food plants grow we could go to Fair Oaks. Help my parents.'

Becca let out a gasp of protest. 'Oh, no, Janny. I know it's been hard here, but you'll feel better after we get a house to live in.'

But Harry understood. He took Jan's hand. She felt an almost overwhelming relief at the gesture, which his words confirmed. 'It's something to be considered,' he said.

Becca sighed.

'We all have to be happy, Becca,' Harry went on. 'Maybe we're being selfish doing what we want. Your grandmother is hard-pressed with that house and garden. Besides, I can't be a workforce any longer. You have to have a husband to help . . .'

'But we only just *got* here!'

Harry, however, had taken over Jan's suggestion and began to elaborate on the possibilities. 'I could stay here with Hanuman. Couldn't leave him behind. You two could go. They'd want to see you two. We promised Becca a visit ages ago, but I couldn't let her travel alone, not with the world the way it is today.'

Over the days that followed, they went over the implications and possible arrangements many times. Jan said she couldn't possibly leave Harry. They'd be away far too long – there would be little point going away for less than a year, if they were to make a good job of their parents' garden and Becca was to receive any benefit of learning American ways. Hanuman, of course, would be a problem. Perhaps, Jan suggested, they could find someone in Cucuí to look after him.

'No,' said Harry, 'He can come with us to Fair Oaks. They'd love to have you, wouldn't they, boy?'

The more they talked, the more Harry began to see advantages in the trip. He could finish writing the story of Rima's life, he could collect his manuscripts, he could make new approaches to publishers.

There were details to be settled, of course, like money (they would probably have to send for more) and travelling clothes. No problem, Harry said, they could make their own. They had time before the cargo-men returned and they had cloth enough with them.

'But, Harry, we'll need better clothes than that.'

'No, Jan, that's one thing I'm not going to do – change our ways to suit city people,' Harry replied. 'We have plenty of good Brazilian cotton. It'll make distinctive clothes, jungle-cut, jungle-sewn.'

So, while they waited for the cargo men to come, Jan made the patterns, feeling her way round the edge of old clothes laid out on the new cloth. Becca did the cutting, and Harry the sewing.

🐝

Since Harry did not admit how much in need of help he was, the change of direction seemed to Jan a miracle. Harry had understood. His confidence in her was untouched by her sugges-tion. Moreover, he remained considerate. He read to her for an hour each day, which kept her mind off Hanuman, and the horseflies, and her own recent depression. Her relief grew day by day into heartfelt gratitude.

Her gratitude, like her depression, was internal, and equally powerful. Indeed, the two were complementary. Black despair vanished; euphoric gratitude took its place, gratitude that demanded both an objective focus and a formal expression. Harry was the focus, but she could not have expressed it in mere words to him. Something more than words was needed, some other way.

She found her way on a Sunday at the beginning of November.

Harry had suggested a Quaker observance. It was a simple enough ceremony, a reading, a hymn and a few minutes of quiet meditation. While Jan and Becca sat on crates, he played a hymn tune on his recorder. She didn't know which hymn it was because she was already lost in her own thoughts, reciting to herself the reasons for her gratitude to Harry: his resilience, the purity of his aims, his readiness to go along with her wishes, his thoughtfulness in reading to her. Then Harry and Becca played a duet on their recorders, and sang a hymn together. The hymn was one of her favourites. The words and the stately tune broke her train of thought:

> A charge to keep I have,
> A God to glorify,
> A never-dying soul to save,
> And fit it for the sky.

'A charge to keep I have.' If her gratitude was to find expression, it could only be by fulfilling the promises already made. Her own charge, accepted at her wedding ('Shall we stick by each other as long as we live?') was to remain loyal to Harry. She had been loyal, loyal to what was best in him. Now he would need her loyalty more than ever. He was a hermit; a man of uncompromising rusticity; a self-righteous patriarch about to step into a world oiled by little hypocrisies and into the house of a matriarch. He was not strong enough to bend, and any suggestion of criticism, any breath of opposition, could shatter him. There must be none, no hint of *disloyalty*.

> And let me ne'er my trust betray,
> But press to realms on high.

She would not betray her trust. Come what may, she would keep faith.

🝤

Three days later, on 6 November, they heard a shout from somewhere among the trees.

'Don Enrique!'

It was Pelon. A swish of footsteps on leaves, and there he was, clearly relieved to see them. 'Don Enrique!' he said, putting his arms round Harry and slapping his shoulders. He handed over a packet of mail, and went off to unload cargo. Harry flipped through the letters. Two were from the US Treasury, addressed to Jan.

'Cheque,' said Harry, tearing open the first of them. 'Oh, no. Becca: read this. My eyes are playing tricks on me.'

Becca took the stiff rectangle of paper and read deliberately: 'Two thousand, seven hundred and thirty-six dollars.'

'That's what I thought it said. Couldn't believe it. I guess this means we can afford the trip. But where does it come from? Why is the Treasury sending you all this money, Jan? Wait. What's this other one? Maybe a letter telling us it's all a mistake. No. More money. A hundred and fifty-two dollars. Perhaps we ought to stay on here, and they'll just go on sending us money.'

'Harry, don't you remember?' Jan exclaimed, happily. 'That's the social security we applied for in San Cristobal when we applied for new passports. We had to get it notarized, remember?'

'I don't remember anything of the kind. Anyway, I better tell Pelon . . .'

'Don't tell him we have money!'

''Course not. I'll say your parents want to see you.'

Pelon was dismayed by the news. He had anticipated a quick round trip.

'Don Enrique,' he said, 'I cannot stay now. I borrowed a motor from friends and must catch up with them to give it back. I will return tomorrow. Tomorrow, Don Enrique.'

They had no choice but to let him go. Besides, they had fresh food now, enough for weeks. The worst was over.

But Pelon did not return the next day, nor the next. A week passed, and still he did not come.

By now, however, their confidence was restored. They spent the time packing, and working in the gardens. They fought off as best they could both the horseflies and Hanuman, who was fascinated by the packed crates and spent much of his waking time trying to unpack them. 'He's out to destroy us!' shouted Harry angrily, as he hauled the monkey away for the umpteenth time.

Three weeks after Pelon's departure, they celebrated Jan's birthday – 27 November – with the last of the new squashes. The next day, just when anxiety was beginning to set in, Pelon arrived.

This time, he had his uncle with him to help out. He explained the delay with a shrug. 'Don Enrique, we shot a tapir and had to get the meat back to the *sítio*. Then there was no gasoline in Cucuí, and we had to wait for the gasoline barge.'

'I see. Well, you're here now,' Harry said, signalling the two men to load up. They had hardly began to carry boxes down the hillside, however, when Harry proposed an idea, one that he'd mentioned a few days before as a way of mitigating Becca's disappointment about leaving. 'Pelon,' he said, 'Do you know the mountains?'

'Don Enrique?'

'We want to come back. When we come, you know we want to go to the mountains.'

'I know. They are close. It is easy.'

'Then take us now, my daughter and myself, without cargo.'

To Jan's surprise, Pelon agreed readily enough. The three of them vanished upriver, leaving Jan with Pelon's uncle. Jan, knowing hardly a word of the local dialect, was embarrassed by the old man's presence. But he had clearly been warned of her disabilities, and kept his distance. For the entire four hours the others were away, they exchanged not a single word.

When the canoe returned, Harry was jubilant. 'A hill!' he shouted as he climbed up from the river. 'A real hill! Pelon wanted to go further, but it's fine for us! A bank that's not too steep. A fallen tree for access. We even went up and marked a spot for a house. I asked him whether the soil was good for manioc, and like a true peasant he got down on his hands and knees, scratched up earth in his fingers and said it was fine! When we come back, we'll have our homestead.'

It only remained to load some of the cargo into Pelon's canoe, and he was ready to make a first ferry trip through the *paraná*. There, he would transfer his load into *Rima*, and return the next day.

'Pelon!' Harry acted long-suffering suspicion, as Pelon

pushed off from the bank. 'This is for certain? You will not go on downriver with more meat to sell?'

'Tomorrow,' Pelon repeated. 'Tomorrow I will be back, because the river is dropping and we must be quick.'

He was as good as his word.

Though Harry was now as eager as Jan to get started, Becca was clearly depressed at having to leave. When she was loading the cargo with Pelon, Harry accused her of working too slowly. 'It's hard, Harry,' she said, choking back tears. 'I don't think you understand.'

But she cheered up on the journey itself. Once they had passed through the *paraná* and picked up *Rima*, the going was easy. To Jan's relief, Becca began to respond to her surroundings again. She spotted one of her favourite orchids, the Amazonian Blue. She watched for the places where they had camped on the way up, counting the bends in the river. When they reached the spot where she had fallen in, she laughed at the memory of herself waving her machete.

After transferring to the launch at the mouth of the North Fork, they chugged downriver until they reached the Negro, and Jan sensed with relief the immensity of sky and the flash of sun on open water.

'I made that 644 bends, Janny,' Becca said, as Pelon nosed the launch into the main stream; '644 bends between here and the Source Pool. How does the Demiti ever find its way out?'

'Not all of it does, Becca.'

Becca laughed, turning to look back at the cool, dark waters. When she spoke again, her mood had changed. 'I'll have to come back here some day,' she said. 'It's so beautiful.'

7

FAIR OAKS

Early on Sunday, 22 December, just in time for Christmas, the Littles, cold, tired, dirty, and still wearing the jungle cottons made on Difficulty Hill, stepped out into the bus depot in downtown Sacramento. And there, impeccably made up, statuesque as ever, and dressed in an imitation jaguar coat, was Jessie Muller.

It had, of course, been a gruelling journey, full of crisis and muddle, but from two particular days of chaos emerged a solution to their – or at least Harry's – principal concern: Hanuman. Pelon had taken them over the border to San Carlos and landed them at the National Guard HQ, where Harry intended to arrange a ride north on a military aircraft. The officer on duty told them, yes, there would be a military flight in three days, and yes, there would be seats, but – he had spotted Hanuman – 'But, *señor*, you can't bring *that* into Venezuela. It belongs to the jungle.'

Harry turned back to Jan and Becca. 'This stops us,' he said, grimly. 'Let's go out and talk.'

He led them to the river-wall in front of the HQ. They sat, looking dejectedly over Pelon's launch, which lay moored against the bank below them, across the river to the Colombian settlement of San Felipe, 500 yards away.

Harry broke the silence, muttering aimless thoughts aloud. Couldn't go on, couldn't go back. Not that he didn't approve of the ruling. It was about time they started practising conservation. He just didn't expect it to be used against *him*. There he was, hoist with his own petard, whatever a petard was. Sounded like a pet ard, whatever an ard was. He was still rambling on when Pelon and his wife came out of the store near by and began to load their launch. Harry's thoughts wandered further. He'd really like to have gone with them. He dreaded leaving Hanuman there. This was where they'd found him being treated so badly.

'There's Luciano,' Harry went on, as Pelon cast off and headed downstream. Jan peered to see the shadowy figure walking down the beach to the water's edge. Luciano was a strange character. He had no front teeth and hardly ever spoke. Harry used to say he'd opened his mouth once and someone had knocked his teeth out, so now he kept it closed.

'Looks like he's got his own canoe now,' Harry said slowly. 'Must be doing well . . .' He broke off, as if in thought, then suddenly leaped to his feet. 'I'm going back!' he announced. 'Luciano!'

But Luciano had already tugged his outboard into life, and did not hear.

'Harry!' said Jan, appalled. 'No! Eighteen hours in an open canoe . . .'

'I can overtake Pelon if we hurry. Luciano!' Luciano looked round. Harry pointed to the vanishing launch. '*Puede llegar al launche ahorita?*'

Luciano, still steering out into midstream, stared down river, then turned back to Harry.

'I'll pay 12 bolivares!'

Jan heard the note of the engine change.

'Quick!' Harry ordered. 'Help me pack what I need! I don't want to go to California. You two go on and have your visit. When you come back, I'll have your homestead ready for you. I'll take care of Hanuman. C'mon, boy!'

'But, Harry!' Jan protested. 'Not back to Difficulty Hill!'

'I'll stay at Pelon's. They'll take care of me. We'll go back and forth. This is the best way. Why didn't I think of it before? My recorder! Becca, my clothes!'

Jan could hardly believe what Harry was doing. It seemed a quixotic gesture, inconceivably reckless. But Becca was already frantically burrowing about in the baggage, scrambling together Harry's things. By the time Luciano pulled alongside, the bag was ready. With Hanuman on his shoulder, Harry climbed in. 'I'll have a homestead waiting for you!' he shouted as Luciano accelerated out into midstream. Jan waved forlornly, and kept on waving until Becca told her to stop because the canoe was out of sight.

Several conflicting emotions began to heave about inside Jan. She was relieved that the problems posed by Hanuman's destiny and Harry's prickly personality had so dramatically been removed, yet she could not admit any such relief to herself, let alone Becca; she felt guilty that there would be no one looking after Harry – he had after all trained them both for years to accommodate themselves to his incapacity. She was also puzzled and aggrieved at Harry's action. It was the first time ever that Harry had left them on their own without clear instructions. He would have described such an act as irresponsible, if anyone but he had done it. Feeling at once abandoned and released, she turned away from the river, moved to tears by her confusion, regaining control of herself only when Rebecca suggested something to eat.

Next morning, after being offered a room by acquaintances from their previous visit, they decided that things would be all right, after all. Without Harry, travel would be simpler, cheaper, and more enjoyable, and life in Fair Oaks would be more peaceful. Soon, they had a plan: they would stay on in their room until the plane came, fly to San Fernando on the Apure, then take the bus the 150 miles north to Caracas. From there, they would take a commercial flight home. Restored by their decision, they repacked their untidy cases, and in doing so found some more of Harry's things. Jan had Becca set them aside in a duffel bag, intending to find someone going downriver who could drop them off with Pelon.

Once again, they made their way back to the river, to wait for a boat heading downstream. Jan liked being there, with Becca. It was the first moment of peace she had known in a long while. Below them, the broad, dark river ran quietly by. A group of women were washing clothes; barefoot children splashed and screamed in the water, sleek as seals; a canoe purred away from the bank, heading across the river towards the matchbox houses of San Felipe.

Suddenly Becca broke the mood with a shout: 'There's a boat coming – fast!'

Jan strained to hear, and after a few seconds picked up the roar of a powerful engine, and then the swish of a bow-wave. A speedboat. That was a surprise. There were only two or three on the upper Negro, and they always drew attention.

'Oh, no!' Becca drew in her breath sharply. 'It can't be!'

'What?'

'Harry. It's Harry back. Why would he do that?'

As the engine died, and the boat swung round to the beach. Harry waved. 'Jan! Becca! Incredible!' he yelled, and even before he stepped ashore, he began to tell his story. He spoke loudly and melodramatically, switching to Spanish, addressing the growing crowd rather than Jan and Becca: '*Increible!*' he boomed. 'Pelon ran into trouble. Alfredo had to come to the rescue and take us to Guadalupe. That's where I found the answer. The Colombian border official there took one look at Hanuman and decided he'd have him. Good company for his capuchin, he said. I wasn't sure about leaving Hanuman, but he had no doubts! This morning, I asked Don Fausto to take me back upriver. When I got in the canoe, Hanuman stayed on the bank. I called him – 'Hanuman, let's go!' He gave me an answering chirp – 'Not now! I like it here!' It was his decision! *Increible!*'

Yes, incredible, she thought wryly, as he made her sign away $100 for his high-speed return, and not only in the way Harry meant.

The first Jan knew of her mother's presence was her urgent voice: 'Hullo, you three!' She felt Jessie's arms round her, but her own nervous greeting – 'Mother, it's good . . .' – was lost in Jessie's: 'Do you have your bags? We're double-parked outside!' She sounded disconcerted, as well she might, Jan realized, at the thought of welcoming three ragamuffin peasants in jungle cottons and Rio Negro straw hats.

Harry led Jan out to the waiting car, and guided her into the back seat. A voice came from in front of her, and more voices from behind as Harry and Becca stowed the baggage. Suddenly she recognized the person in the car with her.

'Chris!' she said. It was her cousin, much altered, judging from her voice, by the passing of the years. 'I'm so glad you're driving!' She was about to say: could you stop by a nursery so I can buy bulbs as a house-gift, when Chris pre-empted her.

'Your mother is driving – and she drives *beautifully*.'

A door slammed, and the car started.

'I didn't mean . . .' Jan broke off lamely. She felt lost suddenly, frightened as she had been in childhood, and isolated by her blindness. Everything was happening too quickly.

As the voices talked on, remote and strange, she tried to concentrate on her surroundings. The streets – busy freeways rather than the once familiar little lanes – passed in a blur. Jessie was explaining where they were. This was Carmichael, this was the brick house where they lived before they moved to Fair Oaks, here was Jan's school, here the local church. Jan stared round vacantly. She was back in the place where she grew up, and she saw only phantoms. She forgot about the bulbs.

The car swung into the driveway. Jan, peering round anxiously, tried to make out the hawthorn trees that had led to the house.

'No trees, mother?' she asked.

'We have a new driveway, Jan. We put that in when they doubled the width of the highway. Here's your father now, and your uncle Lauren.' Lauren, whose wife had died a few months previously, was now staying with Bill and Jessie.

The car stopped. Harry led Jan from the car and up steps over the terraced lawn. Suddenly, she felt her father's hands grasp hers. She knew he would be trying to speak. She saved him the effort, and herself the embarrassment of not understanding, by embracing him.

Inside, everything was different. When Jan had last been in Fair Oaks, fifteen years before, the house had been three rooms hitched on to a garage. Now, the garage had become the living-room. There were thick rugs on a tiled floor, low tables, lamps. The profusion of objects made a clutter in which Jan scarcely dared move. She sat, bewildered, while her mother served tea and cake, thinking how bizarre they must look against the suburban decor. Harry and Jessie were discussing the journey. Jan, fearful and lost in her own twilight world, could contribute nothing. She was a stranger in her own home.

She heard Uncle Lauren's voice. 'Would you be more comfortable over on the couch?' he asked. Jan allowed him to guide her across the room and seat her. Uncle Lauren was a gentle man, reticent, withdrawn. There were reasons for that. The last time they met had been in the company of Lauren's son, Mike. Now Mike was dead. He had committed suicide years before in a peculiar but efficient way, by taking a lawnmower into a closet, starting it up and gassing himself. Lauren had never really recovered.

Lauren, sitting beside her on the couch, began to fill her in on family affairs. Barney was head of a whole department now. Buzz was a postmaster, a very good job. Molly's husband was an executive vice-president. She had forgotten how people back here lived. The concern with money and material success amazed her. Jim was still an auditor. Jim's youngest daughter graduated last year. And Gary, well, Gary was brilliant, of course – graduated at sixteen, and . . .

'Where's Harry, Uncle Lauren?' Jan interrupted, aware of a sudden silence in the rest of the room.

'In the den, I think. Yes, I'm sure he's in the den. Let me show you where it is.' He led her into her old bedroom. 'This is the dining-room,' he said, 'and this' – leading her into what had been her parents' bedroom – 'is the den.'

'Hullo!' Harry's voice. He was sitting in a rocking-chair. Becca and Jessie were on a couch. 'We're having a good talk,' Harry went on. 'I'm doing very well for myself! This'll be a good chair for me to sleep in. You two can have the room upstairs.'

Becca explained that Grandmother had shown her round already, 'and Grandmother says we can go upstairs to have a bath, Janny'. She sounded excited by the idea. Jan allowed Becca to guide her through the living-room and up the stairs to the bathroom.

'Here's the tub, Janny. A bit more hot, I think. Grandmother showed me how to work the bathtub faucet.' Jan climbed in, smiling, reminded of bath times together in San Francisco and San Cristobal, when Becca was a baby. 'Could you do my back for me, Becca?' she asked.

Under Becca's gentle touch, Jan gradually felt the shock of the arrival slipping from her. It was a relief to hear the note in Becca's voice. She seemed genuinely happy to be there. She would find many things strange, of course, but she should be able to adapt, and make the best of this world as well as her jungle home.

🐉

There were nine for Christmas dinner: three Littles, two Mullers, Uncle Lauren, Jessie's nephew Boyd, his wife Nancy and their son Scott. While everyone else talked in the living-room, Boyd carved in the kitchen. Becca, dressed in one of Jessie's trousersuits, carried dishes to the table. Her hair hung loose over her shoulders, a concession by Harry to the occasion, for it was the first and only time he had allowed her to display such overt femininity.

'Is that everything?' Jan heard her ask.

'What about the turkey dressing, Becca?' Jessie asked.

'Dressing?' Becca was puzzled. 'What do you dress a turkey in?' She picked up a towel. 'Something like this?'

Boyd laughed gently. He was a tall, genial redhead, with a reassuring, quietly humorous manner. 'No, Becca – this, the stuffing.' He pointed to a dish.

With a shamefaced smile, Becca carried the dish to the table. As she moved out of earshot, Jessie said affectionately, 'You know, Boyd, she thought she'd broken the vacuum cleaner this morning. You know what she'd done? Pulled the plug out by mistake!' They both laughed good-naturedly. 'All right, everyone, let's eat!'

Bill and Jessie took their places at opposite ends of the table. Jessie, pointing out who should sit where, put Jan beside Bill. Harry was about to help Jan in, when Bill stepped round beside her, guiding her with a hand on her arm. He patted the chair, and then reversed his hand and patted her on the behind, signalling her to sit down.

'Chestnuts, Harry?' Jessie offered.

'Not for me! I don't have the equipment!' He had only a few broken stubs of teeth left now, and kept his moustache carefully combed over his mouth to disguise the fact.

Jan tensed. He'd agreed to eat turkey, abandoning his vegetarianism as a concession to the occasion and the company. She'd been praying he wouldn't give or take offence over some other issue. Jessie would hardly find his dentition a fit topic for Christmas dinner.

Scott broke the silence. 'I believe there are new aids now available,' he said.

Dentures? Harry said, loudly. No, no. His heart. He'd never survive the treatment.

Such tiny, unimportant comments, but they reduced Jan to an agony of anticipation, for she knew both Harry's inner tensions and her own impotence to limit his responses. But Boyd, with easy charm, changed the subject, and the rest of the meal passed without incident.

After the visitors had gone, Bill came over to Jan. 'Let me get you a glass of brandy,' he said.

'No, thank you, Daddy.'

'Just a little one,' he insisted, taking her right hand in both of his. 'It would do you so much good.'

'No thanks, really.'

'Just for me –'

'No!' Harry cut in harshly. 'She said "no", Bill. That ought to be enough!'

Bill dropped Jan's hand suddenly, and opened his mouth to speak.

'Oh, Bill,' Jessie said quickly. 'I meant to mention – the garage door seems to be stuck. Would you take a look at it?' As Bill left, she turned to Harry, and said with studied calm, 'Please, Harry, be patient with Bill. You have to remember he's an old man now.'

'And he has to understand that "no" is "no",' retorted Harry.

'Harry,' Jan interceded. 'It's all right, you don't have to –'

'I *do* have to! Now don't say any more!' A shocked silence fell, broken to Jan's relief, by Harry himself: 'I think we better have our goodnight and get to bed. It's been a long day.'

In the den, the three of them sat on the couch to hear Becca read a passage from the Bible. When she'd finished and they'd said the Lord's Prayer together, Harry made a little speech. They had to be strong, he said. They were facing some very difficult situations, things they'd never faced before, things that could smash them before they knew it.

Jan's heart sank. It was as if he was determined to see life in Fair Oaks as a war: us against them. But that would be disastrous. It was only her parents' feelings for her and Becca that enabled them to tolerate Harry. At all costs, she should try to keep him calm until his anxieties were laid to rest, as they would be eventually, she was sure, by Jessie's determined generosity.

'Harry,' she said soothingly, 'I know it's hard, but everyone's doing their best –'

'How can you say that, after what he did to you?'

'What do you mean?'

'The way he seated you. The way he *handled* you.'

It took her a moment to remember her father's friendly gesture. 'Harry, that was nothing. He did that to help me.'

'That is *not* how a father touches a daughter. I don't touch Rebecca like that. If he will try something like that when I'm standing right there, there's no telling what he might try some other time after he's been drinking.'

Jan was incredulous. Could he really think that her own father, at eighty-two, would – ? It was ridiculous. But she had to be careful. She shouldn't antagonize. Placate, stall, delay. She took a breath. 'I don't think there's anything for you to worry about,' she said, as reassuringly as she could.

'There you go, dodging reality!' His voice began to rise. 'You won't face up to the obvious, Jan! That's how you got so fouled up with men in the first place. If this is how you think, how can I ever trust you to take responsibility for Rebecca if something should happen to me? You have to draw a line, Jan. That's something you can't do. I have to do it for you. That business with the brandy. I wouldn't have said anything if I'd thought you could draw the line yourself. But you can't. Not with him. Even after . . .' He broke off, as if too shocked to express his thoughts in words.

'Yes, Harry, but you don't have to mention it, do you?' she said, pleadingly.

'How could I? I couldn't say anything. It's too awful.'

She allowed herself to relax. He would let it go after all. Relieved that the crisis had been averted, Jan allowed Becca to lead her up to bed, where she lay for a while, puzzling over Harry's reaction. Such a little thing, and so much fuss. Well, she thought, as she drifted into sleep, it's over now.

But the next day, as soon as she went in to say good morning, she knew something had gone dreadfully wrong. Not that Harry was excited. Far from it. As he told her what had happened, he sounded quite relaxed, even self-satisfied.

After she had gone to bed, Bill had come in to see him, under instructions from Jessie. 'He wanted to know why I had been angry,' Harry said, lightly. 'I had to show him.' Jan waited, puzzled and tense. 'I didn't waste time with talk,' Harry went on. 'I reached out and grabbed him *underneath*.' He smiled, as if at a job well done. 'I said to him, "How would you like some man doing that to *your* wife, Bill?" That shocked him. He just stood there. All he could say was "My daughter . . . my daughter." I said, "That's just it, Bill!" He has quite a temper, Jan!' He raised his eyebrows, as if in grudging respect. 'He was so furious he couldn't get a word out, just went to the door and clapped his hands to get Jessie's attention. I give her credit. She came in and said to Bill, "I don't want any of your Dutch pig-headedness. You work it out between you, and make sure you don't do anything to hurt those two upstairs." She's really concerned about you two. Well, after that, I told Bill a thing or two about how to behave. I think he understood. When I'd finished, I put a hand on his shoulder and said I was glad it was settled, man to man.'

Jan, her face a blank, was too appalled to speak. Of course her father would not have said anything. He would not have known how to deal with such outrageous behaviour. Anyway, there was nothing she could have said, she was sure, to turn him from his belief that he had accomplished something positive.

'It's all right now, Jan,' he said, seeing her expression. 'No need to worry. He needed to be told. They know when they need it, and they even respect you for telling them. Well, that's it.' He stood up. 'Shall we have some breakfast?'

All day, Jan waited for some reaction from her father, or her mother. None came. Either he'd been extraordinarily forgiving, or extraordinarily pusillanimous. Or perhaps Harry had exaggerated the incident. In any event, Jan allowed herself to hope that the whole thing would be ignored.

The next day, the incident receded further in her mind under the impact of another crisis. Jessie took Rebecca shopping. When they got back, Becca seemed upset. 'I don't think I did it right at all, Janny,' she confided to her mother, as soon as they were alone.

'What?'

'Grandmother wanted me to try on a pant suit, so I did. It was kind of bright, a print with orange flowers. I said it was pretty, and she said she'd buy it for me. I know it was generous of her, but it was $32! I said no . . .' Her voice trailed away unhappily. 'But she bought it anyway,' she finished. 'I shouldn't have said it was pretty, should I?'

'I guess it would be hard for her to understand how we feel about clothes and money. $32! That would buy food for all three of us for a month.'

'I know.' Becca hesitated again, for she was unused to expressing any criticism. 'You're right, Janny. She doesn't understand at all. I heard them talking yesterday, and Grandmother was saying things about Harry. I didn't mean to hear, but I was in the bathroom and I couldn't help it. I came out, I was so embarrassed, Janny, but almost angry as well, and I said, "You shouldn't talk about my father like that." Grandmother said, "He's not your father," and I said, "He's the only father I've ever had." Oh, dear. I didn't mean to sound so cross.' Becca paused again. Jan didn't want to say anything to interrupt. Becca so seldom unburdened herself. It was important she say whatever was on her mind. She had been as stunned as Jan — more so, perhaps — by the contrast between their seventeen years of jungle living and this $100,000 house with all its faucets and doors and electricity and kitchen utensils and new foods, and there must have been a weight of unexpressed feelings inside her.

'No, she doesn't understand,' Becca went on, sadly. 'I was looking at a picture of a blue orchid in one of her books, and it reminded me of the one I found as we were coming down the Demiti with Pelon. I showed it to her and she just asked "Isn't it lonely there?" I didn't know how to begin to tell her. I just said I didn't have time to be lonely, and that I've always lived an isolated life. I couldn't say any more, tell her what I felt about all *this* – ' she waved a hand '– because I didn't want to hurt her.'

'I know, Becca.'

'It's just that sometimes I feel I'm as much a creature of the jungle as any bird or serpent or monkey.'

'What will you do about the suit?'

'I haven't said anything to Harry, yet. Perhaps I can give it back to her, somehow.'

'Well, she can't force it on you.'

'It's not like that, Janny. She did say she didn't want me taking anything I didn't want. I just don't want to hurt her.'

🐞

Over the next three days, the precarious peace in the household degenerated into a cold war. Harry declared that, now Christmas was over, he would prepare food for himself, Jan and Becca. For breakfast and lunch, they would eat their own food, at their own times. But he generously agreed to join the others for supper, as long as Jessie restricted the amount of salt, and as long as the food was vegetarian.

As it happened, Jan played little part in the drawing of the lines between the two sides. She woke the night after her talk with Becca trembling and sweating. She realized at once that it was malaria, a relapse probably brought on by the change in climate and food. It was not a severe attack, but it kept her in bed or in her room for most of the time.

She was unaware, therefore, of the rising level of tension – of Jessie's distress when Becca returned the suit; of her restrained fury at Harry's cooking, which banned her from the kitchen at crucial times; and of a rumbling dispute over Harry's need for fresh air.

By the time Jan was on her feet again, still desperately weak, Jessie could hardly bring herself to speak to Harry.

🐾

On New Year's Day, Jan decided she was well enough to appear downstairs again. It was early evening. Harry had just begun to read to Jan when Becca came in.

'Harry,' she said. 'Grandmother˜just told me she really wished you wouldn't leave the window open in here and let all the heat out.'

'Why did she tell you and not me?' Harry demanded. 'We'll have to get this settled right now.'

Jan, hearing the anger in his voice, kept silent. There was nothing she could do, she knew that, even if she hadn't been feeling so weak from the effects of the malaria. Any word or action from her would only make things worse. Harry took her hand and strode through to the kitchen, followed by Becca. They found Jessie setting the table for supper. Bill was already in the room. There was no sign of Lauren.

'What's this about my window, Jessie?' demanded Harry.

Jessie turned, and faced him. 'I've told you before. You open your window and leave the heat on at the same time. Heating this house is expensive enough as it is.' Jan's knees were weak. She wanted very much to sit down. 'Last night we were watching TV and every time you came out of the den there was a blast of cold air.'

'Jessie, I thought you understood. We're not used to a closed house. I have to have fresh air because of my heart.' It was his usual pattern. He would now begin to lecture Jessie, battering her with his own cast-iron assumptions. 'The jungle was ideal because the trees give off oxygen at night, and as long as –'

'If you want fresh air,' Jessie interrupted forcefully, 'Why don't you sleep in the garage?'

'I'm very comfortable where I am. I didn't think it would make much difference.'

'Becca and I leave our window open at night, mother,' Jan said, struggling to forestall a confrontation.

'Your room is all right, Jan. You keep the door closed, and the heat is off during the day.'

'You know your trouble,' Harry said. 'Your standard of living is too high. You try to heat all the house all the time. If –'

'We're quite comfortable! Or we were before you came! My God!' Jessie burst out, 'I hate the sight of you!'

Harry's eyes widened, and he turned to Jan in amazement. 'Did you hear what she said?' he asked.

'Shall I repeat myself?' Jessie shouted at him. 'I – hate – your – guts!'

Jan's mind went blank. My head, she thought. I must sit down. If I could sit down, I would know what to do.

Harry, too, seemed at a loss. 'I knew I shouldn't have come,' he said. 'I don't belong here. But –' His voice strengthened again. 'But I have a responsibility towards Jan. She needs me. She –'

'Oh, you think you came out of everything looking so damned wonderful!' Jessie interrupted. 'But you don't care who you hurt, do you? The way you treat Bill is unforgivable. He's had a hell of time with you right from the start, right from that first trip to Mexico!'

'Bill?' Harry turned to him in apparent surprise. 'How can you say that? We drank together.'

'Yes,' he grunted. 'And you stopped me.'

'Oh, that,' Harry said, dismissively.

'Yes, that!' Jessie broke in. 'And everything else! My God, you arrive out of the blue, expecting to stay for a year – a whole year! You come in here, dressed like a peasant, you keep my daughter and granddaughter from me, you drive me out of my own kitchen, you criticize everything we do to help, you think yourself so damned superior, you waste my money, and then, on top of all that you hurt Bill, you hurt him dreadfully . . . My God, I didn't even know what had happened until I asked him last night. He cried! He cried when he told me! He said you had . . .' Outrage made the words stick in her throat. '. . . you had accused him of *laying hands* on . . . on Jan!'

Jan felt her head spinning. We should never have come, she thought, clutching at Harry's hand. In a minute I'll lie down. I'll just keep standing up for one more minute, and then . . .

And then she became aware that her mother was talking to her.

'Has your father *ever* laid hands on you?'

No, of course not. The shadow of her mother swam before her. No. She should say 'no'. But 'no' would mean to counter Harry, deny him, reject him, break him, break the family, break the promise she had made herself on Difficulty Hill.

'Has your father *ever* laid hands on you?'

Harry's hand tightened on hers. Fear encased her. She became a blank, but for one thought: 'A charge to keep I have', a charge, a charge, and both of them, mother and husband, were waiting for her answer.

She had already answered, with silence. The words she finally spoke merely echoed her silence. 'Only kissing me on the mouth . . .' she mumbled, lamely. 'Nothing wrong . . .'

She heard her father interrupt, but couldn't make out what he said.

'What, Daddy?'

'He says,' Harry told her, calmly. 'If you don't retract your words, you are disowned.' His voice came from a great distance. 'You won't be his daughter any more.'

'You can't *disown* me, Daddy.' The words made no sense to her. 'I'll still be your daughter, no matter what.'

For several seconds, no one spoke. Becca wiped tears from her eyes. It should never have come to a choice, Jan thought. No one should have to choose between husband and mother.

It was Harry who broke the silence. 'We will begin our preparations tomorrow to return to the Rio Negro,' he said, stiffly. Then, still holding Jan firmly by the arm, he led her out.

Next morning, Jessie stayed in bed. But even in her absence every tiny event, every word was charged with danger, of which Harry remained supremely unaware.

There was for instance a question of money. The only available source was Becca's college account. Harry pointed out that Becca would not now need it for college, but it would be vital for the development of the homestead. She had better go to her grandmother and ask for it.

There were other parting shots fired. When Harry asked Bill how to get to the bus station, Bill replied 'Let God get you to the bus station!' 'He's never let me down yet!' Harry countered. Later, when Jessie got up to go to the bank, Harry waved some letters at her and asked her cheerily for some stamps. Without a word, she gave him some. 'Thanks,' he said, 'Here's a dollar. Keep the change.' To which, much to his surprise, she said, 'Get out of the way, you clown!' leaving him to explain knowingly to Jan that Jessie was upset because she had never been bested by a man before. And when, on a subsequent chance encounter, Bill told Harry he wasn't supporting Jan and Becca properly, Harry was outright amazed. As if he didn't have a house and place for them to live! 'You see what he's doing, Jan? He's trying to transfer his own failings on to me. People who can't face their own faults do that.'

When Jessie returned from the bank, she called Becca in. 'She said you'd still be disowned, Janny,' Becca told her mother later, 'Because of *him*, she said. But she didn't want to think of us going hungry. She said I would inherit because . . .' The memory forced her to stifle a sob. 'Because I would always take care of you, Janny. Then she put her arms round me and said she was sorry, and I said I was sorry.'

'We're all sorry, Becca,' Jan whispered.

When the time came for departure, and friends of Jan's were waiting for them outside, Jessie came to the hallway. Jan felt her mother's arms round her. There were no words. It did not feel like a reconciliation; but it left Jan with a feeling that reconciliation might one day be possible.

With that small hope to cling to, Jan allowed Becca to lead her to the car. No one spoke. No one came with them to say goodbye.

Nevertheless, this time the goodbye was final, of that she was certain. She was weak, too weak to work. The thought of returning to the jungle again in her present state filled her with dread. This time, she thought, this time the Rio Negro will be the death of me.

8

HOMESTEAD HILL

'A mountain!'

Harry's voice broke the darkness of her mood. They were back on the Demiti, and just past Difficulty. The awareness of its presence had been enough to revive fears that there might lie ahead another, more terrible struggle. But Harry's excitement, and his glowing description of the river, was irresistible. There, no more than two miles away, standing clear of the jungle and framed by trees on either bank, was a perfect, steep-sided, jungle-covered cone. 'Isn't it beautiful?' shouted Harry. 'Couldn't see it for cloud before. Where are the others, Pelon?'

'You will see them, Don Enrique, from the top of your hill.'

On either side, trees loomed over the dark waters, as black in shadow and as sharp with reflected light as wet tar. Dead branches and trailing vines formed mirror images of such baffling perfection that it was hard to tell where water ended and vegetation began. They swerved round a submerged trunk, slowed to duck beneath the arch of a fallen tree, and then, at a spot with nothing to distinguish it but a tree-trunk sloping into the water and a rough path macheted through the riverside saplings, Pelon cut the engine and let the bows ride gently up on mud.

'Homestead Hill!' shouted Harry. 'This is it!'

Becca eagerly seized a basket and hurried ahead. Harry grabbed Jan by the hand and urged her ashore, hurrying her up the steep, root-entangled trail.

At the top of the bank, hemmed in and overshadowed by

trees, was the hut Pelon and Natal had built while the Littles had been camping downriver. This was a good size, its haystack roof drooping to within two feet of the ground. Harry took Jan, still panting with exertion, over the rough floor, her feet knocking against protruding roots and stumps, and sat her down out of the way.

As the others unloaded and prepared for the night, Jan, hearing the murmur of voices, grew impatient at her own enforced idleness, until she felt the roughness of the floor around her and was reassured. She would be busy soon, clearing roots. Already Homestead felt very different from Difficulty. The house was large, the site gently sloping. There was something about the place she liked, and for the first time in weeks she allowed herself to believe that the strain of the last few weeks would be worthwhile.

The return from Fair Oaks had been as stressful as any journey with Harry. For Becca's sake, Jessie had parted with the $3,000 saved up for her granddaughter's college education. Much of this money Harry had spent on the bus to Mexico, a plane to Caracas, a cab to take them the full 150 miles to San Fernando on the Apure, an outboard motor and a canoe that were supposedly to take them on 800 miles down the Orinoco to the Negro, and finally, after the canoe turned out to be stolen and was impounded by the police, a plane-ride to San Carlos and a boat passage downriver to the Brazilian border.

There, at the border post of Guadalupe, a brief halt brought a surprising, bitter-sweet reunion. Jan heard Harry bellow: 'Guess who? Incredible!' and felt at the same moment hairy arms around her neck and heard an impassioned chattering in her ear. Hanuman. Tears had sprung to her eyes, tears of happiness at his obvious delight and of apprehension at what he would do to her. 'Has he ever had adventures!' Harry declaimed. 'Ran away, lived in the woods, saved himself from being shot by throwing his arms round a hunter's neck! The family's together again! Can't believe it!' Becca couldn't believe it either. She burst into tears. 'There won't be any peace now Hanuman's back,' she wept.

Then, in Cucuí, more delay. The river had been too low to travel. Waiting, they bought more supplies (which, to Jan's delight, included a radio) and a second, smaller canoe, *Piaroa*, the name of a tribe of Venezuelan Indians. The journey up the Demiti had been ill-starred, beginning with a strange farewell by the Commandante: 'If you find gold, let us know.' Perhaps he knew something they didn't, for at a couple of their campsites, there had been signs of digging. Gold-miners, Pelon said. Then Pelon's helper had fallen ill, and had to be taken home, leaving the Littles camping. After a month, he had returned to ferry their supplies through the *paraná* and build their house. At last, lured on by the rumbles of distant thunder from the unseen hills, they had weaved through the Stygian *paraná* and eased past Difficulty to the smooth and silent waters at the base of Homestead Hill.

Right from the start, she was busy, hacking roots out of the floor, turning a makeshift camp into the beginnings of a home, while Harry and Rebecca built a hearth, finished the trail down to the water's edge, and set up liana railings along the fallen tree, giving Jan safe access to the river.

All three were eager to start clearing and planting. There was space enough within easy reach of the river, for the gently sloping shelf on which the house stood ran back about 100 yards before the forest swooped up steeply again towards the hilltop.

Not that it would be an easy job. Even Jan could sense that the forest here was very different from Mexico's jungle. There was virtually no dense undergrowth. Ghostly grey and brown trunks rose straight from the forest floor through a veil of thick-leafed saplings. The trees were slow-growing, and of very hard wood. Many held resins and gums, which, to Jan, with her acute sense of smell, gave the forest a light aromatic fragrance.

Harry decided that the first clearing – the Nursery Clearing, as they later called it – would be sixty yards from the house, back up the slope, far enough away to avoid cutting the trees shading the house. The best way to establish seeds would be to build special boxes for them – tree-trunks stacked two or three deep, the joints stuffed with earth and wood chips. Within a couple of months, in the Nursery Clearing and a second plantation, the Garden Clearing, they had made half a dozen beds, with the first growths – tiny shoots of banana plants, pineapples, coconuts, peach-palms, mangoes, avocados, cashews, oranges and lemons – ready for transplanting.

Harry, showing a strength that surprised them all, worked harder than he had worked in years. Impatient to expand operations, he began a third clearing, and talked grandly of building a proper house there, a big one, with a loft.

He also dreamed of the views and the cooling breezes awaiting him once he had the hilltop cleared. He would live there, he said, and he would be buried there. He'd even found the perfect site for his grave: a flat shelf, a parapet, a natural lookout point towards the mountains, which he was sure would make a magnificent view when the trees were cut. Every Saturday he would take Rebecca up the hill to chop a few more trees, returning with excited reports of his progress. First, to the south, emerged the cone they had seen from the river, the gloriously symmetrical head of a towering, 2,000-foot backbone of rock called the Serra do Padre – the Priest's Range. Harry named the peak Sentinel. Though Jan seldom made the tortuous journey to the hilltop in the early days – she wanted to consolidate the plantings near the river first – Sentinel soon became as much a part of their daily lives as Jan's Mountain had been in Mexico. Harry assured her that when more trees fell, more mountains – including, he felt sure, Neblina itself – would be revealed, and he would at last be able to discover where exactly they had settled.

Key

1 Marimba	6 Walkway
2 Jan's hammock	7 Bench
3 Wash-stand	8 Harry's hammock
4 Bench	9 Becca's hammock
5 Hearth	

The Riverside Hut, in cutaway.

Life once again acquired routine, and the beginnings of contentment. Harry, who still refused to sleep through the night, would rise about three to push the fire together, then return to the corner he had made for himself behind a line of boxes, to read or write in his hammock. Before dawn, he called Becca, who prepared breakfast. Jan had to stay in her hammock at the far end of the hut to be out of the way. They had no table; Harry and Jan usually ate in their hammocks, while Becca sat by the hearth. After breakfast, Becca would read a section of *Science and Health*, in both English and Portuguese, and Harry would allot tasks for the day. Hanuman, impatient to be going, chittered at them from the roof as they sharpened their tools, banked the fire, and put soup to simmer over the hard-wood embers for the midday meal.

Once again, Sunday became their rest-day, now they no longer had to take visitors into account. They breakfasted later, treating themselves to small luxuries: some sardines, perhaps, or a fruit dessert. Usually, Harry would read aloud; and there was always the radio.

Those first few weeks breathed new life into Jan. She soon knew the short, straight trail to the Nursery Clearing and sharp left-hand bend to the Garden Clearing. She could haul back branches to the saw-horse beside the house and cut them into logs, measuring their length by feel with her forearm; she could wash clothes in a big pan up on the washstand, rinsing them in the river. She and Becca, both dressed only in shorts, with sweat streaming down their bare torsos, grubbed out tree roots, levered tree-trunks into position for the seed beds and carried unusable bits of wood to fire-pits to be burned into fertilizer ash.

She was just as happy working on her own, as long as the trail and her work area had been checked for snakes. As in Mexico, snakes were their major concern. Harry and Becca saw perhaps two or three a week, and dealt with them by carrying them away into the forest on a long stick – using an eleven-foot pole, Harry joked, for something you wouldn't touch with a ten-foot pole. Jan found she had developed a hyper-sensitivity to their presence, an electric tingle of apprehension that inspired her to tell the others to look around. Only after one of them had guided Jan by the hand or with a leading-stick over the trail to ensure it was free of snakes would she walk back and forth alone.

As the weeks passed, and as Jan's sense of independence grew, she began to feel that only Hanuman marred her idyll. After she had been working for an hour or so, he would come and pester her, apparently unwilling for one member of his troup to remain separated from the others for too long. But when free of his attentions, she could feel truly part of the softly aromatic forest, the misty mornings, the sudden bursts of rain and sun, the living entity that had meant so much to her in Mexico. She had her homestead, she wrote, 'in full measure, pressed down and running over.'

🐾

Harry had only one major complaint about Homestead Hill: the jungle was oddly devoid of life. Few monkeys, few birds. Only once in their first year did the forest seem to promise more. They had been on Homestead several months. Becca was up in the Nursery Clearing. Harry was reading out aloud to Jan in the Riverside Hut. Suddenly, he was interrupted by a ringing call, a mellow, musical shout, with a questioning inflection: 'Who? Who? Who?' Jan felt the hair on her scalp prickle, as if an icy draught had brushed her. 'Who? Who?' came the call again. Hanuman, as astonished as Harry and Jan, leaped wildly up to the roof.

Harry looked up, open-mouthed. 'Seemed to come from the Third Clearing,' he said, after a shocked silence.

Seconds latter, Becca appeared at the doorway, panting.

'What was *that*?' she asked, wide-eyed, as Hanuman, trembling, climbed down and nestled into her arms.

'Strangely human,' muttered Harry. 'Maybe we'll have company.'

'Company?' Jan repeated, nervously.

'Indians. Used to be Indians here, years ago, remember. Maybe they're back. Best be prepared.'

Jan became frightened. Harry's words reminded her of Pelon's story about Indians kidnapping a young white girl (Helena Valero, the daughter of Italian missionaries) from the campsite downriver. Years ago, he'd said, and no one had seen Indians since. But it was deeper in the wilderness here. Maybe they had come back, as Harry said. Maybe they'd never really left. She wondered nervously what they would think of her, cut off by her blindness and deafness. A witch, perhaps.

Silence.

After a while, Harry handed round plates of food. They ate, listening apprehensively.

The food, or perhaps the silence, seemed to restore Becca's nerve. 'Nothing's happening,' she said. 'I'm going to work.'

'Becca,' Jan pleaded. 'Leave it until tomorrow, won't you?'

'If I get shot at, I get shot at,' Becca replied, and left.

'Wait, Becca,' called Harry, to Jan's relief. 'I'll go with you.'

He returned an hour or so later. 'Well,' he reported. 'No Man Friday footprints. No arrows sticking out of any trees.'

The mystery was only solved when the cargo-men made their next delivery. Harry imitated the noise for them and they identified it at once as the cry of a rare subspecies of spider monkey, the red-faced spider.

That visitation was all the more startling because there were so few encounters with wildlife. In one way this was to their advantage. The tea-coloured waters of the Demiti were virtually insect-free. Dragonflies patrolled its surface, but there were few mosquitoes. The only regular annoyances were the horseflies, which punctured exposed skin unmercifully, especially in the dry season, and the sweat-bees, harmless but irritating, which penetrated ever more remote parts of the anatomy if not brushed off. Otherwise, though, the jungle creatures were invisible. Every day, every hour was punctuated by sharp, clear bird-calls – the warning whistles of screaming pihas and the bell-like notes of tinamous – but the birds themselves were seldom seen. At night, frogs burped and whistled. Often at dawn howler monkeys roared out their territorial warnings – Harry said they were greeting the sun or calling out for rain – but they were far away. Sometimes, they heard the howl of a wild dog. Macaws, parrots and guans flapped by, but so infrequently that every sighting was an event. There were occasional visits from boisterous little capuchin monkeys and large-eyed owl-monkeys, nocturnal creatures which sometimes at dawn called to Hanuman, and on several occasions they were lucky enough to see river dolphins, which apparently lived in a great U-bend just upriver. But compared with Mexico, the jungle was empty.

🐾

They had been there six months before Jan began to realize that their heady confidence was not being borne out by results. It was she and Becca who discovered what was wrong.

Just before Christmas, Harry declared the Third Clearing finished, and decided to transplant bananas into it.

'Those bananas in the Garden Clearing,' he said, as the three of them stood together surrounded by the head-high confusion of newly cut trees, 'some of them just aren't growing. They look bad.'

'They're *all* bad,' said Becca sourly.

'Well, you better do something about putting them in the right places, then, right here.'

'I don't know if there are right places in this clearing. When it rains, there's just too much water.'

Harry was irritated by her comment. 'If you're going to be discouraged about everything, maybe we better just quit!' Jan got the impression he was even more irritable than he used to be. It was probably the heat. He couldn't stand the heat. Or the insects. With his fair skin, he had never hardened up. Often, when Jan was perfectly comfortable, he would stand in his shorts with the sweat pouring off him, slapping at himself as if suffering some peculiar nervous malfunction, complaining that the sweat-bees were trying to crawl behind his eyeballs. 'Maybe we better just live in the toolshed in Cucuí,' he went on, 'And buy all our food and watch the highway come by our front door.'

'I didn't say that, Harry. There's something wrong with this clearing, and I don't know what it is.'

'Well, I'm going to dig up the ailing ones. You do as you like.'

As he strode off along the path between the felled trees, Jan placed a hand on Becca's arm.

'Come on, Janny,' said Becca with a sigh, 'We better make some holes, or there'll be no chance of saving them.'

When Harry returned, his arms were full of banana plants. 'I went to look for the bad ones and found all these,' he said in surprise.

'We don't have places for them,' said Becca. 'It's just too wet here.'

'It is *not* too wet here! This is a very good place. Are you trying to tell me that you won't use this clearing after the hard work – the *hard work* – we put in here?'

Becca remained silent.

'Very well. If you won't do it, I suppose I'll have to.'

'No,' she said, poker-faced. 'Janny and I will do it.'

So, as Harry went back to the hut, flapping his hands at sweat-bees, Becca showed Jan to a spot to dig and then went off to collect another load of ailing bananas. After a few minutes digging into soft, sandy soil, the hole suddenly seemed to dig itself. She shoved her grub-axe down the hole. Nothing. Just empty space.

'Becca!' she called. 'I've found the way to China!'

Becca was returning with a load of bananas slung from a tump-line round her forehead. 'Don't go, Janny! We need you

206

here!' she shouted with a laugh. 'Let me look,' she went on, dumping her load beside Jan. She probed the hole with a stick. 'Hm. Eighteen inches, maybe more. It goes down to sand, and *through* sand.'

'It's not an animal's den. More like a channel.'

'More than a channel, Janny. The ground is all springy round here. I think I see what it means. The water must be running away beneath us all the time. It's like we're on the floor and you just dug through to the basement.'

'A floor made of roots and sand under a thin carpet of earth. Not very encouraging.'

'Well,' said Becca, philosophically, 'Maybe the soil will be better up on the hill.'

They planted the bananas anyway, of course, and then prepared to return to the hut. Jan felt for Becca's shoulder. 'Sentinel's out,' Becca said. 'Very blue today. Here, Janny, take the end of this shovel. Don't flap your hand. That's a butterfly.'

They set off together across the clearing back to the hut, winding round stumps and stepping over fallen trunks.

☙

Nevertheless, the first Christmas on Homestead Hill was one of true thanksgiving. It had been years since they had felt at peace for Christmas. In 1972, they had been on the Santa Maria, tense over their uncertain future. Christmas 1973 had been spent in the lean-to in Cucuí and 1974, disastrously, in Fair Oaks. By comparison, by Christmas 1975 there was much to celebrate. Becca prepared a lavish meal: soup made of the leaves of sweet potato and manioc; spaghetti with grated cheese and their own home-grown vegetables – parsley-like garland chrysanthemum, talinum, a squash and some beans. For dessert, Harry made an Indian pudding, steaming cornmeal, oatmeal, spices and sugar together in a tin.

Afterwards, Harry passed verdict. 'That was as good a Christmas dinner as we have ever had, especially good for a first year on a new homestead. I don't know that I've ever had as good a meal.'

'Not even in Vermont?' teased Jan.

'We sure didn't have home-grown squash for our first Christmas there.'

'The best part is being in our own place,' said Becca.

'Yes, it's beautiful,' Harry agreed. 'Wonder what's on the BBC? See if I can find something Christmassy.'

While Harry turned the radio dial, Jan gathered up the dishes, with Becca's help, and made her way across the hut, marking her course with the glow of the fire against the surrounding shadows. Then, with the washing-up finished, she returned to sit on the box beside Harry's hammock.

'Can't get the BBC,' he said. 'Atmospherics. I've got Canada, from Montreal. You're just in time. They're going to do the *Christmas Carol.*' Jan put the radio tight up against her ear, loud enough for the others to hear as well. After the excerpt from *A Christmas Carol*, there followed Canadian reminiscences of Christmases past, of sleigh-rides and feasts and the giving of gifts in the far north. And at the end came a solo male voice singing *Silent Night* in the Eskimo language, an odd and moving reminder of a world beyond the hum of insects and the silence of the surrounding jungle.

A few weeks into the new year of 1976, Jan was reading Braille in her hammock when Becca came back from the Garden Clearing carrying some fresh greens and a tomato. 'What's Hanuman got?' Becca asked crossly, as she set her load down on a kitchen box. 'Oh! Janny! It's your hearing-aid! Hanuman, drop that!'

'My hearing-aid!' Jan wailed. The hearing-aid had assumed a special significance over the last year. With all vision gone except a vague awareness of sharp contrasts, the hearing-aid was more than simply a tool – it was a talisman that kept isolation at bay. Though she seldom used it – she'd be out of batteries far too quickly if she did – it was good to know she could at any time put it in and be back in touch with what was going on around her. She had been keeping it in a cloth bag beside her hammock. She'd wanted to hide it away in a safer place, but Harry had told her not to bother. 'I knew I should have moved it!'

'Now don't blow your top!' Harry called from his hammock. 'He's never got it before!'

'But it's so important!'

'I've got it, Janny,' Becca said. 'Here. Is this all of it?'

Jan felt: torn plastic bag, batteries, ear-mould, but not the hearing-aid itself. 'No!' She stood up, staring round uselessly. 'Oh, I didn't want to keep it there . . .'

'I said: don't blow your top!' shouted Harry. 'It's bad for your heart!'

'Harry, I *need* it.'

'That's your problem!' he went on, remorselessly. 'If you can't handle it, go off by yourself somewhere. I don't want a broken woman around. You make it hard for the rest of us.'

Jan, only too glad to be on her own, felt her way up the familiar track to the Nursery Clearing. She sat down on one of the seed-boxes, put her face in her hands and sobbed. If he'd only offered a little comfort, she could have controlled the panic, the –

'Janny.' Becca's hand fell hesitantly on her shoulder.

'Oh, Becca.' Jan sniffed back her tears. 'I'm all right. Just sitting here feeling sorry for myself.'

'I got the hearing-aid back from Hanuman. Can you tell if it's working?'

'Turn it on. If it whistles, it works.'

'It whistles.'

'Oh, thank goodness.' Her relief spilled over into words. 'All that upset. I'm sorry. I was more angry with Harry than Hanuman. I'd wanted to store it in a better place, but he insisted Hanuman wouldn't get it.' Talking about it brought anger surging back. 'The way he does things – it seems to make trouble, and then he gets mad at one of us. Don't know why he thinks beating us over the head helps us stand up straight. Anyway, what's he doing now?'

'I gave him lunch. He's all right. He said for you to stay until you're ready to come back. He was fighting with Hanuman over pieces of tomato. I had to get away. Sometimes I can't stand Hanuman a second longer.'

Becca handed Jan a large leaf. Jan blew her nose on it, tucked the leaf under the log beneath her, and managed a laugh. 'So we get to *sit* here, because we can't *stand* them.'

'That's about it.' Jan could tell from the direction of Becca's voice that she was looking around her. 'It's nice here,' she said, and fell silent.

Jan's mind turned back to her criticism of Harry. It was the first time she had spoken like that about him to Becca. But Becca understood. Since arriving on Homestead, she had taken over so much of the responsibility for the place that she and Jan had become more like sisters than mother and daughter, both of them treating Harry as if he were a tetchy and un-predictable uncle. 'I would never have married him if I'd had the choice,' she blurted out, with a bitterness that surprised her. 'He asked me and never waited for an answer. I guess he never does.' She felt tears coming again, and controlled herself with a tight smile. 'I wanted a homestead for us, and I didn't know how else a woman gets a homestead, except by marrying for it or inheriting it.'

Becca remained silent. Jan, knowing that her words touched on underlying truths she had never mentioned before, and that they also smacked of disloyalty to the assumptions on which the homestead had been built, wondered how Becca would respond.

'I'm glad I grew up on a homestead,' Becca said at last. 'And I'm glad I don't have to marry for one. I don't think I want to marry.' She paused, and then added forcefully. 'I can't *stand* the idea of a man lying on top of me.'

'Becca, it isn't like that. There are feelings . . .' Jan's voice trailed away uncertainly. Any explanation of sexual pleasure or the satisfactions of a sexual relationship could only derive from experiences she had never mentioned, could not have mentioned, for they had been tabooed by Harry. As a sister, she would have talked; as a mother, she could not.

Jan tried another tack. 'You don't have a good example of a happy marriage in Harry and me, Becca. It's a good working partnership, but not much more. I . . . I can't . . . *enjoy* him. I never could. That wasn't why I married him. It's hard now to remember why I did marry him. You'll just have to believe that the human race has survived because men and women have mostly found it a happy and fulfilling way to be together . . .' She stopped, embarrassed by the emptiness of her words. She wanted to say so much. But there was no way of conveying her own experience to Becca, and perhaps, she thought bleakly, it would be unfair to raise the matter, since Becca had no chance to develop any relationship of her own.

'I can't imagine it,' Becca said. 'I . . . I like children. I think I'd like to have children of my own, even though I don't know the first thing about looking after them.'

'I'd help,' said Jan, eagerly. 'You just have to get used to it. What really counts, Becca, is that you and the man . . .'

'I hear Hanuman,' Becca said. 'Guess he's come looking for us. Misery loves company. We should have named that monkey Misery.'

'Yes.'

The moment had passed.

🐒

There never was another moment like that one.

But if Jan kept her deeper thoughts to herself, so did Becca. She wrote her own journal, but she wrote it in Portuguese to prevent the possibility of Harry reading it. Jan never knew what was in it. But Rebecca also wrote to friends, particularly to Josie Moore in Georgetown. Years later, Jan found some of

Becca's letters, unsent, superseded, perhaps, by later ones.

Becca wrote of the homestead, and of her happiness there. She wrote of the riverside, her favourite spot, her church. When she went for water, she would often sit for minutes on the fallen tree, drinking in the beauty of the softly flowing water and the dark jungle. She liked to use the tar-black surface of the river as a mirror to look for orchids beneath the bushes on the opposite bank. She liked the birds, too. Once she told her mother she didn't think she'd be happy in a heaven without birds. The jungle was not a world she had any desire to leave. Becca wrote,

> No, I don't want to get married – yet. The older I get the more convinced I am that too early marriages are bad. I am not in a hurry, but the desire for children is growing on me. Like you, I wouldn't dream of marrying somebody I didn't expect to stay in love with. It's hard enough to stay married as it is.
>
> I also have the feeling which I cannot back up or explain that both men and women cheapen themselves by premarital sex. Perhaps you won't understand what I mean by cheapening; after all, the standards have been relaxed since my parents were growing up, which still doesn't make black white. I won't say any more on the subject, which I don't much enjoy.

She had, then, been confused by her own sexual nature. But she had been content to live with the problems unresolved. It was as if she, like a nun, believed resolution was to be found in the life she had chosen, a life of hard work and austerity. Though she did not discuss religion, Becca had always seemed to Jan a more integrated, a more natural Christian than either of her parents. She did not talk Christianity; she simply *was* Christian.

She allowed Emily Dickinson, her favourite poet, to whose collection of verse she returned again and again, to speak for her, quoting the lines in full to Josie:

This world is not conclusion,
A sequel stands beyond
Invisible as music
But positive as sound
It beckons and it baffles
Philosophies don't know
And through a riddle at the last
Sagacity must go.
To guess it puzzles scholars,
To gain it men have shown
Contempt for generations
And crucifixion known.

'This world is not conclusion.' Was that what she had believed? Had she, nun-like, set aside her own problems for the sake of a higher good?

I would not mind, I believe, living on here as a hermit. Well, I needn't worry yet, there isn't even anyone coming to visit. After all, we are five winding-river days from Cucuí.

    Yours aff. Rebecca.

🦋

In early 1976, Harry declared the Third Clearing to be a lost cause. The other two clearings were also disappointing. The soil was poor. It was too hot, or too shady, or too damp. The greens were worm-eaten, the pineapples, taro and bananas would all take time (if they grew at all), and their diet remained principally beans, rice, *farinha*, and leaf-of-sweet-potato soup, with the Sunday addition of a sardine and tomato sauce.

In search of better soils, better living conditions, and some more landmarks, Harry opened a good trail to the hilltop, cut more trees and began to clear a site for a second hut.

Jan still wasn't attracted to the hilltop. The crest was a quarter of a mile away, 250 feet up, along winding, rooty, steep and slippery trails she didn't know and couldn't travel

Homestead Hill, looking south.

Key

1	Sentinel	6	Garden Clearing
2	Hilltop Hut	7	Nursery Clearing
3	Pineapple Clearing	8	Third Clearing
4	Long Trail	9	Riverside Hut
5	Fourth Clearing	10	Rio Demiti

alone. But she conceded that another clearing would, or should, be an asset, and went along with Harry's decision to make a Fourth Clearing on the second shelf, half-way up the hillside, where the soils were heavier and drier.

As the weeks went by, and Harry continued to cut trees at the hilltop, his descriptions of the unfolding view won her over. As more trees fell, peak after peak came into view, a sweep of thirty or more ranging through a ninety-degree arc from south to east. Though few days were totally clear, most revealed some of the peaks, and Harry and Becca would paint word-pictures of them to Jan. Harry gave all the main peaks their own names. To the south reared Sentinel, with the jungle frothing up its base like surf and stretching away across lowlands to vanish into grey-green haze. Next to Sentinel stood the Three Sisters, making up the rest of the Serra do Padre ridge. Beyond lay Thunder Mountain, the Green Mountains (reminiscent to Harry of his beloved Vermont), Paradise, the Well of Rains where so much of their weather seemed to originate, Breadloaf, Seal Mountain, the softly rounded Little Hills and a family group he called Hen-and-Chicks. Forty miles away to the east, visible usually at dawn silhouetted against skies of eggshell purity like a promise of good things to come, was Neblina itself, the Mountain of Mists, craggy sides rising gently from a massive base to a plateau, and then on to the camel's-hump knoll that marked its 10,000-foot summit.

Slowly the mountains became a part of Jan, as she came to feel a part of them. Equally slowly, and without formal thought, she built her own relationship with her surroundings, with the Presence she had come to know in Mexico.

As always, she and Harry and Becca prayed together, reading from Mary Baker Eddy and the Bible. But she needed more. She could accept Jesus as one who showed the Way, but she could not see that he was himself the Way, for neither he nor his church said very much about the natural world, in which she found her God. It seemed strange to her that Jesus pointed to the kinship of the human family, and said virtually nothing about the kinship of mankind and nature. Conservation and Christianity – at least the Christianity of the Gospels – had little in common. Yet their concerns should overlap: 'The Earth is the Lord's and the fullness thereof.' Here, on Homestead Hill, it was nature, not mankind, not Christ, certainly not any of the churches founded in his name, that gave her life. Her very presence here depended on the larger Presence around her.

Once again, as in Mexico, but in a much deeper sense, she believed – no, *knew* – that the course they had chosen was correct, that they were 'under guidance'. 'I have a conversational relationship with God,' she explained to Toni Martin. 'I suppose it sounds presumptuous or affected, but this is my private "beacon" and I couldn't live without it. It is rather like the way we live alongside the mountains. The mountains are very close, have much influence on our lives, indeed are our reason for being here, our quest. I do not *see* the mountains, nor do I go there, but I know in many ways the presence of the mountains and feel that presence as a bulwark.'

With such sustaining help, no difficulty (whether imposed by Harry's personality or by nature) seemed too formidable. 'Pioneering is tough for the first year,' she wrote. 'But as Harry affirmed yesterday, "There isn't anything else I'd rather be doing anywhere else." The mountains are compellingly beautiful. Harry and Becca talk of them every day, the cloud and mists and what the sun and shadows newly reveal . . . We are sustained by Promise.'

But Promise was about all the sustenance they were to have in the second half of 1976, and beyond. From April to September, there was virtually no rain. Plants that had previously sagged in the damp dried out and died. Even the three of them working together could not carry enough water from the river to sustain their precious seedlings.

Though the river never dried up – there was always a good ten feet of water running past the end of the fallen tree – it dropped so much that they knew the *paraná* must have dried out completely, cutting them off from all direct contact with the outside world.

On top of this, Hanuman became more pestilential than ever. He was now almost fully grown, with canine teeth that he used to good effect on anyone who tried to correct him, usually Rebecca. He needed constant correcting. He had developed a revolting habit of eating soap, chewing it and sucking it as if it were chocolate. He would then retire to the rafters, and later, in the middle of the night, throw up. Since he usually slept above Harry, Harry often got it quite literally in the neck, waking with a start and a shout of disgust. Still, they endured him, for the reasons devised on Difficulty Hill. 'He has tested us all to the edge,' Jan wrote. 'But the discipline reinforces the lessons of how we have to live and to carry our burdens and help one another, including the "ape-let".'

The cargo-men were due in August. August came, and went. There was no telling when the *paraná* would be high enough to carry them through. Food ran low, and the Littles anxiously began to plan for the worst. Harry imposed an austerity diet to stretch the supply, so that they would have enough to last for several months – half a cup of *farinha* a day, with some 'leaf soup' made from a plant they had seen Hanuman eating, the soup being enriched with a tiny cube chipped from a bar of dried fish. Hanuman started to forage for himself in the tree tops.

After four months of this, they were all too weak to do more than essential work. For Harry, that meant principally keeping the fire going. He simply hated the idea of not having a fire burning twenty-four hours a day. Jan could do some washing and sawing. But it was Becca who did most of the hard labour – chopping, gathering leaves for soup, and climbing down to the river for water every day. Most days, the three of them went down to wash. But they did little else.

Harry, often running with sweat while just sitting in his hammock, complained of 'air-pockets behind the knees' whenever he stood up.

Death was close, they all knew that. For Harry, of course, it always had been and neither he nor Jan had any compunction about discussing the matter.

'If I die,' Harry said thoughtfully after their *farinha* breakfast one morning, 'If I die, you two wouldn't last long without me. Becca would have to take you out, Jan.'

'If you die, Harry, Becca will have more things to worry about than me – she'll have Hanuman. He'll be impossible.' Jan paused, and gathered her thoughts. 'But . . . there is a solution. You and I could take Hanuman down to Difficulty Hill. That way, we could leave all the food for Becca, and she would have a chance.'

'No,' Harry countered. 'I like it here. I want to end it here, on the hilltop.'

Becca, who had listened to morbid conversations like this many times before, kept silent.

'It had better be the hilltop,' Harry continued, as if pondering an obscure theoretical point. 'I can't die down here. You couldn't bury me even if you had sixteen men with picks and shovels. And the two of you could never get my corpse up the hill. You'd have to cremate me.'

'No,' Becca put in. 'The Rio Negro people would be horrified. They never cremate.'

'You might not have an alternative,' Jan pointed out.

'Wait,' Harry interrupted. 'There's a risk with cremation. You might burn the house down.'

'And if I died as well –'

'Shut up, the two of you!' snapped Becca. 'You're both foolish!'

'No, there's no alternative.' Harry went on remorselessly. 'You'd have to get the cargo-men to bury us on the hill. On the shelf, with the view of Neblina. Becca, do you think there's room for two up there?'

'Probably, Harry, but –'

'Listen, I want you to promise me –'

'Harry –'

'Promise me, Becca, that if anything happens to me, you'll leave here, take your mother out. Promise.'

'Harry –'

'I want you to promise!'

'All right, I promise, if I must.'

'You must. It's the only way I could die in peace.'

By the end of September, they had been totally on their own for five months. It seemed to Jan that the end might not be far off. She discovered how close she was to total collapse when she volunteered to help Becca carry water up from the river.

She followed Becca down the zigzag trail and along the smooth-barked tree-trunk that gave access to the river. There, hanging on to the liana guard-rail, she edged along the trunk until she could reach down and fill her bucket. Suddenly, as she heaved it out, she knew her strength was all used up.

'Oh, Becca,' Jan said, panting. 'I didn't know I was so weak.'

'Take this then, Janny,' Becca said, and passed her mother a half-full bucket.

The return journey was a fearful struggle. She managed to stay on her feet, but only by pausing at each root and stone step. Even then, she found when she got to the top that she had splashed out much of the water she was carrying.

It was all she could do to set the bucket safely on the water-stand before she collapsed into her hammock, thinking: if I'm this weak, what must it be like for Becca? How much longer can we last? She began to pray: Father, give me the strength to accept what's happening. I can't ask for a miracle, can't expect to hear Becca say 'They're here!', though that, suddenly, was what she seemed to be hearing. 'No, no,' she muttered. 'I mustn't think that.'

'They're here! They're here!' The words were not part of

her reverie at all. Becca had said them, and was repeating them in delight as she ran out of the hut.

Nilo had arrived.

For a minute, everyone was laughing and talking at once. As the hubbub died, Harry offered coffee to Nilo, and then, even before they reached the hut, began to bombard him with questions.

'We were expecting Rufino,' Harry said in Spanish, 'What happened?'

Rufino had come, but the *paraná* had been empty. He had sat in his boat on the river for many days waiting for the water to rise, and then returned. So Nilo knew when Don Armindo sent him that, even after the rains, he could bring only a small load. Even the water on the main river was low. He had had to paddle all the way along the North Fork.

Nilo stayed barely an hour, just long enough to unload and receive the bundle of mail. Then he was off. 'I will return when I can!' he called, disappearing down the path into river-bank jungle, leaving them once again to their isolation.

※

The arrival of supplies inspired Harry to start work again on the Hilltop Hut. He was eager now to establish it as a second house for them all, and wanted Jan to share his enthusiasm. Day after day, he urged Jan up and down the newly cut trail. At first, the trek made her so tense she dreaded it. She didn't like to use up her precious batteries, and without her hearing-aid she couldn't tell the difference between Harry's shouts of 'Left!' and 'Right!'. Her fumbling infuriated him, until she persuaded him to make a distinction in word length, replacing 'left' and 'right' with 'port' and 'starboard'.

Once she had covered the trail a few times, however, her confidence grew, and she began to make the trip regularly. With her hand on Becca's shoulder, or gripping a leading-stick, she would make the easy walk past the turning to the Nursery Clearing, left into the Glade, and past the turn to the

221

Garden Clearing; then on up a steep zigzag, negotiating root steps that seemed just a little different each time she felt them; over some exposed rocks; across the edge of the Fourth Clearing; over a huge fallen tree, to begin what they called the Long Trail (to distinguish it from the short cut straight up the hill favoured by Becca); along the side of a hill that would eventually become the Pineapple Clearing; and finally straight up the final fifty yards, emerging from jungle on to the hilltop.

Becca bore the brunt of the work on the Hilltop Hut. To compensate for his own infirmity, Harry drove her unremittingly, as if she were an able-bodied male, telling her which trees to cut for posts, where to dig the holes, where to put the crossbeams, where to tie.

But Becca had more than Harry to cope with. Hanuman pestered her unmercifully. Harry said it was because he saw her as a sibling, and only wanted to play. In any event, she was often too absorbed in work to notice what he was doing, and he found her an easy target, nipping her heels and hands, stealing her tools and newly gathered tie-vines. Shouting at him did her no good. Harry blamed her for her lack of tolerance. 'Look at her! Look at her!' he'd bellow. 'She's breaking down! She's breaking down! I told you not to do that!' And anyway, Hanuman simply returned to the attack, nipping away at her resolve until she was reduced to grim, embattled silence and, on rare occasions, to tears of frustration.

🐾

Becca endured Hanuman – they all endured him – until one blessed day, just before their second Christmas.

Nilo had arrived with the first part of the next load of supplies. The river was still low, and he hadn't brought much. He'd said the rest of the cargo was still at the Source Pool, and it had taken him two days to paddle through the depleted *paraná*. After unloading, he'd left, saying he'd be back in a few days with the rest of the cargo.

Two days later, while they were eagerly awaiting Nilo's

return, Harry was preparing mail, with Hanuman on his shoulder. It was very hot, and Harry, as usual, was suffering. 'Elizabeth was right,' he grumbled, flapping his hand at sweat-bees. 'She would never have taken this heat. It's too much for me. Get off, Hanuman! It's too much, just too much! I'll never get to the mountains, I know I won't.' He began to sob at the thought. 'If only I could *accept* . . . Once I accept, I'll be all right . . . Get *away*, Hanuman, get *away*!'

Hanuman, scared by Harry's anger, scampered across the floor to Jan. As he climbed up to her lap, Jan sighed. Harry wouldn't let them break down, but he was always doing it himself. Poor Hanuman, she thought, cuddling him.

Suddenly, unaccountably, he leaned forward and gave her one of his eye-kisses – inserting his tiny tongue, with exquisite delicacy, into the corner of her eyelid. She remained motionless for several seconds, entranced by this extraordinary assertion of the closeness between them. He had done it before, several times, but only when she had been crying. This time, there were no tears to inspire his affection. It was a kiss without reason, a gesture that – in the light of what happened next – seemed to Jan to say: Remember, whatever happens, every-thing will be all right between us.

Shortly after that, Becca went up to the Garden Clearing. Hanuman followed her. He wouldn't bother her there. When she was gardening, he always settled up in a nearby tree to watch her work.

Harry suddenly stopped moaning about the heat, and looked up. 'What's that?' he asked. Then: 'Nilo!' he yelled, 'I hear him coming! Yay!' – and strode out of the hut.

In a minute he was back inside.

'Pigs!' he shouted, grabbing Jan. 'A herd, coming this way. Quick, where's Becca? *Becca!*' he bellowed. 'Jan, in the loft!'

From below, on the lower part of the river bank, came the cracking and rustling sounds of scores of pigs, white-lipped peccary, scavenging their way through the forest. The white-lipped peccary are the only Amazonian creatures to travel in herds; they keep themselves in food by remaining constantly on the move. They are squat, tough and fast, with teeth that can give a ferocious gash to anyone who happens to be in their way. Whether scavenging slowly or in panic-stricken flight, they can lay waste gardens in no time.

Becca came in at a run just as Harry was shoving Jan unceremoniously up the loft ladder.

'Peccary!' he shouted. 'Pans! Quick! Make a noise!'

The two of them dashed out, grabbed pans from the washstand and ran to the top of the bank, banging and shouting as they went. They were just in time. Scores of pigs were running along through the riverside forest. Jan, safe in the loft, listened anxiously as Harry and Becca yelled and bashed pans, while the herd scampered past below them. There was a brief lull; then, from downriver, came the sound of more crashing.

'Quick!' yelled Harry. 'Up the hill! They're turning up the hill! Head them off!' And he and Becca ran past the hut, up through the Garden Clearing to the hilltop, making as much of a din as they could.

From her perch, Jan heard the noise die away. After some twenty minutes, the two of them returned. Jan climbed back down to find Harry panting with the exertion, but apparently none the worse.

'Hanuman with you, Janny?' Becca asked.

'No, haven't seen him.'

'Must have been frightened,' said Harry. 'Not surprising. Those pigs were under pressure – we heard a wild dog barking. Hanuman must have thought we'd all gone insane.' He looked around and called: 'Hanuman!' Then he wandered off up the trail, still calling.

He came back after half an hour, saying he guessed Hanuman would be back by nightfall. But he wasn't.

Nor did he appear the next day, when Nilo arrived with the second part of his small load. Harry went on calling for several days after that. But Hanuman had simply vanished. For months, no one had fed him properly and he had been forced into semi-independence, foraging in the tree-tops. The hour of chaos with the pigs must have been the last straw.

For those first few days, Harry mourned his disappearance as if he had lost a child, breaking down a number of times. Then he took comfort by starting to scribble out a sequel to his book on Rima – the history of their own adventures with Hanuman over the past four years. 'Most likely he joined up with the spider monkeys,' he concluded.

That, in the end, was what they all decided to believe.

Though the drought had still not completely broken, Nilo's two deliveries brought them a few weeks of relief from famine, enough for them to celebrate Christmas in the newly built Hilltop Hut.

Jan found that Harry had been right – it *was* pleasant up there. The climate was better, the air lighter, the soil richer, and the view, described to her daily by Harry, was superb. That was the best thing about being on the hilltop – the unseen, ever-present view. Almost as soon as the trees were felled from the Observation Ledge, Harry took to reading the mountains and the weather to Jan whenever they happened to be passing. 'Sentinel is out,' he would say. 'Wonderfully clear today. You know, Jan, if someone came visiting from outer space and asked "What is a mountain?", that's the mountain you'd show them. It's perfect . . . Hen-and-Chicks are out too . . . Neblina's in mist . . . there's a storm brewing in the Well of Rains beside Paradise, but Thunder and Seal are clear . . .', and on he'd go about rain sweeping towards them across the intervening forest plain only to dissipate before it reached them; or about clouds forming above one of the peaks, building into a cap, a cape, a blanket; about bright sunlight, high mist, or drifting shadows formed by herds of fluffy little clouds; and even, when for some reason she woke with him in the small hours, about the moonlight that turned the ranges into negative, tinted greys against black; and on and on until she saw the mountains so clearly in her mind's eye that she had no conscious notion any more of not seeing. It was like standing in front of a great proscenium, with patterns of cloud, and rain, and light, and shadow making new scenes every hour and every day. A word or two from Harry or Becca, combined with sensations of light or shade, and of dry or damp in the wind, would conjure up for her the whole panorama.

೪

It was in part the new appreciation of the beauty of the place that gave them all the strength to endure the final stages of the drought and famine. Supplies would remain restricted until the start of the wet season, probably in April. But there was no lessening of their commitment. They were experienced. They knew how to survive in these conditions. It was only a matter of enduring.

As their food dwindled once again, and with it their strength, they spent more and more time in the Riverside Hut to avoid the labour of carrying water up the hill. There was very little to do. They read a great deal. Becca read the whole Bible right through in Spanish, notes and all, interspersed by lighter-weight works: Marjorie Kinnan Rawlings's classic account of homesteading in Florida, *Cross Creek*, and Saint-Exupéry's *The Little Prince*. When not reading or doing essential chores, she caught up on schoolwork (she was behind on her French). Harry wrote his journal daily, and finished volume after volume of *Groundlings, Treelings and Skylings*, his account of their time with Hanuman.

He also turned once again to his idea, first mentioned in Mexico, that the homestead should be made the focal point of a wildlife study centre. He dictated to Jan a memorandum to leading conservationists proposing a 2,000-square-kilometre national park, going on to suggest that Brazil should stock the park with gorillas, pygmy chimpanzees and other threatened species imported from Africa. When Jan timidly suggested that this might change the local ecology, Harry brushed the objection aside. 'Jan, don't counter me! This is just to get their attention!'

Sometimes, Harry and Rebecca read to Jan. But much of the time, if she wasn't typing letters, she lay silently in her hammock. Once before, such inactivity had driven her to the brink of madness. But this period of hardship was not, for Jan, another Difficulty Hill. For one thing, she was active and knew her way around. For another, she had come more to terms with her disabilities. She was no longer lost either in the real wilderness or in the wilderness of her own mind. With the first, she was at peace; the second, she could control. She did so by building for herself another, inner, reality.

Day by day, week by week, she made for herself a fantasy world founded on the fulfilment of several childhood wishes, bringing to imaginary but minutely detailed life a landscape and a society eroded by neglect.

Her fantasy began in the Depression years, around the time of her birth. Sacramento was growing then, and people were hungry. She imagined her father and her uncle Gerrit (the one who had vanished in the Spanish Civil War) going into business collecting garbage under contract to the city. Instead of having them throw the garbage away, she arranged for them to dump it on arid rubble, the tailings left behind by the mechanical dredgers searching for any gold left after the great rush of the previous century. On this unpromising foundation, she saw her father, her uncle and a growing cooperative of workers sorting through the garbage, separating out organic waste from glass and metal. Iron, copper and bronze were sent to craftsmen for reworking. Other metals went for scrap. The glass acquired an original use: she had it melted and used as a coating for adobe bricks, thus turning ephemeral mud into hard, non-eroding, beautiful objects that would last for centuries.

With these materials, a few impoverished families – migrant farm-workers, hobos, minority groups – began to grow food and to build a new society, with cooperative schools, clinics and services. There was no money; goods were exchanged, or acquired, by barter. For hours each day, and for uncounted days, Jan worked on the details of her little community, arranging townships and parklands and complex schemes by which food and labour and medical treatment could all be exchanged to build an economy based on subsistence living, reversing the cancerous growth of the city.

This dreamworld, rooted in the reality of her childhood, never escaped from it, for she could not see a way to carry it beyond 1941. War, with its demands for men and labour and goods, popped her bubble utopia, and at that point – pausing perhaps to answer a question from Harry or thank Becca for a cup of leaf tea – she would turn back her clock to refine some further detail of food growth and distribution.

茶

In March, the drought broke, the river rose, and the cargo-men came, marking an end to famine. Their arrival also marked, or seemed to mark, the beginning of lasting success. Undeterred by insect pests, and leafcutters, and the poverty of the soil, asserting their confidence that their difficulties could all be overcome in the end, they laboured on.

Deciding that the plants needed more calcium, Becca spent more time burning unlogged wood to make fertilizer ash. In addition, she and Jan collected leaves – a slurry of rotting leaves carted in *Piaroa* from downriver, and dry leaves carried uphill in a canvas sack specially stitched by Becca for the purpose.

Through 1977, Homestead Hill became again a place of real promise, with rich harvests always chimerically imminent. Within months, Becca and Jan had planted almost fifty species of vegetable and fruit. With the promise of such a harvest, they could, at last, hope to fulfil their aim as 'peasant intellectuals': to prove that it was possible for a peasant family, a small community perhaps, to live in one spot, as vegetarians, without burning or hunting, and therefore without upsetting the jungle's ecological balance. They were certain it would eventually be as fine a homestead as the Caverna.

As if to assert their faith, Harry rebuilt the marimba. He and Becca began to practise again, struggling to recall the tunes they had known in Mexico, and learning a few new ones from Harry's collection of folksongs, delighting Jan with recollections of other happy times – the wedding, the Santa Maria, Becca's teenage years with the Indian girls, all additional confirmation that their decision to return here had been the right one.

For all that was good about this time, however, there was one insoluble problem: Harry's health. He made no mention any more of the growth on his neck. It was 'quiet'. Christian Science had seen to that. But his heart remained a worry to him. He was convinced that he should not lie down, and insisted on sitting and sleeping propped up in his hammock, enthroned by a padded backrest of cushions, foam-rubber and cardboard.

Then there was the heat. He needed to bathe two or three times a day to cope with it. He was simply not suited to the tropics, and never had been. He would sit in his hammock in temperatures that Jan found perfectly acceptable – 82, 83, 84 – and even without a shirt the perspiration would pour down him.

Now, in addition, his skin complaint – psoriasis – worsened. Early in 1978, the disease broke out again, more virulently, attacking a large part of his back and legs. The skin became dry and inflamed, as if he had been badly sunburned, and then cracked open and oozed blood. There was nothing to be done to heal it. He sat in his hammock with the sweat running down him into the cracks in his skin, almost beside himself with the torment of it.

It pained Jan that she could do so little for him. She would rub oil into the roughened areas to ease the pain, and listen in silence to his litany of complaints. 'Jan,' he would say, weeping with pain and frustration. 'I'm willing to starve for what I believe in, but I never expected to do it in a scalding skin . . . Becca must have used oil in the cooking – she knows it's bad for me . . . The trouble is, I need better food . . . The heat, Jan, that's what I can't stand . . . We're still too low here! I need to be over 1,000 feet! That's what I've always wanted! We should be nearer the mountains!'

It was as if he was weeping for Neblina. Unable to reach it, he was literally cracking up.

⚘

For almost three years, they had lived in total isolation. Except for a hunting party from Cucuí, with whom hardly a word was exchanged, the only human beings they saw in all that time were the cargo-men, and they only came once every four or five months.

In mid-1978, however, they were down in the Riverside Hut, having their midday meal, when Becca announced nervously, 'Someone coming. With boots on.'

Harry went outside and called. Becca, peering out under the thatch, told her mother what was happening. A man stepped out of the jungle, wearing jungle boots, dressed in khaki. A soldier? Perhaps, but he was followed by two wary teenagers in shorts and sandals. None of them said anything. Harry grinned a welcome, and waved them forward to the house, where they sat in a line on the log-bench outside. There, Harry could talk to them from his hammock, with Becca interpreting softly from hers, out of sight of the men.

They were, they said, members of a group surveying a route for the road.

The road! The idea of a 100-mile highway through virgin forest joining São Gabriel and Cucuí had come to seem mere fantasy. They had practically forgotten that the threat of the road had been a major reason for leaving Cucuí. Now,

suddenly, the threat seemed on the point of becoming a horrifying reality.

The older man, the foreman, explained that while out
looking for a bridge site they had seen Harry's boat. Could
they borrow it for a while?

Harry agreed, with the affability he always showed to
strangers. But when the men left, his mood changed. 'Well,
it's happened,' he said. 'That's it. Mexico all over again. We're
finished.'

Over the next few weeks, he became increasingly convinced
he was right. There were regular visits from the highway
workers. An engineer said that 'if all went well' the road
would cross the Demiti in a year or so. The road had apparently
already penetrated northwards from São Gabriel to a point not
far from Sentinel, for sometimes they could hear the roar of
bulldozers pushing aside trees and scooping mud into swamps.
The road itself could hardly be far behind.

Harry foresaw catastrophe. The road would be built right
by them. There would be a great bridge. Colonists would
stream in, ripping up the jungle and killing the wildlife. The
men would bother Becca. These thoughts reduced him to tears,
and he would not be comforted. Every morning, he would
work through the implications, deciding, for the last time, that
they could not stay. By lunch, he would have decided with
equal finality that they *must* stay and fight for the recognition
of the park. 'Look, Jan, Becca, everything on my plate comes
from our own gardens. We *can't* let this go to waste!'

Privately, Jan had her doubts about the imminence of disaster. To Harry's rantings she made only token comments. *If
all went well*. How often did things go well in these remote and
forbidding jungles? How often had their own plans been
shattered by illness, climate and erratic supplies? The workers
had a heavy struggle ahead of them. They, and their machines,
were a good eighty miles from São Gabriel. Every kilometre
extended the supply line. Men would die, machines would
break, bridges would collapse, rains would eat away at the

road, the money might run out. It was simply too soon to make decisions. They would stay, as she wrote to Toni Martin, 'until it is absolutely clear it is the Divine Will that we go.'

In the end, God decided for the Littles. After several months, the highway engineer paid a second visit. He seemed sombre, and for a moment Jan feared he had come to announce the start of work on the bridge.

Far from it. The highway workers were leaving, he said, at least for the present.

'Will you come back?' asked Harry.

'Perhaps. It will be hard. The machines break down. The spare parts do not come. The food does not come. The jungle is difficult.'

'So perhaps you will not come back?'

'Perhaps. My opinion is, we could build the road. But keeping it in good condition, that is a different matter.'

After the engineer left, and the bulldozers fell silent, and their isolation was once again complete, Harry rejoiced. This was all the proof they needed that they had chosen the right place. Not even the Brazilian military could fight its way in here. This was one jungle that wasn't going to be defeated!

※

Rebecca knew where the letter came from by the address on the outside: INPA, the Amazonian Research Institute in Manaus. She knew it was in response to the request she had sent the previous year for information about planting. She was not therefore prepared for the shock of its contents. It was signed Roberto – Carlos Roberto Bueno – the memory of whose warm handshake and soft grey eyes she had buried almost as soon as she left Manaus four years previously. To her even greater amazement, it began, informally, with the words 'Cara Rebeca'.

'Who is this man, addressing you by your first name?' asked Harry disapprovingly. 'A man doesn't address a woman that

232

way unless he wants to court her.' When Jan told him about the brief meeting in Manaus, he added, 'Well, if he comes here, he better understand that he has to deal with me first.'

'*Cara Rebeca*'! The words, and Harry's reaction, threw Becca into turmoil. For the first time on Homestead Hill, she recalled, with sudden longing, the meeting in Manaus four years previously. With Jan, she began to anatomize that occasion, and her own reactions to it. Looking back, she found it hard to understand why she had behaved as she had done. 'You know, Janny,' she said, 'When we left Cucuí for Manaus, I remember I had the feeling I was going to meet the right person. And I just forgot about it. So when I met him, I didn't recognize what was happening. I shouldn't have said we didn't have time to see him again . . .'

'Well, perhaps we shouldn't take it all that seriously,' Jan replied. 'It may not mean anything.'

'But, Janny, in Brazil, it *does* mean something!'

Jan was dubious about that. Perhaps he was just being friendly. But perhaps not. Perhaps Becca's reaction to him had been matched by his response. Anyway, she certainly couldn't snatch from Becca her dream of a romantic attachment.

'Are you going to answer?' she asked.

'Yes.'

That was fine. Bueno's reply would make all things clear.

🐒

One day not long before Christmas 1978, the silence of Homestead was shattered by a gunshot from downriver. Both Jan and Becca, together in the Hilltop Hut preparing correspondence, looked up.

'The cargo-men!' Becca said in a pained voice. 'They should know better than that.'

Jan remained working on the hilltop, while Becca made her way down to help Harry with unloading.

An hour later, they walked back up together.

'They want to give us a baby monkey,' Harry told Jan. 'A

very rare species, too. They shot the mother downriver. But I can't accept it because Becca says "No".'

Jan paused. After Hanuman, she understood Becca's reaction well enough, but . . . 'Becca,' she responded. 'How can you say "no" when it's the only chance for the little creature to live?'

For a few moments, Becca was silent. Then, in a small voice, she said: 'No – I can't say "no".'

'I thought she might change her mind,' Harry exclaimed happily, and hurried back down to the men, leaving Jan to wonder what she had forced Becca into.

So they acquired their third monkey-child, a little bundle of dark fur, with round brown eyes and a melancholy, oddly human expression. Harry and Becca recognized the baby as a uakari, for they had seen several of the cat-sized, short-tailed adults before. There are three species of uakari, all rare. Two of the species have startling red faces and bald heads, but this baby, which the men said was a male, belonged to the third species, the rarest and the most charming, the black-headed uakari.

'He's a child of the jungle,' Harry declared. 'We ought to call him Mowgli, after Kipling's jungle boy. Here, Jan, you take him. Let him sleep with you, the same way Rima did.'

For that night, Jan put the baby to sleep on her neck, happy to feel again a tiny, racing heart and furry arms. Not that she was allowed to keep their new orphan for long. Harry soon took him over, feeding him on milk soaked into cotton wool, as he had fed Rima, and allowing him to sleep spread-eagled on the top of his head – 'it'll remind him of riding on his mother's back in the jungle,' he said.

Harry tried to wean the baby on to *farinha* mixed with oil and sugar. The little thing promptly developed severe diarrhoea. Cleaning up, and applying oil to the sore rump, Harry made a discovery. 'We've been living in error,' he announced. 'We have a little girl monkey!'

So Mowgli became Maggie, and like Rima and Hanuman,

proved a handful. The major problem was toilet training. Since Maggie slept on Harry's head, if she messed at night, Harry would wake up with a shout of disgust, calling for Becca to bring water, complaining bitterly – 'I can't stand this! I don't know how I'll handle this!' Only when he was cleaned up did he quieten down, settling Maggie on his head again like a skullcap.

Yet they soon grew fond of her. Perhaps because she came to them so young, she lacked Hanuman's frenetic naughtiness. When content, she purred like a cat and smiled a disconcertingly human smile. As she grew, she became inky black, except for some auburn hair on her shoulders. The dark colouring was relieved only by her small white teeth and tiny pink tongue. Even Becca was won over – 'If only she weren't so affectionate,' she complained, with a smile. Harry gave up practically everything – writing, sewing, marimba practice, gardening – to sit in the hut caring for Maggie.

1979, like 1978, was a swings-and-roundabouts sort of year, a two-steps-forward-two-steps-back dance with planting, and transplanting, and Maggie, and reading, and ill health, and always the near-certainty that they were 'making it'.

Things changed, and things stayed much the same. The Hilltop Hut was re-roofed by the cargo-men. Becca received new seeds – sun-hemp, roselle, egg-plant, shoigoin turnip, radish, ornamental basil, New Zealand spinach – and planted them in cans. Harry scrawled urgent comments in the margin of Bronowski's *Ascent of Man*, berating the author for his failure to emphasize vegetarianism and spirituality. Old cans were flattened and set around the pineapples to give them any minerals that might come from the rusting metal. Maggie was treated for a bot-fly in the forearm. The book box was invaded by termites ('Twenty-five years of living with these things,' lamented Harry, 'and we still don't learn!'). The cargo-men came again in March, bringing a thick and indigestible pile of

Braille sermons from the Christian Science Publishing House in Boston. Harry worked on a family history, *Rooted in Granite*, and scribbled his jungle journal illegibly on Jan's old Braille magazines. He finished *Groundlings, Treelings and Skylings* and began gathering material for *Mag, the Monkey's Little Baby*.

Beneath the business of normality, however, there was change. Harry's health worsened. In April, his psoriasis returned, worse than before, putting him in an agony from which he found no release other than in constant bathing. The rash affected every part of his body except his face. In addition, his legs swelled from thigh to instep. And he insisted on limiting his diet still further in the belief that oil, salt, milk powder and starch all contributed to his condition. He sought relief in Christian Science, and found less and less. 'Pain not real!' he grimaced. 'Mrs Eddy should try walking on these legs!'

In May, Harry, still in constant pain, recalled that 25 May was the anniversary of his Illumination. He wondered why he had never had a similar experience again. 'I've been too close to everyday living, like Martha in the Gospels,' he said. 'Too much concerned with hard work, and looking after you two, to detach myself.'

In July, the cargo-men came again, but without food. They explained that the Coimbras' launch had gone over the São Gabriel rapids and that supplies would be delayed. They did, however, bring mail, including some Braille magazines published by the Brazilian Ministry of Education, ordered for them by a Christian Science contact of the Moores.

There was nothing for Rebecca.

❧

She never did hear from Roberto Bueno. She hadn't heard from anyone in quite a while now. Thinking herself as free as any serpent or bird (her words), and not lacking intellectual stimulation, Rebecca was emotionally starved — caged, isolated, stunted, shut off in ways she could never have imagined, in ways Harry would never have acknowledged, in ways Jan could never have mentioned. Bueno remained a last, and desperate, hope.

Over and over again, she discussed the problem with Jan, vainly seeking an explanation. Eventually, towards the end of 1979, over a year after she had received his letter, she wrote of her unhappiness to one of Jan's correspondents, Eleanor Miner:

It occurred to me out of the blue that he had made up his mind about me, and I thought 'This is preposterous.' I felt abashed, confused, defiant, but at the last I looked him square in the eyes and afterwards I told my mother, 'He is one I would like to know.'

Later – last year – it came to me that I would have another chance before the year was out. I almost spoke of this warning to my father one morning, but I thought 'It can't be – how can anything happen after four and a half years?' In August I received a reply to a seed request, and when I read the salutation I was astonished – the writer had addressed me by my first name, and as my father commented, in Latin America a man doesn't address a woman or girl *that* way unless they are very intimate or he wants to court her. Before replying I had an intuition that I had thought to leave marriage out of my life but that I would have to change my mind.

Later, I was working up here alone. I had fretted through the intervening two weeks, wondering if he would answer and now that it was irremediable wondering if I had done right. I was seized by a moment of anguish – I was waiting for something important to be revealed and had no idea what. Then I saw a figure standing alone on a high place and around the figure it was like an overcast dawn and I said 'I don't know what my future holds, but I know it holds a challenge and a promise.' Then I returned to material vision again, and a voice – the same? – said 'Whether or not you hear from him, it will be for the best.'

As you know I have not heard from him. My father

thinks he tried again and the postal service got in the way. This that I have written is every bit true, and I still puzzle over the whole business.

She puzzled; but she did not complain. She hoped; but she never dared ask. For their life was a gift, the consequence of divine guidance, and to ask would be to criticize and doubt. Like Jan, she simply waited, immersing herself in work, concealing almost all her pain, even from herself.

❡

Perhaps it was because Harry had weakened and aged; or because Rebecca now did most of the work on the homestead; or because Jan herself had changed; in any event, Jan found that she was less affected by his moods and demands. Only once did she allow the change in her to show.

Jan and Becca were raking leaves for mulch in the forest, carrying them up the hill in the green canvas bag Becca had made. 'Janny, why don't you do this area?' Becca suggested. 'I'll start up the hill.'

'All right, Becca, I'll . . .' Jan stopped, caught by that strange, hair-crawling instinct she had learned to trust. 'You better check around again, Becca. There's a snake here somewhere.'

She waited, rigid with fear, while Becca hunted about. After a minute, Becca said: 'Oh-oh. Here it is, in a hollow under this fallen tree. It's really hard to see. Just keep clear. Maybe I'll shift it later.'

Jan, reassured, went on with her work. When Becca returned, she checked on the snake again. 'It's still in the same position, Janny. I think I'll leave it. You know, it's a funny snake. I don't even know if it has any eyes.'

Later that evening, when they were up in the Hilltop Hut, they told Harry about the snake. But he was more interested in the rain-barrel. The rain-barrel, a gasoline drum brought in two years before, needed painting underneath. Up there on the hill, it collected water from the roof via a piece of wooden guttering. Harry wasn't fond of the taste – too metallic, too warm, he said, and he was used to cold New England water – but it was worth keeping the barrel in good condition. Becca had tipped it upside down so that it would dry out, but Harry was concerned that it might rain, and the water go to waste.

That night it rained.

Deep in the night, Jan was woken by Harry shouting. 'Becca! Wake up! Get out to the barrel! Set it up straight again so we can catch the rain!'

Becca sighed and ducked under the drooping thatch. Jan knew she would be feeling around in the dark and the wet. He shouldn't drive her like this, she thought. Becca had begun to develop a dry cough that worried Jan. He should have protected her from exposure, not driven her out in the rain like that.

Jan was woken again by Harry at dawn, as usual. He was angry at Becca. He had gone out to check the barrel, and seen the guttering wasn't set up correctly. 'I told you I wanted to collect water!' he shouted at her. 'Now a lot of water's wasted. That was really a slovenly piece of work, Becca. How can I trust you if you can't even put a rain-barrel straight when I ask you?' He went on at her right through breakfast.

Jan listened in silence, and then, choosing her moment, she said, 'Well, Becca, shall we do some more raking?'

'All right, Janny. The pineapples up here can do with all the help they can get.'

'I hope you do a better job on the leaves than Becca did on the rain-barrel!' Harry grumbled.

'Oh dear, oh dear,' sighed Jan.

She realized her mistake at once. Instantly Harry picked up her tone of mild criticism. 'So you don't think it's important, is that it? Well, let me tell you it is. I have to have water up here, and it has to be clean . . .' And off he went again, bemoaning his responsibilities and the inadequacies of the two women, while Jan and Becca listened, as usual, in stony silence.

Except this time, as he ranted on, Jan's mind wandered, away from Harry and out of the hut. She saw Homestead Hill as if from above. There they were, the three of them on top of a hill, with swamps and rivers all around them, in the middle of an immense and timeless wilderness, and here was this lunatic raving on about an inch of rainwater in a barrel, water he didn't even like the taste of. It suddenly struck her as very funny. Harry was shouting that if that was the best they could do, then it was a pretty poor lookout for them all, when Jan laughed.

Harry broke off in mid-sentence, and stared at her.

'Oh, it's funny, is it?' Jan heard the shift in his voice, the sudden increase in tension. It didn't matter. She sat there, smiling. 'That's just like you!' he bellowed. 'You know your trouble, don't you? You're *not responsible*, and you've taught her to be the same, in spite of everything I've tried to do for her. It doesn't matter to you. Well, you can just leave, that's what you can do! We don't need you any more!'

Her smile faded. Suddenly, there was nothing to laugh at, because she knew that if she ever did leave, Becca wouldn't stay. Harry couldn't run the place on his own. It would mean the end of the homestead. But the homestead was Becca's future. None of them would set that at risk. He was talking nonsense, mere empty anger, and she wondered idly how he would bring his ranting to an end.

'Becca and I can manage things perfectly well without you!' he went on. 'When the men come next time, you just tell them you're finished here, they can take you away, be glad to do so, you don't belong here, you're just a burden to both of us . . .' Suddenly, he stopped. In an instant, his mood changed. 'It was that snake,' he said matter-of-factly. 'I've been worried about the snake. That's why all this happened.'

'Yes, Harry,' Jan said, calmly.

'You shouldn't be working out in the woods, Jan, especially alone. You're not to rake leaves any more. Take care of your work down by the river, and we'll have an early lunch.'

Jan heard Becca pick up a bucket, and she followed her example. With her hand on Becca's shoulder, the two of them set off down the Long Trail. Becca said nothing for several minutes. Then, with an edge to her voice, she commented: 'You should have known better, Janny.' Jan realized, to her surprise, that Becca was angry with her. 'When he's like that, you have to be as a stone idol.'

'I suppose so,' Jan said, with a shrug. 'I just can't . . .'

'*A stone idol*,' Becca repeated.

A stone idol. Yes, she would have to remember that. There was nothing to be gained from needling him. She should control herself, if only for Becca's sake. Becca was the strong one, the one who made the homestead work. By comparison, Harry seemed to be disintegrating.

Towards the end of the year, he fell several times. Once, after repairing the marimba, he stepped outside the Riverside Hut and slipped flat on his back on the pole walkway. Shortly afterwards, there was an accident in the privy of the Hilltop Hut. When he leaned back against the support, it broke, tumbling him into shit.

A third fall proved rather more serious. He was coming up from bathing, leaning against the liana railings to put on his sandals, when the railings broke. He fell forwards down the ten-foot bank, turning a complete somersault before landing on his back beside the river. He managed to climb back up, but he had hurt his ribs badly.

A few days later, in the Riverside Hut, Jan heard him cry out.

'What, Harry?' she asked anxiously.

'If I could only remember not to turn!' he moaned.

'Oh,' she said, 'Your ribs. I'm sorry.'

'You're not sorry!' he said, petulantly. 'You smiled! You think just because you can't see people, people can't see you. I saw you smile, so don't tell me you're sorry.'

He was silent for a few minutes. Then he asked, abruptly, 'Is it old age?' He'd clearly been worrying about his accidents. Maybe it had even occurred to him that the falls were signs of uncertainty, self-doubt about the course he had dictated to his family. But before she could reply, he answered his own question. 'Don't see why it should be. All of those falls could have happened as well to a six-year-old as a sixty-three-year-old.'

A few days later, as if to prove that his homesteading skills were as sharp as ever, he began to make a rough haft, cut by Rufino the year before, into an axe handle for Becca. She had been complaining that the axe she used was too small for her; she would be able to do much more, she said, if she could use the three-pound head, which was lying unused. So he began to cut the length of wood to her specifications, shaping it with a machete into a neatly tapering handle that fitted right through the axe head. That way, each swing of the axe would jam the razor-sharp head on to the base.

He finished it in early December. 'There,' he said, handing it to Becca with pride. 'If you take care of it, it'll last you a lifetime.'

***

The final cargo delivery that year arrived on 14 December.

Jan received a letter from Toni Martin. Strangely, in view of what happened later, Toni asked: 'If you should die tonight, would you be sure of eternal life?'

In her reply – which, together with letters from Harry and Becca, made up the last batch of mail to leave Homestead – Jan spoke for both herself and Harry. Harry, she said, looked no further than his favourite verses from St John: 'I am the resurrection and the life, saith the Lord.' Jan, for her part, recalled her own personal relationship with her God, the God of the natural world around her and the strength she drew from the 'bulwark' of the mountains. She needed that strength now more than ever. 'The food problem here is tough,' she wrote,

'So too the soil problem and our labouring stamina. We don't see any other guidance for us. We do have blessings and more to be realized. It is hard, sometimes quite impossible and I have wondered about it many times, about the sacrifice it costs us. It seems patience and suffering is necessary. If it must be, I can hold.'

Becca, resting after a heavy days work machete-ing the Pineapple Clearing, was still obsessed by the lack of a reply from Roberto Bueno. Coughing now and then with a hard, dry noise that was beginning to worry Jan, she wrote: 'I am beginning to understand the feelings expressed in that song of which the announcer on Radio Brazil Central and myself disapprove: "Bullets of gold for the one who does not want to be my treasure." Or plain leaden bullets for some demoralized, underpaid postal clerks who don't appreciate just how much can hang on this or that letter.'

Just before the cargo-men left on 17 December, Harry scribbled a final, cheery note: 'All goes very well. We need more fresh food, but do not complain, remembering the man who did complain about having no shoes until he met someone who had no feet! We stagger along like a horse on three legs. Season's best, as for all seasons, from the Upper Demiti.'

9

'SHE'S FINISHED'

The end began in ordinary ways.

Dawn. A gentle tapping on her hammock – Rebecca bringing a cup of coffee. No sound of rain on the palm-leaf thatch. Through the grey wall of her blindness, a sense of growing brightness. A feeling of peace and contentment. All was as it should be. Jan sipped her coffee, listening. Even without her hearing-aid, she could hear reassuring little sounds: the radio, Rebecca at the hearth, Harry talking.

Harry had been awake for hours, of course. Death was closest before dawn, he always said, and he had no intention of being taken unawares. He would have woken in darkness, lit the lamp, combed his lank white hair and beard, switched on the radio and written up his jungle journal. Now, although she couldn't make out the words, Jan could hear him berating Maggie and exchanging remarks with Rebecca.

Normally, at dawn, there would be a discussion of work to be done, but today was a Sunday, a day of rest. She lay back in her hammock, wondering what they were discussing – the radio programme, perhaps, or the macaws commuting overhead with a squawk and a clatter of wings. Everyday things. She was content, waiting for the day's pattern to unfold.

Rebecca came to her again, bringing breakfast – a bowl of manioc meal mixed with water, bland and pasty. Jan ate, and then changed from the slacks and sweater in which she slept into her day clothes. She folded her blanket, and sat back in her hammock, until Harry summoned them for their regular Sunday observance: a reading, a prayer, a silent thanksgiving.

Then Harry announced that they would go down the hill for the day. There would be no work, of course, but they would need to wash and collect fresh water from the river. Harry gathered his things. Rebecca set about preparing two containers, one for food, the other for glowing embers to rekindle the fire in the Riverside Hut.

'I'm set, Harry,' Rebecca said. Then she added: 'But I must get a hold of *this*.'

A shadow of concern brushed Jan's mind. The words, referring back to some unheard exchange with Harry, seemed to hint at a problem of some kind.

No time now to ask what she meant. Jan was used to missing quick little remarks between Rebecca and Harry, and had long since learned not to interrupt talk and work with questions. Questions like that irritated Harry. She would wait, and find out later, without imposing.

It was time to go. They stepped out through the drooping thatch, into the hilltop clearing. Jan sensed the sudden brightness of the morning sky, cut off to her left by the crowding trees. Rebecca set off at once, heading surefootedly down the shorter, steeper trail, the one that would lead her to the Riverside Hut in just a few minutes. While Jan stood holding her leading-stick, Harry, with Maggie on his shoulder, strode over the coarse grass to the Observation Ledge to look out over the surrounding jungle at the mountains, checking the distant weather and drinking in the beauty of the jungle-covered peaks.

'Fine day,' he said, as he returned. 'Mist's clearing already. Lots of mountains. No details, though, just silhouettes against the morning sky.' Jan nodded and smiled. His words were enough to conjure the view in her mind: the perfect cone of Sentinel right ahead, close enough to touch; the wall of peaks to the left; the plain of jungle, now white with mist; range upon range of distant mountains; and on the horizon, the broad, blunt lump of Neblina itself.

Jan felt Harry take the leading-stick. The picture vanished.

She fell into step, responding with the unconscious expertise of a dancer. They set off, moving from the open clearing, over the shoulder of the hill, and down the Long Trail, dim and enclosed.

'What was Becca talking about? What did she have to get a hold of?' Jan asked, as the shadows closed over her, and she felt the first tree roots of the descending path beneath her feet.

'Malaria,' Harry replied, loudly.

Malaria? Surely not. This whole area of Brazilian jungle was almost free of malaria, not just along their isolated little river, but all the immense slab of Amazonia – the dozens of unmapped rivers, the thousands of square miles of uninhabited jungle – that ran from the Rio Negro clear up to the mountains on the Venezuelan border, and beyond. They'd had no trouble from mosquitoes, let alone malaria, in all their four and a half years on Homestead Hill. Rebecca hadn't had malaria since she was a teenager in Mexico.

At the Riverside Hut, Harry went into his area, a corner marked off by storage crates. Rebecca had already made up the fire and was down at the river, filling a water-bucket. Jan stood irresolutely by her own hammock, still worrying about Rebecca's remark. It was so unlike Rebecca to admit to feeling unwell. She would never ask for help, but Jan wanted to give all the support she could.

On Rebecca's return, as she heaved the bucket with a thud on to the wash-stand, Jan called out to her: 'Becca, you take my hammock. I'll get another one down.' Jan's hammock had a better view of the trees, which Rebecca might appreciate if she was feeling low. Rebecca accepted gratefully.

Jan fumbled down a spare hammock from the rafters, and hung it in the aisle beside the hearth, tying it carefully the way Harry had taught her. The hammock crowded the passageway, but it was right by Harry's corner. If need be, she could talk to him across the line of crates without disturbing Rebecca.

There was, however, no talk. Rebecca dozed. Harry put a Braille magazine, the *National Geographic*, in Jan's hands and

246

then immersed himself in Darwin's *Voyage of the Beagle*. Maggie bounced off to play outside. Jan, too, began to read. She wasn't fast at reading Braille and as always the effort so wearied her that she dozed off.

About noon, Jan awoke to discover she was shivering. She felt weak. A cold, perhaps.

Food would help, Harry said. He made up three plates of rice with some chicory and sweetcorn. But Rebecca refused it, listlessly, and Jan could manage only a few mouthfuls.

'By the look of things, you two won't want to go back up on the hill this evening,' Harry remarked, as he took Jan's bowl. They always preferred to sleep on the hill if they could, to take advantage of the fresher night air. 'I better go up and get the lantern.'

In his absence, Rebecca stayed in her hammock. Jan heard her talking to Maggie in a soft murmur. At one point, no doubt after the impatient monkey had jumped right on her, Rebecca's voice rose. 'It's all right, Maggie. Today's a rest day. Tomorrow I'll be up to give you an outing.' Inconsequential words, given consequence only by the events that followed.

On his return, Harry was subdued. He bathed in the river, and made tea. 'Shouldn't have bathed,' he said, as he handed Jan her cup. 'Now I'm getting chills.'

The next day was New Year's Eve, the last day of 1979. Jan awoke as Rebecca came past her, panting, carrying a bucket of water from the river. 'Oh, Becca,' she said, worried by her daughter's refusal to slow down, 'You shouldn't have done that. I could have gone for you.'

'Now, Jan,' came Harry's voice, loud and assertive. 'You know there's no need for that. There are two of us here.'

'It's all right, Janny,' Rebecca added softly from the hearth beside her. 'I needed the wash. Besides, it was nice down there.' Her words were a reassurance. It was good to know

that Rebecca was still fit enough to appreciate the secluded beauty of the riverside – the dark and silent water, shiny as
wet tar, reflecting sombre foliage slashed by the white of trailing lianas and punctuated by the occasional, sudden brilliance
of an orchid.

The day passed in near silence: a few drinks of water, a few
mouthfuls of manioc, a little reading. Late in the afternoon,
Harry announced they'd better go up the hill. Rebecca made
no objections. Jan, shivering, and also a little groggy, preferred
not to argue.

🦌

Harry woke Jan with tea well before dawn. 'Want to welcome
the New Year with "The Farming World" on the BBC?' he
asked. They all liked this programme, with its discussion of
agricultural problems worldwide. Jan would listen to it with
the radio tucked tight against her ear, sitting by Harry's
hammock. But, even as she awoke, she knew she was worse.
'No, not this morning, Harry,' she said, shivering. After a sip
of tea, she rolled her blanket tightly around her, cocooning
herself protectively.

But there was something else nagging at her besides the
fever. Something was missing. It took her a few minutes to
realize: she couldn't hear the usual little clinkings and scrapings.
No one at the fire, no one getting breakfast. Rebecca was still
in her hammock – Jan could feel the hut shake as she turned
restlessly. That was worrying. Rebecca would never stay in
her hammock unless she was worse than she had admitted.

Some time later, Harry said: 'We shouldn't be up here.
We'll run out of fresh water.'

🦌

By Thursday, the illness was worse. They had all forced themselves back down the hill. Now Jan began to slip in and out of
consciousness. This was no simple infection, she realized. It
affected her sense of time. The hours seemed either to drag or

to race. Soon after she awoke, Rebecca brought her water; the next she knew it was late afternoon. Past and present, existence and non-existence began to merge.

The disease seemed to affect Harry the same way. When he came to write his journal that evening, he said: 'What happened yesterday? I can't remember yesterday.'

'It was New Year's Day.'

'Was it? I thought that was two days ago.'

Sometimes malaria had that effect. But it was not malaria, she told herself in one of her increasingly rare moments of clarity, she was sure of that now. It didn't have the dead, brick-dust taste of malaria; and malaria would not strike all three of them together; and there was no regular cycle of chills and fever, only a steady downward drift.

Slowly, as day merged unnoticed into night, the world around her dissolved. The present lost all significance. Dreams, or memories, took its place. She was aware only that Harry and Becca were still active. Someone fetched water, for there was always a cup to hand. Someone cooked. Someone put logs on the fire.

There was much that she missed. At some point on the evening of her first descent into unconsciousness, Harry wrote up his journal again. '4th day with the "ague",' he scribbled in a shaky hand, 'but sleep improving and appetites. After a good thunder shower by night which Mag and I only ever hear Becca even made a cargo trip up on the hill, but I find trips to the bath too much. As cooking and eating resume, we all take courage, except Mag, who simply insists those who eat must take exercise! And so pressure from her mounts steadily at our small convalescence.' He ended with a Christian Science quotation from Mary Baker Eddy. '"God always has and always will meet every human need."'

At the time, though, Jan knew nothing of the thunder shower during the night or of Becca's trip up the hill. Perhaps – the thought occurred to her later – perhaps she allowed herself her hours of unconsciousness because she was still certain that everything would be all right. Harry and Becca would certainly have encouraged that attitude. 'Our small convalescence': that's all any of their illnesses ever were.

All she registered, therefore, were those snippets of conversation that carried some emotional weight. Events planted themselves randomly in the quagmire of her mind, appearing later in her memory like the topmost branches of flooded trees, clear enough in themselves, but with no connection to an underlying reality.

At some point that evening, she heard Harry's voice, raised in anger, but couldn't catch his words. 'Harry, what's the matter?' she called.

'It's the oatmeal,' he said petulantly. The oatmeal – Quaker Oats – was a precious item, bought for making cakes on special occasions. Harry had decided to have some, but found there was none. 'Becca put all that was left in the sour-dough mix, without even checking with me,' he complained. 'I can't eat the sour-dough, she lets it stand too long, that's how you and she have it, so what am I going to have to eat?'

Then Jan heard Becca speak, in a soothing murmur. She sounded as if she were explaining something. As always, she refused to rise to Harry's irritability, working to calm him down again. Whatever she said solved the problem. 'Good,' Harry said, after a while. 'All right. If you can do it.'

After that, all was quiet. Jan dozed.

Later, or perhaps it was the following day – yes, the following day, because she registered the fact that she had not been woken by Rebecca offering tea or coffee – she regained consciousness for a few minutes to the soft murmur of the radio on the other side of the kitchen boxes.

Then, whole days ceased to exist. There was no pain, just unbeing. Occasionally, Maggie pestered, jumping up on her hammock and peering anxiously into her face, bouncing on her, pulling at her clothes and hair, gently nibbling her cheek, until Jan flapped a hand and muttered and pulled her blanket over her head and then, briefly aware of tasks undone and her own helplessness, sank gratefully back into dreamy darkness.

※

A few uncounted days after her descent into recurrent unconsciousness, as the light was beginning to fade, Jan heard Harry's voice raised again in anger. Rebecca's replies were, as usual, calm and patient. It seemed to Jan that they were discussing how to deal with a large snake. It must have been close by. Rebecca was saying she could do this and that to take care of it. Harry was in near hysteria, shouting that it wouldn't work, she couldn't do it that way. Yes, Rebecca assured him, she would manage it, it would work, she wouldn't take such a risk if she wasn't sure it would work. Gradually, he became calmer. The danger had passed. Jan relaxed.

Later, when Rebecca came past her hammock, Jan asked, 'Was it a big snake, Becca?'

'Snake? What snake, Janny?'

'I thought you and Harry were talking about a snake.'

Harry's voice broke in, loudly: 'No!'

'No snake?'

'No, Janny. We were just fixing his hammock.'

Harry was for ever re-setting his hammock strings since the fall that had injured his ribs. Finding it almost impossible to get comfortable, he would fiddle about tying and retying knots in the support strings several times a day. Now, apparently, he was demanding help from Rebecca just when she needed all the rest she could get.

※

During the night – that night, perhaps, or the next – Jan was awoken by a bump against her hammock and a heavy crash beside her. Puzzled, she put out a hand. She felt a kitchen box tilted over against her hammock, then another, then . . . Harry's shoulder. Harry was sprawled among fallen boxes.

'Oh, Harry,' she groaned, feeling around him. 'What happened?'

There was no reply. Then she heard Rebecca right beside her saying, 'We have to get him up.' Jan sensed the vague, darting beam of a flashlight, and driven by sudden anxiety tipped herself out of her hammock on to her knees. 'Here, Janny, can you pull his arm?'

Still Harry said nothing. Together, she and Rebecca pulled at Harry until he was sitting upright against the boxes, facing the hearth. The effort had taken all her strength. She knelt, exhausted, her hand on his shoulder.

'Pick me up!' Harry demanded, suddenly. 'Pick me up!'

Jan felt a surge of anger. He was always making these ridiculous demands. Pick him up? How could they possibly do that? There was no way that two women prostrate with sickness could lift a 160 lb man. She and Rebecca had already worn themselves out helping him. He didn't know what he was asking. He would just have to sit there for a while. He was confortable enough, surely. He would have to let them rest and regain their strength.

'You're asking something I can't do,' she said, panting, still kneeling, leaning on him.

'I'm not asking anything of you,' he said impatiently, slapping her hand away. 'Get back to your hammock.'

She felt for the edge of her hammock, and collapsed back into it. Then, a minute later, she heard Rebecca say soothingly, 'Here, Harry, have some coffee.' Harry would be all right, she told herself, feeling the fever wash over her again. In half an hour, maybe, they'd be able to lift him.

But not long afterwards, she heard him speak again, and realized he was back in his hammock. Remorse flooded through her. He hadn't meant 'Pick me up bodily'; he'd meant 'Help me'. Rebecca had understood, and done the work by herself, weak as she was, without saying a word. Jan was appalled at her own pettiness, and the whole misunderstanding. She should never, never have let that happen.

She was still berating herself when she fell asleep.

In the morning, when she sat up groggily to scoop a cup of water from the bucket beside her, Harry asked her: 'What was I doing sitting on the floor?'

'We pulled you into that position,' Jan replied, thickly.

'But how did I get there? Why was I there?'

'I don't know, Harry. We just knew you were there when we heard the crash of the boxes.'

'I fell among the boxes?'

'Yes.'

A pause. She felt herself slipping into unconsciousness again.

'I was coming back from urinating,' he said. 'I was getting into my hammock and missed.'

Peculiar, she thought, her mind falling. He must be weaker, or more confused, than she had . . .

❧

More days passed, unremembered.

But gradually, sometime in the second week of her illness, Jan became more aware of what was happening. She began to look after herself again, and remember what she was doing, reaching out now and then to take water from the blue bucket beside her, the bucket that was always full, with water that was always fresh. Although she must have performed the action all through her illness, she was also now aware that she got up two or three times a day to use the pot. Sometimes, she even emptied it herself, going out past the marimba to pour it down the slope towards the river. Sometimes, someone else emptied it for her – Rebecca, certainly, though Jan did not yet notice her movements.

And it was Rebecca who made the next diary entry (not that Jan knew anything about it until later). She would have done so only on Harry's instructions, for her words followed on from his previous entry of the week before. He must have decided he was too weak to make the effort himself. 'Friday, 11 January,' Becca wrote, in a hand made childish by weakness,

'Mag is the only one of us holding her own – tries to steal the pen but we are still struggling. God's will be done.'

Only once, when Jan asked for tea, did she register what Rebecca was doing.

'There isn't any, Janny,' came Becca's voice. 'I'll get more herb.'

Later, she nudged Jan awake to drink the tea. It seemed that the walk to fetch more herb had done her good.

'There's help for Maggie!' she said, sounding more like her old self. 'I was going up to the Garden Clearing when I heard monkeys. Then I saw them – a troop of uakaris, lots of them.'

The Garden Clearing. She shouldn't have let Becca go. Becca had too much to do as it was, she thought as she sipped her tea – the water, of course, that would be the major chore; but also the fire; the food; and, everlastingly, helping Harry with his hammock.

It was good to know she was up to his demands. Whatever disease they had, Becca at least seemed to be getting a hold of it at last.

🐾

It must have been hunger that forced Jan back to consciousness again, hunger or the need to relieve herself. No one had brought her food, and that worried her, for Harry, always solicitous *in extremis*, had been taking regular care of their eating. First, though, she had to use the pot. It was full – still full – and not wishing to impose on Becca, she rose groggily to her feet to empty it.

'Janny.' Becca's voice. She must have seen what her mother was doing. 'Don't empty your pot out the back any more. It's getting foul out there.'

Jan was surprised. The bank was steep and long. Well, perhaps she hadn't been taking it far enough. 'All right,' she said. 'Where, then?'

'Take it out the front.' Jan hesitated. Becca could only mean the pot should be emptied in or beyond the drainage ditch, a trip that was longer by several paces. She wasn't sure she had the strength. 'It's all right, Janny,' she heard Becca say then, for Becca must have seen her mother's weakness, 'I'll do it.'

With that task removed from her, Jan, impelled by her hunger pangs, went to Harry. 'Harry,' she asked, sitting down heavily on the box beside his hammock. 'What are you doing for food?' She didn't like to ask for food directly. That might have seemed like a criticism of him.

'Soaked *farinha*,' he said. 'I'm doing very well. What about you?'

'I'm hungry. I don't know what to eat.'

'That's no problem if you're willing to eat *farinha*. Tell Becca what you want, and she'll fix it.'

But it wasn't quite that simple. She didn't want to impose on Becca, didn't want to ask Harry, and had herself been banned from the kitchen area for years because she only got in the way. The unexplained, almost casual change of routine left her feeling lost.

'I'll get some,' she said, bleakly. She took her cup, and felt about clumsily until she found the *farinha* can, scooped out some of the coarse meal, topped it up with water, sat back in her hammock, and began to eat the soggy mixture with a spoon.

'You don't have to do that, Janny.' It was Becca again, right beside her now. 'I'll fix it for you properly.'

'No need, Becca. Are you still struggling with fever?'

'No. The fever's gone. I'm just so terribly weak.'

'Rest. Take your food. We have some good stuff from the last cargo delivery. This isn't the time to be saving it. We'll be in better shape to scrimp later on.'

As Jan's consciousness cleared, she attempted to impose some order on the chaos of the previous fever-ridden days. She recalled some comment about it being Sunday. We can't have a Sunday dinner, Harry had said, but next week we'll be better. She pieced together each little disconnected incident, placing it in order, and decided it must have been exactly two weeks since the disease struck.

Later, after dark on that first day of returning clarity, she heard Harry demanding Becca's help with his hammock. It seemed to Jan incredible, incomprehensible that he could make such demands at such a time. It was almost as if he used pain and discomfort as proof of his own vitality, as if to prove that those who didn't suffer as he did were insensible and foolish. She was still working through this idea in her mind when she heard Becca speak. 'I have to have your hammock, Janny.' Her tone was abrupt. 'I'm sorry, but it's necessary.'

'All right,' mumbled Jan. She wasn't feeling generous towards Harry, but she knew that if she protested, it would be Becca who would be blamed. 'I'll go back to my old hammock.'

'No. I had to take that for Harry as well. I had to take it apart. It didn't work. That's why I have to try this one.'

Becca sounded tense. Jan didn't know why Harry should be making such a fuss about different hammocks, but whatever the trouble was he shouldn't be putting such pressure on Becca. Still, Jan, thought, arguing herself into a calmer frame of mind, she might well not know enough about what was happening to risk a comment. After all, she couldn't hear much of what was going on – her hearing-aid was in its place in the box by Harry – and she reminded herself again how irritating it was for others to be asked for explanations all the time. Without demur, therefore, she gathered up her blanket, and moved.

While Becca untied the hammock, Jan went to lie on the pole flooring between Becca's hammock and the marimba. For a rough mattress, she felt for a ragbag of old clothes she knew was stuffed into the corner. When Becca came to check on her, Jan pretended to be asleep. She didn't want Becca offering her own hammock.

Next morning when Jan awoke, that was, of course, precisely what Becca did. '*Please* take it,' she urged. 'It'll make it easier for me to work out another place for yours.'

She sounded much better. Jan, relieved and grateful, lay down in Becca's hammock.

A little later, Becca brought over a small saucepan of soaked *farinha* with some sardines. 'Here, Janny, you can eat what you want now,' she said. 'It has a lid on, so you can keep the pan by you for later.'

Jan murmured her thanks. Those problems of the previous day about the food and Harry's hammock seemed to be solved. They were all on the mend, she thought as she ate. It had been a testing time, certainly, the worst they had had since their arrival on Homestead Hill, but not all that much worse than the six months of famine. At least this time they had food.

She lay back, and dozed, waking occasionally during the morning to sip water or eat, thinking ruefully of the time they had lost and the tasks to be done. Their first project of the new year – the rebuilding of the hearth – well, that might have to wait while they caught up on other tasks – mulching, weeding, more transplanting, harvesting pineapples, cleaning the house. She herself hadn't bathed for over two weeks. They must all be dirty and smelly. The house itself was damp, as always, and the flooring leaves were beginning to decay. So, too, was the pile of spare thatching leaves that lay behind the marimba. Yes, a lot to do, once they were strong enough to start work again.

If they were all improving, Jan thought when she next awoke, she ought to be more in touch. For that, she needed her hearing-aid. She stood up, felt for the pole shelf, and edged her way to Harry's corner, to the box which she used as a seat and in which she kept her hearing-aid, along with other objects of occasional use: batteries, pillowcases, string. Harry said nothing. He must have been asleep.

After she returned, her awareness suddenly expanded by her hearing-aid, she heard Becca moving about near her. Something about the way she moved worried Jan. There was an urgency, a tension, in the hurried, or ungainly, way she stepped on the bottom rungs of the loft-ladder to retrieve something from the rafters – food, perhaps, or a hammock. She seemed driven, too preoccupied to explain what she was doing, and Jan did not distract her with questions.

Later, though, in the early afternoon, when Becca brought her a cup of water, Jan took the opportunity to seek reassurance by asking, 'Have we enough water, Becca?'

'Some.'

'You don't have to go down to the river, do you?'

'There are storms out there, over the mountains. We can set out buckets to catch rain.'

Rain. That would be welcome. Harry would have relief from the heat, and it would save Becca the gruelling daily climb down to the river and back. Poor Becca. She must still be terribly weak, yet she went on, without complaint. Jan's heart went out to her. 'Becca, I love you,' she said, reaching out.

'I know you do, Janny,' Becca answered, stooping to give her mother a fond and gentle hug.

What Becca did for the rest of the afternoon Jan did not know at the time, and could only guess at later. After that exchange of hammocks the previous day, she had said she would put up another one for herself. She had time enough to do so now, yet for some reason did not. Perhaps instead of establishing herself in the house, she took a spare hammock outside, and tied it between two trees to sleep in the fresh air for an hour or two. She often did that for her afternoon siesta. In any event, the coming rain promised a cool spell, and she put on a cotton jacket in addition to her blouse, red sweater and heavy cotton skirt, the one which came down to below the calf as a protection against insects.

Perhaps she was already bringing the hammock inside again after her siesta, perhaps she had already begun to set it up in the aisle, beside the hearth – for that was where Jan later found it – and perhaps Harry, waking, interrupted her after a glimpse outside, urging her into action with quick, decisive phrases that Jan did not register. Hurry, Becca, the storm's coming, he might have said. Be dark in no time once that cloud gets here. The lantern. The buckets. The flashlight. Don't want to be caught out in the dark. Perhaps that was why Becca left the hammock half-hung, and why they were both outside as the light faded and the storm rolled towards them.

Jan, lying in her hammock, had no knowledge of where Harry and Becca were or what they were doing. She was aware only of the looming storm, of the day dying, of the heavy clouds curtaining off the remaining light. There were rumbles of thunder, coming closer.

She heard no noises, no conversation. From Becca's words earlier, she guessed the other two would already be outside with the buckets. Thinking she might be called upon to help, and determined not to risk wetting her hearing-aid, she got up again and replaced it in its box beside Harry's hammock.

She was pleased she had thought of doing that. It was a sign she was beginning to think straight again, a sure sign of recovery.

Then, as the storm clouds blanketed the mountains, and the light died, Jan realized she needed to use the pot. It was already full. Remembering Becca's request not to empty it down the river-bank, she set off with it towards the front, along the pole walkway, past the hearth. She hadn't walked without support for days, and not wishing to risk a spill by slipping or bumping into anything, she began to crawl, lifting the pot carefully in front of her, feeling her way.

She had scarcely moved more than a yard or two when she heard Harry call out, right beside her. 'Jan! Where are you going with that?'

'To empty it out of the front.'

'You don't have to do that!' A distant roll of thunder threatened to drown his words. 'There are two of us here to help!' he explained, loudly, but not unkindly. She recognized his tone. This is a well-run ship, he was saying, and her action was unnecessary. 'Get back to your hammock!'

She left the pot where it was, tucked in tight out of the way beside the kitchen boxes, and did as she was told. A flurry of rain, a forerunner of the storm, pattered briefly on the thatch. At any minute, she thought, pulling her blanket over her legs, Harry or Becca would tell her that the pot had been emptied and hand it to her to use.

But no one came to her, and no one spoke.

Her need to use it grew more urgent. Harry must have gone out again. Well, he was busy, obviously. They both were. She didn't want to be a nuisance. She felt around among the objects lined up under the eaves, and came across an old powdered milk can stored with the garden tools for use as a plant pot. She put it by her hammock, planning to take it outside and use that, if no one came.

The air was still now, breathless, the silence broken by the approaching thunder. If she had had her hearing-aid, she would have heard the faint murmur of rain sweeping in across the jungle, lashing at a billion leaves. Yes, the other two would be outside, setting the buckets on the washstand or under the eaves. But why were they taking so long? Perhaps they were still cleaning the buckets, perhaps they couldn't see well in the darkness, even with the flashlight. Or perhaps there was some other problem – thatching leaves that needed to be reset before the storm struck, the canoe's mooring to be checked.

Well, she couldn't wait any longer. She took her can, crawled along the pole walkway, reached for the stick she kept leaning beside the entrance, stood up shakily, and felt her way out. They would be around the corner, by the washstand, so there was a good chance they wouldn't see her. That was important. She didn't want to interrupt them at their work by revealing the urgency of her need, for Harry could easily see that as an implied criticism, and she didn't want to be seen disobeying the rule about not going out alone at night. She walked out unsteadily, leaning on her stick, breathing in the dampness that presaged the storm, feeling her way with her feet across the little log bridge that spanned the drainage ditch, past the chopping block to the spot where the path entered the forest. She used the can, and left it there, by a tree-trunk, so that Becca would find it the next morning, and be able to dispose of it where she wanted.

She walked back a few paces, and paused. No one called her, no one came to her. But between the claps of thunder, she could hear voices, raised and urgent, as if they were giving each other directions. Yes, they were busy at some new and vital task round the other side of the hut. She would be able to get back in without being seen.

She stepped forward again, and suddenly realized that, in pausing to listen, she had lost her sense of direction. She felt the ground rise beneath her feet. That told her she was heading the wrong way, towards the jungle. She turned, and this time felt the dip of the drainage ditch. Following it, she bumped into thatch. With a sharp sense of relief, she felt her way in, replaced her stick, walked back to Becca's hammock, supporting herself on the kitchen boxes and the shelf, and rolled the blanket tight around her for warmth to wait for Harry and Becca.

She felt quite pleased with herself. After two weeks of collapse, it was good to have accomplished such a trip on her own, without being a burden to the others.

She had returned just in time. The low roar of the approaching rain rose to a surf-like hiss. The storm struck. Outside, the forest dissolved into a pale mist, shot through every second by lightning. The thatch crackled like the trees themselves under the impact of the rain. Water cascaded from the eaves, the splashing torrents combining with cataclysmic claps of thunder to overwhelm the hissing of the rain on the surrounding forest. Jan felt the sudden cold the storm brought and wrapped herself up tighter, relieved at escaping the deluge, feeling a tingle of child-like excitement at the power and noise of the storm.

Surely they would be back soon. It should not take long to finish whatever they were doing, and they would want to get dry. Any moment now, they'd be in, and then it would be time for their evening drink – hot milk perhaps, made with milk powder and hot water – their goodnight prayer, and then sleep, with the fire banked up for the night.

Within a minute, the storm spent its first fury, and settled into a steady, drumming downpour. The torrents from the thatch became rivulets trickling from each pointed leaf.

Now that she had begun to eat again, the idea of hot milk seemed particularly good. She heard a movement from the other side of the hut. That would be Becca at the hearth, pushing the fire together, opening a kitchen box by the light of the lantern.

She asked loudly, to make her voice carry above the noise of the rain: 'What's the prospect of a cup of hot milk?'

It was not Becca. It was Harry. He called out. She couldn't make out what he said, but his tone, harrassed and urgent, implied he was too busy to attend to her right then. Perhaps he was already making the milk. That would explain why he didn't tell her what was happening. He was usually careful to explain things. Something was holding him up, then. He would be along soon as he could.

But no one came with hot milk. Well, there could be reasons for that. A new can to be opened, the fire to be built up. She wouldn't say anything or try to help. Any action by her might make her seem demanding. Besides, if the others were busy, she knew it would merely be a hindrance to have her wandering about, feeling with her arms out, getting in the way, forcing someone to stop and help her. Likely as not, there was no problem. So often in the past, she'd been crazy with anxiety, only to find that nothing was wrong at all. Nothing was wrong now, she told herself. No cause for anxiety. As the storm passed, and the downpour slackened to a drizzle, and the thunder became no more than a distant murmur, she willed herself to be patient. As far as she was concerned, they were all on the verge of recovery. Insisting to herself that all was well, she stretched her legs to ease the stiffness, rolled the blankets around her, and dozed.

🐝

When Jan awoke, she realized with a shock that she had heard nothing from either of them for far too long. At last, the need to make contact overwhelmed her.

'Aren't we going to foregather for our goodnight?' she called, with a trace of perplexity in her voice. Wherever they were, they would hear her now that the rain had stopped.

A moment later, Harry was beside her. He must have been somewhere close, in his hammock probably, to have responded so quickly. He sat down on the floor beside her, and said loud and clear: 'I'm not going to leave you alone at a time like this.'

His words did not seem strange. It had been a harsh time, and it was understandable that, in the wake of the storm, he should choose to be closer to her, to reassure her, especially as he had left her alone for so long.

He said nothing else for a minute, then: 'Our marriage is for ever, Jan.' His voice had dropped, and she leaned forward to hear him. 'We've had our difficulties, but nothing has ever really separated us.'

He'd switched tracks, but that, too, was usual. Jan waited for him to work through whatever thought was possessing him and tell her about Becca.

She felt him shift position. 'Harry, what are you doing?' she asked.

'Backrest,' he said. He felt for the sack of old clothing on which Jan had lain the previous night, and set it against the hammock at her waist. Then he leant against it, so that his back was cradled in the curve of her body, holding her firmly against the screen. 'Can't use a hammock any more. You don't know the struggle I've had to find a position free of pain.'

When he had settled himself, he said, 'You weren't here in the hammock earlier?'

'I . . . I had to go out,' she replied hesitantly, afraid of prompting his anger by admitting her disobedience. 'I didn't have the pot. How did you know I was out?'

'I sent Becca to get you. She came back saying you had gone, she didn't know where.'

Jan, dismayed at the image of Becca looking at the empty hammock, seemed to hear Becca's forlorn voice repeating: 'Janny's gone, Janny's gone.' But why had Becca not simply called for her? And why, when Becca reported her absence, hadn't they looked for her?

'I waited for you to empty the pot,' she said. 'But you didn't, so I had to go out with a can.'

'What? Don't remember anything about a pot.'

'Well, I went out.'

'Oh. So that's why she couldn't find you. We had no light. Maggie was up to her usual tricks again. She'd snatched the flashlight. Becca couldn't remember where the other one was.' Again, a shadow entered Jan's mind. Becca always knew where everything was. 'We just went round and round in the dark looking for it.'

He shivered, and she touched his shoulder. 'Are you having more chills?' she asked.

'No. This is cold. I'm past the chills. But I'm in dry clothes now. I'll be warm soon.'

He fell silent, and her mind began to wander, drawn by the image of the two of them hunting round for the flashlight in the rain and the dark, until she suddenly realized he was speaking again. '. . . Becca and I,' he was saying, 'Lying out there in the rain.'

'What?' she asked, startled.

'I thought she was behind me . . .' He spoke flatly, without emotion. 'But she was *under* me.'

Jan was puzzled. *Under* him? His words, without a context, summoned only a flurry of jarring images – someone slipping on rain-slick mud, a collision, the memory of Becca's words: 'I can't *stand* the idea of a man lying on top of me.' She cut the

264

images off. She could make no sense of them. She'd talk to Becca about it in the morning. Becca would explain.

'Neither of us could get up.' Harry went on, too quietly for her to hear every word. '. . . raining harder by then . . . All I know is, I sure was surprised when I picked up that bucket and there was nothing in it.'

They *had* fallen, then. But why? Some sort of outburst? Was that what he meant by 'surprised'? Sudden anger at something, at the loss of the flashlight, or a spilled bucket?

There had to be more. She waited, scarcely breathing.

'You know what she said?' he went on, after a pause. 'She said "There's more than one kind of martyr in this world."' He quoted her words in mild surprise, as if he found the remark inexplicable.

Strange words, she thought, but not a cause for surprise. Becca knew the price she was paying. She always had known. But what had Harry said or done to prompt such a remark? She made no comment, waiting for him to explain. He said nothing. It was she who broke the silence. 'And Becca's tired?' she asked, casually, not wishing to betray anxiety. 'She's gone to sleep already?'

He gave her no warning, no warning at all.

'She's finished,' he said, in the sort of voice he used when telling her something she should have known.

The shadows that had flitted briefly into her mind suddenly gathered together into a universe of storms, a nightmarish blackness, a gulf so horrific that her only defence was not to have heard. 'What?' she asked.

'She's finished. She didn't make it. She's gone, and we're going too.'

BOOK
II

10

'I'M GOING TO TRY FOR IT'

Shock erased her. She became pure shock, without body or mind.

She mouthed his word: 'Finished', but made no sound.

She knew that what he said was true. The horror had been with her for years, hidden, waiting. Now it had sprung at her, at last, from the darkness, and she accepted its presence utterly and instantly. Becca's spirit had broken free, and gone ahead to show them the way to a new beginning. She was gone, and they were going too.

'Mag had to be fed,' Harry said. 'And I told her to get Mag's milk. She said, "I can't", or groaned, and fell in front of the hearth. She never moved. I covered her with the old medium . . . no, the light . . .' He dithered, trying to decide which of the two spare hammocks he had used, '. . . no, the *medium* hammock, and got Mag's milk.'

'You fed Maggie?' Jan couldn't take in the incongruities – Becca had fallen, and died, and he had covered her, and then, calmly –

'You fed Maggie?' she asked again.

'Yes, I did. She's been taken care of. It was all I could manage, but I did it.'

Well, what did his words matter, now that she was only a breath away from following Becca? She was eager to follow, eager to escape the pain which she knew would engulf her if she lived. All she had to do was break through the fragile barrier of her body, and she too would be free.

'If she had lived,' Harry said, 'She would have married José. That would have been nothing but physical abuse.'

'Who?'

'José. That was what it was coming to. It's good she's the first to go. Without me to protect her, it would have been physical abuse, you understand that, don't you?'

'José?'

'José!' he said, impatient at her incomprehension. 'He brings the cargo!'

'Oh.'

Why did he go on speaking? There was no need for him to say anything. Becca was out there, watching, and listening, and waiting. There was no need for Harry to explain, or justify. Becca would explain everything, soon.

'The music on the radio is horrible,' Harry said. It was the first Jan knew of the radio being on. 'It was pretty good earlier, from Manaus. I have to try to turn it off.'

She felt him get up, laboriously. He returned a few minutes later.

'I only just about made that,' he said, panting. 'I can't walk any more. No matter. I'm ready. It may not be long. I checked. She hasn't moved.'

No, of course not. Becca had left her body behind. Had he forgotten?

'The news will get out, back in the States,' he went on. '"Americans dead in the jungle." How do you think it will get out first?'

'I don't know.' She didn't understand what his concern was. It was as if she was too removed to understand. But then his words penetrated her, and summoned an image: strangers looking into the hut, seeing bodies. 'It will look like Jonestown,' she said. The Jonestown suicides: 900 bodies decaying in the jungle. The image had haunted her for weeks after they heard the news on the radio fourteen months before. 'No one will know what happened.'

'I had Becca write a note in my journal when it looked as if we weren't going to make it. I've written as well. It's all there. They'll find it.'

270

Later, she wondered what his words – 'It's all there' – had implied. While Becca lay by the hearth, and Jan waited restless and puzzled for their goodnight, he had, instead of going to Jan, changed out of his wet clothes, fed Maggie, and gone to his hammock; and done what? Written up his journal? At the time, he told her nothing, and she, in her acceptance, asked him nothing. She simply waited for the end, in silence, numb, until sleep took her.

At one point during the night, she awoke, and felt a surge of impatience at her own continued existence. She reached out and touched Harry.

'You're still there,' he said. Then, a moment later: 'It could take some time.'

🦂

Jan awoke. It was daylight. She could hear a noise, a whiplash thudding that was familiar, yet so out of place it took time for her to recognize it. She touched Harry.

'Helicopter,' he said thickly. 'Engineers, looking at a bridge site, I guess. They better leave soon if they want to get home before dark.'

So it was late afternoon. She had been asleep, or unconscious, for twelve, perhaps fifteen hours. A helicopter. The men in it would be worried about the coming dark and about the jungle. They would be wrapped in their concerns, bound to the physical world. She pitied them their dependence, and welcomed her coming release the more.

But she couldn't go before Harry. She couldn't leave him behind, alone. Once he was gone, she would simply let go and allow herself to slip across the threshold to rejoin Becca.

She felt a pain in her stomach. Stomach cramps. Collapsing stomach, she thought, recalling the pain Harry described during his starvation in prison. The pain held her back. It annoyed her that such a useless atrophied body should continue to function, should refuse to let her go. She let herself slip, away from the pain, towards release, falling, falling . . .

No. Something held her. Harry was not coming with her. He was at a ceremony. There was a huge open field, a crowd, a podium. Harry was on the podium. He had saved the lives of twenty-seven dogs. Billy Graham was presenting Harry with a medal for saving the lives of the dogs, and making a long speech about how sympathetic and brave Harry was. Come *on*, Harry. Let *go*. But no: the speech went on and on, and Harry couldn't leave, and there was no going forward without him.

She woke briefly, knowing she had to hold on; then fell again into darkness.

🜩

But the darkness was not the darkness of death.

Deep in that night, Jan saw a face, saw it almost as clearly as if her eyes were healed. It was a female face, vibrant, luminous, achingly beautiful, familiar, but not consciously known. It seemed to promise so much, and she longed to recognize it. She struggled, in anguish, to know the face, to resolve the conflict between its loved and loving familiarity and her inability to put a name to it. She wrestled for knowledge as one wrestles to lever a forgotten word from the tip of the tongue. But the effort stirred up her conscious mind, and the image that hung before her began to dissipate and drift away. The more she struggled, the faster the image blurred.

She saw; and she also felt. As the face blurred, hands seemed to take her by the shoulders, and shake her, in a particular way, as a loving and indignant parent might shake a child to bring it to its senses, to force in upon it a heartfelt plea. The vision, now no more than a wraith, did not speak. But words formed in her mind, giving meaning to what she saw and felt: 'Don't *do* this! Just don't *do* this!'

The face vanished. The light died. Jan became conscious, with the feel of the hands as clearly imprinted on her as if she had just been thrown backwards in her hammock.

She lay trembling, too astonished to move. Slowly, as the

shock ebbed from her, she realized that the reality of the experience was within her. If she had been physically shaken, Harry, leaning against her, his back fitting precariously into the curve of her waist, would also have been moved. But no. He was still breathing heavily and regularly, asleep.

She was shaken, nevertheless, shaken into life and thought.

Becca was dead, that she accepted. But if Jan, in her anguish and her desire to be reunited with Becca, also accepted her own death, then Becca's life, the life Becca had chosen, would have been for nothing. Becca had always borne responsibility for her life. The decision to return to the jungle had been as much hers as theirs; she knew as much of the dangers; she had been as eager – more eager – to build the homestead. She should have lived to see the fruits of her work. But her death did not destroy what she had achieved; that could endure, through Jan. Surely Jan's aim should be not to emulate Becca's death, but to give meaning to her young life, and redeem her unlived years. She couldn't do that by dying. Dying for Becca – no, that was easy, she'd always been ready to do that. What she had to do was *live* for her, or try to.

There was no guarantee she could make it, she knew that. She was weak and ill and burdened both by her own infirmities and Harry's. If Harry died, she had no idea how she could cope with her blindness on her own. She might die anyway. But she knew now that her strength had not been tested to its limits. She would go on until it had.

At dawn, Harry woke. Jan felt the rhythm of his breathing change. 'Are you there?' he said, raising his head.

'Yes,' she answered, and then, without preamble: 'Harry, I think . . .' Her voice was faint. She had to force the words out. 'I think I'm going to try for it.'

There was a long silence. Then he said: 'All right.' That was all. No argument. No encouragement. 'It is taking a long time,' he added, after another silence. 'You're going to have to eat something. If you could eat something it would help.'

'When I get up I'll find something,' she said. She had not

prepared food for a long time. She hadn't been allowed near the fire for years. She didn't even know where the food stores were.

'There are the Sunday cans in back of you.' He was referring to the two or three dozen cans of vegetables they kept for Sunday meals as a supplement to their daily diet of *farinha*. 'Reach around.'

'There's no way to open a can,' she said, making no move.

'I can reach a machete down by my feet. I think I can make a stab at a can, if you get it for me.'

'All right,' she said, hardly registering that over the past two days he had apparently become so weak he couldn't reach the cans for himself.

She turned, felt along the floor under the screen, found a can, and handed it to Harry. The movement made her breathe more deeply. She became suddenly aware of the dampness of the house. The storm would have sent little trails of water winding in under the flooring leaves, wetting any old clothing on the floor.

'It's corn,' he said. She felt his jerky movements and heard the clink of metal on tin. 'I've got an opening in it. If you shake it, you can get a kernel at a time. I poured the juice away – too salty.'

'What about you?'

'Can't. But Mag will be hungry. She'll come. Feed her.'

Jan took the can, tipped it, and shook it. She felt a corn kernel fall into the palm of her hand. She ate it, chewing slowly.

Her action drew Maggie to her, as Harry had predicted. She gave the monkey a kernel, and ate another herself. It took a good shake to get the corn out. For an hour or more, she shook it out kernel by kernel, feeding herself and Maggie alternately.

As she ate, her mind cleared more. Maggie must have been in the hammock with her more often than she knew over the past two days, for she could feel items stolen from other parts of the house – a cup, a spoon, an old can-opener, a worn file – lying in the folds of her blanket. As she ate, she surreptitiously gathered them up and squirrelled them away to prevent them being taken again. After a while, exhausted, she set the can down beside her and slept.

She woke again to Harry's insistent calling. 'Jan! Jan! I'll give you milk if you reach some. There's a can close to you, to the right of the vegetables.'

'I'll have to get water to mix it.'

'The blue bucket is by the post, full. Reach back and you'll feel it. You need a cup.'

The blue bucket full? That puzzled her. The blue bucket had been taken outside with the others before the storm. Becca must have brought it in and placed it near her when she, Jan, had been out with her can. Again, she wondered why Becca, seeing her hammock empty, had not called out for her.

'I have a cup,' she said.

'Get me the can of milk, the spoon and a cup of water.'

She did as she was told. Harry levered the top off the can, and mixed up a slurry of milk for her. She drank it in silence, sharing it with him.

Abruptly, Harry half-turned and said: 'If you're going to make it, get out of the hammock and let me have it.'

He must have been painfully uncomfortable on the floor. He had been there for two nights and a day, without moving, as far as she knew. Later, she wondered why he didn't just go back to his own hammock, and concluded he was either too weak or wanted to be near her to be looked after. But at the time, she was too struck by the harshness of his tone – a tone he'd never used to her before during sickness – to question his actions. They changed places, laboriously. Jan resettled the clothes-bag to form a pillow, laid out some of her old Braille magazines to act as a protection against the rough saplings, and lay down.

'I could make you another cup,' he said, when he was settled.

275

She thanked him, drank the second cup, and asked for a third. After that, she felt she could eat something. 'I think I know where there's some guava preserve,' she said. 'Give me the spoon.'

She leaned to the end of the hammock and felt for a jar in which Becca had stored some leftover guava jam. Wiping the spoon clean on a sheet of Braille paper, she took a mouthful of the sweet, sticky mass. 'Want some?' she asked, offering a spoonful to Harry.

'Can't.'

'What?'

'Can't swallow. Sore throat. Even the milk burns.'

Jan ate several spoonfuls of the preserve, sharing it with Maggie. Then she wrapped her utensils – spoon, cup and file – in a rag to prevent the monkey stealing them.

'I can't stand this hammock any more,' Harry said after a while. 'Help me get out and fix up the bed.' Jan held the hammock steady while he levered himself out and rolled on to the floor. 'Prop me up!' he grunted. 'Give me my backrest! Hurry up, hurry up!'

Jan found some of Becca's discarded clothes on the ground, and shoved them under him, helping him to sit up. Then, holding the sack in position to act as his backrest until he said he was all right, she climbed again into the hammock.

An hour later, he wanted the hammock again. After another hour, he demanded the floor. So it went on, a move every hour or two, half a dozen moves through the night. Each time, Jan couldn't believe she had the strength to move, couldn't believe he could demand it of her, yet each time she responded, gasping for breath, sobbing as she forced her weak and wasted limbs to act.

🐒

Next morning, she again woke before Harry, and recalled how rarely she had not been woken by his voice. Sitting on her crumpled magazines, with Harry dozing in the hammock, she felt carefully round, made milk for herself and drank two cups straight off.

As she finished, Harry awoke. His first words made her freeze, cup in hand. 'You have to get the body out,' he said.

She didn't move, didn't want to move anywhere. The little space defined by her rough bed and the hammock beside her was a universe quite large enough. And the thought of acknowledging Becca's death directly, of touching her, was too awful to contemplate.

'Why?' she asked, fending off his demand.

'I heard animals in the night, coming in.'

'No animals,' she said quickly. Determined not to move, she cast about for reasons not to do so. 'No animals . . . I can't move.'

'You have to.'

No. She willed him to leave her alone.

'I don't know how,' she said desperately, thinking: not this, anything but this. She knew what happened to bodies in the tropics, and how quickly.

'Take a hold of the feet,' Harry went on, remorselessly, 'Take a hold of the feet and drag it out.' He said 'it', not her.' 'Take it as far as the ditch.'

'No. I . . .' She pulled herself into a sitting position, gasping, about to fight him again. But there was no escape, for she knew he was right. Animals or no, someone had to move the body before decay set in, or it would be too late. The insects would come, and perhaps even predators. He was too weak to move. It was up to her. 'I'll have to rest,' she whispered.

'Don't lie down!' he said sharply. For once, she felt perversely grateful for his harshness. He knew how to drive her, and she needed to be driven. 'If you lie down, you won't get up. Just sit if you have to rest, but you better get started. It has to be today.'

She knew she couldn't walk. Two days without food and the shock of Becca's death, on top of the illness, had left her too weak. She would have to crawl. She felt with her feet for her sandals, and tipped herself forward on to her hands and knees, feeling her sandalled feet scuff up pages of Braille, feeling dampness come through her slacks.

She began to crawl.

Becca's body lay fifteen feet away, round the corner from her, on the walkway beside the hearth. As she turned the corner, she felt a tumbled pile of paper and a dropped cup. The thin saplings of the walkway were rough with peeling bark. Two of them were half rotten, and oozed mud on to her hands and knees. Something brushed her face. A hammock, right in the passageway, hanging loose. Becca must have put it there the afternoon of the storm, and been interrupted in her task. She shouldered the hammock aside, feeling it slide along her body.

She became aware of the weakness of her failing limbs and the chaos around her, the mouldy stench of wet cardboard, of storm-dampened palm leaves with the slick mud beneath, the scatterings of food, the flotsam of their ruined lives. The chaos wove itself around her. She was not much more than an arm's length from the body when she knew suddenly that she couldn't do it, couldn't. What Harry asked was impossible. Everything was impossible: moving, eating, living. She stopped, bound by the horror and the chaos.

As she knelt, empty and incapable, her mind slowly opened, and into it trickled a germ of feeling – a yearning, a curiosity, not expressed in words, to know what lay beyond the impossible. Kneeling on the muddy poles, unmoving, she became aware that she possessed strength beyond anything she had guessed at, and remembered where it came from. It was hers by right of birth, inherited from her father. 'Well,' she told herself firmly, and if she had spoken the words aloud they would have come out in a cheery, conversational tone, quite inappropriate, 'Well, I'm still Bill Muller's daughter.'

The words cut her free.

She crawled forward.

She felt something – cloth, yes, the hammock that Harry

278

had placed over her, and an arm. It was as if Becca were asleep. Perhaps, Jan thought, grabbing at this possible shred of comfort, perhaps she didn't need to go on. Perhaps Becca was just that, asleep. That was the way she always handled illness. She'd sleep for a long time, not saying anything. Soon she would wake up, and they would tell Harry and laugh and, in days to come, talk about the time when they thought Becca had died.

Her fingers brushed skin – Becca's cheek, uncovered. It was cold, and soft, almost as if ready to dissolve.

She drew back and sat, empty, all thought erased again by the certainty of Becca's death.

Take a hold of the feet.

How? She would not have the strength to grasp. She needed something to pull with. Something of Becca's, something suitable. She turned to the line of kitchen boxes alongside her. In one was a collection of towels. She opened the hinged top and felt through the box until she found the towel she was looking for, one that Becca had embroidered herself with a pattern of leaves and flowers. She lifted it out, and crawled with it to Becca's feet.

One leg was partly drawn up. Becca had fallen in step, as it were, on her front, with her face turned sideways. She was barefoot, and her clothes damp. She would have been chilled, coming in from the rain. The image filled Jan's eyes with tears. The fire had gone out, and Jan had been lying snug in her hammock, while Becca, dying, had lain there in the cold and wet.

Weeping, Jan looped the towel round the ankles, levered herself into a squat, took up the towel and leant back.

At that moment, from right behind her, there came a sharp cry.

'Cat!' she thought, recalling Harry's words, and was frozen by a double certainty – that she was about to feel the weight of a jaguar or puma on her shoulders, and that she could not abandon Becca's body.

She waited, every fibre rigid with anticipation.

Nothing happened.

She braced herself, and again, as if in response to her slight movement, came the cry. Again she paused, and leant back, and again the cry came. Three cries, strange and otherworldly, as if from the heart of the anguished forest itself.

A fourth time, she took the strain. Now the silence remained unbroken. She leaned back, straining against the weight of her burden. Nothing happened. She felt she was about to slip. Her feet in the rubber-soled sandals had no grip.

She pulled herself up against a hearth post, and pushed off her sandals. Then she squatted down again, feeling her feet forming themselves to the roundness of the poles, and heaved. Still no response. Again she pulled, to the limits of her strength. This time, the body slipped two inches towards her.

Perhaps if she could get a better purchase it would be easier. Right alongside her was the box in which rope was kept. She took out a rope, one they had used for mooring *Piaroa*, wound it round the feet over the towel, and tried again.

No good. The rope was harder to grip than the cloth. She untied the rope, replaced it, and repeated her first set of actions – two initial tugs to take the strain, then a final desperate, lung-wrenching heave that moved her burden a few inches. The effort drained her. She paused, panting, squatting on her haunches. After a minute, she pulled again, and then again, with long pauses to recover.

For an hour, she worked. In that time, she moved Becca's body six feet, so that it lay just outside the hut.

She could do no more.

She crawled back to the entrance, feeling for the hearth to guide herself in. Then, to find her sandals, she raised herself against the hearth and reached with her foot across the sapling floor, feeling back and forth.

Beneath her foot, she felt something soft and furry. She bent down to retrieve the object – a misplaced cloth, perhaps, or a piece of clothing, though she gave no thought to what it might be. She lifted it, and felt it, and with a shock that drained the life from her limbs she realized:

She was holding Becca's scalp.

Her mind went blank. She became a void, waiting for whatever might happen to her. If I am going to go mad, she thought, it will be now, *this minute*. Feeling the hair fall loosely over her hand, she stood ready to welcome any release.

None came.

As the shock of her discovery flowed from her, thought returned, strangely rational: Now I know why Indians took scalps. Scalps come loose after death. Only much later did she understand (or thought she understood) why it had come loose. The rough saplings had caught Becca's hair, and sheared the decomposing skin.

She felt her sandals, slipped them on and dropped again to her knees. She knew what she had to do. She would find a pillowcase, one of those Harry kept in his box. She crawled forward, with the hand carrying the scalp bunched into a fist, back into Harry's corner, without attracting his attention. She took out the pillowcase, and gently placed the scalp in it, folding the end of the material over. Then she replaced the little parcel in the box, right at the bottom, where it would not be easily found either by Harry or by the cargo-men, when they came.

Finally, she moved slowly back around the centre post to Becca's hammock, where Harry still lay.

'Done?' he asked, hoarsely. He seemed to be having trouble speaking.

'Yes.' No need to go into details. Instead, she had a question of her own. 'Those cries – you heard them?'

'Hawk.'

'Hawk?' The explanation was too simple. It didn't match the power of her experience: the fear, the apprehension, the significance. 'What kind?'

'Don't know.'

She didn't question him further. She'd never heard a hawk.

Even if he was right – and he knew his birds, after all – the noises were not to be so easily explained away. The sorrow and the loss were not hers alone. Rebecca was of the wilderness, and the wilderness had cried out in anguish at her death.

🦁

The next morning, after making herself a cup of *farinha* and water flavoured with chocolate powder, Jan crawled back along the walkway to continue her task. This time, she felt the pot she had placed carefully by the kitchen boxes on the night of the storm. Lifting it in front of her as she crawled, she emptied it outside, and placed it under the marimba.

Outside again, feeling her way to Becca's feet, she set herself to repeat her actions of the previous day, squatting, pulling, resting, moving back. After several heaves, as she moved backwards, her foot struck something hard. She picked it up. It was the flashlight, the one Harry and Becca had been searching for on the night of the storm. She set it aside, and continued with her labour, inch by inch, for perhaps two hours, or a century, until exhaustion overcame her will.

Inside, she showed the flashlight to Harry. Astonished, he asked where she had found it. When she told him, he said they'd been looking much further away. 'We went round and round,' he said, puzzled.

Throughout the day, every hour or two, Harry insisted on changing from floor, to hammock, to floor again, to gain some relief from discomfort. Late in the afternoon, he called her and grunted something. His voice seemed to be worse, and she had trouble understanding him. She bent her head right down to his mouth. 'Oil,' he said, hoarsely. 'Oil.' He meant palm oil. When she brought it to him from its place in one of the kitchen boxes, he said, 'Rub.' She tried to open the can, and struggled vainly for a few minutes, until she thought of using the file as a lever. Pouring oil into her cupped hands, she felt him guide her to the sore spot beneath his buttock. She noticed for the first time that he wasn't wearing trousers, just a long, loose shirt. He must have taken his wet trousers off when he came in past Becca, and not bothered to put on dry ones. When she felt the spot, she found it was a raw area the size of her hand. Anything like clothing or a hammock against that must have been agony. She understood his pain, and rubbed him gently. He could, of course, have applied the oil himself, but she was so used to ministering to him that the thought never even occurred to her.

The next day, when Jan went to prepare food, she found that Maggie had taken all the kitchen utensils from their place in one of the kitchen boxes. Maggie, you pest, she thought, scavenging under the hearth for a piece of bark to use as a spoon. For Harry's breakfast, she used the only good tin-opener to open some tomato purée, which she diluted. When she offered it to Harry, he said 'Thank you', but took only a few sips.

After that, Jan crawled out, and for the third time dragged Becca's body until she reached a small depression, which she thought must be the drainage ditch. It was far enough. There she left the body, still clothed, and still covered by the cotton hammock.

Now she had to find out where the rest of the food was. She spent the remainder of the day on her knees feeling through the boxes to identify the cans of fish, the chocolate, the powdered milk, the preserves, some cloves of garlic. In one large can, which had once contained food, she found the second flashlight. This was exactly where it should have been, yet Becca had forgotten it was there, Harry had said. So many mysteries, such sorrow that Becca should have been too weak, too driven, too ill to remember. She put the flashlight with the other in Harry's box, to protect them both from Maggie's predatory hands. Then, although she was still too weak to walk, she did manage to climb the loft-ladder far enough to feel the food stored in the rafters – a case of canned sardines, a bag of beans and a dozen leaf-lined baskets of *farinha*.

When she came down, exhausted, she collapsed to her knees by Harry, scooped out some water from the blue bucket, drank, and offered Harry a cup. He tried to say something.

'What, Harry?'

He made a noise.

'What?'

He took her arm, and began to write letters with his finger: C. H. O. C. . . .

'Chocolate?'

'Uh.'

She mixed powdered milk and chocolate with the water, and handed it to him. But after only a few sips, he passed the cup to Maggie. Then he insisted on moving again from hammock to floor, leaning on her heavily. Once there, he ordered her to arrange and rearrange the clothes-bag – 'Take something out,' he snapped. 'No good . . . build it up . . . build it *up*' – until she was weeping with fatigue and frustration. Only when he had grunted his satisfaction could she fall into an exhausted sleep in the hammock beside him.

Several more times during the night, he nudged her awake to change places. Eventually to escape his demands, she felt her way round behind the kitchen boxes, to his old hammock, and collapsed at last into undisturbed sleep.

🦌

Early the next morning, she awoke to Harry's insistent calling. There was something else, too, something she couldn't bear to think about. Becca's body had been out in the sun no more than three days, yet already the nauseating smell of it permeated the house.

Still unable to stand well enough to walk, she crawled to him.

'Ar-ha!' he said. 'Ar-ha!'

'Harry, I don't understand.'

'Ar-ha!'

Suddenly she felt a sharp blow on her head, and a cup thrust into her hand.

'Water?'

'Aha.'

She scooped up some water for him, and crawled back to her corner, until, a few minutes later, he called her to him again.

'Where is Rebecca?' he asked.

The question appalled her. She had no idea how to describe where she had left the body. She didn't know if she had fulfilled his instructions – 'Take it as far as the ditch' – or not. She tried to speak, and failed.

But he was not, after all, referring to the location of her body. 'Where is Rebecca?' he repeated. 'She used to come around sometimes during the day, you know.' His tone was quite conversational. He might have been referring to a casual acquaintance. 'Where is she?'

The implications of his words – derangement? denial? – were too much for her to take in. She replied only to the question as she had first understood it. 'In the ditch, Harry – where you told me to –'

'What day is it?' he interrupted, as if he had suddenly remembered the truth, and was unwilling to face it.

'I don't know.'

'Are we –' his voice sank as an appalling thought struck him. 'Are we . . . *all alone*?'

'Yes.'

She sat beside him in blank silence for a while. Then he asked for more water. She dipped the cup into the blue bucket. There was hardly anything left in it. 'Water's outside, Harry,' she said.

She crawled out past the hearth and round the corner to the washstand. This time, when she returned, she walked in order to keep the water from spilling, reaching for post after post for support.

When she offered him the cup, he said, 'You first,' in what she thought was an odd tone. Perhaps he was being considerate. Sometimes, when reminded of the sufferings of others, he was capable of that. But there was a slyness in his voice, as if he didn't trust her, almost as if he thought the water might be contaminated, poisoned even. He added something else she couldn't hear. He didn't repeat it, but, as she sipped, it struck her how isolated they were from each other by his weakness and by her deafness. She needed her hearing-aid. The battery was weak, but it would be better than nothing.

She made her way to Harry's box, where she had carefully replaced the aid before the storm. It was a finicky thing, and she knew it would be attractive to Maggie in her present mood. She hunched over the box, protectively, even though Maggie didn't seem to be around. She felt for the aid, and lifted it, and in that instant, felt it jerk in her hand.

'Maggie, no!'

Too late: she had not thought to hold tight to the little lead and the ear-mould. With horrified apprehension, she felt along the lead. The mould was gone, snatched right off its connection.

She sat for a moment, struggling to bring her anger and despair under control. 'Maggie!' she shouted, her voice breaking. But shouting for Maggie would do no good. By now, she would have bitten the mould and dropped it somewhere on the floor amidst the mud and damp leaves. 'This finishes me!' she said out loud, weeping. 'Finishes me!'

It took her several minutes to regain control of herself. Then she countered self-pity with action. She replaced the useless hearing-aid, and began crawling among the flooring leaves, sifting through them with her fingers, ranging methodically back and forth to trace the things that Maggie had stolen. After a while, she had gathered a small pile of spoons, cups, and two or three knives, but no ear-mould. She wiped the utensils clean, put them in the kitchen-box, and carefully closed the lid.

Her work was all for nothing. The next day, when she went for a cup and a spoon to make her *farinha* breakfast, all the utensils were gone again. She knelt, overwhelmed by renewed despair and confusion, feeling the box incredulously, until her hands told her what had happened. The box had two hand-holes in its sides. Maggie had reached in and teased out each knife, fork and spoon one at a time. Relieved to have solved the mystery, she blocked the holes by lining the insides of the box with a couple of sheets of cardboard, and then wearily started her search all over again, fingering through the flooring leaves. What else, Jan wondered despairingly, what else could Maggie do to undermine her?

🦇

Now the days and nights, the successive periods of activity and collapse, began to run together in her mind. Harry's demands and her own exhaustion were like a second illness. Incessantly, every hour or two, Harry called her. She would register the sharp single syllable, and know that he had called her name. It was peculiar. Before, he had always called for Becca. Now, only Jan. He knew Becca was dead, then. Yet not once did he mention her.

In the mornings, he was particularly insistent. When she awoke, she needed food. She had to have energy to operate at all. But he demanded instant attention, hurrying her to help him take off his nightshirt and his socks, to fetch the water, to wash his face, to comb his hair.

Sometimes, by the time she got to him, he was asleep again. Sometimes, he had forgotten what he wanted. Sometimes, it was drinking water he wanted, or an oil-rub. Occasionally, but less frequently as time went by, he wanted to move from hammock to floor, or floor to hammock.

Over this time – perhaps a week, perhaps ten days – she gained strength enough to walk again. Along the walkway, about five feet from the ground, above the kitchen boxes, ran the strong pole shelf. By pulling herself up to the shelf, and then using it as a support, she managed several paces. After a few days of practice, she found she could stand up and walk out to the drink-stand with no help other than her stick.

Now based in Harry's hammock, and able to give herself food, she became the homesteader, responding like an automaton to the practical demands of existence, drawing on her years of disciplined and self-disciplined training. If she was to remain active, if she was to go on helping Harry, she could not afford to face what had happened. She would drown in grief. Any spare moments between work and sleep she filled with the radio. Sitting on Harry's box, with the radio tucked up on her shoulder against her ear, she could hear well enough, or thought she could, and became eager to establish the date. On three successive days, she tuned in to the BBC's World Service, and managed to hear the day of the week: Tuesday, Wednesday, Thursday.

But only on the Friday of that week, listening to 'Voice of America', did she also hear the date: 29 January. That was the first concrete piece of information she had had from the outside world for almost a month. It gave her enough of an anchor in the sea of her confusion to begin working out a chronology of events over the past month. On 30 December, the disease had struck; for so many days had she been conscious; she had made this move and that move from hammock to hammock, and then – nothing. She worked backwards from the present, counting the days since her re-emergence into full consciousness, and thus, repeating and checking her fuddled memories, she worked out that Becca had died on 19 January.

She climbed out of her hammock to tell Harry the date she'd heard.

'Not right,' he protested. 'February's gone.'

'No. It's still January. Friday, 29 January.'

In fact, they were both wrong. In 1980, 29 January was a Tuesday.

🐝

Maggie, meanwhile, was becoming increasingly distraught at the collapse of her little world. Jan's slow, stumbling movements must have destroyed the last shreds of Maggie's confidence. Frustrated and fearful, she turned from acts of vandalism to outright violence, directed at Jan. She took to leaping on Jan's shoulders, especially when she was crawling, as if attempting to force her out of such unusual behaviour. She would nip at her exposed arms and scratch and bite at her head in random, unexpected assaults that left Jan weeping, and shouting 'Maggie! No!' So vicious were the attacks that Jan took to wearing a headscarf and a long-sleeved shirt for protection.

After two days of this, it became clear to Jan that Maggie might soon threaten her survival. Maggie could bite through nuts that were hard to crack even with a stone. One full-power bite in the head could incapacitate her, Jan realized, and even a lesser nip in a foot, ankle or knee could cripple her for days, prevent her getting food and water, and reduce her, and Harry, to starvation. She realized that she might have to defend herself by force. There seemed only one way of doing so. She set aside a piece of rope in the box beside Harry's hammock, and decided that if the worst came she would seize the rope and strangle Maggie. The idea of killing anything appalled her; the idea of killing Maggie, whose life they had saved, who trusted them for protection, who was as much their jungle child as Rima had been, hardly bore thinking about. Yet she might have no choice, if the attacks continued.

She confided her dilemma to Harry, not so much hoping that he would have a solution as seeking to resolve the problem in her own mind. 'I might have to do it, Harry,' she finished, her voice trembling, 'But I just can't imagine what it would be like afterwards, having to live with such a thing.'

He held her hand, and pulled her head down to his mouth. 'No,' he said, 'Love will be your way.'

Love? She didn't see how that helped her in practical terms, but his words did give her strength. She would endure the next few days, at least. Perhaps in that time she would find a solution.

That decision suggested an idea. Perhaps, she thought, she could recreate for Maggie something of her lost security by feeding her mouth-to-mouth, as she had fed Rima. Perhaps that would calm her.

She was grateful for Harry's idealism. But it also puzzled her. 'Love will be your way.' He could talk of love for Maggie; yet he had still made no mention of Becca, nor any acknowledgement of Jan's loss.

'Harry,' she said, after a long silence. 'Don't you grieve for Becca?'

'No. I think of Cambodia.'

She was stunned. How could he find it in him to grieve for the world's children, yet express no grief for his own step-daughter? He had wept for Es, for Rima, and for Hanuman, yet never a tear for Becca. She could not understand how he could so absolutely reject what had happened. Was it fear, she wondered, fear of her overwhelming grief?

Or of his own?

🦋

One evening, around the turn of the month, after she had settled him down and gone to sleep, she heard him calling her. He was shouting her name over and over again, and making a banging noise with something. When she reached him, she found he was striking the ground with the flat of his machete. 'Animals!' he shouted, between blows. 'I heard animals! No light! Can't see!'

She felt a momentary pang of fear, and dismissed it. Never, in almost five years, had a large animal come into the house. Anyway, even if he had heard something, the noise would have driven it away by now.

'There's nothing I can do, Harry,' she said wearily, and returned to her hammock.

As she lay there, though, she felt a fresh wave of pity for

him. No doubt that his fear was genuine. She was used to darkness; but he had not slept without fire, or a light of some kind, for twenty years.

The following morning, Harry asked for a flashlight. She gave one to him. He flicked the switch a few times. 'Doesn't work!' he said, concerned perhaps at his inability to see if any animal should come in at night. 'New batteries.'

Jan found some new batteries in the box beside his hammock, and gave them to him.

An hour later, he called her again.

'New batteries!' he commanded.

'Harry, I gave them to you.'

'Oh. Yes. Four batteries here, in my lap. Asleep.' He paused. 'Which ones?' he asked. Jan was puzzled. She supposed he wasn't certain which were the new and which the old batteries.

'Harry, how should I know?'

'New batteries! New batteries!' he demanded.

'I *gave* you new batteries, Harry.'

'Oh. Yes.' Then: 'Other flashlight.'

She gave that one to him as well. He fiddled with them both for a while, then called her again. Pulling her down so that he could speak directly into her ear, he said, 'You can use this one by moving this part here.' He spoke slowly, forcing the words out. 'Remember you can't use the switch.'

'That's fine, Harry. Thank you,' she said, as she took the flashlight. 'But it's all right. I won't be using it.'

'Why not?'

'Harry, I can't see.'

'Can't *see*?' He sounded astonished at the news. 'Can't see,' he repeated, thoughtfully. 'Can't see.'

🦂

Two or three days later, Jan found she was shivering.

'Harry,' she said, as she offered him some diluted tomato purée. 'I have to lie down. Chills starting. It's malaria.'

This time, she knew it really was malaria, a relapse brought on by illness. The disease, long dormant, had crept out of some recess – liver, probably – and re-established its hold. She also knew there would be a pattern to the disease – a daily bout of icy shaking and sweating, sleep, then release until the next day. If the attacks were not too bad, she could plan for them, and arrange her work accordingly.

Over the next few days, as the severity of the attacks increased, she established a rigid schedule for herself. In the morning, she fed Maggie, who was calmer now that routine was re-established, and ate her regular meal of *farinha*, sardines, guava preserve and garlic. Then she tended to Harry, helping him change his nightshirt and socks, providing him with water and offering a little food, which he never touched. Sometimes, he wanted his sore patch of skin oiled. After she had set him up for the day, she returned to her own hammock to endure, in near unconsciousness, the three or four hours of chills and fever, awaking in the late afternoon to eat and drink again.

Often, she woke during the night, even when he hadn't called. The smell from outside was worst at night. It was during these times, when she was free both of Harry's demands and of the fever, that she began the struggle to confront what had happened. She failed; time and again she failed. She knew Becca was dead. But she simply could not take in the enormity of it. She was still wrapped up in the practicalities of survival. 'Becca's gone, Becca's gone,' she would say, but the words had no impact. For the moment, there were few tears. She could find no way to understand, to reach, to release the grief that lay buried within her.

And still Harry did not speak Becca's name. For a while, she focused on that grief – a substitute for the larger grief – and felt a bitterness towards him. That was wrong, she told herself. Harry must surely be suffering, as she was. She fought to make herself believe that he was grieving.

To help her in her struggles, she read Braille sermons, the

292

sermons that had been coming to her for a year or so from the Christian Science publishing house in Boston, and which had so often gone unread. There was comfort in the very act of reading, and in the subject-matter: love and forgiveness. She clung to those words, seeking to rise above Harry's refusal to sympathize, and his demands, and the poison of her own bitterness.

Only once did she manage to approach the subject of Becca's death with Harry. One morning, she told him: 'I dreamed of Becca last night. I dreamed we came to a garden . . .' Her voice faltered and died.

She felt his hand on hers: the first, and only, acknowledgement of her loss.

🐾

Then, as the malaria attacks increased in severity, she had no clear idea of anything. She must have followed her schedule, but all memories were erased, except one. She noticed that the water on the washstand outside was getting low. It had been almost a month since the storm, and there had been no rain since.

'Harry,' she said, as she gave him his cup of water that morning. 'I'll have to go the river for water.'

'No. Too much. There's enough water.'

He was wrong. They would soon run out of drinking water, and besides, she had to wash – she'd been getting in and out of the same pyjamas and slacks since before Becca's death. But she welcomed the excuse not to try, for another day or two at least.

🐾

Three days later, the water was too low to be ignored any longer. Still there was no sign of rain.

'Harry,' she told him, 'I'm going to have to try to go down to the river.'

'We can get by.'

'No, we can't. I'll have to go.'

'All right,' he said, after a pause. 'But I want to see.'

'How?'

'Get me into the aisle. Other spare hammock. Close weave.'

She understood he didn't want to go into the hammock Becca had half-hung in the passageway. She would have to take that down, he said. The weave was wrong – too loose. She would have to replace it with a close-weave hammock that lay stored in the rafters.

The business of finding and tying up the close-weave hammock took hours. She couldn't hear his shouted instructions, failed to find the hammock in the loft, and had to return to him for more detailed guidance. Then it took her an age to find the right poles, tie the knots correctly, with the rope at just the right length to keep the hammock taut.

When it was finally done – it must have taken two or three hours in all – and she was back beside him, he reached for her shoulder and heaved himself up. Leaning on her heavily, he shuffled round the corner and settled into the aisle hammock. By then it was too late to go for water. She would go the next morning.

An hour later, he called her again. When she reached him, she couldn't understand what he was saying. He seemed to be giving little grunts. She put her ear to his mouth, and discovered he was crying. 'Meal,' he sobbed. 'Falling.'

She felt something dribbling on her head. Maggie had poked a hole in one of the leaf-lined *farinha* baskets above him, and grains were trickling on to him. He was weeping with frustration.

She stood on the hearth-bench, felt for the opening in the basket lining, and pulled a leaf across the hole to seal it. But Maggie was still up there. As soon as Jan stepped down, Maggie playfully pulled her handiwork apart, releasing another stream of grains on to Harry. Twice more, she sealed the leak; and each time, Maggie undid the repair.

'Move me back!' Harry commanded. But when she tried to support him, he couldn't even stand.

There was only one solution: she would have to rig a tarpaulin above him. For an hour, two hours she worked. To find the tarpaulin, to set it in position, to recall by touch where exactly she was meant to tie it, to fix each corner – each action demanded that she hold a model of the hut in the forefront of her mind as she worked. Any lapse, any noise from Harry or touch from Maggie, was likely to disturb her, leaving her standing in stony concentration, feeling gently with hands and feet, to restore the image and continue her labour.

🦎

Next morning, she told Harry she was going for water. He insisted he would watch her go, and added, 'When you get to the water, shout,' not that there was anything he could do if she was in trouble.

Jan took one of the buckets from the washstand, picked up her snake-stick, and, with Maggie capering round her, tapped her way out of the house towards the bank. She closed her mind to the smell coming from the ditch to her left, and concentrated on her direction. It was her first time away from the house for weeks, her first solo trip to the river for months, and the first time ever that she'd had no one to check the trail for snakes.

On the descent, all went well. The steps down the bank were still familiar. Jan checked her position with the big tree at the bend two thirds of the way down, felt the stone step beneath her sandalled feet, and, sliding her hand along the guard-rail, picked her way down over roots and across the fifteen feet of gently sloping flood plain until she came to the smooth-barked tree, with its own guard-rail still intact, sloping down into the water.

She parked her snake-stick, took off her shoes, stepped on to the trunk, and gingerly edged her way towards the water, gripping the pole railing, feeling the narrow, barkless wood steep and dangerously smooth beneath her bare feet. The trunk seemed to go on for ever, for it was the dry season, and the river was very low. Eventually, her feet splashed into water. Remembering her instructions, she yelled: 'I'm here!' She looked about her, hoping to sense some familiar shadow, but she saw only flashes of water-reflected light, dim reminders of good times spent down here with Becca.

Still holding the guard-rail, she squatted, dipped the bucket, and heaved it back on to the trunk between her legs. With one hand, she splashed some water from the bucket on to her sweaty face, and had a sudden image of how filthy she must be. Filthy body, filthy clothes. But she couldn't risk bathing, not yet.

The return journey would, she knew, be incomparably harder. 'I'm coming back!' she yelled. She didn't dare stand, not with the full bucket. If she slipped, the guard-rail wouldn't hold her. She crouched and shuffled sideways, lifting the bucket a foot at a time beside her, splashing herself with water.

At the far end of the trunk, she stood up, stepped carefully on to the ground, and put on her sandals. She left her snake-stick, planning to fetch it later. 'Come on, Maggie,' she said, and carried the bucket to the trail leading up the bank.

The effort had already exhausted her. Even as she felt the ground rise and roughen beneath her, she realized she would not be able to walk up. She would have to crawl. She hefted the bucket up the first few steep feet, knelt beside it, and lifted again.

Suddenly, something smacked into her head, tearing at her hair.

'Maggie! No!' she shouted. 'No! No! No!'

With a couple of quick bites, delivered as Jan slammed the bucket down and flailed with her arms, Maggie fled back into the darkness from which she had sprung, leaving Jan stunned, staring round uselessly, slowly realizing what must have happened. Maggie, seeing Jan change again from an ordinary human into a four-legged monster, had attacked as she had a few days before in the hut.

For a moment, Jan thought the incident was over. She raised the bucket again, lifted – and again came the weight of quick little limbs, hands scrabbling at her scalp, the sharp pain of teeth on her head and neck, a cry from Jan, arms flailing, and a sudden retreat.

Jan felt panic rising in her.

She paused, ready for another attack. None came. But she couldn't stay on the alert for ever. She stood, irresolute, wondering in desperation what she could do. Nothing. She had no choice but to continue, knowing that from now on every step would be a skirmish.

So it was. She needed all her strength and all her concentration to move at all, yet at every movement Maggie was there to torment and shatter her. Lift, stand, kneel, lift, 'Maggie! No!', stand, kneel, an eternity of effort, and pain, and panic, until finally, distraught, bleeding from a dozen little bites, she was at the top.

Only to find no familiar path beneath her feet. Maggie had destroyed her sense of direction. Somehow on the way up she had taken a wrong turn. She felt with her feet, hands tight around the bucket handle, but no, nothing was familiar any more. No shadowy clues filtered through the grey of her blindness. There was no way of telling which way she had come, or what lay ahead. Just a few steps more, and she could be permanently lost, wandering in the maze of the surrounding jungle.

And then, as if to punish her for failure, Maggie came at her again, scratching and biting at her head.

Jan, gripping the bucket, helpless to defend herself, shook her head in an agony of frustration, and, at last, screamed.

Maggie fled.

Silence fell.

In the silence, she heard, vaguely, a noise, an irregular thumping.

Harry. Harry was hitting something, hitting the hearth with a stick.

The sound came from close by, in front of her and a little to the right.

All at once, she knew where she was – by the washstand. Under the disturbing impact of Maggie's assaults, she had come up by a much steeper path, a short cut favoured by Becca.

Confidence flooded back. Maggie, reassured, stayed clear. Jan covered the last few feet, lifted the bucket on to the stand, found a cup, and brought Harry some water.

He muttered something.

'What, Harry?' she asked, lowering her head.

'Earned your rest,' he said. 'Don't go again.'

'Don't worry,' she said with a confidence she didn't feel, 'Now I've made it, I can get water whenever we need it.'

She collapsed into her hammock, pleased with her achievement, ready for the midday onset of malaria.

🐝

That one bucketful – or rather what was left of it by the time she reached the top of the bank – was enough for no more than a day. The next day, however, the trip was easier. She knew the way, knew the technique, and had more confidence, and Maggie stayed out of the way. After several days, the journey became more or less routine. She decided to risk bathing. The need to do so had become paramount. Besides being filthy, she now had fleas in her hammock and in her clothes. Soon, the dirt would become a danger.

One morning, perhaps toward the end of the second week of February, she got out clean slacks and shirt, and carried them down to the river. There, still in her old slacks and shirt, she worked her way gingerly down the log into the water until it was up to her knees, and then sat down.

The feel of the cool water flooding up over her legs, waist and shoulders was exquisite. It lifted her foul clothes and massaged her skin, gently easing away the filth of weeks. She sat, delighting in the sensation, for long enough to ensure that the fleas were all drowned, reluctant to put an end to such a glorious experience. Finally, she splashed her face, rubbed herself as clean as she could through her clothes, stood up, and set off back along the tree-trunk, made treacherous by the water dripping from her.

Back on the bank, she undressed. As she did so, for the first time in weeks she became aware of her body. What she felt made her see herself as if with the eyes of someone else. The unfamiliarity of the image horrified her – gaunt rib cage, protruding hips, drawn-in stem of a waist, bones protruding grotesquely through a thin covering of skin. She was a creature so mutilated by starvation and disease as to seem near death. That was not how she felt, not how she wished to imagine herself. To hide away the evidence of her condition, she dressed hastily, gathered up the wet clothing, and made her way back up the path.

꒰

Despite the food, the assured water supply and now the bathing, Jan could not be certain she would survive the malaria. For two weeks, now, she had spent every afternoon shivering in her hammock, lost in a haze of semiconsciousness. If she did die, Harry would go soon afterwards, and there would be nothing to explain to the cargo-men and the outside world what had happened, or what to do with their possessions.

'Harry, I don't know if I can make it,' she said one morning, after breakfast. 'I want you to write up your journal.'

He was lucid that day, and was speaking more clearly. 'All right,' he said. 'My journal is the one on top.'

She went to his corner, and felt for the pile of Braille magazines in which he wrote his journal. She brought him the topmost folder. He began to write, laboriously, reading aloud what he wrote. 'Saws for Nilo. Axes for Rufino. Binocs for Armindo.' Making a will, she thought, was not much of an explanation, but it would do for a start. 'Jan and I,' he was saying, but she missed what came next. 'Severe fever. God's will be done. Cloth and clothing to Pelon and Nilo and Rufino. Bury us on hilltop, please.' So he still planned on her death. Even if he had accepted her decision to 'try for it', he did not really believe she would be able to survive if he died.

※

Some time in the third week in February, it seemed to Jan the malaria was receding. The attacks were brief and less severe, and came a little later each day.

When she was going for water one morning, weaving her way from the hut to the top of the bank, for it was still hard for her to hold a straight course, she kicked something hard and heavy. She stooped to pick it up, and felt shock weaken her. She was holding Becca's skull, quite clean after a month's exposure to the effects of the heat, humidity and insects.

She stood, breathing deeply. It was as well she could not see what lay in her hands and at her feet, for the image she had in mind was of Becca, not what Becca had become. It was for Becca that she stood there, shocked and still, for her sake that she was able both to weep and consider what to do for the best. She had vaguely assumed that the cargo-men would arrive and help her gather the remains. Now, she knew that it was not a task she wanted to leave to someone else. She would collect the bones herself.

By the time she got back to the hut, she knew what she would use – a plastic sack. She found the sack, and walked back past Harry, trying to keep it out of sight. Her actions, however, prompted the very suspicions she feared.

'What have you got there?' he demanded, snatching at her as she went past.

'A sack, Harry.'

'What for?'

She drew a breath and sagged down on the floor beside him. 'I came on Becca's skull. I . . . I want to keep it –'

300

'Don't do it!'

'Why?'

'Can't keep it – can't *cling*. Have to burn it.'

'I wasn't going to keep it in that way.' It dawned on her that he thought she planned to preserve the skull as some sort of relic. 'I wanted to gather . . . the remains . . . when the men come . . . we'll make a burial, a place with a cross . . .' Her voice died away.

'All right.' He put his hand on her shoulder briefly. 'All right.'

She picked herself up, took the plastic sack, and moved out of the house, feeling with her feet until she reached the spot where Becca's remains lay. She lifted the skull, and was struck again by the memory of Becca as she had been, full of strength, and character, and purpose. She could feel her strength still, out there, a part of the forest, watching.

Fortified, she began to gather up the other bones. Almost at once, she came upon a candle stub. That's what she must have been holding when she came to check on me, Jan thought. Strange, though, that she was still holding it when she fell.

Most of the bones were inside clothing. Carefully, reverentially, Jan separated them out, setting the clothes aside for washing. Then she carried the plastic bag and the clothes into the hut, entering by the marimba so that she would not have to squeeze past Harry. Inside, she put the plastic bag into the green canvas leaf-carrying sack Becca had made, and set it by the marimba.

She returned to Harry, sitting down beside him on the bench by the hearth.

'Did you manage it?' he asked.

'Yes. Harry, I found a chip broken off one of the hip bones. Would that have happened when she fell or was she limping before?'

'She,' he said with great deliberation, 'fainted.'

'But was it something from before, or did it happen that night?'

'I don't think so.'

He was no help. But perhaps now she had begun to speak of Becca she could attempt again the task of coming to terms with her loss.

'It troubles me . . .' she began, not knowing how to begin. 'She worked so hard, and there was so little reward . . . she never knew –'

Harry broke in. 'You are falling,' he said, as deliberately as before, 'into the trap of unhappiness.'

※

The next day was clear. At midday, when the sun was shining directly down into their little clearing, Jan went out to wash Becca's clothes. She put them to dry, and sat down in the sun. It would be an hour or more before the fever struck, and it was a chance to sunbathe. Sunbathing helped suppress malarial chills, or so it had seemed when she'd tried it in Chiapas. She removed her blouse, and sat on the log bench in the sun.

After a few minutes, as the sun moved behind trees, she concluded that it was too enclosed down there for extended sunbathing. But by then the sun had given her an idea. Fire. If she was to give herself a better diet, she would need fire. There were no matches in the house, but there were other ways of making fire.

She dressed again, and fetched Harry's binoculars and a Braille magazine. Back outside, she placed the paper on the ground, and held the binoculars over it, pointing them at the sun. She knelt there for perhaps a minute, and then realized how foolish the scheme was. She couldn't tell if the dot of light ever shone through, let alone if it was in focus or stationary. She couldn't even be certain that the binoculars were not obscured by foliage.

But the attempt had served to concentrate her mind on the problem. Thinking through what else she might try, she realized there were, after all, matches in the house. She herself had put a box aside, in the toolbox, beneath the rope, as part of an emergency kit prepared for a boat trip two years previously.

Back in the house, she found the matches, and a candle, and took both to Harry.

'Harry, I want to start a fire,' she said. 'Can you light this candle?'

She was afraid the suggestion might prompt an irate refusal, and a criticism of her for endangering herself and him. But no. He meekly fumbled out a match and tried to light it. Brazilian matches, dwarfish things with a tiny dab of sulphur, are inadequate at the best of times, and are usually effective only if used in pairs. Harry was too weak and clumsy to strike even one, let alone two.

'No good,' he muttered. 'Too old. Damp.'

'Give them to me,' she said. His action and his words had summoned up an old memory: Mexico, the morning after the first night in the jungle. She picked up some Braille paper, kindling and a few small logs, and carried them outside. It would be dangerous to make a fire inside, for it might blaze up and catch the roof.

Back inside again, she set two candles in jars, placed them on one of the boxes, and opened the matches. If Harry was watching, he said nothing. Holding two matches together, she positioned them between the heels of her hands, and rubbed her hands back and forth, warming and drying the match heads. Then she brought the matches against the box, and struck. To her utter astonishment, the matches blazed into life, sending a flare of light through the grey haze around her.

Harry was equally astonished. 'How did you do *that*?' he asked.

'The way you taught me the first night in the jungle,' she said, pleased and excited, feeling for the candles.

Lifting one of the candle-jars, she carried it outside and placed it against the pile of paper and wood. It caught. She saw the orange glow, felt the heat, and stood back, delighted with her success. It was her first fire for six weeks, and the first time she had *started* a fire in fifteen years.

She fetched a kettle of water and the hotplate, a slab of metal cut from the gasoline drum being used as a water-butt on the hilltop. Then she built up the blaze with more logs, and put the kettle on to boil, checking it now and then by listening to it closely.

As soon as she heard the water bubbling, she made a hot chocolate drink for Harry, and added some hot water to a tin of tomato purée to make a soup. He thanked her, but took no more than a few sips of each.

After that, she tried to boil up some beans. This was not a success. She had cooked nothing for fifteen years and had no real notion any longer of how much water to put in or how long to boil the beans for. When she came to check them, the smell told her she was too late. The water had evaporated, and the beans were burned. She pulled the pan away, tipped in some water to cool the mess, and then tried a spoonful. She pulled a face: diluted charcoal. She scraped out the unappetizing slurry on to the ground, and called Maggie over. 'Come on,' she said, 'And no complaints. Charcoal is good for the stomach.'

A fire outside was no long-term solution, she knew that, for it would rain some time. But she tended her fire for two days, burning the logs that were lying already chopped by the path, and getting up several times each night to push the fire together.

The third morning, when Harry warned her it looked like rain, she decided it was time to take things a stage further. She would start a fire on the hearth. Harry would disapprove, but once she had shown she knew what she was doing, he would accept.

She went to her fire, and felt for a log cool enough to pull out by one end. Carefully, she lifted it to the hearth, and returned to fetch a second. As she laid the logs together, adding the last of the kindling, she imagined what Harry would have said in the old days. 'Jan, what's that you're doing? Pure idiocy! What if there's a flare-up? Might catch your clothing, the boxes, the roof, anything.'

But she was confident enough, after her success outside, to take the risk. Bit by bit, she felt the heat building, and saw the sudden burst of orange flame. She was already congratulating herself on a second success when she smelt burning. She sniffed, wondering what she had set fire to. A cloth lying close to the hearth perhaps?

'Are you all right, Harry?' she called. If there was something seriously wrong, he would surely shout.

'Yes.'

But the smell was stronger now, coming from close by.

She felt a sharp pain on her thigh. Burning. Her slacks. She jumped back, slapping at the smouldering polyester, restraining the urge to cry out.

The pain died, and the scorched material cooled. As she brushed at the mark, her back to Harry, she damned herself for taking such a stupid risk. I can't afford a mistake, she thought. Not a single one.

After that she let the hearth fire go out. Better no fire at all than set fire to herself or the house.

That night, rain dowsed the fire outside. She tried to rekindle it the next day, but the logs were too wet. She'd used all the kindling, and now the matches, exposed to the air, really were too damp to use. There would be no more fires for a while.

She knew what her solution would have to be. She also knew how Harry would react to her suggestion, but it was only fair to discuss the idea with him first.

'Harry, the fire's out,' she told him, sitting down beside his hammock.

'Yes. More kindling. Start it again.'

'There's no more kindling, Harry. Anyway, the matches are too damp now. But there are matches up on the hill.'

'No!' he said emphatically, grasping her hands. 'Too dangerous. You get lost! Don't go!'

'Harry —'

'Promise me you won't go.'

She made no further protest, allowing silence to seem like consent. She would have to go some time, though, she knew that, with or without his permission.

🦋

Now that she was doing laundry again, she needed an open, sunny space in which to dry clothes. The sun didn't penetrate the overhung area around the Riverside Hut for long enough, but up in the Garden Clearing there was a pole frame that stood clear of any trees. It had been planned for tomatoes, but the tomatoes hadn't flourished, and she and Becca had often used it as a drying-frame. She knew, however, what Harry's reaction would be if she suggested that she go anywhere else other than the river. She would have to arrange her trips surreptitiously.

One morning, perhaps in the third week of February, she told Harry she was going outside to sunbathe. But instead of lying down in the sun, she picked up her pile of washing and her stick, and felt her way over the drainage ditch, up the slope to the beginning of the trail. It was well worn, and she remembered the way clearly.

After fifty yards, she felt a small fallen tree, and knew she was at the Glade. She turned, took a few more steps, reached out with her stick and touched the fallen tree through which Becca had cut the gap they called Grandfather's Gate. Then she was in the Garden Clearing, tapping her way across the three beds of sweet potato and manioc, until she reached the spot where the pole framework stood.

Pleased that she had managed the walk so easily, she threw her damp clothes over the rungs, and returned, hoping that Harry had not noticed her absence. He hadn't; he'd fallen asleep.

Every morning after that, she would make the five-minute

trip to the Garden Clearing, both to dry clothes and empty urine, which, she realized, she could use as fertilizer on the sweet potatoes and manioc.

※

Though Harry drank a little every day, he ate practically nothing. He had scarcely had a mouthful since Becca's death, some five weeks before. He never complained of hunger. Far from it: when she offered him food, he insisted he wasn't hungry. He hardly even complained about his sores any more. Most of the time, he slept, or listened to the radio. Words seemed to tire him, and he preferred classical music.

Every evening, Jan would help him with his socks and his sleeping-jacket. Every morning, she would hand him his wash-cloth and comb, help him sit up a little straighter in his hammock, fix his pillows, and take off his night clothes.

Day by day, imperceptibly, he weakened, and as he slipped away, his mind became steadily more removed from reality. Since Jan could not see his gauntness, the routine she had established allowed her to believe that he might still do what he had done before when near death: start eating again, put on weight, get back to work. For a while, she was reassured, too, by his conversation, so slowly did the real give way to the unreal. Jan would sit beside him, her face on his chest, her ear by his mouth, and they would talk of the future. The men were due in April. Both of them knew from the radio that April was little more than a month away. Then there would be fresh food, and they would both get better. What then? With one part of her mind, Jan knew that there would be no return to a homesteading life with Harry, not with Becca gone. But so absolute was his denial of Becca, and so absolute Jan's past dependence on Harry, that part of her still went along with the fond notion that one day he would start eating, and recover, and talk as usual about how close to death he was, and set about rebuilding.

Not on Homestead Hill though. 'We'll go to Vermont,' Harry said once. 'There's no malaria in the Green Mountains.' Pause. 'Maybe we should go to northern California. What are your favourite fruits?'

'Avocado and citrus, maybe mango.'

'We'll grow avocados and oranges. We'll buy an orange grove with the money your mother leaves you. Where shall we grow them?'

'I don't know, Harry. How about . . . southern Brazil?'

'How about Guyana? Are we in Guyana?'

'No. We're in Brazil.'

'Oh. What part of Brazil?'

'Northern Brazil, near the Venezuelan border.'

'Oh. Thank you. Thank you very much.'

🦂

One evening, in the last days of February, he called her, begging for orange juice.

'We don't have any orange juice, Harry.'

'Please, *please*, orange juice.'

'Harry —' His suffering and her impotence brought tears to her eyes. 'Harry, there is none.'

'Where is Don Armindo?'

'He's not here.'

'I always did right by him, paid him the money I owed, and now I want to buy orange juice, he isn't here. He should be here. You understand my position.'

'Yes.'

'I want orange juice. I beg you, please, orange juice.'

At some point during that night, he woke her shouting, not shouting for her, but ranting in a loud voice, in terrible anger, an anger so terrible she didn't dare go to him. He sounded wild with rage, but she had no idea what it was all about. Minute after minute the voice bellowed from the darkness, and there was not one single word that she understood. She

308

listened in fearful silence until his voice became more subdued, and finally stopped.

※

And on the evening of 28 February, he called her again, with the same request, and the same desperation. 'Please, please, I beg you, orange juice.'

'There isn't any, Harry.'

'Orange juice, ple-e-e-ease . . .'

'Oh, Harry,' she said, and explained again, as patiently as she could, that there was no orange juice, that there was nothing she could do.

Later, she heard his voice again. When she went to him, and put her head on his chest to hear him, she found his mood had changed.

'Where is Jan?' he asked, abruptly. This too sounded like an accusation, as if it was the old Harry talking. You're not the person you should be, he seemed to be saying, where is the real Jan? Sudden fear gripped her. If he became angry, as he had the night before, if he held her, or hit her, she would have no defence. She had a sudden nightmare vision: a madman attacking a blind woman. She had no answer to his question, and waited in helpless apprehension for his accusation to be made specific.

But he was not making an accusation. He was puzzled. 'Where is my wife, Jan?' he asked.

She made no reply, baffled by the question. He knew she was there, beside him, so he must, she thought, mean something she could not even guess at.

'Where is her mother?' he asked.

'In California, in Fair Oaks.'

He shifted his position, as if facing someone else.

'Where is your daughter?'

Jan was overwhelmed with grief and confusion. That he should talk of Becca now, when he was incapable of offering comfort, was almost unbearable. She said, weeping: 'She – is – dead.'

But he hadn't been talking to her. He'd been talking to Jessie.

'So,' he said thoughtfully, 'Jan is dead.' Then insistently: 'Where is your *living* daughter?'

Again, Jan was lost. She wondered desperately what answer he could possibly be wanting, for it sounded almost like a trick question, as if he were testing her. At last she faltered: 'She is . . . in . . . heaven.'

'So: Jan . . . is . . . dead,' he repeated.

'No, Harry, no. I am Jan. It is Rebecca who is dead.'

'Oh! I se-e-ee.' He drew the word out and spoke it gently, as if in genuine gratitude that she had so enlightened him. 'Thank you.'

Jan stood up, confused by his confusion. He had abandoned her physically weeks ago, but somehow the loss of his mind was not something she had yet accepted. He had always been the logical one, he had been the head. Now there was no more guidance, and she did not know what else to do, other than settle him for the night, as she always had. She slipped his sleeping-jacket on, and then his socks. She took his hand. 'Our Father, which art in Heaven . . .' she began as usual, hearing him join in weakly – 'in Earth as it is in Heaven' – after the first few words.

She was about to leave him, when he spoke again. 'Do you have any money?' he asked.

She paused to think when she had last handled money. Manaus, perhaps, five years previously? No, Becca had dealt with the money. She hadn't touched money since a shopping trip in San Cristobal, thirteen years before.

'No, Harry, I don't.'

'Oh. Have you studied Greek?' an oblique reference, she realized after a pause, to his researches into Jewish history back in Mexico and his regret at never having studied Greek.

'No.' She paused, praying he would allow her to sleep now.

310

'Now goodnight, Harry,' she said, at last. There was silence. She went to her own hammock.

In the night, she began to shiver with the belated, final stages of her malaria, breathing in the peculiar dank smell of malarial sweat. She wrapped her blanket tight around her, and slept.

Later, an unmeasured time later, she heard him shout. She struggled up, and went to him, her limbs like jelly, her teeth chattering. Even with her head on his chest, she couldn't understand him.

'Ot ocla.'

'What?'

'Ot ocla.'

'Hot chocolate?'

'Aha.'

'I can give you chocolate, but not hot.'

'Ocla.'

Forcing herself to concentrate, she mixed some chocolate powder and water with a spoon and handed the cup to him. She heard a tapping, and knew he was indicating the box beside him.

'Do you want anything else, Harry?' she asked, setting the cup down. 'I don't think I can get up again.'

'No.'

She settled back in her hammock, shivering, wet with sweat, gripping the blanket around her, unable to summon the will to face the cold or change her soaked clothes.

'Jan!'

'I can't come,' she called. Her patience and her strength were all used up. 'What do you want?'

There was no reply. She drifted into a troubled sleep.

Deep in the night, he woke her again: 'JAN!' The cry was loud and urgent enough to spur Jan from her hammock and summon Maggie from her perch in the rafters. As Jan stumbled to him, Maggie came to her arms. She reached out and felt Harry.

He was silent again, asleep. Jan, with Maggie on her arm,

remembered the spoon and the cup of chocolate beside him. She took the spoon to the kitchen box for safekeeping, leaving the untouched chocolate. Maggie, reassured, retired to the roof. Jan returned to her hammock, weak with exhaustion, and slept.

※

In the morning, she awoke to silence. It was only the third time in years she had awoken before him. Perhaps he was still asleep after his disturbed night.

Her fever was gone, but, as she swung her legs to the floor, she felt she was too weak to risk walking. There was some *farinha* within reach. She mixed it with water and guava preserve, and ate slowly. After a few minutes, she summoned her strength, and went to Harry's hammock.

'Harry?'

He didn't move.

She reached out and felt for his shoulder. He had slumped sideways. But his feet were still up in the hammock, as for sleep. She should wake him, she thought, sit him up, ready for the day.

She pulled a leg clear of the hammock. It swung and bounced up and down, without straightening. The knee joint was locked.

He had been dead for hours.

11

SURVIVAL

She felt again up along the body, over the still-warm torso. It was dotted with bits of *farinha* dropped by Maggie when she visited him. One arm was resting on the ground, almost as if he had fallen back, as if he had seen something coming at him from the forest.

She felt up the long grizzled beard towards the place on the throat where he had the growth. Perhaps it had become worse. Perhaps that was why he'd been unable to eat and talk. She felt around his throat. No, there was only a circular ridge. The growth had receded, starved away like the rest of him.

Something in her still refused to accept that he was finally dead. Seventeen years before, he'd told her 'I have discovered you *will* your death,' and she had believed him, believed that he would embrace death boldly, purposefully, asserting the power of his will even at the end. So often in the intervening years he had seemed to stand at the brink, only to draw back and say 'Not yet.' But he would never have willed this wretched end, this slow collapse into confusion. Perhaps, once again, she would hear him say 'Not yet.'

She felt his heart. It was still warm. She remembered other words, from years before: 'Just make sure that I'm dead . . . might be in a coma . . . quite easy . . . check the pulse.' There was no heart beat, no pulse.

She was convinced. There was no grief, not yet. Instead, she felt relief that his pain was over.

She knew what to do, having done it once already. Besides, it was his wish. He'd told her back on the Santa Maria: 'Just drag the body out into the yard.' She loosened the hammock, letting the cord slip through her fingers, then edged along the pole walkway, checking for snags by sliding her foot from side to side. Finding none, she returned, and undressed the body, surprised at how light he had become and how much stronger she was. Forty days (or thereabouts) without food had reduced him to a shadow. This, at least, was as he had wished it: to be laid out in irreducible, Franciscan simplicity, cold skin to cold earth. 'Naked came I out of my mother's womb, and naked shall I return thither.'

This time, she found the dragging easier. Every heave moved her burden, not two or three inches, but a foot or more. Foot by foot, she moved backwards, past the hearth and across the ten intervening yards, beyond the spot where she had exposed Becca's body. This time, she felt with her feet that she had reached the drainage channel, and there she stopped.

She felt the early morning sun striking through leaves on to her face. As if concerned for some kernel of consciousness that might still remain in the corpse, she thought: He shouldn't be left lying out here in the sun uncovered.

She went back to the house and felt her way round to the washstand, where there were some spare thatching leaves. The huge fronds were falling apart with age, but they would serve her purpose. She gathered the stems of half a dozen, dragged them across the yard, and laid them over the corpse.

Back in the house, she collapsed into her hammock, and let grief engulf her. For the first time, she wept in a way that had not been possible while Harry was alive. She wept for Becca, for Harry, for what Harry had become, for their ruined lives, and for the homestead, which was already returning their years of labour to the jungle.

But even as she mourned, she saw that Harry had been right. There was a trap in unhappiness. There was so much to mourn that she was in danger of doing nothing else. Only in action, in concentrated action, could she avoid the over-whelming chaos of grief.

There was much to do. She had to stay healthy and clean.

The house had to be set straight. She needed food, better food, fresh food, cooked food. For that, she would need fire, which required firewood and matches. Beyond all that, impossibly far into the future, the cargo-men would come, and she wanted to be ready, though ready for what exactly she could not yet imagine.

Weeping gave way, for a while, to action. For an hour, she cleaned the house, starting in Harry's corner. As usual, she found some cups and cutlery quite quickly, but groping her way across the floor served only to show the extent of the task, She would have to clear out the whole damp mass of flooring leaves, and sift through them as well, if everything – especially her hearing-aid mould – was to be found. It would require all her concentration and many days' work.

First, though, she had to eat, not because she felt hungry, but because she knew she had to preserve and build her strength. She mixed herself some *farinha*, adding in guava preserve, going over the tasks, trying to impose on them some logical order. Maggie, as usual, appeared beside her to receive a share. Jan didn't want Maggie's hands in the food. She offered a mouthful from her lips, and she felt Maggie take it.

'I'm not thinking, Maggie,' she said, as she ate. Then, to herself: We need good food. Fire. Matches. They're on the hill. We have to go up on the hill. That's what we have to do first.

She'd never walked the trail on her own. She would have to mark it, mark it so carefully there was no chance of getting lost. That would take time. How could she mark it? String, rope, poles – yes, there were poles lying up in the Garden Clearing.

But wait – no point thinking about the fire, and matches, and the trail to the hilltop, if she couldn't keep a fire going. Firewood. That should come first. There was wood enough, fingertip-to-elbow lengths piled up by the saw-horse. They would need splitting. If she could split them, there would be enough of the hard, dense, coal-like wood for several weeks' burning. After that, perhaps, she would have to cut more in the forest. Chopping. *That* should come first.

Very well. She had a plan, and had kept control. Now, exhausted, she slept.

Next morning, her determination restored, she pulled out Becca's axe – the one Harry had made for her before Christmas – from among the tools stored beneath the marimba. She was wary of it, remembering Harry warning her years before that she should never do any chopping. She felt the tapered shaft, and swung it experimentally. When was the last time she had used an axe? At the Caverna, a good thirteen years ago.

A sudden, shocking memory sprang into her mind: a sawed section of wood, ready for chopping; her hand sliding down the haft; raising the axe; the swing, and in that instant the feel of something brushing her scalp; the axe striking the log dully, and bouncing off; her gasp of horror at what she had done – the axe held upside down, the inverted blade kissing her scalp, her legs turning to jelly, the appalled vision of herself as she might have been, flat on her back, her head split open, Rebecca looking down at her, mouth agape. She had sat down, weak-kneed, and worked to regain composure by telling herself she was under guidance, that there was no need to lose confidence because of a near miss, that she just had to concentrate more. Confidence and concentration. Blind people learned to play golf, so they ought to be able to chop wood.

She went over to the saw-horse, leaned the axe against it, felt for a log, placed it on the ground near the chopping-block and reached for the axe. What on earth would Harry have said? She could almost hear his stern rebuke. 'Jan! I told you never to chop! And that's Becca's axe! Put it down!' She glanced round apprehensively, and then smiled at her own foolishness. Come on, Harry she thought – or perhaps she even said the words out loud – we've been through this before, just before your heart attack, remember? Yes, that time she nearly cut her foot open. 'Now, Jan, I don't want any accidents!'

She turned to the log. Setting her feet together, as Harry had taught her, she tapped the axe a couple of times to feel for the top of the log, lifted and swung down. The blade struck, and glanced sideways. Again she positioned herself, tapped, and swung.

The blade bit true.

'Got it!'

She swung again. This time, she missed completely. The head dived into the earth. Well, at least that was safe.

A fourth swing, and a fifth, and the log fell in two. She smiled in relief. Well, that proves ghosts don't exist, she thought. If they did, he'd have been here to stop me.

She set aside the split lengths, chopped another log, and then a third. After a while, she established a pattern. About half the swings struck home. Keeping the handle low, she found that glancing blows bounced off safely into the earth. After two hours' steady work, she had a score of cut lengths, enough for a good fire, with a whole stack of logs remaining to be cut.

She carried the axe back to the house, made herself a bowl of *farinha*, drank some water, and lay down in her hammock to recover her strength. Exhaustion and satisfaction gave way almost at once to grief. Tears seemed to come as easily as breath itself. To keep the tears at bay, she went out again to fetch the split wood, storing the logs beside the hearth. She didn't stop until she felt the evening air cool the sweat through her shirt, and then, exhausted, pausing only to change into old but dry work clothes, she allowed her need for sleep to overcome her.

Next morning, over breakfast – *farinha* and a can of sardines shared with Maggie – she listed to herself what she could use to mark the trail. Typewriter ribbon – she had four spools, washed and ready for tying plants. They were in a plastic bag, hanging from a support post. Ribbon was long and light, but it tangled easily and would be hard to unknot. To give herself a choice, she would take a twenty-five-foot rope used for mooring *Piaroa* and fifteen feet of lighter-weight cord stored in the toolbox. There were also some strips of cotton rag she could use as string, and the three twenty-foot poles lying in the Garden Clearing, useful as railings, perhaps, once she reached them.

Walking to the Garden Clearing wouldn't be a problem. She had already been there many times to dry laundry and to empty the urine bucket on the sweet potatoes and manioc plants. But beyond, on the trail up to the hilltop, marking would be a matter of life or death. To stray from the trail even by a yard might leave her stumbling, lost, in a grey, undifferentiated world. It would take time to establish a path, but time didn't matter. She had plenty of that. Care was all.

There was another danger: snakes. No one had been up the trail for two months. In that time, vegetation would have grown enough to provide good cover. Well, she would have her stick to give plenty of warning, and she would be travelling slowly. There was no point in worrying about snakes.

She put the typewriter ribbons in her gardening bag, tied it at her waist, wound the rope round her, and tucked in the cotton rags.

'Come on, Maggie,' she said, feeling for her stick. 'We're going for a walk. And let's hope I don't blunder into any serpents.'

Tapping her stick from side to side in front of her, she crossed the ditch, walked through the forest, veered left through the Glade, and, with Maggie scampering around her, felt her way through Grandfather's Gate, the gap in the fallen tree, to the Garden Clearing. Just at the edge of the clearing, she leant against a tree. Near her lay the poles. She reached out a foot and touched them. There were three of them. She lifted the ends of them, all three together, and dragged them back to the main trail, and round to the left, back to the corner of the Garden Clearing, across which the path cut.

Thirty or forty feet away across the clearing was a particular light-coloured tree marking the start of the climb up the ridge. Harry had tied railings to it. But finding the tree would not be easy. The trail across the clearing was now overgrown with grass and made a sharp turn round a fallen tree. She would need to mark her way meticulously if she was ever to find the spot where the trail entered the jungle again.

She tied one end of the cord to the tree and the other end to her belt, carefully winding the rest of it in her hand. Then, feeling for the openness of the path with her feet, and dragging a pole behind her, she ranged forward to the dog-leg. She checked she was still on the path, moving from side to side, from open path to overgrown garden, then tied one end of the pole on to a bush. She turned back, finished tying the first pole, and dragged the second forward to mark the dog-leg. Feeling secure now about the first few yards of this section, she turned back again, using the poles as a guide, undid the rope, and took the last pole to her forward position.

There, she tied herself on again with rope, and walked slowly forward across the twenty-foot gap, hauling the pole with one hand, using the other to feel with her stick, scanning the grey and darker grey to pick out a hint of lightness that might be the tree she sought. Aha – a light patch, right in front of her. She felt it with one hand, and peered close. No telling if it was the right one. She moved left. 'Dammit, Maggie, here's an-other!' She felt a slight pang of guilt at her words. It had been years since she had sworn. Harry always said it denoted hardness in a woman. 'I want *one* light-coloured tree, not a forest of them.'

She moved back to her right, and checked out the first tree. Yes, this *was* the one: she could feel the end of the railings. She tied the pole at right angles to her course, so that as she crossed the gap, the pole would catch her at her waist height and lead her to the start of the uphill trail.

She had completely lost track of time. No need to court exhaustion. It had been a good day's work. Pleased with her achievement, she wound in the rope, called Maggie, and headed home.

Back in the hut, she mixed up some *farinha*, and thought: with this stuff, I won't die of hunger, but I might die of boredom. She remembered Harry reading Wallace to her, an extract in which Wallace made a big thing out of being reduced to a cold-water cup of *farinha* for one whole day. He wrote as if that made him a really hardened explorer. One day! Well, Mr Wallace, I should be so lucky, she thought, taking another mouthful of the pasty mixture.

'You want some of this, Maggie?' She thrust her jaw forward, and Maggie came to nibble gently from her mouth. Maybe Wallace had felt lonely, Jan thought. At least I have Maggie, if nothing else.

'Nothing else.' The phrase brought tears to her eyes. Anything, any pause, seemed to open a wound in her through which her sorrow poured. While Maggie, reassured by the ritual, retreated to the rafters, Jan gave way to sobs, crying until exhaustion overcame her.

Twice that night she got up to relieve herself. The second time, knowing the pot was full, she went out into the night to empty it. Maggie was there to welcome her back in, reaching down from a beam. Jan held her hand briefly. 'Don't worry, Maggie,' she reassured her. 'There's no danger here.' Not that she would know if there was. Perhaps Harry really had seen something, when he banged with his machete, and when he shouted so loudly on the night of his death. But she was simply not concerned. The jaguar was a gentleman, Harry always said, a danger only to rival meat-eaters. Protected by ignorance, for she had no real concept of how fast and powerful a fully grown jaguar was, she told herself she wouldn't worry about jaguars. Snakes, yes, she would take as much care as she could, but not jaguars.

Next morning, she took an early trip to the Garden Clearing, taking the bucket along with her to fertilize the manioc. It would be some time before the plants produced any of the long white tubers, but she would use the leaves to make soup just as soon as she had a fire going.

That second day marking the trail was easier. The path up the ridge to the Fourth Clearing was steep and rough with exposed roots, but still well defined by Harry's railings. In the shade, there was little undergrowth.

The Fourth Clearing was, initially, straightforward. The trail led out of the trees across the cleared area to the little space in the middle. She had no difficulty making herself a guideline of typewriter ribbon across to the spot. At this point, Harry and Becca would often stop to look out towards the hills and read the weather for Jan. She was already turning, wondering if it would rain, when Becca's voice came into her mind – 'Sentinel's out, Janny, there's a storm-cloud building round Thunder Mountain.' *No.* She cut the voice off, and felt hastily for a bush to act as a support for the end of her ribbon.

Here, the trail divided, and she faced a greater difficulty. The left fork, heading straight up the hill, was the more direct, but too steep. She needed to get on to the Long Trail, which led off to the right on a slower climb along the side of the hill. The start of the Long Trail, at the edge of the Fourth Clearing, was a mere forty feet away from her, but the intervening gardens were a jumble of little paths where she, Harry and Becca had crossed back and forth from trail to trail. Moreover, she knew the entrance to the trail was blocked by a fallen tree. The approach involved a detour. The rope was not long enough to bridge the gap; yet she couldn't risk wandering about trailing typewriter ribbon. It could get tangled, and if that happened she would have to cut herself clear, and risk becoming lost.

'Maggie!' she called, and set off back to the house, thinking this would take some time.

The next morning, she armed herself with a machete to clear her way through the overgrown bushes to the Long Trail. She would have to be careful with the machete. She hadn't used one for some time, and the thought of what a misplaced swipe would do to an arm or leg did not bear thinking about.

Back up at the open space in the Fourth Clearing, she tied on to her bush with the rope, edged forward as far as she could go, and then, with the rope taut, began to work her way sideways, searching for some clue to the direction she should be taking. Nothing: no path, no trees, just plants and grass brushing her legs.

To give herself greater range, she would, after all, have to use the typewriter ribbon, fixing it to bushes at intervals to stop it tangling. She replaced the rope with ribbon, tying it on with rags, then ranged forward again.

She came up against leaves. She felt: jungle, bushes, leaves, no trail.

'Back we go, Maggie,' she said, and started the whole process over again, untying and re-tying. Each time she tied the knot, she carefully set down the machete. Then, when she had finished tying, she retrieved it and worked her way forward, one arm outstretched to feel for a gap in the wall of vegetation, the other swinging randomly with the machete to ease her way through the growth.

It was painfully slow work, for she had no idea which direction she had chosen to explore, or even if that direction was much different from the previous one. Hour after hour she worked, with dogged persistence. Midday passed. Still she found no way forward.

After retying her lines a dozen times, after fiddling with scores of knots on scores of different bushes, she made her first mistake. Instead of laying the machete down beside her feet while working on a knot, she stuck it in the ground. When next she reached for it, she found it had fallen over. 'Idiot!' she shouted, and damned herself for her carelessness. She debated briefly whether it would be worth feeling around her among the roots of the grass and garden plants. No, she thought, I don't want to cut myself or grab a snake by mistake. I'll have to abandon it.

Even this loss did not anger her for long. She had established a system that was safe and would, eventually, be effective. It didn't matter how long it took. In a way, she was grateful for the challenge. It forced her to face the present, only the present, and keep the past at bay. She worked on, forming and re-forming the mental image of the area she was exploring, until she felt the heat begin to die from the sun.

'Come on, Mag,' she called. 'Tomorrow we'll be there.'

On the afternoon of the next day, after several more hours' work, as she tried doubling back around a bush she was sure she had felt a dozen times before, she found what she was looking for. The foliage seemed to evaporate under her waving hands, and she stepped through into the welcome shade of the forest, and on to a firm path edged with spindly vegetation grown high enough now to brush her legs.

From here on, it would be easy. Tying on ribbon to mark the final join between the start of the Long Trail and the open space in the Fourth Clearing, she felt her way home to the reward of an exhausted sleep.

On the fifth day, ready for the final leg of her ascent, she moved easily back to the Fourth Clearing, so easily that she had the freedom to wonder about the weather. If rain came, the hard-packed trail would dissolve into mud, and be difficult to follow. She was wondering how much warning she would have when she arrived at the spot where the trail divided. Before she was aware of what she was doing, she turned to read the weather, ready to see the horizon painted in her mind by Harry's words.

It was a clear day, the sun was hot on her shoulders, and Sentinel would surely be out. But nothing of that great panorama penetrated her walled vision. The sudden apprehension of her lack, the contrast between the mind's-eye view she knew so well and the blank grey before her, made her throat ache. Before the tears could rise, however, she set her mouth, felt for the ribbon, and set off through the tangled garden towards the Long Trail.

Feeling the firmness of the forest path, she decided she didn't need to mark it. 'Come on, Maggie, this is clear enough,' she said, and set off, holding her stick out in front of her, guided by the saplings that brushed her on either side, moving faster

323

up over the roots than she had dared move in the previous five days.

After twenty yards, the trail was blocked by a fallen tree, over which she climbed; then came a sharp left turn; and another fallen tree. She was panting hard now, and sat to rest, as she used to do with Becca. At that thought, her panting turned to weeping. She took a breath, and held it. No, she would not think, would not give way. 'Come on, Maggie,' she said. She stood up, resolute, and walked on.

At the Pineapple Clearing, the path came out into the open. It held tight to the edge of the clearing, and shouldn't have been a problem. In a practical sense, it wasn't. But the sudden burst of light had a strange effect upon her mind. The past came crowding back to her. Here, Becca had been working until just before Christmas, overworking herself, Harry had said. The very air spoke of the past – the smell of the plants, the sudden warmth, the slope of the ground falling away to her right. She stifled a sob. It was as if Becca and Harry were standing like shadow-players in the darkness of the forest, constantly waiting for their chance to step on stage. She couldn't allow that to happen. Replaying those scenes would undo all her resolution.

She walked on, to the sharp left turn that led up steeply to the crest of the hill. Within a minute she was out in the Hilltop Clearing. The path disappeared in long grass, but it was a mere twenty feet from the top of the trail to the hut, and the slope told her the direction. And then there she was, fingering the palm-leaf thatch, trying to find her way in.

She felt around for some minutes, unable to decide which part of the hut she had arrived at. Then she remembered the clothesline that led away from the front entrance. With one arm upraised, she worked her way around the edge of the roof until she bumped into the line. She followed it to the front entrance and ducked under the thatch.

Inside, she stood silent, breathing in the place that had been so much Becca's. It was dry up here, and the air had a sweetness to it after the rank, damp smells of the riverside. She could feel the openness of the hut, sense the light streaming in under the thatch. Suddenly, her mind was full of images again. She saw the vista of forest and mountain so often described by Harry and Becca. She heard, in memory, Becca's early-morning radio programme, and pictured water boiling on the fire. As she felt around, each familiar object lit another scene. The sour-dough pan was still on the hearth, as if Becca would be making cakes as usual the next morning. Jan's hammock was slung up out of the way, but Becca's hung down from the beams, as she always left it when she thought she would back soon.

Jan set her mind again on what she had been working towards over the last week. Yes, there, in the empty powdered-milk can, hanging by the hearth, was the little cache of matches, safe and dry.

Would one box be enough? No: she would take several, along with some other things stored above Becca's hammock –the big cooking spoon, some cans of fish, a sweater, radio batteries, bark for kindling. She gathered them up, and put them in a sack.

There was nothing more to do. She had all she wanted for the moment. But she paused, nevertheless, unable to break away from the intense reminders of her past.

A line of Walt Whitman's came to her:

Is there a single, final farewell?

Not for her, not yet. There would be many returns here, and each return would mean another farewell.

She turned, picked up her stick, felt for the thatch, called Maggie, and stepped out, allowing the slope to guide her feet to the beginning of the Long Trail.

By midday, she was home, in amongst the damp, the gloom and the smell of putrefaction. She went to her hammock and switched on the radio to check the time. Lying back, she put the radio to her ear. Her mind already held two worlds – vivid past and obscure present. Now there was a third: the outside.

She listened, reassured, until she heard the midday signal.

She had been away no more than three hours.

That same afternoon, she started on the fire. It was a dry day, and she decided to build it outside, in order not to risk another accident inside.

With Maggie scampering and squeaking curiously around her, she carried out a Braille magazine, matches, kindling, and the hotplate. Then she scrumpled up a page, set some kindling on the paper, and laid split wood across the top. She screwed up another page of Braille to act as a taper, sat down, laid the paper out in her lap, and took out two matches.

Holding them firmly at the heads, she struck. No good. The striking surface had torn. She tried again. Still no good. Each attempted strike wore away a little more of the box. At this rate, she would soon run out of boxes. If she was going to conserve her supply, she realized, she would have to keep the fire alight twenty-four hours a day. She would have to keep it covered with the hotplate as a protection against rain.

She fumbled for a new box, resettled herself with the paper in her lap, took two matches and struck. They flared. She saw the sudden burst of light through the fog of her blindness, and felt the heat on her fingers. She dabbed downwards, but failed to find the paper. The matches died. Clenching her teeth with impatience, she threw the matches away.

She needed a better taper. She remembered a trick she'd learned from Harry a long time ago, and made little tears along the edge of the paper. She took out another pair of matches, and tried again. This time, the matches caught, and so did the paper.

Before the flame could die, she snatched up the paper and set it against the base of the fire. Paper and kindling caught, with a rush of flames. Delighted by the bright flare, the crackle and the surge of heat, she shouted out exultantly, scaring Maggie into a scampering retreat; and fell silent, suddenly anxious that the kindling might burn away before the logs caught. After a few minutes, however, the logs settled into a steady burn, and Maggie returned.

'There you are, Mag. Look, isn't that good?' she said with a satisfied smile, as the monkey climbed on to her arm.

She stood up, and returned to the house to gather rubbish from the hearth. When she had added this to the blaze, she covered the whole thing with the hotplate. Certain now that she had a fire that would burn for hours untended, she brought over a pan of water and set it to heat, throwing in a handful of beans to act as the base for a soup. While that was heating, she went up to the Garden Clearing and picked some manioc and sweet-potato leaves to add to the soup.

Within two hours, she had her first hot meal for two months.

'Here Mag, bean soup,' Jan said, as she dipped her cup in. Offering the cup to Maggie, Jan felt her draw back. 'Too hot? All right, you stick to the *farinha*. Sticking is about all it's good for.'

She sipped her soup, and forced herself to think ahead, beyond her present misery. Her thoughts ran, as they did increasingly now, in a series of detailed conversations. She constantly improvised Harry's opinions, until he seemed to her like an independent voice, advising, encouraging, warning. She heard, but not as before. He was apart now, had been for some time before his death, and she did not have to obey. Becca, too, sometimes spoke; but mostly she was simply close, an ever-watching presence. Every now and then, Jan spoke out loud, to herself or Maggie, surprising herself with the sudden, intrusive noise of her own voice.

In a month or so, the cargo-men would come. What then? 'Oh, Maggie, they won't let me stay.' Not a woman on her own in the jungle. The homestead should live on, for Becca's sake. But the Commandante wouldn't allow it. Besides, so much would be impossible. Even if Jan could look after herself and the gardens, she couldn't see to sign cheques or to answer mail. She would be vulnerable. Hunters or highway workers might come and steal. There was no alternative: she had to be prepared to leave.

'A month,' she said out loud. What should she aim to do in that time? One thing, certainly: she would have to fulfil Harry's wishes. 'One good thing –' She remembered his cheerful remark the first day on Homestead Hill '– I found a place for my grave-site!' Yes, the Observation Ledge. Your view. I guess I can manage that. What would it mean? Carrying the remains up the hill, finding the way to the Ledge, and digging there. The thought of doing that, of immersing herself in a place that had been so much part of Harry and Becca, suddenly racked her with sobs, 'Come on, Jan!' It was as if she could hear him, as clearly as she had ever heard him in real life. 'You know I can't stand it when you break down.' It's hard, Harry, you don't understand, she might have said once. Now things were different. Who's breaking down, Harry? Not me. I'm on my own now, and I'll do as I think best.

A month.

The cargo-men would come, and she, and her possessions, would be taken away. So many possessions. The tools – well, the men could have those, that much was in Harry's will. But the papers, Becca's things, the books, the marimba, everything else would have to be ferried out. The men would, as usual, be in a hurry. They wouldn't be able to take everything with them at once. There would have to be two journeys, at least. So much opportunity for loss, damage and theft, so little chance for her – blind, deaf, and, with her non-existent Portuguese, effectively dumb as well – to control events.

'A month, Maggie. We have a lot to do.'

🜚

Jan – exploring her growing capacities, imbued with such a sense of independence that she felt quite newly hatched, fascinated by what she might achieve, as if she were the subject of

328

a unique experiment – worked as meticulously for herself as Harry had once, many years before, worked for her. Once or twice through the night, and again at dawn, she would push the fire together. As soon as she had eaten, she went out to split wood for the day. For a few days, she kept the fire going outside, underneath the hotplate. As her confidence grew, however, she decided to try again to light a fire inside. This time, there was no mistake, and from then on she had a regular supply of hot water for making soups and tea.

Not that she kept regular hours. A morning's work would exhaust her, and she would often fall asleep for the afternoon. Then, later, she would be unable to sleep for more than an hour or two. She would wake to make breakfast, only to discover from the radio that it was 2 a.m.

As it happened, this suited her, for during the night Maggie retired to the rafters, and Jan was free from her. Those night-time hours, she discovered, were good for going through the boxes, to discover exactly where everything was.

One night, when she was working, her hair-band broke. Her long hair, uncut on Harry's instruction for the last twenty years, tumbled down around her shoulders. She couldn't allow it to remain loose. It would singe as she made up the fire and dangle in her food. She felt through one of the boxes to see if she could find another band. There was none. She had decided to use a cloth, and was on the point of closing the box when she felt a pair of scissors.

Well, this is my chance, she thought, lifting them out. I've been wanting to do this for years. It had always been im-practical, having long hair in the jungle. She began to snip away, and as she worked, she remembered Harry's words that night in the Granja before they were married, when he had begun the process of remoulding her. 'I don't want you cutting your hair,' he'd said. 'You'll have to take your new life seriously.' Growing her hair had been a sign to him that she had rejected her former life, and accepted his in its place. Now, equally deliberately, she asserted her own freedom, laying the eighteen-inch locks carefully down beside her, then gathering them up to burn them.

The next morning, when Maggie came down from the rafters, she explored Jan's head with interest, but seemed not at all put out by the sudden change in her mistress's hairstyle. 'That's right, Maggie, it's still me!' Jan reassured her, and gave her a spoonful of *farinha* and guava preserve to show that nothing fundamental had changed.

When it was wet, or threatened rain – which it did with increasing frequency, for the weather was turning cooler now – Jan stayed down by the river. She would leave the packing up of the riverside house until later, but meantime she set about making sure their boxes were in good repair.

Of the six wooden boxes they had brought with them from Mexico, four were badly damaged by rot and termites, and needed new planking. As it happened, there were spare planks – three eighteen-foot boards with which Harry had intended to make another gutter – stored on blocks behind the marimba.

For many wet days at a time, Jan worked on her carpentry. First, determined to keep Becca's remains safe and dry for burial, she hung the sack up on a crossbeam. Then she heaved the planks out, measured the broken boxes with string, and marked off rough lengths on the planks, using the carpenter's saw to make nicks in the wood. She cut the planks as best she could, making rough right angles with a straight-edged piece of cardboard. She could feel that the results were amateur. 'Foolishness, Jan!' she could hear his voice berating her. Well, Harry, it's up to me now, and I've done it, and it's not a bad job for a beginner.

Next came the business of hammering the cut pieces into place. The frames of the boxes were still firm, providing her with solid bases. But the wood itself was so dense that, as often as not, the nail would slide sideways beneath the hammer. It took many more wet days of concentrated, frustrating work for her to complete the task to her satisfaction. So intense was her concentration that several times as she worked, she bumped the sack containing Rebecca's remains. So close did Becca seem, though, so much part of her daily work, that, far from being appalled by the action, she found herself muttering an absent-minded 'Oh, excuse me,' only realizing when she heard the sound of her voice how incongruous her words were. When she finished her work, she knew the repairs were rough, but she could feel that they were strong enough to withstand the journey back to Cucuí.

On dry days, with Maggie running back and forth in front of her, she would walk up the trail, sliding her hands along the trail markers, to the Hilltop Hut. There, she sorted through the possessions, area by area, moving from Becca's corner to the hearth, to Harry's corner, to her own place, feeling for objects – hammocks, food, utensils, a duffel bag of Harry's, books, binoculars, garden tools. At first, she was wary of Maggie – she didn't want her thieving hands to make her task more difficult – but Maggie seemed to understand what was expected of her, for most of the time at least.

Only once did Maggie frighten her. Jan had dropped a knife in the sack, ready to take it down the hill, but a few minutes later, as she checked through what she had, she found the knife was gone. There was a hole in the bottom of the sack. Maggie must have seen or made the hole, and teased the knife out through it. The thought sent a shiver of trepidation through her. If Maggie jumped on her shoulder with a knife in her hand, there was no telling what damage might be done. She stood up hastily, and hurried out of the hut, hoping that her action would cause Maggie to drop the knife right there on the floor, where it could easily be found later. Which was exactly what happened: on her next visit, Jan, feeling across the floor with her feet, found the knife by the hearth, not a yard from where she had lost it.

As Jan's strength and confidence grew, she began to plan for the burial. There was nothing yet she could do for Harry. But she did, on one of her trips, take the sack containing Becca's remains with her. She feared, as she lifted the sack down from its crossbeam, that the journey would be a hard one. But no: Becca, surviving in spirit, had no connection with what she, Jan, held in her hands. The remains were a symbol of what had been, and of what endured. By concentrating on each step and each handhold, Jan again held grief in check.

One day, after a dozen journeys spread over two weeks, she realized she had almost finished. There were two large boxes she would have to leave up there – they were too much for her to carry, and would have to wait there until the cargo-men came. Another trip or two would be enough to clear up anything else, she thought as she set off. On this occasion, she had with her the last bundle of food, hanging down her back from a cloth tump-line round her forehead.

Almost as soon as she left the house, she smelled pineapple. She paused. She had smelled the fruit on the way up earlier, and had failed to find it. Having had no fresh food, certainly no fruit, for almost three months, the wonderful, fragrant, pervasive smell enticed her into a more thorough-going search. She stopped and sniffed the air, trying to work out exactly where the ripe fruit must be. Following her nose, she stepped cautiously off the trail. It was a risk, but a small one, for the slope would guide her back up to the hut if she couldn't find her way across to the trail.

She had taken no more than a few steps when her stick whacked into something. She stopped, smelled pineapple more strongly, reached out, felt spindly leaves, and then to her amazement, as much by luck as by following her sense of smell, she found the ripe fruit itself. She felt enormously pleased, as if she had made a great discovery or been given a wonderful present. It was the homestead's greatest gift to her in all the time she had been alone. She picked it, swung the food package round to the front, stuffed the pineapple into it, and sidled back up the slope to the trail. She called Maggie, and, delighted with her find, hurried on down the hill.

Once she was in the forest on the Long Trail, she felt she was as good as home. Another ten minutes, and she would be able to eat her sweet-smelling pineapple. Moving fast, she crossed the Pineapple Clearing, re-entered the forest, and was about to take a right-hand bend that would lead her down the Long Trail to the Fourth Clearing, and –

And suddenly, the mud and roots beneath her feet were foreign – too steep, too rough, and quite definitely not the Long Trail. By the time she realized she had taken a wrong turn, she must have been ten or fifteen feet off course. The path was steeper now, and she couldn't stop. She felt for footholds with increasing desperation, hardly daring to admit to herself what she had done. She had taken a short cut favoured by Becca and Harry when they wanted to stay in the shade, or wanted to get down to the Nursery Clearing quickly. It went straight down the ridge slope for perhaps sixty yards, and came out somewhere at the far end of the Nursery Clearing. There was no retracing her steps. She was too weak to carry her burden back up the hill, and she certainly had no intention of abandoning it.

She staggered on down the slope, her feet fumbling for holds, bumping into trees, until, she didn't know how, she burst out of the jungle shadows into the Nursery Clearing.

She stood panting and apprehensive. Where now? The clearing was overgrown. There was no trail to guide her, no slope to give her a sense of direction.

She felt Maggie's hand on her leg.

'Maggie?' she said, shakily, 'You going to be my seeing-eye monkey?'

But Maggie couldn't help. Jan twisted her head around, trying to pick up any clues from her surroundings. Nothing but shadow and darker shadow.

'Well, no use standing around here all day. Come on.'

She knew what she should aim for: the far end of the clearing, where the narrow entrance led out to the main trail.

But with the sun almost overhead, disoriented as she was, she couldn't tell which way to go. She aimed towards shadow that she guessed would be jungle, stepping over the overgrown remnants of the nursery beds. Her feet found no pattern there, and after several yards she came up against bushes and saplings. She turned, and tried again. More bushes, more leaves, more trees.

She backed off, feeling not fear, so much as the knowledge that fear was waiting for her, out there, a shape in the darkness, a beast that could be kept at a distance if only she could face the worst that could happen to her.

What, then, if she couldn't find her way back? She had food with her. She even had a fresh pineapple. It was the pineapple that fortified her. That gift from the homestead, that recompense for their labour, seemed to be an assurance that she was, in some odd way, being looked after. Perhaps she could just . . . stay there, until the men came? It would be cold at night, but she wasn't going to *die*. The thought comforted her. There was no hurry. She had, she guessed, two weeks. She could surely survive out there for two weeks alone, even without shelter and without fire.

Freed from the threat of paralysing fear, without considering the real implications of the idea, she began to wonder what might then happen. Oh – how would the men know she was there? She couldn't hear them. True, they could hear her, but she couldn't shout every daylight hour for the next two weeks. She decided she had better, after all, make a more thorough-going effort to find her way back.

She consulted the map of the homestead laid down in her mind. The path from the Nursery Clearing led to the trail, which led through the Glade to the Garden Clearing. The Glade, then the Garden Clearing. That meant the trees should be a good deal thinner in that part of the forest. She could distinguish between the light grey of sky and the dark grey of jungle shadow. Perhaps she would be able to make out a difference between the heavy shade of the surrounding forest

334

and the lightness of the sky shining through the trees from the Garden Clearing.

She backed away further, to even out the shadows around her. She scanned experimentally. Yes, there, *there* the shadow paled. She fixed on the spot, and aimed towards its centre.

Suddenly, after a few paces, the pattern of raised beds made sense beneath her feet. She breathed a sigh of relief. She knew precisely where she was. She felt her way through the beds, through scanty bushes, towards the middle of the patch of light, and then she was out of the Nursery Clearing and on to the main trail.

Waving her stick in front of her, she reached the hut, and swung her parcel to the ground. Back in her hammock, she felt for her knife, sliced the pineapple in half, scooped it into a bowl, and after a moment of delicious anticipation, tasted the first spoonful. It was the sweetest sensation since her first bath in the river. The tang of the juices trickling over her tongue sent through her depleted body a shiver of delight, a joy so intense that it made the experience of being lost seem trivial.

🕭

She knew from the radio that Easter was approaching. Easter that year was on 6 April. That was about the time the cargo-men were due. But back in Cucuí, it was a holiday. The men wouldn't even set off until after Easter. Meanwhile, there was still work to do.

In particular, she had not yet been able to start on the terrible task of the burials. She planned to treat Harry's remains with the same reverence as Rebecca's. But the cooler weather had slowed the process of decay and the smell told her she could not yet approach.

There was, however, another vital task waiting to be done. She wanted to make sure that the information she had was clearly recorded, ready to be taken out to Cucuí. Her friends, her family, Harry's family, and numerous officials would all want a clear statement of what had happened. Besides, if the cargo-men were late, and she herself died, no one would ever know what had happened. She had no idea what Harry had written in his journal, and anyway the Brazilians would not be able to read it. She wanted to leave her own typed record of events, to be formally despatched through the mail, rather than rely on anything Harry may have scribbled.

There was a second reason behind her decision to write down what had happened. She had to remain in control – *responsible*. In the outside world, events would sweep her along with bewildering speed, unless she could assert herself. She'd always been bad at that, even before her marriage. It would be harder now, much harder, after so many years of dependency and isolation. Without proof that she was functioning well, and could take decisions for her own life, there would be a risk that someone – a judge, an officer, an embassy official, even some well-meaning friend or relative – would think her incompetent, and snatch the power of decision from her.

She began to type again, sitting by the hearth with the typewriter on her lap. For the first time, she sought words to summarize what had happened. She did not try to express her grief. On the contrary: she contained it, in an austere recital of events. She wrote to her parents; to Harry's sister, Junetta; to Armindo; to the Commandante in Cucuí; to the American Embassy; to Jaime Bulnes; to Eleanor Miner; to Toni Martin. For ten days, on and off, she wrote, breaking off only to split wood, fetch water, wash, eat and sleep. 'Dear Mother and Daddy, This letter has tragic news . . .', 'Dearest Toni, This is the saddest latter I shall ever write to you . . .', 'Dear George and Kay, I am using the Easter feeling of hope to write this letter of tragedy . . .', 'Dearest Eleanor . . .', '*Querido* Jaime . . .' To each she wrote a two-page summary of events, transforming the ruin of her life into words.

Still there was no collapse into grief. As with everything she had done on her own since dragging Becca's body, the raw practicality of the task served to protect her from her emotions a while longer. Her ribbon was too worn to use, so she reverted to a trick she had employed before of typing without a ribbon, using two sheets and carbon paper to 'make a copy of something that doesn't exist'. It took concentration to set the sheets right, square up the carbon, and then, afterwards, keep the pages arranged in the right order and the right envelopes. Her task was made even more difficult by Maggie, who was disturbed by the change in routine and sat on her shoulder waiting to snatch any loose sheets she could lay her hands on.

Thus distracted, Jan was able to hold herself in check until she had finished her last letter:

> I have collected Becca's bones and carried them up to the other hut for burial there, which I have been putting off, and finally decided to wait until the men can open the path to the lookout, which is where H. wanted his grave. His bones are not yet ready to be picked up and the men are due after Easter.
>
> I shall stay in Cucuí until I know where I am going and have settled with Armindo. I want to stay in Brazil, where I can garden, have enough to eat and have someone read my mail to me, and thread a needle – I pin everything now. I would like to do something for children. Becca delighted in them so and she loved flowers and it makes my grief seemingly unhealable that she had so little of either joy in her young life. I don't understand what happened to end it so suddenly. I trust life is good and you two are taking care of yourselves,
> My love,
> Jan

12

INQUISITION

Understanding was the hardest part. Only now, after weeks of work, after the brutal, formal exercise of letter-writing, did she risk moving beyond mere knowledge towards understanding.

On Easter Sunday, for the first time, she asked: Why? The question opened a new and terrible chapter, for a simple examination of the events surrounding Becca's death led, step by step, to an inquisition that twisted her mental and emotional universe upside down.

Why? What had happened out there in the rain and the darkness? They had fallen, with Harry somehow on top of Becca. But why? Had they both slipped, simultaneously? Unlikely. There must have been a collision. Perhaps – and here she reverted to her first thought when hearing his words – perhaps he had been the cause of the collision. He had been 'surprised' at finding the bucket empty. That could only mean he had thought it would be full, as it should have been after all that rain. Perhaps there had been a spill. He had always been sensitive about water. If a bucket had been spilled, and with the main downpour over, he might well have exploded into sudden anger at the idea of anyone having to fetch more water from the river. He could have lashed out. He had not struck Becca since childhood, but with the disease, and his pain, and the urgency of the task in hand, and the infuriating loss of the flashlight to Maggie's thieving hands, and then (perhaps) the spilling of water so carefully caught, who knew how he might have reacted? She could see Becca, exhausted out of mind, standing meekly by him, could see him jerking the bucket upwards, snatching it from her grasp, swinging it in explosive and uncoordinated anger, losing his balance, falling, falling as she fell, falling on her. A sudden silence, perhaps. The rain pattering down on them both. His shock. Her injury. (Where? Some vital but painless tear in her abdomen, or – Jan recalled that nightmarish moment when she stooped to pick up the strange, soft object from the floor of the hut – an agonizing wound in the head?) Him helping her up. She stumbling inside, hanging on to a hearth post, and then falling with a groan, even as he, as usual, glossed over the whole incident with some inconsequential remark about Maggie.

It couldn't be worse than that, could it? It couldn't be of any significance, no, it couldn't surely, that when she first started to look after him, she found he had no trousers on. No, he said he had changed when he came in. Yet the connections – Harry half undressed (perhaps), his phrase 'She was under me' (why hadn't he said simply, 'I fell on her?') and Becca's pitiful words 'I can't *stand* the idea of a man lying on top of me' – made terrible equations in her mind.

They made no sense, yet refused to go away. Harry had not been sexually active for years, had made no reference to sexual matters for she could not remember how long. He evaded the subject. He had always been so protective of Becca; but that had meant insisting that she appear as unfeminine as possible. He was determined to hide her femininity. Who from? Himself? So that he should never, ever 'touch Rebecca like that' (his words in Fair Oaks)? Ridiculous. He was old, and ill. Yet his behaviour and his words sanctioned such thoughts, because he himself had given her so little information, as if, by not telling her of Becca's fate, he were guiltily concealing some fearful deed.

And not simply concealing – actively seeking to excuse it, if his odd remarks about José were anything to go by. 'It would have been physical abuse, you know that, don't you? It's good she's the first to go,' he'd said, as if he were determined to avoid accepting any burden of guilt, though there was reason enough for guilt even if he had had no direct role in her fall; as if he were determined to justify her death, and his part in it, by claiming to have saved her from a fate worse than death.

Why? She could find no answers by repeating the events and the words of that evening. All was hidden in darkness, the darkness of that night, and the darkness of Harry's own soul. Why? The very question, driving her to look beyond the events themselves, evoked a violent, unfocused, childish anger.

She railed at first against misfortune. It shouldn't have happened! They had been 'under guidance' – it shouldn't have been *allowed* to happen. They were expert homesteaders, they knew what they were about. So many things might have shaped events differently. If she hadn't moved hammocks, she would have been right by the hearth when Becca fell. If she had kept her hearing-aid in, she would have heard Becca fall. If she hadn't taken her can outside, Becca would have been with her instead of with Harry.

Why? For two days she lived in rage, raging that she had nothing on which she could vent her rage. There was Harry, of course. There was reason enough to rage at Harry. Twenty years of marriage, and never a word of endearment (no: one, just one, and that from the time before they were married. 'God put those words in your mouth, *honey*.') Had he ever really loved her, or just seen her as a prop for his own personality? Had he just needed her to confirm his view of himself as controlled, definite, truthful, masterful, so thoroughly adequate? From the start, he had convinced her he knew how life should be lived, he knew what was wrong with the world, he knew how it should be set right. He knew, he knew so well he had no need to examine himself any more, no need to question what effect he had on others, no need to think. He'd set himself so carefully beyond all criticism, outside society, in a place where no one could get at him, turned himself into a hermit, protecting a mask that would have been shattered by

340

contact with normal people, turning every inadequacy into a virtue, dismissing his mistakes as the will of providence, a voice crying in the wilderness, preparing the way for nothing and no one, because he could make no one listen.

There was in all this enough reason for bitterness, which, if released, would cast his whole history in a new light. Throughout his life, he had been afraid of security, had consistently rejected it. On the point of any achievement – college, the cooperative movement, the Vermont homestead, his first marriage, two homesteads in Mexico – he cast aside what had been built, as if success were the ultimate failure because it might deprive him of control, as if he could keep his vision intact only by rejecting success to take up some other challenge, until he had to throw aside life itself, or face what he had become, the embodiment of sins he condemned in others. Christian! What was this talk of love, from a man who mourned for pet monkeys, yet refused to acknowledge the death of his own stepdaughter? Who could preach forgiveness, yet find fault at every turn? Who could preach the glories of God, yet never bother to keep a single record of all the work they performed to preserve those glories? Who could so inhibit the two women who cared for him that they preferred to strangle their own emotions rather than risk exposing themselves to his ridicule?

And at the end, he had deceived them both, by preaching unselfishness and then driving Becca to death with the selfishness of his demands. Knowing that Becca was life itself to Jan, he had not even given Jan the chance to save her. He had chosen to do the most ordinary things – changing clothes, feeding Maggie – while Becca lay dying upon the floor. By his silence, his unforgivable silence, he had deceived Jan into thinking that all was well, when Becca was already dead. And then only: 'She's finished. She didn't make it.' Surely, surely he had done enough for her to lay all blame on him?

Yes, he had; but no, she couldn't.

If there was anything of all this in her anger, it was too

341

unfocused to settle on Harry. She did not escape by blaming him. She was still too imbued with his ideals, too conditioned to the belief that to criticize him was nothing more than pettiness. Besides, to reject Harry would be to reject the world that Becca accepted, and she was not ready for the complex implications of that. Even if she had blamed him then, she would have found no enduring comfort in doing so. There was still too much unanswered about herself.

After a week, on the first Sunday after Easter, her anguish leaped to another, yet more painful level. From the moment she awoke, unanswered questions battered her. For a time, she tried blocking out the questions by turning on the radio and holding it against her ear. But those voices had no chance against her inner voices. She sat in her hammock, the radio unheard on her shoulder, weeping helplessly.

Hoping that physical exhaustion would silence the voices in her head, she went out to chop wood. There were some logs left to split, knotty recalcitrant things. But this activity, which might once have controlled her grief, only plunged her deeper into it – these reject pieces had been Becca's, fuel for one of her ash-fires. Sometimes the axe stuck. With gritted teeth and sobs of frustration, she hammered at it with a branch to get it free or force it through. Sometimes the twisted grain threw the blade uselessly sideways. Eventually, exhausted, she stopped, her sweaty blouse and slacks clinging to her. She returned to her hammock, and her unresolved turmoil.

Becca had been lying there, alive perhaps, and she had not gone to her. Why, why had she believed Harry? Becca had lain cold upon the ground while she, Jan, had had warmth to spare, a blanket, even strength to spare, and when her child's need was at its most intense, she, the mother, had been simply unaware, cut off in selfish isolation. Oh, Father, she prayed, help me to know *why*.

Rebecca's words echoed in her mind – 'There's more than one kind of martyr in this world.' What had Harry said to prompt that enigmatic statement? She could imagine – he'd so often said he was a martyr himself, to physical affliction, to the burden of being responsible for Jan and Becca (my cross, he'd called them on more than one occasion, my cross). Becca, driven beyond endurance, might then have made her comment, a criticism he could not acknowledge despite its mildness, and therefore had expressed in a tone of equally mild bewilderment, for any other tone would have meant understanding what she meant, and admitting a part in her martyrdom. To Jan, there was no puzzle. Becca had been a martyr many times over, martyred by the work, by the failure to make the Homestead flourish. If Becca had put one third of that labour into a homestead in Vermont or California, it would have shown twice, three times the results. Martyred by isolation, by the lack of friends, by the lack of a mate, by Harry's incessant demands. Yes, more than one kind of martyr, for she was many kinds in one, crucified by labour, by isolation, by disappointment, by disease, by Harry.

And by Jan?

There was no twisting away. She, too, was guilty, and not simply of being unaware. It went deeper. Because she had known herself to be unworthy, inadequate, guilty in some way she could never quite define, she had, right from the start, accepted her own suffering as just; she had cast *herself* in the role of martyr; she had accepted Harry's emulation of Jesus and sought with him a way to virtue; she had trusted that in all they did they were under guidance; she had accepted Harry's direction, she had worked to develop that acceptance; she had so worked to be subservient that subservience had come to seem a virtue. If it was true that Harry had driven Becca to her death, it was also true that Becca had let him drive her; and where else had she learned her determination to accept, and accept, and accept, if not from Jan? Where else had she learned to be so fatally vulnerable, so passive, if not from Jan? The voice crying in the wilderness had been heard, by Jan. *She* had listened, uncritically, for far too long, and taught Rebecca to do the same. As a result they had – *she* had – killed the truest

343

Christian of the three of them. From a seedbed of undefined guilt this monstrous growth had sprung: she, she, not Harry, was guilty of Rebecca's death.

She sat, racked by her own inquisition, immobilized by grief, for hours on end. Only in the late afternoon did she see that if she stayed there, her will to live would die, as she had always feared it might once she allowed herself to look into the darkness within her. For her own sake, and for Becca's, she must move.

What else was there to do? The logs were in. The fire was burning. She had food.

Water. That was it. She could fetch more water. Extra water might come in handy tomorrow, or the day after.

She stood, walked to the drink-stand, picked up a half-full bucket, poured its contents into the aluminium basin to serve as washing-up water, and set off to the river. She found her way down the steep first section, towards the dog-leg, by the tree, the place where she had got lost on her first lone trip to fetch water after Becca's death.

Becca, always Becca.

Down here by the river, Becca seemed more alive than ever. She remembered Becca as she looked out over her favourite spot. 'Janny, I can see the dolphins upriver.' Jan recalled occasions of quiet contentment down at the river, and Becca's gentle voice describing the scene: the dark foliage, the trailing vines, the black, black water, the silence. 'There's a tree in bloom up there; the blossoms are drifting down on the current.' The remembered words cut at her through her frail resolve, and left her again without defence.

But what happened next had nothing to do with memory. Suddenly, other words came to her, heard, yet unheard, like a voice breaking in upon a dream:

'Don't carry on so, Janny. It's all right with me.'

She stopped, and said out loud: 'Becca, how can you . . .' She was about to say: '. . . let go so willingly?' but her voice sounded so incongruous in the surrounding silence of the jungle and the river that she broke off.

At once, she distrusted. There had been no voice. There was nothing but the jungle, and the river, and the silence. Her mind was playing tricks to take away the burden of guilt and grief.

Yet the words, the words were Becca's. 'Don't carry on so' – typical, folksy Becca. And if the words were Becca's, to deny them would be like denying Becca herself. She had always felt, with a certainty amounting to knowledge, that Becca's spirit was free of her body, that Becca was there, a part of the surrounding forest, waiting and watching. If Becca was there, as real in spirit as the forest was materially, then she, Jan, had to accept that Becca's words must also be true.

As she stood, astonished, she became certain that it was indeed Becca herself who had offered reassurance and forgiveness.

A great weight lifted from her.

❦

By mid-April, the cargo-men still had not arrived. Perhaps there was a gasoline shortage. Perhaps Armindo was ill. Perhaps they *had* come, seen the frond-covered body, called out, received no reply, and fled.

As before, anxiety found relief in action. Her logs were almost gone, and she needed a longer-term supply of firewood. There was a source, close to hand – a tree lying in the forest, twenty or thirty yards away, its roots near the trail. Harry had let it lie because the wood was too hard to cut.

One morning, she took the rope, her stick and the thirty-inch pulp-saw, and went a few yards up the trail to the spot near where she thought the tree had fallen. Maggie dashed past her into the forest.

Even here, so close to the house, she could get lost. She tied on to a trail-side sapling and stepped tentatively between trees and bushes, feeling her way with the stick, the rope unravelling behind her.

'Don't know why I bother with this stick, Maggie.' Heavens knows what I'd do if I picked up a snake, she thought, as she felt the rope go taut. Well, it's not this far. Let's try another direction.

She pulled herself back, then set off again. Within a couple of minutes, she came up against a hard tree-trunk, smoothed to a gloss by time and rain.

'Made it, Maggie. Let's get to work.'

She explored the trunk back and forth. The bole was long, sixty-foot or so probably, and eighteen inches across. It was raised a foot off the ground, still resting on its branches at one end and on its roots at the other. It'll grip the blade when it begins to go, she thought. Better be careful, or I'll end up losing the saw.

Cutting the tree up would be quite an operation, but she knew how it could be done. She returned to the house to fetch the axe and two logs. Not bothering now to secure herself with her rope, for she could feel the newly opened trail with her feet, she slid the logs under the trunk to make sure that it remained raised after she had made her first cut.

Then she started sawing, feeling the taut blade bite into the wood. It was slow work, with many pauses to allow her aching shoulders to recover. After an hour or so, she felt a slight stiffness in the saw. Now, don't let the blade *bite*, Jan, that would be just plain foolish – Harry's instructions echoed in her mind – stop *now*, or you'll be in trouble! She drew the saw out, and laid it down beside the trunk.

She stood back, picked up the axe, swung the head up on the trunk, felt for the cut she made, and began to chop, aiming to hack away the wood either side of the saw-cut so that the trunk could break downwards without seizing the saw. Now, remember, Janny – that was Becca's voice now – it's best to chop only one side of the cut. I never understood that, Becca. I'll try it on both sides to make a good V-shape.

After a while, with the sweat soaking her blouse, she changed tools again. She was there for two or three hours, sawing and chopping, slowing up as exhaustion overtook her, but persevering until the trunk was almost through. Then she chose a spot a yard to her right, and began again. For another two hours she worked, with ever longer pauses to allow her aching limbs and pounding heart to recover. Finally, first one side then the other cracked, and the whole section fell clear, with a thump. 'Maggie! It's OK!' She called out, exhilaration momentarily overcoming her exhaustion. 'We can keep our fire!'

But she couldn't rest yet. First she took the saw and axe back. Then she rolled the log out of the forest, along the trail to the saw-horse. Tomorrow she could chop it.

A day to cut a single log, she thought, as she collapsed into her hammock. Well, it'll be quicker now I've opened it up.

⚕

She knew now she could survive for a while longer, not indefinitely, but almost certainly until the cargo-men came. Sometime, they *would* come; if not the cargo-men, then the military. And there was still a lot to do.

Routine chores took up much of her day. To her usual tasks, she had added another, which gave her considerable satisfaction. She had been surviving for much of this time on sardines, and had amassed dozens of empty sardine cans. Every few days, she would carry them out to the chopping block and hammer them all flat with a piece of firewood. Some of them she would use as tiles, to pave over the muddy doorway; the rest she placed around pineapple plants, to add minerals to the soil.

Now that her routines were well established, she had time to start on another chore: cleaning out the flooring leaves, and at the same time sifting through the soggy mass to find whatever had been dropped. What she was really after was her good ear-mould. Day to day, it would make little difference to

347

her, for if she used the hearing-aid, the batteries would soon be dead. She hadn't heard a bird, a monkey or the insects since the day of the storm, and she had lived so long in silence that it no longer bothered her. But she was eager to have the aid working again so that she would be able to hear the cargo-men properly when they came.

For hours, she knelt, working her way down the hut, raking leaves into piles, then raising handfuls of leafmould, feeling through it and transferring it to a basket. She checked every nook as carefully as she could – noting, as she did so, that one of the house-posts, her own hammock-support, was almost eaten through by termites. The sifted mass she took to the Garden Clearing to use as mulch. In the course of her work, which took a week to finish, she found several spoons, a couple of forks, a few pencil stubs, and a candle or two; but no ear-mould.

𝍠

She needed to be clear in her mind about what to do when the men came. They would, as always, be eager to deliver their supplies and be gone back to their families. There would be the burials to arrange, for by now, at last, she had gathered Harry's remains. But the men would not want to spend days packing. They would not want, would not be able, to take loads of packages back with them. As Indians, they would be shocked at having to escort a woman with neither husband nor chaperone; a white woman at that, and a disabled one. How would she ensure against loss, damage, or outright theft? How, in brief, could she remain in control?

One thing was certain: she would have to make her wishes plain, and her Portuguese was almost non-existent. For years, she had been in Harry's shadow. Irrespective of her poor command of Portuguese and her disabilities, the culture demanded the public subservience of women. Becca had learned the language, but she had been Harry's translator. In five years, she, Jan, had never had an extended conversation with Cleonisia, let alone Armindo. She had the respect of others as a wife and mother, she assumed, but she was never addressed directly. She didn't even have a name in Portuguese. Occasionally, she was Dona Juana, but more often no more than 'my wife' or 'my mother'.

Now she would have to speak for herself, and that meant learning Portuguese. The means to do so were at hand. She had already made an attempt to start learning the language with the Brazilian Ministry of Education's Braille magazine. Her Spanish was useful, and Portuguese Braille used the same letter symbols as English except for the accented vowels, so she could make out some words.

She also had her radio. She was used to listening to the BBC's World Service, and had formed a particular attachment to the short stories and the book programme. She always listened to the news. Now, by twiddling the dial, she found the Portuguese service. The news provided her with her foundation. American hostages were being held in Iran. Guerrillas were fighting Russians in Afghanistan. The authorities were recommending the evacuation of areas around Mount St Helen's. World leaders gathered in Belgrade for Tito's funeral. In London, special forces stormed the Iranian embassy. Knowing the gist of the stories from the English broadcasts, she forced herself to concentrate on the Portuguese, dividing it down into words, building up her knowledge of grammar, vocabulary and pronunciation, reinforcing her growing skills with the Braille magazines.

As she broke through the symbols to the meaning, she became obsessively fascinated with the content of the pieces. There was one on the Big Bang theory of the creation of the universe. Another was on the behaviour of the emperor penguin. That was her favourite. She was moved to tears by the devotion of the emperor penguins to their young. They inhabited a world much harsher than hers, yet they did not fail as she had failed. Pictures formed in her mind, vistas of ice and snow empty but for the huge, flightless birds huddled against the icy wind, their precious eggs tucked between their feet. It was astonishing to her that she and the emperor penguins should be living on the same planet.

※

So there was work, always work, either mental or physical. She did not feel her isolation. Besides, she had a companion: Maggie. Maggie was a sounding-board for ideas, a constant presence scampering in from the yard or down from the ceiling whenever she heard Jan preparing food, a reassurance that the trail was free of snakes, and, on one occasion, an insurance against danger of a different sort.

It happened when Jan was preparing soup. She wanted to add some cooking oil. She felt about among her cans, and found a slightly rusty one, an old oil-can, one that she should use up. She felt Maggie's soft, questing hand on her arm.

'You want your share right now, do you, Maggie? Just a moment so we don't spill it.'

She unscrewed the top, dipped her finger into the can, and offered it to Maggie. The monkey sucked her finger and gave a sudden *psssst!* of disgust. Jan sniffed at the can. Insecticide! No wonder Becca had placed it out of the way; no wonder the can was old and rusty. She shook her head incredulously, remembering the time when Maggie had been so tyrannical she had considered killing her. Love had been her way, after all.

But love would not be enough in the future, for Maggie posed a long-term problem. How would she live after the cargo-men came? Like Rima and Hanuman, she was neither a jungle monkey nor a house monkey. As time drew on, the problem, obvious from the start, became more pressing.

One afternoon early in May, Jan came in from washing her lunch plate at the washstand. As she poured herself a cup of freshly brewed leaf tea, Maggie jumped up on to the hearth and tugged at her hand. 'Wait a moment, Maggie,' she scolded. 'It's too hot for you.' She added some cold water from the cup. 'Come on,' she coaxed, scooping Maggie up in the crook of her arm. 'We'll go out and sit on the log.'

The sun was still high. Jan carried Maggie to the log bench, and sat down. Gripping the mug firmly to resist Maggie's urgent fingers, she allowed her to drink her fill. When the monkey had finished, she lay down in Jan's lap, belly up in the sun. Jan began to stroke her gently, pausing occasionally to brush sweat-bees from her face.

'We could go on like this for a long time, couldn't we, girl? The sardines are running low, but there are enough beans to last for weeks, and the manioc leaves are fine. We've got the garlic, and the taro will be ready, if I can get around to digging it up. We should have more moments like this, Maggie. I should have sat out in the sun with Becca more. But there was just so much work. Perhaps things will be different now. It's our choice, isn't it? I don't owe anything to anyone. I can work when I choose, rest when I choose . . .' She scratched Maggie's flat stomach thoughtfully.

I can be as sensible, or as foolish as I like, she thought. I can live or die, and there's no one to answer to for my decision. I can make sure that Maggie is returned to her proper place, in the tree-tops. I could take her there myself. I could make a ladder, a jungle ladder of sharpened stakes driven into the trunk, the way they do it in Malaya. Yes, Maggie, if I want, I can show you the tree-tops, and die there too if I want. She smiled at the thought.

But they will come. The knowledge brought her back to reality. They will come, and I shall have to act the grateful survivor. I'll do my best, I know I will. But what about Maggie? 'Cucuí is no place for you, Maggie,' she said out loud. 'It's a different climate, a different world. You'd never survive. But I can't leave you. You're not a jungle monkey. You're not even like Hanuman. No one has forced you to fend for yourself.'

The problem of Maggie's future saddened her. There was, as far as she could see, no answer. She began to weep. She stroked Maggie's tummy and raised her head as if she could see over the tree-tops to the mountains. 'Father,' she prayed. 'I can't take her, and I can't leave her. I don't have a solution. I have to be given one.'

The sun dipped behind the trees, throwing the yard into shadow.

'Come on, Maggie. Let's have an early dinner. I'm hungry already.'

She went in, and put some bean soup to reheat. A few minutes later, she poured out a bowl and began to eat, standing up. Maggie climbed up to the shelf, and leant down to take beans from Jan's pursed lips. When the soup was finished, Maggie bounced off through the hut as usual, to play out in the yard.

Jan went to her hammock, then remembered that the upright to which it was tied had been eaten through by termites. She untied it, and carried it to the place behind the screen where Becca had slept. Maggie was nowhere around. That was normal: she always retired to the rafters at dusk, never coming down until dawn.

But the next morning, she did not reappear. That had never happened before, not once in the previous two months.

Suddenly anxious, Jan called: 'Magg-ie! Magg-ie!' But the sound of her voice was small and lonely, as if swallowed up in the surrounding silence. Maggie did not come, and Jan suddenly knew, with absolute certainty, that she would never come again.

The knowledge cast her into mourning all over again. For two months, Maggie had been her only friend, her only family, providing not simply companionship, but a distraction that helped keep grief at bay. 'I know I asked for a resolution, Father,' she prayed. 'But I didn't know it would be so hard.'

Now, for the first time, she was utterly alone.

𝕩

Isolation forced her deeper inside herself. There were more layers yet to be probed and stripped, in her attempt to understand what had happened.

In the beginning, there had been a simplicity to their aims. They had seen themselves as peasant intellectuals seeking to live in harmony with nature, following Christ, mapping a way of life that might also be a pattern for many thousands of others living in the tropics. Hard to do, yes, but any suffering, hers or Harry's, would be part of the human condition, the common cup. They had chosen to count themselves among the have-nots, the suffering majority. If the rewards were slow in coming, at least they were assured – the satisfaction of living with nature; spiritual growth; the acquisition of experience and knowledge; a lasting homestead, which Becca could inherit; the certainty that she, that they, were 'under guidance', a certainty that 'all things work together for good to them that love God,' a certainty confirmed by her sense of intimacy with the Source, the Presence, the forest, God-in-Nature manifested in his own creation. Against all this, the idea of her own death seemed insignificant indeed.

All that, her past, her life, was now bereft of meaning. Harry, whose guidance she had trusted, and the Christian God to whom she had committed herself had led her to a false Eden. There was no reward. Harry had been reduced, not elevated, by suffering; reduced to a gutted shell of a personality, never once mentioning the faith he had claimed to hold so dear, denying her in death the guidance he had provided in life. What was he now? Was his spirit as confused as it had been before his death? Or had he somehow, in spirit, assumed the gentleness and refined perception he advocated? If that were so, he must see what he had always been, and had become, and suffer a torment no less awful than the physical torment in which he died. What sense did all this make of spiritual survival?

What sense, too, in the fact that she, Jan, had not died; that she had been condemned to live, while that for which she would have given her life – Becca – had perished, chilled and alone?

She had believed that virtue had its rewards. To believe that, to remain true to her faith, she would have to accept that Becca's death, which was all the reward she received, on this earth, for her innocent commitment to Christian virtue, was good and right. Becca herself had said it was all right, but no, no, it was not all right, it was not right at all. She could not believe that God's purpose could be served by Becca's death. Good could not come out of evil.

'It is not all right!' Jan cried out, railing at the silent wilderness. 'It is not all right! How can she say it is?'

Grief was a maze, a city of criss-crossed streets, a San Cristobal with just one way back to the high road of faith, and she couldn't find it. There was no way out of grief, because there was no way to accept Becca's death. She knew what Christ taught: acceptance of suffering. For Christ, for Christians, suffering had meaning and purpose. But in this, there was no meaning. What meaning could there possibly be in disabilities that left her impotent to help a dying daughter, in Harry's inadequacies, in a forest that promised so much and gave so little? There was no meaning, and there could be no acceptance.

She heard the words, she felt the urge from the forest, the wilderness, the Presence: accept, you must accept. Accept and be healed of your grief. And she cried out from the wilderness within her:

'No! I cannot accept! The grief is all I have left of Becca! Do not ask me to give that up!'

All around her, the shadows crowded in, waiting for her response.

She wept. 'Father, I know I must accept, but I cannot.' Her voice was no more than a croak through the paroxysm of weeping. 'I cannot accept. I am too wounded. Let me go. I will come back, if I can.'

She fell silent, and waited.

Words came into her mind: 'All right, my child'.

The words were both a release and an abandonment. She felt a great void around her, as if a circle of loving friends had understood her need, and withdrawn.

From then on, she ceased all prayer.

※

Saturday afternoons were good listening on the BBC. One Saturday, the last day of May, four and a half months after Becca's death and three months almost to the day after Harry's, she was listening to the book programme. The programme was in two halves. As the first half came to an end, she got up to make sure the fire was together, because she didn't want to interrupt the second half – an interview with Han Suyin, author of *A Many-Splendoured Thing*, a book she had read when young. She set the soup to one side, added a log, enough to keep the fire going for several hours, and turned to go back to her hammock.

As she turned, she felt the touch of something smooth and warm on her bare arm.

A hand.

13

WITHDRAWAL

Her whole body leapt with shock.

A voice said: 'Don Enrique?'

She turned, trembling, and said in faltering Portuguese: *'Com quem estou falando?'* – 'With whom am I speaking?'

The voice said: 'José.'

The cargo-men had arrived.

'Don Enrique is here?' asked José.

Still trembling with shock, Jan asked: 'Who is with you?'

'My brother, Gerao. And Angelico – he works for Don Armindo.'

She took a breath. 'Two weeks after you left, we became ill,' she said, feeling for the words. 'I am the only survivor.'

Silence. They received the news impassively. They were used to remaining aloof in the presence of whites, and José was even more taciturn than most Indians. But they might well, in addition, have been too shocked by what they had found to say anything. For the Homestead Hill of Jan's mind – a place as intimate as a suburban garden, overgrown now, but with every path clearly marked, and the lower hut as spick and span as she could possibly have made it – was very different from the grim physical reality. From the river, the hill was not even a hill to anyone who hadn't been there. From ten yards down-river, there was nothing to mark it off from any other bank of trees and overhanging saplings. The trail up from the river was like any other trail. When the men landed, they would have called, and been met only by a disturbing silence. The hut, its thatch already decaying, would have seemed strangely desolate. All around lay evidence not so much of Jan's meticulous work

356

but of squalor and decay. She had not found quite all the bones. Three or four of Harry's lay white out on the mud. Scattered apparently at random lay old cans, some strangely crumpled. Inside were more cans, piled up with plastic sandals, papers, and rough boxes. And Jan herself, though a model of health and sanity compared to the horror and confusion through which she had lived, was, by comparison with the Indians, a corpse-like creature, a witch with staring hair and only four teeth in her head. They must have watched her in fear and amazement, for several minutes perhaps, as she worked at the hearth, before they dared approach her, a woman with whom they had never had direct dealings. No wonder they were silent, until it became clear that Jan was not about to add anything else. Then, finally, José said: 'Don Armindo will be sad. He had much affection for Don Enrique.'

'It was malaria,' said Jan. It seemed as well to give the disease a name, and she didn't know what else to call it. 'Have you had malaria?'

'No.'

'Could you have brought it in with you?'

'Yes,' José said. Her question made no sense – if they hadn't had malaria, they couldn't have brought it with them – but José said what he thought she wanted to hear. They stood in silence for a few moments, before the slow, formal exchange continued. José said, 'There are letters. There is a letter from Don Armindo.' He placed a bundle of letters in her hand, and then Armindo's note.

She was at a loss. He must know I can't see, she thought. But she hesitated to ask for help – perhaps he had never learned to read. Perhaps a request for help would be an embarrassment.

'Is Don Armindo well?' she asked, to give herself time.

'Yes. He has gone to São Gabriel.'

'Could you help me . . . by reading the letter from Don Armindo?'

José didn't answer at first. Then she heard him talking in

lingua geral, the local dialect, with Gerao and Angelico. Eventually, José said, 'My brother will read.'

As it turned out, the note was nothing more than a brief apology that delivery was almost two months late.

'I have letters,' she said, when Gerao had finished. 'And I need help with the house. The termites have eaten a roof-post. Will you stay to work?'

There were low murmurs. No doubt they were talking over her request. Perhaps they were wondering what to do about her. She had made no mention of leaving. Best to show them, without discussion, that there was no question of her going. There was still work to do, the marimba to be packed away, the burials to be made. She had no intention of being rushed into departure, leaving her goods to be picked over by scavengers. They were responsible to Don Armindo and the Commandante for her, and would take her if she were in a state of collapse; but the journey with her would be a difficult one, and if she were obviously in control, she thought they would accept her decision readily enough.

'Yes,' José said. 'We will stay until tomorrow.'

'Thank you. The supplies . . . I will not need all the supplies ordered by Don Enrique.'

'No.'

'We will go to the boat. You will tell me what you have. I will tell you what I need.'

Guided by José, she accompanied the men down the bank to the canoe. There, José checked through the cargo, shouting out each item. As he did so, she told him what she wanted. When she had made her selection, they unloaded, and then carried the supplies up to the house.

'I will make a list of what I have,' she said, as they put the boxes on the floor. 'Wait.'

'Yes,' José said. Then, after a pause, he added, 'We wish to go up the hill.'

It was their usual request. They liked to climb the hill for the view across the jungle, back towards Cucuí, to see at a glance sweeps of jungle that took many days to paddle through. At the time, it did not strike Jan that there may have been other motives behind the request.

As they left the clearing, Jan remembered the two boxes that were to be brought down from the hill. 'José!' she called, but they were already out of earshot.

She sat down on the hearth bench, put the typewriter on one of the boxes, and typed her letter to Armindo. '*Estimable amigo Don Armindo*, You will know from the men that I have lost my two beloved ones from malaria.' As always, the mention of what had happened brought tears to her eyes.

I wanted to die also, but it seems that God wanted me to live to complete some task in the interests and desires of Don Enrique and my daughter Rebecca. Because of this, I do not want to abandon this place, but I am not able to live here without family. We shall talk of this . . . I do not know why this tragedy occurred . . . keep this place for the scientists to visit, without hunting animals. This will be Rebecca's memorial. I trust in God, Don Armindo. I hope all is well with you and your family. Please pardon my bad Portuguese. I am going to learn better.

> *Afectuosamente,*
> Juana Little.

She rolled in a second sheet, and made out a list of the supplies she had chosen, explaining that she would settle his account when she arrived in Cucuí, when she had a chance to discover how much money she had. Then, finally, she wiped the tears from her cheeks and returned to her hammock. There was nothing to do now but wait for the men to return.

She took the time to consider her plans in more detail. They would leave without her; but they would be back some time. Then what? Travel with the cargo-men would be an imposition on them, and hard for her. She would need looking after. She would need to be apart from them sometimes, for propriety. Would she go alone, and risk the danger? Or embarrass one of the men by asking him to guide her? No, she could do neither. But there was a way, a way that would make things easier for them all.

She heard a shout from outside. The men were back. It was nearly dusk. With only a brief pause to say goodnight, they went off downriver to their camp.

✻

They returned the next morning, soon after dawn. Jan was in her hammock, drinking soup, when José called loudly from the edge of the hut. 'We must go!' he said. 'We cannot work.'

'Why?' she asked, surprised at their sudden change of plan.

'To say what has happened here.'

'But, José, the post. I am afraid the house will fall down.'

There was a murmured conversation, then José said: 'All right.'

She relaxed. 'And there are two boxes in the hut on the hill. I forgot to ask you yesterday. Will you bring them?'

'Yes. We saw them.'

So they had been in the house. Why, she wondered, with a flicker of irritation, had they gone in there without permission? They had never done such a thing when Harry was alive.

They seemed about to go when the boy, Angelico, spoke. 'Shall I get the third box?' he asked.

What box? She couldn't remember a third box, but since he mentioned it, she said 'Yes, if there is one.'

When the men returned, Jan told them to put the boxes in the space where Harry's hammock had been. As soon as they went out to cut a tree for the new post, she took the opportunity to check the 'third box'. It was not a box at all. It was the green canvas sack containing Becca's remains. She wondered apprehensively if curiosity had impelled them to look inside, and if so what would be reported in Cucuí.

After a few minutes, the men returned with a length of wood, cut out the old support and replaced it with the new strut, tying it in position with a vine.

When they had finished, she said: 'José, can you take these books?' She patted one of the boxes they had brought from the hilltop.

'Yes.'

'And this one.' She tapped the box containing the notebooks, pens, pencils, ink and several reams of paper. 'Give them to Don Armindo to store for me.' Then she handed them the list of supplies and all her letters. 'These ones must be mailed,' she said. 'And these are the letters you brought with you. Don Armindo must keep them for me. Someone will read them to me later. You understand?'

'Yes.'

'José, when you return, would you please bring a woman with you?' she asked, wondering what woman would brave such a long and hazardous journey to a place of death. But at least everyone would realize she was quite happy where she was, and that there was no urgency to return. 'Would you bring a wife or a sister?' she asked. 'I will pay her the same as you.'

'Yes.'

'When will you return?'

'August.'

At least two months, perhaps three, the normal time between visits. That would give her the time she needed.

'Good. *Adeus*,' she said, 'Thank you. A good journey.'

Each in turn solemnly shook her hand, and then they were gone.

* * *

She turned and went back to her hammock. In one sense, she felt relief. There would at least be an explanation for what had happened. Yet relief was mixed with foreboding. When the men came back, she would have to face challenges she hardly dared guess at. The abandonment of the homestead, a return to the outside world, dealing with people through a blanket of blindness and deafness, answering questions from Armindo, the Commandante and who knew how many others, in a language of which she had no real command, and then – what? There was as yet no future, just the empty, undefined foreboding.

The next day, she set to work on the marimba. It needed careful handling. Each piece had its place, and it would have to be packed so that it could be reassembled easily and without damage by unpractised hands. To dismantle it, she had first to find out where all the screws were, feeling her way around the instrument, recalling from her years in Mexico what little she knew of the structure. Then she found that the only remaining screwdriver was too large. She spent hours filing it to fit. It took her all day just to remove the first six screws. Over the following days, she wrapped each note of the keyboard separately in typing paper, sealed each with masking tape, and numbered and packed the scores of pieces neatly in the marimba box.

That left the problem of what to do with it. It would be prohibitive to air-freight. Perhaps she should give it to a church in São Gabriel. Whoever puts it together again, she said to herself as she tucked the screwdriver in on the top of the case, I hope he's as persistent as I am.

It had taken ten days to pack the marimba. Then there were other boxes to be packed. One by one, as they were completed, she hauled them to the front of the house, making a neat line, until there were only three of the eight left unfinished.

As she worked, the weather turned colder and wetter. She had been anxious to attend to the burials, but the time never seemed right. Now there was further delay. The damp brought on an attack of migraine that kept her in her hammock for a day and a half. It was all she could do to keep up her chopping, and make her daily trips to the river.

Next week, perhaps, when everything else was ready, the weather would be better and she would be feeling strong enough to face the labour and the anguish the burial would demand of her.

※

She heard a shout.

But it had only been two weeks! Were they back so soon?

'José?' she called, hurrying to the doorway.

'Dona Juana, Dona Juana . . .' To Jan's relief, it was a woman who answered her – Cleonisia, Armindo's wife. 'Dona Juana, we have come to rescue you!' Cleonisia said, bustling up to her, speaking loudly, almost shouting.

'Dona Cleonisia! Thank you. It's good . . .' Her voice caught. It had been almost five years since she had spoken with any woman besides Becca. Controlling herself with an effort, she asked, 'Who else is here?'

'There is José, and two others. And Nazaret, she works for us.' Jan nodded. It would not have been proper for Cleonisia to travel with three men, without either her husband or another female. 'Dona Juana, it is late,' Cleonisia went on, as loudly as before. 'We shall camp now.'

Jan smiled. 'Dona Cleonisia,' she said. 'It's all right, you don't have to shout. If you speak close to me, I can hear.'

'Yes, Dona Juana. In the morning we will return. The other canoe is downriver. My husband's boat is beyond. In the morning we come. *Boa noite*, Dona Juana.'

※

Next morning, Jan was ready at dawn, waiting to explain which boxes were ready to be taken, and which she would finish packing later. But when they arrived, Cleonisia at once led her aside to the hearth bench.

'Dona Cleonisia, I want to explain about . . .'

'Keep calm, Dona Juana,' Cleonisia said. 'The men will do everything. They are already working. No need to worry.'

Jan heard noises: men's voices, questioning, boxes being dragged, objects being moved. In rising concern, she asked: 'But what are they doing?'

'They are packing everything for you. Keep calm. We shall do it all.'

Jan's heart sank. The men were going through every box, examining and discussing the contents, then repacking everything in a totally different way. She suddenly understood, as she listened to the urgent, incomprehensible back-and-forth of movement and conversation, how impotent she really was. So, she thought, this is what it's like being with outsiders. This is what will happen to me all the time, if I'm not careful.

'Keep calm, keep calm!' Cleonisia called to her every few minutes. But Cleonisia herself was anything but calm. She was armed with a supply of disinfectant, and, after explaining at some length her fear of mosquitoes, she began opening several of the canisters, scattering the contents liberally around the house.

As the men worked and Cleonisia sprinkled the pungent liquid, Jan offered food and tea. No one accepted.

Everyone seemed to be working so urgently, to be so anxious to leave. Jan, unaware of the bones, the cans, the sandals, the overwhelming gloom and squalor of the Riverside Hut, was bewildered. It was almost as if they were panic-stricken. The thought gave her a sudden inkling of the truth. They were afraid – afraid of her appearance, afraid she would collapse, afraid of the deaths associated with the house, afraid that she would, with emotional and incomprehensible demands, slow their departure.

By mid-afternoon, the boxes were ready to be taken down to the river. As the men carried them off, Cleonisia noticed Jan's unhappiness, and asked Jan what she wanted. What do I want, thought Jan, miserably. Not one thing in particular. Just for everything to be different, to be done as she had planned. 'Nothing, thank you, Dona Cleonisia,' she said, turning away. 'Nothing.'

When the boxes were loaded to José's satisfaction, Cleonisia told Jan that they would have to go up the hill, to the other *barraca*, to make sure there was nothing else to be brought down. She asked if Jan would like to come. Jan, surprised that all three men wanted to make the trip when there was nothing else to bring down, said she would.

Then she remembered there *was* something. 'José,' she said. 'I want you to look for a machete I lost on the path. I will show you where.'

Cleonisia took Jan firmly by the arm, in the forceful way of sighted people inexperienced with the blind. Then, with Jan tapping her stick in front of her, they all proceeded slowly up the path. At the edge of the Fourth Clearing, the beginning of the Long Trail, Jan stopped, saying she thought the machete must be somewhere around there. Cleonisia was silent. She must be wondering how on earth I managed to lose it so far from the house, Jan thought.

But Cleonisia's attention was on another matter. 'What is *this*?' she asked, in a surprised voice, guiding Jan's hand.

Jan smiled. Cleonisia had seen the yards of weathered typewriter ribbon strung about the bushes. 'I wanted to be sure of following the trail,' Jan explained. 'Like this.' She felt for the ribbon, and walked a few paces. 'With my stick to frighten snakes,' she added, waving it in front of her.

Nazaret, who had said virtually nothing the whole day, suddenly laughed.

The welcome sound of a child's laugh – for Nazaret, she had discovered, was only eight – made Jan smile. 'In all the days here,' she said, 'I did not encounter a single snake.'

'It was the mercy of God,' Cleonisia commented, taking Jan's arm again.

A moment later, there was a shout from one of the men.

'José has found your machete,' Cleonisia explained. 'He will carry it back. We go now.' She began to lead Jan away from the Long Trail, up the steep path through the Fourth Clearing.

'I am used to the other trail,' Jan protested, holding back. Cleonisia didn't argue. Allowing the men to go on ahead, the women slowly walked up the Long Trail.

At the top of the hill, Jan automatically raised her stick to feel for the clothesline she had often used as a marker to guide her to the house.

It was gone.

'The rope?' she said, anxiously. 'Where is the rope?'

'There is enough rope down by the river,' Cleonisia answered quickly.

Jan guessed what had happened. The men had begun to help themselves to the things they thought she wouldn't miss. 'There was much rope here before,' Jan insisted. 'I want that rope.'

'There is no rope here, Dona Juana.'

'There *is* rope here. Or there was. Every time I came to the hut, I felt for it.'

There was a silence. Then José came to her, and put some rope in her hand. She could feel from its weight that it was not the clothesline. 'This is shorter than the rope that was here,' she said, determined to make the point, to do her best to ensure things weren't stolen.

'You mean *that* rope,' said José. '*That* rope is down below. We will give it to you later.'

'That is good,' Jan said.

Inside the house, there was, as Jan knew, very little left. A pile of old Braille magazines; a pot of salt; some old coffee; half a dozen bottles of sugar syrup. But she remembered that behind the hearth there should be a machete and an axe. Jan asked José to make sure to bring them.

As they prepared to leave, Cleonisia, who had had time to admire the clearing with its bananas and pineapples and the view across to Sentinel and the Serra do Padre range, said: 'It is beautiful here.'

'It was a very happy place,' said Jan, her voice breaking at the memory of the mountains, and Becca, and their years of hopeful labour. Cleonisia put a hand on her arm in silent sympathy. 'A very happy place.'

🦋

The next day, the men took a loaded canoe back to Hummock Camp, where their second canoe lay. Cleonisia and Nazaret stayed with Jan.

With the woman and the child, Jan allowed herself to relax. She and Cleonisia prepared some food together. Then, after lunch, Jan gave Nazaret some marbles that Becca had bought years before to give to any children she happened to meet. While Nazaret played with them in the yard, Jan and Cleonisia cleared up. Jan washed, Cleonisia dried. Now, for the first time, they began to talk as friends.

'You know, when I met Armindo,' Cleonisia said, 'He had a child by an Indian woman. I raised the child as my own, and now there are six others . . .' She laughed ruefully, and then, encouraged by Jan's interest, she began to talk about her life running the store and raising her growing family. She had a direct way of talking that conveyed both warmth and intelligence. Jan asked what her children were called. Cleonisia told her: Luciano, Anna Lucy, Anna Alice, Tadeo –

'Tadeo?' Jan said. 'We don't have that name in English.'

'But 'Juana' is both English and Spanish?' asked Cleonisia.

'Juana is not my name,' Jan explained. 'My name is Jan.'

Cleonisia laughed, a high, silvery laugh. 'I cannot say that,' she protested.

Jan thought suddenly of her father, and his Dutch ancestry. 'Jan' was the Dutch for 'John'. 'It is like . . . João,' she said.

Again Cleonisia gave her high little laugh. 'Your name is João?' she asked. 'Shall I call you Dona João?'

Lady John. Why not? It was high time she had a name in Portuguese. 'Yes, if you like,' she said, and smiled, grateful for the change of mood.

They talked on for a while. Then Cleonisia said, 'The Commandante read your letter.' She paused, uncertainly. 'He came to see Armindo. He said . . . he said we must bring the remains back to Cucuí.'

Jan let the words sink in. This was one decision she would make for herself, come what may. But it would need careful handling. 'Dona Cleonisia,' she said, emphasizing her words, 'I wish to comply with the law, but I must also comply with my husband's wishes. He said his bones must be buried here, up on the hill. If I must take them with me, then I will bring them back later to bury them.'

Cleonisia was silent for a moment. 'It is not a question of law, Dona João,' she went on, slowly. 'We wanted to tell you . . . The Commandante would be willing to bury Don Enrique and your daughter in Cucuí.'

'Oh. It is generous, but no.' Then she added, to leave no room for doubt. 'No! I must bury them here!'

'That was Don Enrique's wish?'

'Yes. There is a place that looks out over the forest.'

'You will tell the Commandante?'

'Yes. I will say it was my promise to my husband.'

'Then I will help you, Dona João.'

Jan breathed a sigh of relief. In this, at least, she had managed to assert herself.

When the men returned, Cleonisia explained to them what had to be done. Then she returned to Jan. 'They understand, Dona João,' she said. But it was already near dusk, and too late to do anything before nightfall. They would return the following day.

Jan was drinking her soup the next morning when she heard Cleonisia's voice. Cleonisia explained that José's two helpers had set off through the *paraná* with a second load of boxes, while José had stayed to make coffins and crosses.

While Jan waited, calm in the certainty that her wishes were being granted, José, using planks from old crates, hammered together two makeshift rectangular boxes, about eighteen inches square and three feet high. They were larger than necessary for the remains, Jan realized as she felt them, but their stature was fitting.

Then José cut a tree, a hardwood, from which he made two crosses. One was a good solid five-foot one, and the other smaller. He made grooves with his machete so that the cross-pieces fitted well, and tied them solidly together with vines.

By mid-morning on the fourth day, the last of the goods had been loaded. Jan had sat silently by the hearth while the men worked. Now at last the moment she had planned for, and dreaded, had come.

Cleonisia touched her gently on the arm. 'They are ready, Dona João,' she said.

'Where are the boxes?'

'By the place where Don Enrique cut wood.'

'Wait there for me.'

Jan turned, picked up the sacks containing the remains, and carried them out to the yard.

Cleonisia was there to guide her gently to the boxes. She stood for a moment, feeling the eyes of the others on her. They would be curious, apprehensive perhaps. She must re-assure them, show them that everything was correct, that there was nothing to hide. She didn't want them to face awkward questions back in Cucuí.

Now that the moment had come, her composure broke. As she untied the first sack, the one with Harry's remains, she began to weep. She took out the remains, one by one, and placed them gently in the box. Finally, she folded the sack over on top.

There was no sound, no sigh, no comment from the others. It was as if she were alone with her grief. She reached down for the second sack, the green canvas bag. Again, she laid the remains to rest, with care and reverence, crying softly to herself. Then she lifted out the pillowslip, and took out Becca's hair. She stroked it gently. It was still dry, soft and abundant. She placed the hair in the box, added the candle Becca had been holding, and spread the pillowslip over the remains.

It was done. She began to fold the canvas sack.

'Dona João!' Cleonisia's words rang out sharply. '*Tudo!* Everything!'

Jan stopped, puzzled. What was Cleonisia objecting to? Perhaps she believed that nothing that had touched the dead should remain unburied. Perhaps she thought that, if this ritual continued, it would lead to Jan's collapse. But I'm quite calm, Jan told herself. I'll show her I'm quite calm. She nodded slowly, and carefully placed the sack in the box.

As she stood up, she saw a match flare. Cleonisia had two candles. When she had lit them, she gave one to the little girl, and took Jan's arm. 'Do you want to go up there, Dona João?'

Jan was surprised at the question. 'Of course,' she said. 'It is my place.'

The men took up the boxes and tools, and set off.

'Do they know where to go?' asked Jan, anxiously.

'They know where, Dona João,' Cleonisia replied.

With Nazaret following behind, Cleonisia, holding Jan by the elbow, led her up the Long Trail, asking Jan every now and then, 'Are you all right, Dona João? Are you all right?'

By the time they arrived at the top, the men were already digging the graves on the Observation Shelf. Cleonisia led Jan across the few yards of open space. Strangely, it was the first time Jan had ever stood there. Before, either Harry or Becca had made the quick detour, leaving Jan by the hut. Why, it *is* a shelf, she thought, in surprise, as she stepped across the hard, flat earth. At the far side was a low rock wall, on which she, Cleonisia and Nazaret sat, their backs to Sentinel, while three yards in front of them the men worked at the unyielding quartz soil.

Her mind wandered. It was surprising to her that the men could dig at all in that soil, and in that space. She heard again Harry talking with Becca, checking whether the shelf was large enough for two graves, saying he would like a mangosteen tree planted there after his death. She imagined a mangosteen shading this hard patch, growing up to match the other trees that covered the hillside, beginning to return this little open space to jungle.

Behind her, Homestead Hill dropped away to jungle. She felt the sun, diffused by cloud, warm on her back. Sentinel would be out, and Thunder Mountain, and perhaps the whole great line of mountains, reaching across to the hazy shape of Neblina itself.

After an hour's work, José said the ground was ready. Cleonisia took Jan's elbow and led her forward. Jan felt a candle in her hand, and then, under Cleonisia's guidance, the roughness of the first cross, Harry's. Together, the women dripped wax on the crosspiece, and set the candles in place.

'The earth,' Cleonisia said, 'Like this.' She placed Jan's hand on a pile of soil.

Jan, weeping, raised a handful of earth and tossed it down. Then she took up a second handful, and a third, and would have gone on if Cleonisia had not laid a gentle hand on her arm, allowing the men to move forward and begin filling in the hole.

Then Cleonisia turned Jan to Rebecca's grave. Again, they placed candles, and again Jan tossed in a few handfuls of earth. As she stood back, she raised her head, feeling the sun hot on her face. Yes, she thought, as the scraping shovels smoothed the earth, on a day like this, Neblina should be out.

'Thank you,' she said, through tears. 'Thank you for everything. It is as they would have wished.'

🐾

The candles were still burning as Cleonisia led Jan away from the graves and turned her towards the Long Trail. Jan held back. She was not ready for the final farewell, and the emotions it might release.

'The ... the ...' she faltered. She couldn't think of the word. Cleonisia stopped. 'The box for the rain ... the *thing* for the rain – it should be turned over.' She was thinking of the rain-barrel, the one Becca had been going to paint. It seemed important, suddenly, that it should not be allowed to stand gathering water and breeding mosquitoes.

'José!' Cleonisia called him over to explain what Jan wanted. 'He is doing it, Dona João. Now please ...' She urged Jan on down the path.

Going across the Garden Clearing, Jan's mind turned to the plants around them, the coconuts, cashews, citruses, sweet potatoes. She and Becca had worked so hard here. Perhaps there was something which they should be doing to ensure the survival of the plants. What? At the corner, she stopped, on the point of breaking down.

Cleonisia must have seen her expression, for she said deliberately: 'I know what this is, Dona João. In one month, my brother died, then my father. The same year, my mother died. This passes. This passes, Dona João.'

Jan nodded. Cleonisia's words turned her thoughts away from her own grief for a moment. Cleonisia had left her children to come here. It was the first time she had ever left her two-year-old. She was a strong, compassionate woman. She understood grief. She had good reasons for her haste. Perhaps she thought Jan would collapse under the strain if they delayed. Certainly, they needed to get through the *paraná* before nightfall. As they hurried on down to the river, Jan determined to keep her grief to herself. But still she hesitated.

'Dona Cleonisia, one minute. I must check ..'

What could she check? The fire, the hammocks, the pans, the flooring leaves?

'Dona João,' Cleonisia urged. 'It is all done. Everything is in the canoes. The canoes.'

Cleonisia pressed her on past the hut, down the trail to the river, and into *Piaroa*. There was no time to take in the sunshine sparkling on the black water, no time to recall the hours spent down there with Becca.

The men cast off, and began to paddle.

At that moment, however, she did see something. By some quirky combination of light and position, she caught an astonishing glimpse of dark figures paddling in silhouette against a brilliant patch of reflected sunlight. Just for a second she saw them, and then they were gone, swamped again by the fog of her blindness.

Cleonisia leant over and touched Jan's mouth with something. It was candy. Jan took it, thinking, that's what Harry did with Es to stop her crying. Well, I will not cry, she told herself. I will not cry. What was it Becca said when they left the Santa Maria? I've done all my crying.

She set her mind to the task in hand: keeping steady, as the paddles dug in and the canoe rocked. This is not me, she thought, as she gripped the side of the canoe and sucked her candy. I've just turned myself into someone they can cope with. Most of me has gone off somewhere else.

Homestead Hill, its shadows unseen, slipped away, and was lost.

14

THE FINAL CHALLENGE

They beached briefly at the camp downriver to collect their own belongings. Then they paddled on in silence, past Difficulty Hill, through the *paraná* to Hummock Camp. There, Jan's boxes had been left, along with a third, larger canoe. The men put up Jan's hammock for her, and Cleonisia prepared tapioca for her supper. Still no one had spoken more than a few words.

Next day, they loaded some of Jan's cargo into *Piaroa*, tied *Piaroa* behind the big canoe, and set off down the North Fork, with Jan and Cleonisia in the big canoe. As time passed, the mood lightened. When Jan checked the pronunciation of a word, Cleonisia began to teach her how to say the Portuguese alphabet. Jan explained why she did not wish to go back to the States. 'It is a country of cities. In cities, there are no gardens. I like gardens.' Cleonisia told Jan about one of the Coimbra brothers who had 'many cows – 100 head, *cem cabeças*'. Jan misunderstood. 'What?' she said. '*Sem cabeças* – without heads?' and everyone laughed.

The men paddled on, threading their way past fallen trees. The splash of paddles and the warning shouts brought memories flooding back. This must have been where Becca found her blue orchid, this the stretch where she had fallen in with the machete. Jan heard again the splash, and saw the machete as she had imagined it then waving like Excalibur above the black water.

Suddenly, Jan's reverie was shattered by a crash, and shouts. The canoe lurched sideways to the bank. The men leaped out, still shouting.

What was happening? A tapir?

'Are they hunting? Are they hunting?' asked Jan, anxiously.

'No, Dona João. A tree fell on your canoe.'

The shouts went on. José and Gerao frantically passed boxes from *Piaroa* to the other two canoes, hoisting the marimba clear, making the canoes bob and rock. Then, as the crisis passed, they cast off again.

'What happened to my canoe?' Jan asked.

'It is gone, Dona João. It is broken, in the river.'

It seemed appropriate, somehow. *Piaroa* belonged to the wilderness, like Maggie, and had been similarly reclaimed. Foolish of me, Jan thought, to think I could take her out.

At the fork, the launch rode at her mooring. Cleonisia helped Jan aboard, and hung a hammock for her on deck. 'We must wait, Dona João. José must return for the rest of your things.'

Jan settled down. It would take the men a day, at least a day, to paddle to Hummock and back. It didn't matter. She was in no hurry. The more time she had to adapt, the better.

When José and Gerao returned, at dusk the following day, they stowed Jan's cargo on the deck and cabin roof. By the time they finished, it was dark, but they were too eager to get back to delay. They cast off, with José at the wheel. He had beside him a cymbal which he struck whenever he wanted to tell Gerao, below deck, to slow or increase engine speed. For hours, the boat chugged on slowly through the night, the throb of the engine broken now and then by the silvery clash of José's cymbal.

Some time later, it began to rain. Jan's hammock was moved below deck, beside the engine, where Gerao reclined. She pulled her blanket over her head and sank into sleep.

❧

Early next morning, they swung out on to the Negro. It was the first time Jan had been there for five years. Soon she would meet people again. This was the moment she had been dreading. She would be an object of intense curiosity; yet she would be able to explain virtually nothing, and sense very little of what was happening.

The boat stopped briefly to drop off Nazaret, and then moored at Pelon's *sítio*. Cleonisia took Jan's arm. 'They wish to greet you,' she said. Jan forced a smile. Well, she had to go through it some time. Best make it as easy as possible. She let herself be guided ashore, to greet and be greeted. Members of the family came forward one at a time to shake her hand. She sensed their uncertainty, but also their composure and dignity.

'What will you do?' someone asked.

'I shall go to Cucuí.'

'So! You will go to Cucuí.'

'Yes.'

'Good, good.'

The formality left her feeling oddly stranded. It hurt her that these people, to whom death was familiar enough, never even mentioned Harry or Rebecca, whom they had all known. Perhaps, she thought, she came from a life and a tragedy so remote from common experience, even on the Negro, that it was hard for anyone to find anything suitable to say. But the failure to do so hurt, nevertheless.

At Cucuí, the Commandante stood waiting. On Cleonisia's prompting, Jan offered her hand, to show she was composed. He, like the others, was withdrawn, offering a two-finger, wet-fish handshake, and mumbling something she didn't hear before Cleonisia took her up to the store, to a curtained-off corner of the children's room.

There, Armindo and Cleonisia both came to her. Cleonisia sat apart, deferentially. Armindo drew a chair up close. 'Dona João, what will you do?' he asked.

She hesitated. She had made too many mistakes in her life by acting in haste. Now she had to be doubly cautious. She wanted to take things slowly until she felt a definite sense of direction.

'Don Armindo,' she said. 'I do not want to leave Cucuí until I am sure of where I am going and why. I have so many boxes.

I would like . . . what I would like at this moment is to stay in Cucuí, somewhere where I can garden.'

'Dona João, you have money?'

'I have money from the American government, because I am blind.'

'Yes. You know we have another little house here. Please, you must live with us as long as you wish. I will give you a good price. You may stay *eight years*, if you wish.'

She had no idea what significance she should read into the 'eight years', but there was no mistaking his insistence.

'Thank you. I will try that. Thank you.'

Next morning, Armindo led her to a one-room shack across the garden. It was a simple brick room adjoining the garage, but it had been used as a guest room before. Her possessions – her boxes and her mail – were already in there. There were rings for her hammock. She began to unpack to find some of the things she needed – plates, clothes, the type-writer, paper.

Jan began to set up her room as she wanted, feeling round to build up a map of the place in her mind. She learned the route to the privy – straight ahead to the chicken-run, turn right, twelve steps, turn left, twenty-three steps. When she knew her way around well enough, she began to arrange her possessions, sliding her boxes against the wall and setting up areas for sleeping, cooking and writing.

Everything took a long time. She found she could only be active for an hour or two, and would then have to rest for another hour. But after several days, she was settled enough to turn her attention to more important matters. First, her mail. After counting her letters – fifteen small and nineteen large airmail envelopes, and eight manilla ones – she begged Cleonisia to find someone to read them to her. 'And I have my husband's journals and my daughter's journals,' she added. 'I want to know what they say.' Cleonisia said she was sure she could find someone. Reassured, Jan asked about gardening. Armindo showed her a patch of ground just outside her room which, he said, could be her garden. She began to work it that same day.

It was hard to extend her world much further. She had very few batteries for her hearing-aid, which was anyway inadequate. Armindo had fixed in her spare ear-mould, but it was faulty, and no real help. She had difficulty even fetching water for washing and bathing. Cleonisia guided her a few times to the little inlet behind the store, so that she thought she knew the way. She tried it on her own several times, and each time became hopelessly lost, waving her arms and shouting until someone rescued her. 'I zigzag about feeling rather like a captured forest animal,' she wrote to a friend. 'No one has any comprehension, it seems to me, of the life that was once mine.'

Over the next few days, she caught a cold, which turned into flu. In her weakened state, it made her feel so ill she issued instructions to Cleonisia about what to do with her possessions if she died.

The thought of Jan dying out in their garden shed must have terrified Armindo, for the next day a doctor came, along with the Commandante and two other officers. The doctor peered at her lower lids, asking about the illness on the homestead.

'Malaria?' he asked, sceptically. 'Did your husband and daughter really die of malaria?'

'I think so. Perhaps.' She didn't wish to be an embarrassment: the area was supposedly malaria free. 'But that was in January and February. I do not have malaria now.'

Mutterings and whisperings, then: 'She needs malaria pills,' said the doctor. 'And new clothes.'

After the deputation left, Armindo came back in. 'We have to burn all your clothes,' he said, abruptly.

Jan suddenly understood, or thought she understood, what everyone was thinking, and why Cleonisia and the cargo-men had been so wary of her on Homestead Hill. Plague. They were afraid she had a plague. The idea had a peculiar kind of logic: when colonists penetrated the Amazon and the Negro, they used to give the Indians clothes impregnated with smallpox. As a result, the very thought of contagious disease, especially in association with clothing, would no doubt hold a peculiar horror for them.

'No!' she said angrily, 'They didn't die of a contagious disease! There's no reason to burn my clothes!'

'It is all right, Dona João,' Armindo reassured her. 'We will make you new clothes.'

She allowed herself to be persuaded. Over the next few days, Cleonisia arranged for a seamstress to replace her old slacks and shirt with new ones, patterned on her pyjamas, of all things, but made of black cloth, as befitted a widow.

As she regained her strength, she again began to pester Armindo to find someone to read her mail to her. At least, she insisted, she had to know what money she had. Seeing the wisdom of that, he opened likely looking envelopes for her, and found Social Security cheques for the last eight months. That would be enough to pay him all she owed, and more. He suggested that she sign over the cheques to him, assuring her that he would hold the money on account, set all her purchases against it, and make up regular statements for her.

In theory, it sounded a sensible arrangement, and she had little choice but to agree. But she distrusted her own judgement. Armindo had never been good at accounts, and besides she'd noticed, during the time of her recovery, that he seemed to be drinking too much. On several occasions, when he came to see her, he had embarked on interminable and embarrassing monologues which she could hardly understand. All she could glean was that he'd had a row with his elder brother over the loss of the launch, and that he had borrowed money to buy a sawmill. Perhaps he dreamed of supplying the army, for the army's own sawmill, beside which she, Harry and Rebecca had camped for months before setting off for the Demiti, had never worked properly.

Well, if Armindo had business problems, no doubt he would sort them out. Meanwhile, the letters became her major concern. Any one of them might contain information around which she should be rebuilding her life. In addition to those she already had, she was expecting replies to those she had written on Homestead Hill. None had arrived yet. That was odd. She would have expected *something*. Certainly, when the letters did come, her need would be all the greater.

Yes, yes, Armindo said, perhaps the priest, Padre Miguel, would come. He had once studied English. But he was very busy. Or perhaps the Swiss mechanic who worked downriver would come. Next time he was around, they would ask him. He seemed less than eager to arrange matters that might lead Jan to assume control over her own destiny. Perhaps it was because she had become something of a celebrity. They seemed proud of her, in a strange way, as if eager to make her a fixture.

Not that any of this caused her concern, for she was determined that it should not. Once she had her mail, and knew what was in it, she would make her plans. Having coped with Homestead Hill, and arranged, as she thought, to retain control of her own future, she believed she understood the problems she faced. Her optimism was reinforced by a determination that she should not herself create unnecessary problems. Knowing herself to be an imposition simply by her presence, eager never to make the mistakes that Harry insisted expressed her true nature, she remained compliant.

In fact, her slight confidence was groundless. Far from being in control, she was already caught up in a coil of emotions, motives and interests – selfishness, embarrassment, impatience, incompetence, thoughtlessness – expressed in sidelong glances and sudden silences, all hidden from her by her own disabilities and by a veneer of concern for her well-being. Any move she made to increase her freedom only allowed the grip to tighten further. In the end, even when somewhat more experienced, she was to leave Brazil more by luck than judgement.

By the time she had been in Cucuí a month, Jan had become something of a fixture in the Coimbra household. Armindo even suggested she might like to consider moving to a clearing that he was developing at the end of the newly built section of road. Oh, that place had rich soil, he said; he already had some chickens there; she could dig and plant, and no one would bother her. He was solicitous and protective, yes, but there was something else in his manner, as if he wanted to keep her to himself, as if she possessed knowledge he envied. Perhaps it was because she was American, she thought, an opinion that received some support one day when Armindo came to see her, accompanied by his eldest son, Napolão.

Armindo said that he had a new machine, and wanted Dona João to explain it to him. He had it with him. He placed her hand on something, and then quickly took it away, as if she should know without further ado exactly what it was. For some reason, she assumed it was a sewing-machine. No, no, Armindo replied, testily. Feel it, Dona João, feel it! She felt again. It had a long, thin handle. Ah, a floor polisher, most likely.

'What's it for?' she asked, not wishing to make a fool of herself.

'It finds things, Dona João.'

'Things?'

'It finds –' He paused. 'It finds gold.'

Jan had no idea what a metal-detector was. She had never even heard of such a thing. 'Where did you get it?' she asked. Armindo wasn't taking kindly to her questions. But he admitted he had bought it from a Colombian merchant for the equivalent of $400. Jan gasped. It was an immense amount of money. She assumed Armindo, naïve and ignorant, had been duped into the purchase of a useless bauble. More than that – she couldn't see how he could suddenly have paid over such a sum, if he hadn't used the cheques she had just assigned to him.

'I don't know how to operate it,' she said brusquely, quelling her suspicions and handing it back to him.

Armindo seemed dumbfounded by her ignorance and lack of enthusiasm. 'But, Dona João,' he said, as if he was dealing with a simpleton, 'It was made in your country.'

She could think of nothing that might be used to find gold. Maybe it was a geiger counter. 'I think it is used to find uranium,' she said.

'No, no, gold, Dona João,' Armindo insisted, and began to spell out for her the words written on it as if he were revealing the instructions. 'L-O-W,' he said, laboriously, reading out the letters on the dials. 'H-I-G-H. S-T-O-P.'

'Don Armindo, I don't think you can use this.'

'Oh, yes, we can!' It was Napolão who had spoken. He sounded quite angry at her incomprehension, as if she were deceiving them.

'But there is nothing to find.'

'Oh, yes, there is!'

Armindo had suddenly become silent, as if too much had been said. Now Napolão shut up as well, and the two of them left together, with their machine. Jan puzzled briefly over the incident, and over Armindo's gullibility, and then dismissed the whole thing as foolish. Only weeks later would she see its significance. Meanwhile, she had her own problems.

She still needed someone to read her mail. She was beginning to despair of ever finding anyone to help when one afternoon, soon after lunch, one of the local girls – Anna – came running into her room.

'Dona João, Dona João, there are two *gringos*!'

Gringos! Americans! Perhaps, if she could meet them, her mail could be read at last. She pushed in her defective hearing-aid, and followed the importunate Anna.

❊

Though she didn't know it, Jan was already well known on the upper Rio Negro. José's first report had seen to that. News rapidly turned to rumour. The Americans had been attacked by Indians. The blind lady had refused to leave. She was out of her mind with grief, and wanted to die with her family. By the time Jan arrived in Cucuí, the story, increasingly simplified, dramatized and distorted, had travelled downriver to São Gabriel, and even to Manaus, and upriver across the border to San Carlos.

San Carlos had not changed much since the Littles were there in late 1973, except that a new ecological research programme was now based there. The programme was an international one, backed by the Venezuelan Institute for Scientific Research (IVIC), the University of Georgia and the Max Planck Institut in West Germany. The participants – up to thirty, depending on the time of year – were based in two houses, in one of which lived two of the programme's station managers, an American couple, Howard and Kate Clark.

Strangely, the Clarks had long known the Littles by name because they had been occasional readers of the *Christian Science Monitor*. And locals occasionally mentioned the eccentric American homesteaders who lived somewhere to the south – the old botanist, his blind wife, and his grown-up daughter who was extremely strong. Some in San Carlos still remembered how, five years before, when the Littles were returning from the States, Rebecca had carried the sixty-pound outboard motor down to the river by herself.

Almost a month after Jan's arrival in Cucuí, further news arrived in San Carlos. The blind lady from the jungle was asking for someone to read her mail. Howard and Kate decided they should offer assistance. They spoke to the Commandante, and received permission to bring Mrs Little back upriver, if she wished to come. They were joined in their expedition by another couple and their two children.

In Cucuí, the Americans checked in at the fort and, accompanied by the Commandante, walked on down to the Coimbras' store, with the children chattering beside them. There, they asked Armindo for Jan. Little Anna dashed away to find her.

Knowing Jan's story in outline, the Clarks were more than a little apprehensive. 'You realize this lady could be a real basket case?' Kate warned.

The first sight of Jan seemed to confirm their fears. She was like a concentration-camp victim, gaunt, stooping, with most of her teeth missing, walking uncertainly forward on the Commandante's arm. She looked immeasurably older than her fifty years. But her first words, after the introductions, gave immediate reassurance that here was no basket case. 'It's so nice to hear the sound of American children playing,' she said. 'Would you like a cold beer?'

Typically, neither Anna nor the Commandante had made any mention to Jan of the women and children, just of *gringos* – American men. That was why the sound of children's laughter had been such a delightful surprise.

'Come through to the patio,' she said, 'but I have to tell you, I don't hear well, and my hearing-aid is in bad shape, so I hope you don't mind speaking up.'

Over beers, Howard explained who they were, and why they were there. Was there anything they could do to help?

'Yes, yes! I have six months' of letters, and I've been praying for someone to read them to me!'

Of course. They could read them right now.

Jan, delighted, fetched her bag of mail. But it took only a few minutes for the Americans to realize the size of the task Jan had given them. There was too much to read then and there. Maybe Jan would like to go back with them to San Carlos for a while? They could get acquainted and read her everything at more leisure.

Jan was touched, and pleased. She liked the idea. Howard's measured speech gave the impression of a generous personality. Kate was crisper, more direct and assertive, but no less friendly. There was a refreshing combination of incisiveness and banter in their speech she had not heard since the first months in San

384

Cristobal. There was no reason not to go. She already felt at ease with the group, and was eager to know what work they were doing. She smiled. 'I'd like that,' she said.

🦌

The first thing that surprised Jan on her arrival in San Carlos was the abundance of fresh food. For her first lunch, she ate an apple and a carrot, and marvelled at the tastes.

The second surprise was the ease with which people solved problems that had dogged her for weeks. Howard, a gentle bear of a man with a great dark beard, went to work on her hearing-aid. The ear-mould was clogged with wax, he said, and the battery was dead. He soon fixed that. With a clean mould and a new battery, taken from a camera, she could hear better than she had for six months.

That afternoon, Kate read letters to her. Kate was small, dark-haired, dark-eyed, and very attractive, with a manner Jan sometimes found reassuringly professional and sometimes disconcertingly brusque. The letters were all at least three months old. The only one of interest was from Mexico, from Jaime Bulnes with news of the Lacandon forest, or what remained of it. But it was not in reply to her last letter to him, telling him of the deaths.

Over the next few days, Jan became a temporary part of this community of intellectuals. At communal meals around a huge, rough-hewn kitchen table, people argued the merits of their projects. Jan revelled in it. She could understand; she was with fellow-countrymen; because of her practical immersion in the ecology of the area, she felt she was accepted as a fellow professional; and no one seemed embarrassed by her disabilities. She never quite mastered the way to the outside bathroom, which was at an angle across the yard, and whenever she went out, there would be a chorus of directions – 'Back a bit. Now left. LEFT!' – and bursts of good-natured laughter.

Her stay also gave her a chance to begin the task of coming

385

to terms with what had happened on Homestead Hill. No one pried into her feelings, but she had some of Harry's journals with her. Howard, taking it in turn with other members of the group, read them out loud. By chance, two were the ones in which he had made his last entries.

Her awareness of what had happened during her illness was

still hopelessly blurred. There had been time to mourn Becca's death, but it was a lasting pain that there was still no explanation for what had happened. As she heard Howard's faltering voice trying to decipher the pencilled scrawl on the rough Braille paper, she hoped desperately that Harry's words would give coherence to her confused recollections. She'd had no idea, for instance, that Becca had made a second trip to the Hilltop Hut. She could imagine the strain that must have placed on her.

Then: 'Fever. Becca dead . . .' An illegible squiggle. A date 'Jan 14? [Or maybe the 29th?] Jan and I very weak. Jan 21–22.' Another squiggle. Then the final agonizing entry, the will. 'Saws for Nilo. Axes for Rufino. Binocs for Armindo. Jan and I few days to [. . . to what? To live?] Severe fever. God's will be done. Cloth and clothing to Pelon and Nilo and Rufino. Bury us all on hilltop, please. Thanks. Please all writing to Dr Ball in Canada [a reference to George Ball, Professor of Entomology at the University of Alberta, Edmonton, who had visited the Littles twice in Mexico and once, briefly, in Brazil]. God's will be done.' No one hearing those last despairing entries could have hidden their emotion. With Jan, they wept.

But part of Jan's grief was bitter disappointment. Harry had been devoted to his journal, forever asserting that it would live on as the story of his homestead life. He had written whole books on Rima and Hanuman. Yet the journal contained nothing of importance. It was a chronology as banal as a weather report, as if the purpose of journals was to conceal, rather than reveal. Maybe that was it. Once, on the Santa Maria, she had started her own journal, only to have her efforts condemned by Harry because she expressed emotions and actions of which he disapproved.

And when the homestead ended, when his world collapsed, when Rebecca herself died, he had failed utterly. He was weak, the writing showed how weak, but he could at least write. Yet only four entries (and one of those written by Becca) during those two vital weeks! Nothing more except for the two – or was it three? – final entries. And even they looked suspicious. The writing was identical, and the dates confused by their positions, and by question-marks, as if he had written the entries all at the same time and simply guessed at the date of the most important event – Becca's death. It's all in my journal, he'd said. But it wasn't, it wasn't, and she would never know for sure what had happened.

After two weeks, Jan decided that the time had come to return to Cucuí. Howard tried to dissuade her. He was going back to the States shortly, and offered to escort her home if she liked. She shouldn't worry about her possessions, he said – they could be shipped home separately. Jan thanked him, but said she felt she should return to the Coimbras until she knew what her long-term plans were.

When the Clarks heard of a boat heading downriver, they took Jan to the landing area by the National Guard HQ – the spot, Jan remembered, where she and Becca had been sitting the morning Harry vanished downriver with Hanuman. As she stepped aboard, holding some plant cuttings the Clarks had given her, she heard Howard call goodbye. 'We managed to put some colour back in your cheeks, Jan,' he said. 'Remember we're here if you need any more help.'

'Thanks.' She smiled towards the voice, recalling the time she'd been in San Carlos when soldiers had rummaged through their cargo for gold and diamonds. It was good to be in friendly hands, and free of such misplaced suspicions. 'I'm sure I'll be fine,' she said. 'Just fine.'

🦂

But as soon as she was delivered back to the Coimbra store in Cucuí, she found that everything was not fine. The store was locked. That was peculiar, she thought, knocking at the door. It was the social centre of Cucuí, and was usually open from 6 a.m. to 8 p.m. Finding the store locked like that was like finding Cucuí itself closed.

She went on knocking. Surely there would be someone there – Armindo, Cleonisia, the older children.

After a few minutes, the door opened a few inches, and then all the way. 'Cleonisia?' Jan said.

It was not Cleonisia. It was a woman she had met only once before – Socorro, Armindo's sister-in-law, wife of Germano Coimbra. She had disturbing news. Cleonisia was in São Gabriel and Armindo was in Manaus. She was there, she said, to look after the store, and make sure Jan was all right.

At first, Jan was reassured. She could stay on in her one-room house indefinitely, planting her garden, repacking her possessions, typing. Perhaps in a few days mail would arrive. Armindo would return. They would talk about whether she should establish herself in his *fazenda* at the end of the new road.

Worry only began to gnaw at her when the Coimbra's fifteen-year-old yard-boy, Miguel, came round to borrow a spade. He was always borrowing something, for he knew she had a good collection of tools. In passing, Jan asked about Armindo and Cleonisia.

'A big fight!' said Miguel, to her surprise. 'He hit her, and she left.'

'He *hit* her?' That didn't sound like Armindo. 'Why?'

'He was drinking.'

'You mean . . .' She remembered Armindo's drunken monologues. For the first time, it occurred to her that he might have a real problem. 'You mean, more than just a little?'

'Yes. It is very bad.'

'Why? What will happen?'

'Divorce!'

That scared her. Cleonisia must have been terribly hurt. And her own safe little world suddenly seemed not at all safe. Still, there was nothing to be done yet. She would be all right. She had her house and her garden and her work. She would wait for Armindo's return.

No such luck. Two days later, Arnaldo Coimbra arrived. Arnaldo, the least successful of the brothers, was a gentle and ineffectual man in his late thirties. He walked with a stoop and had the beginnings of a pot-belly. He sat down in the chair beside her hammock, put his head in hands and gave a deep, tragic sigh. It was terrible, terrible. Cleonisia wanted half the business, and she was the one who really ran it. Armindo owed all that money for the sawmill, and the sawmill would not work. The family did not know what to do. So he had come, he said, to lock up the store.

And that same afternoon, the Commandante came to call. He was, as usual, polite. In a stilted mixture of Portuguese and English, he said he was worried about her. He understood that the Coimbras were in São Gabriel. Wouldn't that be a good place for her to be?

'But I am happy here.'

'But, Dona João, Arnaldo is taking Dona Socorro down-river. It would be better if you went with her.'

'No, senhor, I'm sure I will be fine on my own. You are there in case of emergencies. I want to stay.'

'No, no, Dona João. You see . . .' He had become a little hesitant, for he was a well-meaning and sympathetic man, 'The colonel in São Gabriel would like to see you.'

※

Jan packed in a state of irritation. She was ready to plant the cuttings she'd brought back from San Carlos. It was frustrating to have her plans upset, first by the Coimbras, then by the military. If only she wasn't so dependent on others. But then, as she packed two bags with clothes, mail, toilet things, and her typewriter, her mood changed. What could the colonel possibly want? It must be something to do with the highway. Perhaps he wanted to know why Brazilians had failed to conquer the jungle, when Nordamericanos had managed to live there for five years. Yes, that would be it. He'd ask about the weather, wildlife, Indians, water-levels, that sort of thing.

By the time they left, she had convinced herself that the request to see her was really quite flattering.

They reached São Gabriel late the following afternoon. From the broad bay above the rapids where they landed, Socorro guided Jan to a riverside store. 'I don't know where they are going to put you, Dona João,' she said, seating Jan on a bench. 'I will return in an hour.'

While Jan was doing her best to control the niggling fears rising inside her, a man spoke to her. She looked up, eagerly. Encouraged, the man started talking. He was one of the highway workers, he said, and had visited Homestead Hill. He talked for a while, almost incomprehensibly, about Don Enrique, and snakes, and bulldozers, until he suddenly asked her why she was here. Was it to see the Americans?

'What Americans?'

'The missionaries.'

'No.' She recalled from her visits five years previously hearing mention of Baptist missionaires in the town. 'No, I don't think so.'

The man continued his monologue for a while, then left her on her own. After an hour, she was becoming impatient; after two hours, anxiety set in. Finally, after almost three hours, there was the roar of an engine from outside. She heard a yell: 'Dona João, quickly, get in.' It was Armindo. But she scarcely had time to greet him before she felt him pulling her roughly to the truck. He shoved her in beside another man – it was Arnaldo, she realized – and started the engine.

'My things!' she wailed.

'Yes, yes! They are in the back!'

Armindo accelerated away from the river along a pot-holed street, with the two men shouting at each other excitedly over the noise of the engine and the clatter of springs. Then, almost at once, he stamped on the brakes. They were at a military post. Armindo jumped out. Jan, totally confused, and increasingly nervous, heard an exchange of angry words, of which she understood nothing except a final, oddly disturbing cry from Armindo: 'You can't do that to her!'

Then Armindo leaped back in the truck and began to shout across her again to Arnaldo. After several minutes of this, he started the truck and accelerated away with a roaring engine and protesting springs, until a minute later, he stamped on the brakes again, shrieking to a halt on a concrete roadway. The two men ushered her out, and she gathered they were at Arnaldo's house. They sat her down inside, told her to wait, and vanished. Silence fell.

A few minutes later, Arnaldo returned. 'We have a place for you,' he said handing her one of her bags. 'Very quiet.'

'Thank you, Don Arnaldo, but . . . you have my other bag?'

Silence. Then: 'Tomorrow, Dona João. You will have it tomorrow.'

'But where is it? It has all my private things, letters, typewriter, other things.'

He hesitated again. 'The military took it,' he said. He seemed angry and embarrassed, with the officials, with himself and with Jan for making him confess the loss.

'The military? But . . .'

'We will take care of you here, Dona João. Tomorrow, tomorrow.'

And he was gone. She felt another hand on her arm. It was Arnaldo's wife, Cecilina, who led her down a hallway and along a passage. She heard the sound of a key in a lock.

'In here, Dona João.' Jan, wary but still determined never to make a fuss, never to seem out of control, allowed herself to be guided in. 'It will be quiet in here.' She backed away, and Jan heard the door lock.

Jan was puzzled. The room was musty with lack of use. It had, she discovered, feeling around, a bed and a chair, and nothing else. No toilet, no pot.

Cecilina returned a few minutes later with a bowl of noodles, some rice and a mug of water.

'*Escusado*. The toilet,' said Jan. 'Where is the toilet?'

Cecilina, taking Jan by the arm again, led her through a corridor and out into a backyard, where she guided Jan's hands to a tap. There was a smell of pigs.

'No, no,' said Jan. 'The toilet.'

Off they went again, up a steep, grassy slope and through a small plantation to a makeshift privy.

'No, no,' said Jan, insistently, with growing desperation. 'I will not find this at night. I need a pot. There is a pot in my other bag.'

'I will look,' said the woman. She led her back to her room, and locked her in again.

An hour went by. Jan began to feel she had been forgotten, or ignored. She started to bang on the door, shouting: 'Arnaldo! ARNALDO!'

Eventually, he arrived with Cecilina, opening the door impatiently. 'Someone in the street said the American woman was screaming,' he said. He sounded as if he had been insulted. 'What is it, Dona João?'

'Arnaldo,' She spoke slowly and emphatically. She didn't want any misunderstandings about this. 'I cannot go up the hill at night. I must have a pot.'

'There isn't one.'

'Yes, there is. I brought one, I brought it especially in order not to be a nuisance.'

'Dona João.' He hesitated. 'The National Police have it.'

'The National Police have my pot?' Her voice rose.

'Or maybe the Maritime Police.'

'What?' The idiocy of the situation struck her, and she laughed. 'What do the police want with my pot? *My pot*?'

Her laughter changed the mood. Cecilina joined in her laughter. 'I will find one,' she said.

Next morning, Cecilina brought her a cup of coffee and some *farinha*. As she set down the cups, she told Jan. 'Armindo slept at Cleonisia's house last night.' Her tone was confidential, even conspiratorial. So, thought Jan, as she heard the lock turn in the door, if Cleonisia and Armindo were getting together again, perhaps all would be well. Perhaps she had no need to worry after all.

But as the morning passed, her fragile facade of confidence began to crack. Two hours passed, then three. The thought crossed her mind that she would not get out of that place all day. But she had to get out. She would not be shut away like this. She would make a fuss, and demand to be taken to the American missionaries.

She rattled the door and shouted. No response. She shook the door harder, then put her shoulder to it, and threw herself against it, several times. At the fourth attempt, to her surprise, the catch gave and the door crashed open. She found herself standing out in the passage, pleased by her achievement, wondering if the noise would attract anyone's attention. No one came. She turned down the corridor towards the backyard, and went out into the daylight.

'Is there anyone there?' she called. There wasn't. She went on calling – 'Arnaldo! Arnaldo!' – with no idea where she was or whether anyone would ever hear her. But damn it, she thought ('Arnaldo!!') if someone heard the American woman screaming yesterday when she was inside, they should certainly hear her when she was outside.

Five minutes later, Arnaldo himself interrupted her in mid-scream.

'Dona João, what are you doing?'

'I escaped,' she said, ominously. 'Arnaldo, I am desperate. *Desperate*.'

'Yes, Dona João,' he said, unhappily.

'There is an American couple in town. Missionaries. Take me to them. I want to talk to Americans. I must talk to them *now*.'

'Yes, Dona João. I will talk to Armindo.'

She didn't have to wait long. After half an hour, Armindo burst in. He seemed to be doing everything at an insane speed since Cleonisia left him.

'Come, Dona João!' he shouted at her. 'I will take you to the Americans.'

He led her back down the passage, out through the house and to his truck. He drove in silence for a couple of minutes, accelerating viciously uphill, swerving right, bumping down steeply over mud-holes, and finally banging to a halt. He helped her down. 'The door is right there,' he said firmly.

She took three wary paces, waving her arms in front of her, and came up against a door. She knocked. After a moment, a woman's voice, obviously American, said: 'Hullo?'

'Hullo,' said Jan, holding out her hand. 'My name is Jan Little, and I'm . . .'

There was a roar from behind her. Armindo was gone.

'I'm afraid he presumed that I would stay,' Jan said, apologetically.

'Come in, come in, that's all right. We heard about you. We Americans have to stick together. That's understood.'

The woman, who introduced herself as Phyllis Jackson, led Jan in to meet her husband Neil.

The Jacksons, São Gabriel's Baptist missionaries, treated Jan with scrupulous hospitality. They described the house for her – single storey, tin-roof, American furniture, refrigerator, fan, veranda, view across the rapids towards the Sleeping Beauty Mountains – so that Jan soon felt at home. Neil gave up his study for her, fetched her things, and even pried her hearing-aid and her typewriter out of the hands of the police. But what of the letters, she asked? 'They say you can have them when they have read them,' he said.

Read her letters? What did they want with her letters? Her *private* correspondence? Besides, the letters were in English. How long would it take to read them? Neil could only shrug.

What she felt she needed most was to talk. Yet the Jacksons

avoided anything that might prove emotionally demanding. Once again, Jan had the impression that her experience had marked her in some way. She began to wonder if what she had been through simply had no meaning in terms of the religion, emotions, or experience of normal people. Who would ever understand? How would she ever be able to see what had happened clearly?

After her first week with the Jacksons, however, Jan's emotional needs gave way to physical ones. She developed dysentery, and spent the next two days in her hammock, too weak to talk or move much.

She was only just on her feet again when she had a visitor: an army sergeant. He explained that there was an officer who would like to ask Jan a few questions, when she was feeling better. Ah, yes, at last, the colonel. Of course, she said, that would be fine. One thing, though, said the sergeant, as he was on the point of leaving: how many boxes did the *senhora* bring with her from the jungle?

Jan thought back, picturing the boxes along the wall in her little room in Cucuí. 'Seven,' she said. 'No —' There was another box in there, which wasn't with the rest. 'No, eight.' The sergeant thanked her and left.

It was only afterwards that she remembered that she had sent two other boxes ahead from Homestead Hill. They were still in storage in Armindo's house. Well, what did it matter? The question had been asked in passing. There was nothing of interest in the boxes anyway.

Two days later, an officer appeared and told Neil Jackson that Jan was needed at the army headquarters to answer a few questions. He was very polite. When Neil told him that Jan was still in no fit state to go anywhere, he smiled. 'No problem,' he said. 'We will work here.'

He returned half an hour later with a typist and set himself up in the little spick-and-span kitchen, with Neil sitting across the table to act as interpreter.

Jan felt weak, but she supposed she would be all right for

half an hour or so. She just hoped she would be able to provide the kind of scientific detail she was sure they wanted. She looked towards the officer expectantly.

'Now, *senhora*,' he said. 'Tell me: when did you first come to Brazil?'

The question was unexpected, and she hesitated. First come to Brazil? She backtracked to that time seven years previously when they had landed in Boa Vista and travelled down the Branco to Manaus.

'An unusual journey for Americans,' he said. 'Tell me: what was the name of the boat?'

What an extraordinary thing to ask. 'I don't . . . oh, yes. It was the *Fé Im Deus*.'

It became clear almost immediately that if the officer was interested in Jan's experience in the jungle, he was also extremely interested in every other detail of the Littles' activities in Brazil, and indeed in Guyana, Mexico and the United States. Where were you born, he asked. Where were your parents born? When? Your husband's date of birth, his parents, their birth dates? When were you married? Where was Rebecca born? Ah, a previous husband? Why did you leave Mexico? Some trouble with the authorities?

'It was a strife over land,' explained Jan. 'We were pacifists. We wished to defend Indians, but we did not wish to cause bloodshed.'

By this time, the interview had lasted well over an hour, and still he had not asked any questions about how they got to Homestead Hill. When he did, he seemed to want everything – the places, the dates, the reasons, all cross-checked and corroborated with the quirky little details that dotted each paragraph of their lives – the cost of rooms in the Hotel Lar, the name of the captain on the Manaus–São Gabriel launch, the dates of cargo deliveries. How did you pay for supplies? With money. Where did your money come from? The United States. Hm. *Senhora*, how much money do you have in your account?

'We do not have a bank account. We had no money.'

397

Sudden silence. She could almost feel the smile of scepticism, the exchange of glances between officer and typist.

'Americans – without money?'

'Well, we had money from the government. And from a newspaper.'

From the government, and ... What newspaper? Ah, a religious newspaper. How much money, exactly? How often did you receive it? How was it paid? How often? Where was it changed?

Jan answered as though she was in a trance. It never occurred to her to try and hide anything. She was sure the only way to end the interview was to answer as truthfully as possible.

But somehow her answers never seemed to satisfy. Why the Demiti? the officer asked. Was there, perhaps, gold on the Demiti? Did they hope to meet Indians they wished to convert to their Christian Science? How exactly did the girl and the husband die? Malaria? But there is no malaria in that place ...

Later, of course, she realized there were reasons enough for suspicion. There seemed to be no record of their presence. The papers they had fought for and paid for in Manaus had never been processed. Officially, then, they were either illegal immigrants, or, more bizarrely, had never lived there at all.

That initial error over papers was compounded by another, more immediate mistake – Jan's failure to state correctly how many boxes she had. There had been ten, not eight. It was easy enough to check the number. Why, an imaginative and bored intelligence officer might ask, had she lied?

On this foundation, suspicious minds could build – had perhaps already built – epics of intrigue. The Littles were educated Americans. They had many books. But they also said they were poor. Everyone knew that Americans, especially educated Americans, were not poor. Why had they settled in such a remote spot? After all, no one had ever chosen to settle in the remote interior away from the river highways; no locals had ever done it, let alone foreigners. The area was known to be mineral rich, as all highlands supposedly are. Rumours already abounded. Some of the locals had been to the Serra dos Americanos, the Americans' Mountain, and there was talk that Armindo had some secret knowledge of what Don Enrique was really doing there. What did their hermit facade conceal? Why else would they be there, living in such obscurity, if they did not hope somehow to profit?

Oh, there were so many things that were strange about them. They were in a sensitive area, disputed with Venezuela. They had tried to settle in Venezuela, a sure sign, as any Brazilian knows, of derangement. There were those who said that the blind lady was not as blind as she pretended – had people not seen her typing? And had she not been seen staring round as her husband pointed out things to her? What were they really? CIA? Venezuelan spies? Missionaries? Geologists hoping to export their finds illegally?

Beyond all this was the problem of the deaths. It was stated, officially, that there was no malaria on the upper Rio Negro. If the deaths were not from malaria, what had really happened? Perhaps there was another, more sinister explanation. The young girl was the older woman's daughter, but the old man was not her father. What exactly was the relationship between the three of them? After all, the girl was old enough to be married. Might the old man have taken both women as wives? Could there have been a jealous struggle up there in the jungle, a murder, or two, perhaps? Why had the woman gone to such lengths to hide the evidence in boxes, and insist that the bones be buried there, rather than in Cucuí?

If Jan herself had followed through this weird logic, she might have been considerably more nervous of the interviews, especially as she had, in one of her recent letters – a letter which was at that moment in army hands – hinted at her own suspicion that Harry had consciously contributed to Becca's death.

'I think,' she wrote, 'if he thought B. were still alive, he concluded it were better she not survive our death for all the painful problems that could mean for a young woman. That

399

was a terrible mistake, but one I can forgive because I understand his thinking. I don't know if B. could forgive him not helping her the one time she really needed help.' She was referring only to his inaction, but – 'better she not survive', 'terrible mistake' – didn't her words, out of context, to someone who did not speak English well, hint at something very ominous?

In any event, the answers to such questions could only lie with the woman, the letters and the journals. It would take time to read the material. And of course there would be more letters arriving – they, too, might contain interesting revelations. The woman herself might be innocent. But then again, she might not.

It was fortunate for Jan, perhaps, that she was so stunned with fatigue after her five hours of questioning that she did not reason along these lines, that she did not realize how easily she could have been trapped in the jungle of Brazilian bureaucracy. As it was, she was certain she could have left no loopholes through which suspicion might creep.

❦

Three days later, Jan felt recovered enough from both her illness and the strain of the interview to concern herself with Cleonisia. Neil took her round for a visit. Apparently, there had been some sort of a reconciliation, for no sooner had Jan sat down than Armindo himself burst in.

'Dona João!' he shouted excitedly. 'A letter! A letter to me in Portuguese! You have to go back to the United States! I have to send you back! Your parents are worried about you. The letter says I should beg you, *beg* you, Dona João, to return to your grieving parents.'

She breathed a sigh of relief. That was the first indication she had had that any of her letters had actually been received. Not that Armindo had the letter – it was in Cucuí – but never mind that: it was the content that was important. The news was like an answer to a prayer. It offered a bridge over the void that had divided Jan from her parents six years previously. It gave her the guidance she needed. Yes: she would go home.

'How will you go?' Armindo asked. 'Will you go to Manaus?'

'No. I will go to my friends in San Carlos, and travel from there.' Perhaps Howard had not yet gone; perhaps she could travel with him; in any event, they would make arrangements for her.

As soon as she was back in the Jacksons' house, she wrote to her mother. She was grateful for the invitation, she said, and would write again when she knew when and how she would arrive. 'I'm all right,' she finished, reassuringly. 'The loss of Rebecca is an unhealable hurt, but I do not put the burden of my grief on anyone else.'

꽃

When Armindo moored by the store in Cucuí, she went immediately to her old room. Her plans were clear. Germano, who had brought his family upriver with Jan and Armindo, had business in San Carlos, and would take Jan with them. Her boxes could follow later. All she wanted to do now was find some items for the Clarks, pack a few things, and leave. It would take her no more than a few minutes.

She felt around for the few things she would take with her – books, binoculars, clothes. She felt across the top of the line of boxes. She began to check them off. She came to the sixth, and her hands did not find it. Funny. She must have moved it in the rush before departure for São Gabriel. She checked again, counting carefully. Now, where was the next box? She felt along the walls. Nothing. No sixth box, no more boxes *at all*. Her stomach turned to ice. *Someone's been in here.* A thief. What had gone? What was valuable? The marimba. The marimba box was there. She felt for it again. But wait. It had been opened. She pulled the top back, and felt inside. Chaos. Oh, dear God, someone had gone through the box. A resonator

401

lay on top, broken. Here were keys, here more resonators, all unpacked, lying higgledy-piggledy.

She drew back. Keep calm, she told herself. Don't lose control. If you lose control, you're finished, you'll never get out of this maze.

So there's been a robbery. Such things happen. She just had to know exactly what was missing, then she could cope. Armindo must help her.

'Armindo!' She went out, pacing her way past her garden to the store. 'Armindo!'

'Dona João?' He came to meet her on the path.

'Armindo, someone has been in my room.'

'Yes, Dona João.'

Yes? He showed no trace of surprise.

'Boxes have gone.'

'I know.'

'You *know*?' How could he possibly know? Oh: he had been up here, hadn't he? Did that mean that he . . .? No, of course, he's not the thief. 'You know who it was?'

'The police, the police, Dona João.'

'The police? What police? The police from the fort?'

'No, no.' He was having difficulty speaking. 'From São Gabriel. But do not worry. They will return them in two weeks.'

'But why did they take them? How did they get in?'

'They are suspicious, *very* suspicious.'

'Of me?'

'Yes. They are very bad people.'

'But they must have had a key.'

'It was my key, Dona João.' His voice sank. 'They told me to give them the key.'

She fell silent. She knew she was in a maze, yes, but she hadn't realized what sort of a maze. She'd thought it was merely a distortion of normal, everyday events, reality turned into a maze by her disabilities. But no: the confusion had been deliberately created by others. She had been running, running,

402

just as they wanted, staying here, signing this, saying that, going there, and all the time thinking she was fighting her way clear.

And Armindo was a part of it. He had handed over the key in São Gabriel. He had known all along that they would break into her room. And if he, her friend, was part of the maze, who else was involved? What other madness was in store?

At all costs, she had to remain in control, of herself and of events. She wanted to come back to settle her affairs. She couldn't come back if, through fear or hostility, she turned herself into an exile. She was not in control, she knew that now, she never had been. But she had to seem in control, or she would be lost.

'But Armindo, all my letters!' she said, as steadily as she could. 'And writing material! And books and photographs! What do they want?' She remembered the pieces of the marimba. What must they look like to a suspicious officer? What else but elaborate weights and measures or storage containers for mineral samples? 'Do they think I have found gold at my *sítio*?' She gave a mirthless laugh.

'Yes. Gold. They are very bad people, very bad. There is nothing we can do.'

'Armindo, they now have all my letters and I have no money.' She had no money because she had given it all to Armindo, but it was hardly the time to insist on a statement of account. 'There is more money, I think, from the United States government. It will be in other letters, in the post office in the fort. We must call there before we go.'

She paused, gathering herself together. She was fine, she was quite calm, she was not going to panic. She gathered her baggage. It was little enough – her own clothes, her typewriter, Harry's and Becca's binoculars, boots for the Clarks, a box of supplies. Germano was waiting at the launch with Socorro and their son, Julio.

'Germano,' said Jan. 'The fort. The post office. My mail.'

'Yes, Dona João, of course. I will get it for you.' Jan was

glad Germano was taking her. He was the youngest and most compliant of the brothers.

At the fort, twenty minutes upriver, Germano moored, and went ashore.

He was back almost at once.

'Dona João.' His voice was trembling with anger. 'The police have your letters.'

She gasped. So: it was not over yet. But this went far beyond anything she had suspected. Once again, it gave a new meaning to everything that had happened since ... since before she came out. If they had her letters now, they must have had all the letters that should have come to her over the last three months. They must have been seizing her letters ever since news of the deaths emerged, in June. It was intolerable. It was horrifying. It was wrong. And surely, surely it was illegal? 'But, Germano, there are letters there from the United States government. It is my *right* to receive them. They are my cheques. They cannot possibly do anything with them. I need them to live.'

'It's no use, Dona João,' he said, bitterly. 'I have talked to the Commandante. They have orders. They will read the letters. You have to get them when you come back.'

She forced herself to stay calm. 'I see. Then there's nothing we can do. We must go on now.'

So they crossed the border. And since this was not a legal emigration point, there was no record of her departure. Officially, she had never been there in the first place; officially, she never left. Officially, their five years in the jungle had never happened.

In a much more immediate sense, she was still in limbo. She had no money, no means of support, no way of knowing how her friends and family had responded to the news of Harry's and Rebecca's death. Her only comfort was the belief that she would soon be among friends.

But she was not yet out of the maze.

Germano had business in San Felipe, on the Colombian side, opposite San Carlos, 500 yards away across the Negro. He docked for the night, and next morning took his dinghy over to arrange permission to land, leaving Jan and Socorro in the launch.

He was away all morning, and all afternoon. Socorro became worried. Jan secretly thought Germano had gone drinking with friends, though he didn't seem the type. The two women reassured each other. At dusk, when Jan was nearly asleep, Germano returned, shouting as he moored. Coming to Jan's hammock, be began to talk so excitedly he was barely comprehensible to her. She had to keep repeating back to him what she understood him to be saying.

'Yes, Dona João. It's true! I arrived in San Carlos as usual, and they put me in jail!'

Drugs, thought Jan. Must be drugs. Was he actually smuggling, or had they held him on suspicion? But he didn't seem the type for that, either.

'Did you have to pay much to get out?'

'No, no. My friends rescued me. These Venezuelans are crazy.'

'But why did they do it?'

'Venezuela is closed to foreigners! There are too many Colombians. They enter illegally, to work. Now Venezuela makes a census of foreigners. Me, a foreigner! We have been going back and forth between Brazil, Colombia and Venezuela since I was a child, and suddenly we are foreigners. They grabbed me and put me in a dark place.'

Poor Germano, his placid life chugging up and down the Negro disrupted by crisis after crisis.

'They did not even let me send a message to your friends.'

Suddenly her sympathy for Germano receded.

'But they will let *me* in,' she said, with a confidence she didn't feel. 'I am an American citizen. I have to see my friends. The Commandante knows me . . .'

'No foreigners, Dona João! No foreigners at all! I cannot set foot in San Carlos. And I have cargo to sell!'

'But Germano, that means I . . . I have nowhere to go. I cannot stay here. I have no money and . . . and . . . my friends are just over there. They will help, if they know I am here. If they don't, I shall have to go back with you.'

Germano fell into a stunned silence for a moment.

'I shall do something,' he said, 'Tomorrow.'

The next day, he told Jan to write a note to her friends. He said he would pass it to someone for delivery. She dug out her typewriter, and put it on her lap. As usual, since she had no ribbon, she ran two sheets into the machine, separated by a piece of carbon paper. 'Dear Kate and Howard,' she typed. 'I'm sitting here stuck in a boat in San Felipe,' and went on to tell them calmly and clearly what had happened since she left them. She finished by asking them politely to please do what they could to help.

She finished the letter, put the carbon copy in an envelope and held it out to Germano. Moments later, he was heading back across the river in the dinghy.

🐝

Kate was in the IVIC house that morning as usual, when she heard a knock on the door. When she opened it, she was surprised to see a boy carrying a letter. The boy thrust the letter into her hand, and ran off without saying a word.

Kate carried it back inside, opened it, and announced to Howard that it was from Jan. 'Funny,' she said, 'Listen: "Dear Kate and Howard, I'm sitting here stuck in a boat in –" ' She stopped, for there was nothing more to the line.

Jan had, of course, typed exactly where she was. But she had no way of knowing, when she inserted the carbon between her two sheets of paper, that the top of the carbon had been folded over. That part of the carbon copy that should have shown her location was a blank.

Kate read on, repeating Jan's description of her appalling

stay in São Gabriel and her decision to return to the States, if Howard's offer was still open. 'Maybe,' she finished, as polite as always. 'Maybe you can find a way to see me some time. Love, Jan.'

Kate set the letter aside. It was obviously from São Gabriel. Equally obviously, there was nothing to be done until Jan came upriver.

※

Jan, meanwhile, was waiting on Germano's boat, in a state of increasing anxiety. Germano had solved his own problems by trading from out in the river. His business was almost complete, and in another day or two he would be off downriver. Jan started to think she would have to go with him without contacting the Clarks. There would be no alternative.

Hemmed in by cargo, she spent her time reading a *National Geographic* article in Braille about Hans Christian Andersen. With nothing else to do, she read and reread the piece, through the afternoon, and the following morning, developing a strong dislike for Hans Christian Andersen.

Late on the second afternoon, she heard a voice from the river: 'Jan? You there?'

Jan raised her head, puzzled, and then – 'Kate!' she shouted.

Kate and Howard had eventually realized there was something peculiar about the letter. It took them a couple of days for them to work out what it was. The boy. How did the boy get the letter? It could have been brought upriver and handed over, but it was a long way. Wouldn't Jan have posted it? And why was there no address? And why sit in a boat in São Gabriel, for Heaven sakes? Wouldn't it all make more sense if she was actually close by? If so, she would be across the river, because she wouldn't be allowed in. They had to check, fast.

Delighted their hunch had proved correct, they were horrified at Jan's proposal to go back to Cucuí. Even assuming she would be free to travel, the plane could come any day, and they would not have time to fetch her. On no account should she go back over the border. She must stay here, in San Felipe, until they found a way to bring to her in.

🔆

Back in San Carlos, Howard battled with Venezuelan bureaucracy. The lieutenant in command refused to bend the rules. What could a blind, deaf, old widow, demanded Howard angrily, possibly do to undermine Venezuela? The lieutenant was adamant. Howard changed tactics. He said he would try to get permission via Caracas. The lieutenant said he was welcome to try, although unfortunately (a smile, a shrug) the radio-phone was out of order. Howard had his own ideas about that. The local priest had a radio. He proposed to use the radio to get a message to a friend in Caracas, and thence to the American Embassy.

While he was explaining this complicated scheme to the padre, he noticed two women listening in on the conversation. One turned out to be the wife, or daughter, or mistress of an official high up in one of the ministries. She was scandalized that a blind, deaf, old widow should be refused entry. She said she would do what she could, at once, for she was leaving that day for Caracas. Howard thanked her for her concern, though he privately dismissed her words as mere politeness.

Four days later, however, to the amazement of Howard, and everyone else, the lieutenant received a call on the now-repaired radio-phone. On orders from the Interior Minister himself, *la anciana*, the ancient one, was to be admitted instantly.

The next day, Jan found herself, to her relief and delight, once again installed in the IVIC house in San Carlos.

🔆

The military plane did not come. Eventually, with money cabled by Jessie from Fair Oaks, Jan prepared to leave on a commerical flight, accompanied by Becky Holmes, one of those who had come to Cucuí with Kate and Howard Clark to find her. By then, after a month of good food and good companionship, Jan was stronger, physically and emotionally. She had once again been able to set grief aside by involving herself with the routines and discussions of the research team. It was a temporary respite. As she sat waiting for take-off, the roaring engines sending a reassuring vibration through her, she thought again, as she had done every day over the previous weeks, of the past and the future.

There was no separation between them. The past would be the future. She would have to confront them both, the world of people and cities and the world she had left behind on Homestead Hill.

She was, at last, strong enough to face those tasks. She felt a tremor of fear – closed rooms, strange people, her own incapacities. Real fears, but with a difference now. In the past, her fears – fears of her inadequacies, fears induced by Harry, and countless fears of Harry himself – had controlled her. Not any more. She had survived, by luck, perhaps, partly by judgement, and certainly by will. She knew herself and her capacities better. The fear that remained – for life would always mean danger – was positive. For her, as for a mountaineer, fear would be an essential safeguard. She had made her oldest enemy a friend at last.

Nothing would be easy. But her course was clear. She would live with her parents; she would work to heal the rift; she would make new friendships and renew old ones; she would laugh again; above all, she would work at acceptance and understanding. So much to understand: her own grief, Becca's death, her own obscure motives for staying with Harry, and Harry himself, saint and sinner, idealist and tyrant, and a hundred other opposites. And herself: if she had strengths, had they somehow come from him and his insistence that she was weak, irresponsible, careless, degraded, petty and foolish? How much was she Harry's creation? How much her own, despite him?

What could such work possibly bring? She had no idea.

Only that somehow, she must face everything. *Everything.* First, the outside world; then, one day, full circle – a return to the jungle.

As the plane rose, she could see in her mind's eye the jungle stretching away and away into Brazil. She turned to her companion.

'What's it like, Becky, to the south?'

'Rainforest. Some hills. Maybe some mountains right on the horizon.'

'Can you see a big, broad mountain, standing alone?'

'No. It's too hazy. If it's there, I can't see it.'

'It doesn't matter,' Jan said, eyes closed. 'I think I can.'

EPILOGUE: *Full Circle*

Jan arrived home on 25 October 1980. Bill and Jessie, now aged eighty-seven and seventy-seven, welcomed her back. There was no need, any more, for bitterness, and every reason to start afresh, restoring affection with mutual support. A health check showed that Jan had hookworm and amoebic dysentery, both of which responded rapidly to treatment. In other respects, except for the blindness and deafness, she was in remarkably good shape.

Soon afterwards, she visited specialists to check on her disabilities. There was nothing to be done about her hearing; it would remain impaired, even with a hearing-aid. But now, for the first time, she learned that it was not her tunnel vision that had finally blocked off her sight, but cataracts, removable at any time by routine surgery.

In August 1981, she had an operation on her left eye, the poorer of the two, and came out of hospital with three degrees of vision − a tiny field, but enough, in conjunction with a magnifying glass and bright lights, to allow her to struggle through a book, her first in ten years. That Christmas, she saw once again the faces of friends and relatives.

In May, 1982, a second operation restored sight to her right eye, giving her ten degrees of vision − half as much as she had had as a young woman, but sufficient to begin an emotional and intellectual rebirth, and grant her limited independence. She exchanged letters with the US Embassy in Brasilia in an attempt to retrieve the missing mail and journals. (Some were found; the rest vanished, as did the marimba.) She devoted herself to caring for her ageing parents. She made contact with a local self-help group of tunnel-vision sufferers. She checked the proofs of *Rima*, which George Ball had taken with him from the jungle for publication. She involved herself with groups aiding Guatemalan refugees and working for the preservation of rainforest. She allowed herself to dream that there could, one day, be a return to the jungle.

☙

At the time, such a dream was mere fantasy. But by chance, it was shortly after Jan regained her limited vision that I was in southern Venezuela, researching a series of documentaries on human survival. There, I and the series director, Nick Downie, met Kate Clark, who, with her husband, Howard, had contacted Jan in Cucuí and arranged for her return through San Carlos. Kate told Jan of our interest. She wrote to me. We went to Sacramento, and interviewed her for the series. Astonishingly, she had never told her story before in detail. It had always seemed to her so remote from everyday experience that she never knew how to begin. The first time Jan related the details of Becca's and Harry's deaths was on camera.

Soon afterwards, we began work together on this book.

Jan needed to formalize her experiences in order to assimilate them, but the labour of doing so was intensely, often brutally painful. Working on many levels and from several sources – her letters, her friends, Harry's journals, and her own versions of events, both written and spoken – we worked together to sift from her astonishingly detailed memory the significant from the ephemeral.

The most demanding sections were those concerning Becca's death. Jan was almost unconscious for much of the period of the illness, and to make sense of the events leading up to Becca's death was an emotional equivalent of archaeology. Much still remains obscure. Certainly, there is no final explanation of Becca's death. It seems likely that the disease, whatever it was, had affected some internal organ. One effect of malaria, for instance, is to enlarge the spleen. An enlarged spleen can easily be ruptured by a blow, causing internal bleeding. Rebecca would not have known immediately that damage had been done, and would have had the strength to stand up and stagger into the house. The bleeding would eventually have caused severe pain, but it seems that she became unconscious almost at once. Already weak, she would have died soon afterwards. Even if Jan had known what had happened, she could have done nothing.

Right from the start, we were both drawn towards Homestead Hill, Jan to complete the process of coming to terms with what had happened, and to see for the first time the place where she had lived for almost five years, and where Harry and Rebecca were buried; I because I wanted to experience for myself the places and landscapes that had meant so much to Jan.

In 1984, I approached the BBC with the suggestion that Jan's return to Homestead Hill would make a powerful documentary. The following year, under the direction of one of the BBC's most experienced producers, Bob Saunders, we made that trip.

In São Gabriel, after an emotional reunion with Cleonisia, Jan discovered that in her five-year absence a number of strange developments had taken place on the upper Rio Negro.

Armindo had been killed. After Jan's departure, his failing business collapsed. The pretty little store in Cucuí was abandoned. He, Cleonisia and the children came to live in São Gabriel. Less than a year after Jan left, when Armindo was crossing the Negro at São Gabriel, he was swept to his death over the rapids.

He was not deeply missed. Unknown to the Littles, he had always had a reputation as a greedy man – a judgement that had become the keystone of a dramatic rumour by which the locals explained to themselves much about the mysterious Americans living on the Demiti.

The Littles were, it was said, looking for gold. Why else would anyone live by themselves in the jungle? That being so, the rumour ran, Armindo must have known what they were doing. He was thus well placed to know when they struck it rich, and where they had buried their new-found wealth. He therefore poisoned their rice, killed Harry and Rebecca, and stole Harry's metal-detector, with which the gold had been found in the first place. The existence of the metal-detector was proof that this was so. Of course, Armindo failed in his prime aim – to find the gold. But the blind widow knew where it was buried, and Armindo made sure he had her imprisoned. She, however, managed to escape without revealing her secret. And Armindo was punished by God for his greed.

That was not the end of the story. The road, which the Littles fled so precipitately, had, as they knew, followed them. They also knew the road-builders had been forced to retreat. The swamp lands of the upper Demiti, through which the *paraná* threaded its intricate and Stygian course, was unsuitable for a road. The route had therefore been redirected towards high ground: the flanks of Sentinel. By a dreadful irony, Harry, fleeing the road to one of Brazil's remotest spots, chose a hill almost exactly on the road's future course. It aimed like an arrow at the heart of his wilderness, veering left at Sentinel. In the intervening five years, the road had inched forward another twelve miles. That stretch, already badly eroded, included a sturdy wooden bridge that crossed the Demiti just by Difficulty Hill.

The building of the road was also the cause of a curious little incident concerning a man who had already played a minute role in Jan's life: the Swiss mechanic who might, Armindo said, have read her letters to her if and when he came upriver to Cucuí. His name was Jean-Pierre Vuillomenet, and he was an astonishing man. He had trained as a mechanical engineer, but his passion was cycling. He had cycled round the world, and acquired a minor reputation in his native Switzerland as explorer, writer and photographer. On his travels, he had fallen in love with São Gabriel, imported his equipment, built a launch, and rapidly established himself as the best mechanical engineer on the 500 miles of river between São Gabriel and Puerto Ayacucho in Venezuela. With his lanky good looks – hawk nose, hooded eyes, drooping moustache – he made as much of an impression on the Rio Negro people as Harry.

Jean-Pierre's passion for São Gabriel and its surroundings expressed itself in a determination to map the upper Rio Negro with an accuracy notoriously lacking from commercial publications. The road did not appear in detail on any maps. In early 1980, Jean-Pierre, who had never learned to drive, and anyway covered São Gabriel's hummocky roads on his racing bicycle as fast as any local car, decided to cycle the length of the road and chart it.

One hundred kilometres down the road, at the main army camp, the headquarters of the highway engineers, he heard of the Americans, and decided to pay them a visit. The next morning, when he reached the snout of the road in the lee of Sentinel, he decided to climb the mountain to see if he could spot the Americans' camp.

At the top, he took stock of his position. Looking north, he saw smoke drifting lazily up through the trees. Yes, he decided, that would be where the Americans were, on a hill that was almost invisible against the jungle backdrop. He promised himself he would visit them the next day.

But after spending the night on top of Sentinel, he awoke hungry and exhausted. He climbed down, mounted his bicycle and set off home without trekking the final two miles. It didn't matter, he told himself. Now he knew where they were, he could visit them any time.

The smoke Jean-Pierre saw could have been from the fire Jan lit the week before Harry's death. If he had completed his journey, he might have been in time to save Harry's life.

🜪

Accompanied by Cleonisia and Jean-Pierre, we drove to the Demiti, and camped. From there, we explored up and down river, and found Homestead Hill, overgrown, the clearings almost unidentifiable, but with the ruins of the huts and the trails (even sawn logs and riverside railings) still visible. There was the fallen tree down which Jan had felt her way to fetch water; there the remains of the washstand, the drainage ditch and rusted sardine tins; and there, on the hilltop, the rain-barrel Jan had asked to be inverted as she left after the burial. And there, of course, were the mountains. As Indian helpers chopped at bushes and saplings, the falling foliage revealed the stupendous sweep of jungle-clad hills that Harry and Rebecca had described daily to Jan, dominated by the perfect cone of Sentinel.

Across from the Hilltop Hut, amidst the new growth that choked the Observation Ledge, a shock awaited. Rebecca's cross was still standing. But Harry's was uprooted and broken apart. His grave was a mess of mud, desecrated by someone searching for the gold that everyone said was buried some-where on Homestead Hill.

After the initial shock, the guides tidied the graves and made new crosses. Later, at Jan's suggestion, some of us returned. There were six: Jan; Cleonisia; myself; the cameraman, Martin Patmore; the sound engineer, Dave Brinicombe; and a guide, Leje. First, we planted fruit trees brought from Manaus as memorials for Harry and Becca. Then there followed a brief but intensely moving service. There was little choice of hymn: we sang what we could remember – first, a few verses of 'O God our help in ages past'. The strangeness of the scene – the crosses, Jan hand in hand with Cleonisia, three Englishmen singing in uncertain voices on a hill in the depths of the Amazon – struck me so forcibly that I found it hard to keep my emotions under control. I then read Harry's favourite text, from St John, chapter 14: 'Let not your heart be troubled: ye believe in God, believe also in me. In my father's house are many mansions: if it were not so, I would have told you. I go to prepare a place for you.' I followed this by

416

reading, with considerable difficulty, Becca's favourite poem:

> This world is not conclusion
> A sequel stands beyond
> Invisible as music
> But positive as sound.

Then Jan spoke, and there followed a second hymn: 'The Lord's my shepherd, I'll not want', sung to Crimond, and some words from Cleonisia recalling her memories of Don Enrique and Dona Rebecca, and then, finally, tears as the two women comforted each other in a display of grief that had not been possible at the hasty burial itself, five years before.

The heart of the ceremony, though, was Jan's speech. The last words should be hers, spoken against that wonderful view, with Sentinel out and the forested hills ranging away towards Neblina:

'I have a farewell to make to Harry, to the life that ended here in tragedy. There are memories from that life that are dark, that are painful, but there was goodness, *there was goodness* – honesty, love, courage and laughter – and from that goodness comes understanding, and redemption. I have come back, never having been away from what was involved in that life, a life that was private, and remote, and secluded. Now I have been making that life open for many eyes, for many hearts and minds. It might be thought a terrible exposure, but it is for a purpose, for a purpose for us all. In the words he loved, "Ye shall know the truth, and the truth shall make you free."

'And for Rebecca . . . for Rebecca I cannot yet make a farewell. A part of her has gone on, but something of her is always with me, is part of me, as I am of her; and together we are still part of the forest, the forest and the life that it nourishes, and the life that must be cherished.

'We go on together.'

ACKNOWLEDGEMENTS

Together, we wish to thank Jessie Muller and Angy Man, who so generously coped with the needs and demands incurred in the writing of this book; Elspeth Sandys, for her committed editorial involvement; Iradj Bagherzade, for his unflagging support as publisher, editor and friend; George and Kay Ball, Edmonton, Alberta, the only outsiders to visit the Littles in Brazil, with particular thanks for their photographs; Kate and Howard Clark, Athens, Georgia; Derek, Johanna and Josie Moore; Gordon Clyde; George and Kathy Arias, Manaus; Gertrude Duby-Blom, San Cristobal; Marcey Jacobson and Janet Marren, San Cristobal; Nick Downie and the 'Survive' team – Robb Hart, Deborah Isaacs and Carmen O'Rourke; Elizabeth Little, Powell River, BC, for her observations on her husband's early life; the Cooperative College, Loughborough; Gladys Noyes, Tunbridge, Vermont; Linotte Watson, Poole, Dorset; Tim Cloudsley, Glasgow; Christine Hugh Jones, Cambridge; the BBC's 'World About Us' team on the filming of the return to Homestead Hill – Bob Saunders, Dave Brinicombe, Martin Patmore, and Sandra Wellington; Cleonisia Coimbra, São Gabriel; Jean-Pierre Vuillomenet, São Gabriel; and Geraldine Cooke, who edited the MS in its final form.

In addition, Jan wishes to thank 'John Man, whose friendship freed me from the ills of the inarticulate; Mrs Robert A. Martin (Toni), whose dedicated horticultural help and friendship sustained the family in the homesteading years; Dr Harriet Lovitt, who listened and responded always with humanity, perspicacity and humour; Dr John Hudson, whose words "I am with you" validated the lonely exploration of past experiences; and Eleanor A. Miner and Winifred Detwiler, who each served in her own way above the call of friendship.'

Some published works proved useful sources, in particular Herbert Rittlinger's *Jungle Quest* (Odhams, 1961), which includes a portrait of Harry just before Jan met him. Gertrude (Trudi) Duby-Blom has written extensively on the Lacandones and their forest. Her book *Bearing Witness* (Gertrude Blom, Duke University, 1984) contains glorious evocations of the Lacandon Indians and their now vanished forest home. A detailed study, *The Lacandones of Mexico* (Philip Baer and William Merrifield, Summer Institute of Linguistics, 1971) mentions both Harry and Es. *The Last Lords of Palenque* by Victor Perera and Robert D. Bruce (Little, Brown. 1982) is the best general book on the Lacandones. The best history of the area is *La Paz de Dios y del Rey: La conquista de la Selva Lacandona 1525–1821* by Jan de Vos (Colección Ceiba, Gobierna del Estado de Chiapas, 1980). Harry's own book, *Rima, The Monkey's Child*, was published by the University of Alberta Press in 1983, after the MS was brought out of Brazil by George Ball.

John Man, Oxford
Jan Little, Sacramento

FOR THE BEST IN PAPERBACKS, LOOK FOR THE

A CHOICE OF PENGUINS

The Big Red Train Ride Eric Newby

From Moscow to the Pacific on the Trans-Siberian Railway is an eight-day journey of nearly six thousand miles through seven time zones. In 1977 Eric Newby set out with his wife, an official guide and a photographer on this journey. 'The best kind of travel book' – Paul Theroux

Star Wars Edited by E. P. Thompson

With contributions from Rip Bulkeley, John Pike, Ben Thompson and E. P. Thompson, and with a Foreward by Dorothy Hodgkin, OM, this is a major book which assesses all the arguments for Star Wars and proceeds to make a powerful – indeed unanswerable – case against it.

Selected Letters of Malcolm Lowry
Edited by Harvey Breit and Margerie Bonner Lowry

Lowry emerges from these letters not only as an extremely interesting man, but also a lovable one' – Philip Toynbee

PENGUIN CLASSICS OF WORLD ART

Each volume presents the complete paintings of the artist and includes: an introduction by a distinguished art historian, critical comments on the painter from his own time to the present day, 64 pages of full-colour plates, a chronological survey of his life and work, a basic bibliography, a fully illustrated and annotated *catalogue raisonné*.

Titles already published or in preparation

Botticelli, Bruegel, Canaletto, Caravaggio, Cézanne, Dürer, Giorgione, Giotto, Leonardo da Vinci, Manet, Mantegna, Michelangelo, Picasso, Piero della Francesca, Raphael, Rembrandt, Toulouse-Lautrec, van Eyck, Vermeer, Watteau

FOR THE BEST IN PAPERBACKS, LOOK FOR THE 🐧

A CHOICE OF PENGUINS

A Fortunate Grandchild 'Miss Read'

Grandma Read in Lewisham and Grandma Shafe in Walton on the Naze were totally different in appearance and outlook, but united in their affection for their grand-daughter – who grew up to become the much-loved and popular novelist.

The Ultimate Trivia Quiz Game Book   Maureen and Alan Hiron

If you are immersed in trivia, addicted to quiz games, endlessly nosey, then this is the book for you: over 10,000 pieces of utterly dispensable information!

The Diary of Virginia Woolf
Five volumes, edited by Quentin Bell and Anne Olivier Bell

'As an account of the intellectual and cultural life of our century, Virginia Woolf's diaries are invaluable; as the record of one bruised and unquiet mind, they are unique' – Peter Ackroyd in the *Sunday Times*

Voices of the Old Sea   Norman Lewis

'I will wager that *Voices of the Old Sea* will be a classic in the literature about Spain' – *Mail on Sunday*. 'Limpidly and lovingly Norman Lewis has caught the helpless, unwitting, often foolish, but always hopeful village in its dying summers, and saved the tragedy with sublime comedy' – *Observer*

The First World War   A. J. P. Taylor

In this superb illustrated history, A. J. P. Taylor 'manages to say almost everything that is important for an understanding and, indeed, intellectual digestion of that vast event . . . A special text . . . a remarkable collection of photographs' – *Observer*

Ninety-Two Days   Evelyn Waugh

With characteristic honesty, Evelyn Waugh here debunks the romantic notions attached to rough travelling: his journey in Guiana and Brazil is difficult, dangerous and extremely uncomfortable, and his account of it is witty and unquestionably compelling.

A CHOICE OF PENGUINS

The Book Quiz Book Joseph Connolly

Who was literature's performing flea . . .? Who wrote 'Live Now, Pay Later . . .'? Keats and Cartland, Balzac and Braine, Coleridge conundrums, Eliot enigmas, Tolstoy teasers . . . all in this brilliant quiz book. You will be on the shelf without it . . .

Voyage through the Antarctic Richard Adams and Ronald Lockley

Here is the true, authentic Antarctic of today, brought vividly to life by Richard Adams, author of *Watership Down*, and Ronald Lockley, the world-famous naturalist. 'A good adventure story, with a lot of information and a deal of enthusiasm for Antarctica and its animals' – *Nature*

Getting to Know the General Graham Greene

'In August 1981 my bag was packed for my fifth visit to Panama when the news came to me over the telephone of the death of General Omar Torrijos Herrera, my friend and host . . .' 'Vigorous, deeply felt, at times funny, and for Greene surprisingly frank' – *Sunday Times*

Television Today and Tomorrow: Wall to Wall Dallas?
Christopher Dunkley

Virtually every British home has a television, nearly half now have two sets or more, and we are promised that before the end of the century there will be a vast expansion of television delivered via cable and satellite. How did television come to be so central to our lives? Is British television really the best in the world, as politicians like to assert?

Arabian Sands Wilfred Thesiger

'In the tradition of Burton, Doughty, Lawrence, Philby and Thomas, it is, very likely, the book about Arabia to end all books about Arabia' – *Daily Telegraph*

When the Wind Blows Raymond Briggs

'A visual parable against nuclear war: all the more chilling for being in the form of a strip cartoon' – *Sunday Times*. 'The most eloquent anti-Bomb statement you are likely to read' – *Daily Mail*

A CHOICE OF PENGUINS

Adieux: A Farewell to Sartre   Simone de Beauvoir

A devastatingly frank account of the last years of Sartre's life, and his death, by the woman who for more than half a century shared that life. 'A true labour of love, there is about it a touching sadness, a mingling of the personal with the impersonal and timeless which Sartre himself would surely have liked and understood' – *Listener*

Business Wargames   James Barrie

How did BMW overtake Mercedes? Why did Laker crash? How did McDonalds grab the hamburger market? Drawing on the tragic mistakes and brilliant victories of military history, this remarkable book draws countless fascinating parallels with case histories from industry world-wide.

Metamagical Themas   Douglas R. Hofstadter

This astonishing sequel to the best-selling, Pulitzer Prize-winning *Gödel, Escher, Bach* swarms with 'extraordinary ideas, brilliant fables, deep philosophical questions and Carrollian word play' – Martin Gardner

Into the Heart of Borneo   Redmond O'Hanlon

'Perceptive, hilarious and at the same time a serious natural-history journey into one of the last remaining unspoilt paradises' – *New Statesman*. 'Consistently exciting, often funny and erudite without ever being overwhelming' – *Punch*

A Better Class of Person   John Osborne

The playwright's autobiography, 1929–56. 'Splendidly enjoyable' – John Mortimer. 'One of the best, richest and most bitterly truthful autobiographies that I have ever read' – Melvyn Bragg

The Secrets of a Woman's Heart   Hilary Spurling

The later life of Ivy Compton-Burnett, 1920–69. 'A biographical triumph . . . elegant, stylish, witty, tender, immensely acute – dazzles and exhilarates . . . a great achievement' – Kay Dick in the *Literary Review*. 'One of the most important literary biographies of the century' – *New Statesman*

A CHOICE OF PENGUINS

Castaway Lucy Irvine

'Writer seeks "wife" for a year on a tropical island.' This is the extraordinary, candid, sometimes shocking account of what happened when Lucy Irvine answered the advertisement, and found herself embroiled in what was not exactly a desert island dream. 'Fascinating' – *Daily Mail*

Out of Africa Karen Blixen (Isak Dinesen)

After the failure of her coffee-farm in Kenya, where she lived from 1913 to 1931, Karen Blixen went home to Denmark and wrote this unforgettable account of her experiences. 'No reader can put the book down without some share in the author's poignant farewell to her farm' – *Observer*

The Lisle Letters Edited by Muriel St Clare Byrne

An intimate, immediate and wholly fascinating picture of a family in the reign of Henry VIII. 'Remarkable . . . we can really hear the people of early Tudor England talking' – Keith Thomas in the *Sunday Times*. 'One of the most extraordinary works to be published this century' – J. H. Plumb

In My Wildest Dreams Leslie Thomas

The autobiography of Leslie Thomas, author of *The Magic Army* and *The Dearest and the Best*. From Barnardo boy to original virgin soldier, from apprentice journalist to famous novelist, it is an amazing story. 'Hugely enjoyable' – *Daily Express*

India: The Siege Within M. J. Akbar

'A thoughtful and well-researched history of the conflict, 2,500 years old, between centralizing and separatist forces in the sub-continent. And remarkably, for a work of this kind, it's concise, elegantly written and entertaining' – Zareer Masani in the *New Statesman*

The Winning Streak Walter Goldsmith and David Clutterbuck

Marks and Spencer, Saatchi and Saatchi, United Biscuits, G.E.C. . . . The U.K.'s top companies reveal their formulas for success, in an important and stimulating book that no British manager can afford to ignore.

THE PENGUIN TRAVEL LIBRARY – A SELECTION

Hindoo Holiday J. R. Ackerley
The Flight of Ikaros Kevin Andrews
The Path to Rome Hilaire Belloc
Looking for Dilmun Geoffrey Bibby
First Russia, then Tibet Robert Byron
Granite Island Dorothy Carrington
The Worst Journey in the World Apsley Cherry-Garrard
Hashish Henry de Monfreid
Passages from Arabia Deserta C. M. Doughty
Siren Land Norman Douglas
Brazilian Adventure Peter Fleming
The Hill of Devi E. M. Forster
Journey to Kars Philip Glazebrook
Pattern of Islands Arthur Grimble
Writings from Japan Lafcadio Hearn
A Little Tour in France Henry James
Mornings in Mexico D. H. Lawrence
Mani Patrick Leigh Fermor
Stones of Florence and **Venice Observed** Mary McCarthy
They went to Portugal Rose Macaulay
Colossus of Maroussi Henry Miller
Spain Jan Morris
The Big Red Train Ride Eric Newby
The Grand Irish Tour Peter Somerville-Large
Marsh Arabs Wilfred Thesiger
The Sea and The Jungle H. M. Tomlinson
The House of Exile Nora Wain
Ninety-Two Days Evelyn Waugh